PEOPLE, MARKETS, GOODS:
ECONOMIES AND SOCIETIES IN HISTORY

Volume 23

Capitalism

People, Markets, Goods:
Economies and Societies in History
ISSN: 2051-7467

Series editors
Marguerite Dupree – University of Glasgow
Steve Hindle – Washington University in St Louis
Jane Humphries – University of Oxford, London School of Economics
Willem M. Jongman – University of Groningen
John Turner – Queen's University Belfast
Jane Whittle – University of Exeter
Nuala Zahedieh – University of Cambridge

The interactions of economy and society, people and goods, transactions and actions are at the root of most human behaviours. Economic and social historians are participants in the same conversation about how markets have developed historically and how they have been constituted by economic actors and agencies in various social, institutional and geographical contexts. New debates now underpin much research in economic and social, cultural, demographic, urban and political history. Their themes have enduring resonance – financial stability and instability, the costs of health and welfare, the implications of poverty and riches, flows of trade and the centrality of communications. This paperback series aims to attract historians interested in economics and economists with an interest in history by publishing high quality, cutting edge academic research in the broad field of economic and social history from the late medieval/early modern period to the present day. It encourages the interaction of qualitative and quantitative methods through both excellent monographs and collections offering path-breaking overviews of key research concerns. Taking as its benchmark international relevance and excellence it is open to scholars and subjects of any geographical areas from the case study to the multi-nation comparison.

PREVIOUSLY PUBLISHED TITLES IN THE SERIES
ARE LISTED AT THE BACK OF THIS VOLUME

Capitalism

Histories

Edited by Robert G. Ingram and James M. Vaughn

THE BOYDELL PRESS

© Contributors 2025

All Rights Reserved. Except as permitted under current legislation no part of this work may be photocopied, stored in a retrieval system, published, performed in public, adapted, broadcast, transmitted, recorded or reproduced in any form or by any means, without the prior permission of the copyright owner

First published 2025
The Boydell Press, Woodbridge

ISBN 978-1-83765-198-6

The Boydell Press is an imprint of Boydell & Brewer Ltd
PO Box 9, Woodbridge, Suffolk IP12 3DF, UK
and of Boydell & Brewer Inc.
668 Mt Hope Avenue, Rochester, NY 14620-2731, USA
website: www.boydellandbrewer.com

A catalogue record for this book is available
from the British Library

The publisher has no responsibility for the continued existence or accuracy of URLs for external or third-party internet websites referred to in this book, and does not guarantee that any content on such websites is, or will remain, accurate or appropriate

Contents

List of Tables and Figures vii
List of Contributors viii
Acknowledgements x
List of Abbreviations xi

1. Capitalism: Histories and Institutions 1
    Robert G. Ingram

2. Origin Stories: Expressions and Presentations of Capitalism in Early British America 26
    Peter A. Coclanis

3. Creativity and Capitalism in the Nineteenth-Century United States 60
    John Majewski

4. The Trans-Atlantic Slave Trade and the Birth of the Business Cycle 79
    Mark Metzler

5. Violence and Capitalism in Early Modern European Overseas Expansion 99
    Ralph Austen †

6. Capitalism in Africa: Two Histories, 1650s–1940s 123
    Gareth Austin

7. European Empires and the Origins of Global Capitalism 159
    Emma Griffin

8. Capitalism in a Feudal Society? Property Rights and Economic Development in Russia under Serfdom 180
    Tracy Dennison

9. Capitalism in South Asia: Three Transitions 200
    Tirthankar Roy

10. Capitalism, Caste and Subaltern Aspirations in India: Bengal, c.1500–1859 221
    Anirban Karak

11. Chinese Capitalism c.1500–1850: Institutions, Dimensions, Dynamics and Limitations 246
    Kenneth Pomeranz

12. Why the Soybean Export Failed to Trigger the Reemergence of Coercive Labour Control in Eighteenth-Century Manchuria 275
    Horus T'an

13. Property Law at the Transition to Exponential Growth: Examples from Japan 294
    C. Alexander Evans and J. Mark Ramseyer

Index 309

Tables and Figures

Tables

4.1.	Major cycles in the British trans-Atlantic slave trade, by number of people embarked in Africa, 1640s–1690s	86
4.2.	Major cycles in the British trans-Atlantic slave trade, by number of people embarked in Africa, 1690s–1740s	88
4.3.	Major cycles in the British trans-Atlantic slave trade, by number of people embarked in Africa, 1750s–1800s	91
4.4.	Peaks in the share of British slave sales to 'ultimate markets', 1750s–1807	92
6.1.	Annual average exports (£ million, nominal prices) 1900–47	141
6.2.	Average annual cash earnings and labour productivity in South African gold mining, 1911–46	145
6.3.	Real wages and infant mortality in Ghana and South Africa (Black population only), 1910s–1940s	150

Figures

12.1.	The price of rye in Krakow (gram of silver per litre), 1371–1700	280
12.2.	The August price of soybeans in Fengtien prefecture (tael of silver per 100 picul), 1756–1889	282
12.3.	A comparison of August soybean and sorghum price in Fengtien prefecture (tael of silver per 100 picul), 1756–1889	284

Contributors

Ralph Austen was Professor Emeritus of African History at the University of Chicago.

Gareth Austin is Director of Research and Emeritus Professor of Economic History (1928) at the University of Cambridge.

Peter Coclanis is Albert Ray Newsome Distinguished Professor and Director of the Global Research Institute at the University of North Carolina at Chapel Hill.

Tracy Dennison is Edie and Lew Wasserman Professor of Social Science History and Ronald and Maxine Linde Leadership Chair in the Division of Humanities and Social Sciences at the California Institute of Technology.

C.D. Alexander Evans is Visiting Associate Professor at the University of Tokyo.

Emma Griffin is Professor of Modern History at Queen Mary, University of London, and President of the Royal Historical Society.

Robert G. Ingram is Professor of Humanities and Associate Director of the Hamilton Center at the University of Florida.

Anirban Karak is Harper-Schmidt Fellow and Collegiate Assistant Professor at the University of Chicago.

John Majewski is Professor of History at the University of California at Santa Barbara.

Mark Metzler is Giovanni and Amne Costigan Endowed Professor of History at the University of Washington.

Kenneth Pomeranz is University Professor of Modern Chinese History and the College at the University of Chicago.

CONTRIBUTORS

J. Mark Ramseyer is Mitsubishi Professor of Japanese Legal Studies at Harvard Law School.

Tirthankar Roy is Professor of Economic History at the London School of Economics.

Horus T'An is a doctoral student at the University of Texas at Austin.

James M. Vaughn is Assistant Instructional Professor in the College at the University of Chicago.

Acknowledgements

We appreciate the institutions and people who made this book possible, particularly the Menard Family George Washington Forum at Ohio University, the John Templeton Foundation and the Institute for Humane Studies, which provided funding for this project. Maria Rogacheva steadfastly supported this project from the get-go, while Nikki Ohms, Isabella Mershon, James Bohland, Cameron Dunbar and Sebastian Johnson provided invaluable logistical support early on. We also thank the press's anonymous reviewers, whose comments helped sharpen its arguments. This volume is dedicated to the memory of our colleague, Ralph Austen.

Abbreviations

AfEcH	*African Economic History*
AmEcRev	*American Economic Review*
AHR	*American Historical Review*
BHR	*Business History Review*
CEHME	*Cambridge Economic History of Modern Europe*, eds. Stephen Broadberry and Kevin H. O'Rourke, 2 vols. (Cambridge, 2010).
CEHMW	*Cambridge Economic History of the Modern World*, eds. Stephen Broadberry and Kyoji Fukao, 2 vols. (Cambridge, 2021).
CHC	*The Cambridge History of Capitalism*, eds. Larry Neal and Jeffrey G. Williamson, 2 vols. (Cambridge, 2014).
CSSH	*Comparative Studies in Society and History*
E&S	*Enterprise and Society*
EcHR	*Economic History Review*
EEH	*Explorations in Economic History*
EHDR	*Economic History of Developing Regions*
EREH	*European Review of Economic History*
HJ	*Historical Journal*
IESHR	*Indian Economic and Social History Review*
IJAHS	*International Journal of African Historical Studies*
IJMES	*International Journal of Middle Eastern Studies*
JAfH	*Journal of African History*

JAH	*Journal of American History*
JAS	*Journal of American Studies*
JAsS	*Journal of Asian Studies*
JEcH	*Journal of Economic History*
JEMH	*Journal of Early Modern History*
JESHO	*Journal of the Economic and Social History of the Orient*
JGH	*Journal of Global History*
JICH	*Journal of Imperial & Commonwealth History*
JID	*Journal of International Development*
JIH	*Journal of Interdisciplinary History*
JSAS	*Journal of South African Studies*
MAS	*Modern Asian Studies*
MIH	*Modern Intellectual History*
P&P	*Past and Present*
QJE	*Quarterly Journal of Economics*
R&R	*Renaissance and Reformation*
Review	*Review of the Fernand Braudel Center*
RHR	*Radical History Review*
RS	*Renaissance Studies*
TRHS	*Transactions of the Royal Historical Society*
WMQ	*William & Mary Quarterly*

Note on the footnotes

In references to books, unless otherwise noted, the place of publication is London.

I

Capitalism: Histories and Institutions[1]

ROBERT G. INGRAM

This book looks yet again at the history of what Max Weber (1864–1920) called 'the most fateful force in our modern life' – capitalism.[2] Near-endlessly, scholars have debated what is capitalism.[3] But less contested is the notion that capitalism, whatever it might be, has been a radically new form of socio-economic organisation that eventually encompassed and transformed the globe. The conversations about why, how, when and where capitalism emerged have been going on for over two centuries and have fed into the disciplines of history, economics, sociology, political science and philosophy among others. Usually the arguments about why capitalism emerged in the first place slot somewhere onto two axes – *time* and *space*. Most reckon that something wildly discontinuous happened in the early modern period.[4]

---

1 I thank Jill Ingram, Jason Peacey, James Vaughn, Brian Schoen and Bill Bulman for helpful discussions on this subject.
2 Max Weber, *The Protestant Ethic and the Spirit of Capitalism* [1930], trans. Talcott Parsons (2005), xxxi.
3 See, for instance, Jürgen Kocka, *Capitalism: A Short History* (Princeton, 2016), 1–24; Gareth Austin, 'The Return of Capitalism as a Concept', in *Capitalism: The Reemergence of a Historical Concept*, eds. Jürgen Kocka and Marcel van der Linden (2016), 210–214; Albert Hirschman, 'Rival Views of Market Society', in idem, *The Essential Hirschman*, ed. Jeremy Adelman (Princeton, 2013), 214–247; Jerry Z. Muller, *The Mind and the Market: Capitalism in Western Thought* (New York, 2013); Jeffrey Sklansky, 'The elusive sovereign: new intellectual and social histories of capitalism', *MIH*, 9 (2012), 233–248.
4 See, for instance, Weber, *Protestant Ethic, passim*; Karl Marx, *The Communist Manifesto*, ed. Frederic L. Bender (New York, 1988), 55–62. Cf. *CHC*, I, esp. 24–120, which traces capitalism's origins to Babylonia, ancient Greece and ancient Rome.

What changed then was the emergence of something quantifiable – modern economic growth.[5] Its emergence marked a profound shift in human history, one that scholars ever since have sought to explain. Modern economic growth happened first in the West, which Weber attributed mostly to something non-quantifiable – 'the spirit of capitalism'. To gauge whether that is actually the case requires thinking capaciously and comparatively. So, this book brings together scholars working on most of the major world regions and, often, on the connections between the world's various regions. They belong to no one historiographical school nor do they adopt a single, hard-and-fast definition of *capitalism*. That means that they come at the story from different points of entry, with different logics, with different objects of analysis and with different theories of value.[6] But the authors lay out their cases in light of the latest developments in the history of capitalism. Among much else, their essays point anew to the fundamental role of institutions in shaping capitalism's varied and various histories.

I

Properly to appreciate capitalism's histories requires first appreciating the geography, chronology, scope and scale of modern economic growth. Parts of the world underwent profound, at times vertiginous, economic growth beginning in the early modern world. The epicentre of economic growth was the West, particularly Britain.[7] While Britain might have grown more slowly during the Industrial Revolution than once thought, it was first to achieve modern economic growth.[8] As Emma Griffin illustrates in Chapter 7, historians still debate why the Industrial Revolution happened first in Britain; but there were some observable phenomena that attended that revolution and the economic

---

[5] 'Modern economic growth' here signifies growth both in population and in GDP per capita which is both sustained and sustainable. See also Oded Galor, 'Economic Growth in the Very Long Term', in *New Palgrave Dictionary of Economics*, eds. Steven N. Durlauf and Paul A. Johnson (2008), 685–691; Joel Mokyr, *A Culture of Growth: The Origins of the Modern Economy* (Princeton, 2018); Joel Mokyr and Hans-Joachin Voth, 'Understanding Growth in Europe, 1700–1870: Theory and Evidence', in *CEHME*, I: 7–42.

[6] Richard D. Wolff and Stephen A. Resnick, *Contending Economic Theories: Neoclassical, Keynesian and Marxian* (Cambridge, MA, 2012), 347–353.

[7] Many medieval economic historians argue that their period saw greater economic growth than hitherto acknowledged and that it witnessed the first emergence of recognisably capitalist institutions. See, for instance, Karl Gunnar Persson, 'Markets and Coercion in Medieval Europe', in *CHC*, I: 225–266.

[8] Stephen Broadberry, 'Britain, the Industrial Revolution and Modern Economic Growth', in *CEHME*, I: 41.

growth that shot up in its wake.⁹ These included marked technological change; significant capital accumulation; and more workers with more skills.¹⁰ During the stretch between 1700 and 1870, British GDP per capita grew by 150 per cent. Put another way, in 1500, British GDP per capita was two-thirds of Italy's; by 1870, it was more than twice as much.¹¹

The Industrial Revolution affected continental Europe too.¹² As in Britain, continental European countries saw a rise in population: in 1700, Europeans accounted for 19.5 per cent of the world's population; by 1900, they accounted for 27.5 per cent. The Industrial Revolution's effects, though, spread unevenly across Europe. In places like Spain and Italy, a far greater share of GDP came from agriculture than from industry even as late as 1870; the situation was precisely the opposite in places like Britain, Germany, France and the Netherlands. And it showed up in GDP per capita figures, with more industrialised places, mostly in the northwest, having higher GDP per capita than those places which were less industrialised.¹³ During the two centuries of industrialisation in continental Europe, many of the same observable phenomena were on display as had been there in industrialising Britain: more people worked and worked longer; exports rose; and technological changes altered both agriculture and manufacturing.¹⁴ Moreover, there were significant institutional changes, including the modern state's rise and serfdom's decline.¹⁵

---

9   Stephen Broadberry, 'The Industrial Revolution and the Great Divergence: Recent Findings from Historical National Accounting', in *The Handbook of Historical Economics*, eds. Alberto Bisin and Giovanni Fedrico (Amsterdam, 2021), 749–771.
10 Stephen Broadberry *et al*, *British Economic Growth, 1270–1870* (Cambridge, 2015); Joel Mokyr, *The Enlightened Economy: An Economic History of Britain, 1700–1870* (New Haven, 2009).
11 Stephen Broadberry and Kevin H. O'Rourke, 'Introduction to Volume 1', in *CEHME*, I: 2 (Table 1.1).
12 C. Knick Harley, 'British and European Industrialization', in *CHC*, I: 491–532; Stephen Broadberry, Rainer Fremdling and Peter Solar, 'Industry', in *CEHMW*, I: 164–186.
13 Broadberry, Fremdling and Solar, 'Industry', in *CEHMW*, I: 164–186; Giovanni Federico and Andrei Markevich, 'Continental Europe', in *CEHMW*, I: 50 (Table 2.1).
14 Federico and Markevich, 'Continental Europe', 45–66; Peer Vries, 'Europe and the World, 1500–2000', in *Global Economic History*, eds. Tirthankar Roy and Giorgio Riello (2019), 299–318; Jan de Vries, *The Industrious Revolution: Consumer Behavior and the Household Economy, 1650 to the Present* (Cambridge, 2008).
15 Dan Bogart, Mauricio Drelichman, Oscar Gelderblom and Jean-Laurent Rosenthal, 'State and Private Institutions', in *CEHME*, I: 70–95; John Joseph Wallis, 'Institutions', in *CEHMW*, I: 369–390; Charles Maier, *Leviathan 2.0: Inventing Modern Statehood* (Cambridge, MA, 2014); Shane O'Rourke, 'The Emancipation of Serfs in Europe', in *The Cambridge World History of Slavery. Volume 4: AD 1804–AD 2016*, eds. David Eltis *et al* (Cambridge, 2017), 422–440.

Beginning in the late fifteenth century, European nations began to colonise other parts of the world, especially North and South America.[16] Before industrialisation, land was the key natural resource and the American colonies were resource rich. North American British and French colonies experienced particularly stunning economic growth.[17] And after the American Revolution, growth accelerated. In the newly independent nation, the population rose, as did GDP; indeed, real GDP per capita more than doubled between 1790 and 1870. Real GNP also skyrocketed, going up 175-fold between 1774 and 1890, with an average growth of nearly 4 per cent annually.[18] Agriculture predominated in the American economy. In 1800 around three-quarters of all American labour worked on farms; by 1870, fully half still worked on farms. But manufacturing also grew: it accounted for 5 per cent of the total labour force in 1800, while it accounted for 20 per cent by 1870.[19] By World War I's outbreak, the United States had both the largest industrial sector *and* the largest agricultural sector of any country in the world.[20]

There were significant regional economic differences within the United States, most notably between the slave-holding South and other parts of the country during the nineteenth century. Slavery had been the cause of sectional difference from the nation's very beginning. The pre-Civil War South was one of only a handful of actual slave-societies, as opposed to societies in which slavery existed.[21] In the economies of both the South and the West Indies, slaves were hugely important, not only because they were forced to work land under such conditions that no paid labour would work but also because their cost was their upkeep, not their wages. Whether or not slavery is compatible with capitalism

---

16 Gareth Austin, 'Capitalism and the Colonies', in *CHC*, II: 301–347 and idem, 'The Economics of Colonialism', in *Oxford Handbook of Africa and Economics*, eds. Célestina Marga and Justin Lin (Oxford, 2015), 522–535 are excellent introductions to the economic dimensions of this Western expansion beyond Europe's borders.
17 Joshua L. Rosenbloom, 'The Economic History of North America, 1700–1870', in *CEHMW*, I: 193–218. Cf. Regina Graffe, 'Latin America: 1700–1870', in *CEHMW*, I: 219–245 for the uneven economic growth of Latin America, especially after the age of revolution.
18 Robert E. Gallman, 'Economic Growth and Structural Change in the Long Nineteenth Century', in *The Cambridge Economic History of the United States. Volume 2: The Long Nineteenth Century*, eds. Stanley L. Engerman and Robert E. Gallman (Cambridge, 2000), 2.
19 Rosenbloom, 'Economic History of North America', 208–210; Jeremy Atack, 'America: Capitalism's Promised Land', in *CHC*, I: 549–563.
20 Gallman, 'Economic Growth and Structural Change', 55.
21 M.I. Finley, *Ancient Slavery and Modern Ideology* (New York, 1980), 9 identified ancient Greece, ancient Rome, Brazil, the Caribbean and the U.S. South as the only five 'genuine slave societies'. Philip Morgan, 'Slavery in the British Caribbean', and Laurent Dubois, 'Slavery in the French Caribbean, 1635–1804', in *The Cambridge World History of Slavery. Volume 3: AD 1420–AD 1804*, eds. David Eltis and Stanley L. Engerman (Cambridge, 2011), 378–406, 431–449 briefly survey West Indian slavery.

has long been debated; but that Southern planters invested significant amounts of capital into slavery is indisputable.[22]

Slaves helped to grow tobacco in Virginia, rice in coastal Carolina and sugar in Louisiana; but by far the biggest focus of slave labour was on cotton. Both the invention of the cotton gin and the rising British demand for cotton transformed the South economically. By 1850, 75 per cent of slaves worked on cotton plantations. The division of labour and the gang labour system boosted cotton production massively: in 1790, the South produced around 5,000 bales of cotton annually; by the Civil War's outbreak, it produced around 4,000,000 bales per year.[23] Most of this was destined for Europe: in 1860, Europe imported five times as much cotton from the South as it did from the rest of the world combined, something which made the American South a key player in the mid nineteenth-century global economy.[24] The economic growth in the South was not uninterrupted – there was a major economic downturn after 1837, when the prices of both cotton and slaves plummeted. But both rebounded during the 1850s and by the time the Civil War broke out, there was no sense, either in the South or in the North, that slavery was an institution which would collapse because it was not profitable.[25] And yet though some of America's richest individuals lived in the South, it was the North which really boomed during the nineteenth century. Part of this shows up in population figures: in 1780, the North and South had roughly equal populations; by 1860, the population of non-slave states was double that in

---

22 The literature on this subject is vast. Eugene Genovese, *The Political Economy of Slavery: Studies in the Economy and Society in the Slave South* (New York, 1965) and idem and Elizabeth Fox-Genovese, *Fruits of Merchant Capital: Slavery and Bourgeois Property in the Rise and Expansion of Capitalism* (Oxford, 1983), for instance, argue that slavery was not capitalistic. Robert Fogel and Stanley L. Engerman, *Time on the Cross: The Economics of American Negro Slavery* (New York, 1974); Trevor Burnard and John Garrigus, *The Plantation Machine: Atlantic Capitalism in French Saint-Dominigue and British Jamaica* (Philadelphia, 2018); and Trevor Burnard, *Planters, Merchants and Slaves: Plantation Societies in British America, 1650–1820* (Chicago, 2019), by contrast, stress the capitalistic nature of the plantation system.
23 Rosenbloom, 'Economic History of North America', 211 (Figure 8.5).
24 Brian D. Schoen, 'Containing Empire: The United States and the World in the Civil War Era', in *The Cambridge History of America in the World. Volume 2: The Nineteenth Century*, eds. Kristine Hoganson and Jay Sexton (Cambridge, 2021), 141–171; idem, 'The Civil War in Europe', in *The Cambridge History of the American Civil War. Volume 2: Affairs of the State*, ed. Aaron Sheehan-Deen (Cambridge, 2019), 342–366; idem, *The Fragile Fabric of Union: Cotton, Federal Politics and the Global Origins of the Civil War* (Baltimore, 2009).
25 Stanley L. Engerman, 'U.S. Slavery and its Aftermath, 1804–2000', in *The Cambridge History of World Slavery. Volume 4: AD 1804–AD 2016*, eds. David Eltis *et al.* (Cambridge, 2017), 164; idem, 'Slavery and its Consequences for the South in the Nineteenth Century', in *Cambridge Economic History of the United States. Volume 2: The Long Nineteenth Century*, eds. Engerman and Gallman, 351.

slave states.[26] Though the American economy eventually outstripped all competitors during the twentieth century, it took nearly a century after the Civil War for the American South to catch up to the North.[27]

Modern economic growth, then, came first to the West, initially in Europe and then in the United States. Outside of the West the economic picture was less clear. Africa was the external source of the Americas' slave population.[28] Coerced labour of all sorts was a feature not a bug of African economic life for a long time, not least because it, like America, had an abundance of land but a scarcity of labour. Though the economic data is not robust, it is fair to say that Africa achieved modern economic growth later than the West. It now seems likelier than not that the African population stayed roughly the same between 1700 and 1900.[29] During the twentieth century, while places like China, India and Indonesia saw their GDP per capita rise markedly, Africa's has stagnated; it is now the poorest part of the world.[30] So, while Africa was integral to the interconnected world economy from the sixteenth century onwards, its economic story bears few similarities to those of Western countries.[31]

For South Asia, the picture was less dire but still not rosy.[32] It was a region which long had traded with the outside world before encountering Europeans. There was, in South Asia, significant regional diversity, most notably between the Himalayas, the Indo-Gangeatic basin, the Deccan plateau and the littoral. So too were there significant political differences, most notably between the landlocked inland empires and the coastal cities. The former relied on agricultural taxation to fund them and were larger and more powerful than the latter. Beginning in the early sixteenth century, the Mughal Empire was the most powerful polity in South Asia.[33] Though their empire notionally remained intact

---

26   Rosenbloom, 'Economic History of North America', 212–213.
27   Peter Coclanis, 'The Southern Economy in the Long Twentieth Century', in *A New History of the American South*, ed. W. Fitzhugh Brundage (Chapel Hill, 2023), 464–496 expertly surveys the terrain.
28   David Eltis and David Richardson, *Atlas of the Transatlantic Slave Trade* (New Haven, 2010).
29   Patrick Manning, 'Africa: Slavery and the World Economy, 1700–1870', in *CEHMW*, I: 246–264; Gareth Austin, 'Africa: Economic Change South of the Sahara since c.1500', in *Global Economic History*, eds. Roy and Riello, 251–270; Morten Jerven, 'The Emergence of African Capitalism', in *CHC*, I: 431–454.
30   Ewout Frankema, 'African Economic Development: Growth, Reversals and Deep Transitions', in *CEHMW*, II: 276–305 at 277 (Table 10.1).
31   Cf. Stephen Broadberry and Leigh Gardner, 'Economic growth in Sub-Saharan Africa, 1885–2008: Evidence from eight countries', *EEH* 83 (2022), 1–21.
32   Tirthankar Roy, *An Economic History of India, 1707–1857* (2022) and Anad V. Samy, 'From the Mughals to the Raj: India, 1700–1858', in *CEHMW*: I, 123–145 ably survey the subject. For an earlier period, see Tapan Raychaudhuri and Ifran Habib (eds.), *The Cambridge Economic History of India. Volume I: c.1200–c.1750* (Cambridge, 1982).
33   John F. Richards, *The Mughal Empire* (Cambridge, 1995).

until 1858, the Mughals had, by the early nineteenth century, lost control to the British, who consolidated their hold on the whole subcontinent across the nineteenth century.[34]

In the mid nineteenth century, as in centuries before, agriculture accounted for most of the South Asian economy. During the stretch of time from the Mughal empire's rise to its demise three centuries later, South Asians' standards of living declined.[35] Where in 1600, Indian GDP per capita had been 60 per cent of British GDP per capita, by 1871, it amounted to only 15 per cent of British GDP per capita.[36] So too did relative Indian wages decline across the early modern period. In the mid sixteenth century, Indian silver wages were 21 per cent and grain wages were 83 per cent of English wages; by the mid nineteenth century, Indian silver wages were 12 per cent and grain wages were 29 per cent of English wages.[37] By any accounting, then, Indian living standards were declining at the very same time that British and northwest European living standards were rising.[38]

This gap between European economic growth and Indian economic stagnation was mirrored in China, a phenomenon scholars have dubbed the Great Divergence.[39] In the mid sixteenth century, Chinese silver wages were 39 per cent and grain wages were 87 per cent of English wages. By the mid nineteenth century, Chinese silver wages were 15 per cent and grain wages were

---

34 James M. Vaughn, *The Politics of Empire at the Accession of George III: The East India Company and the Crisis and Transformation of Britain's Imperial State* (New Haven, 2019); Philip J. Stern, *The Company-State: Corporate Sovereignty and the Early Modern Foundations of the British Empire in India* (Oxford, 2012); P.J. Marshall, *Bengal: The British Bridgehead: East India, 1740–1828* (Cambridge, 1988) and C.A. Bayly, *Indian Society and the Making of the British Empire* (Cambridge, 1988) recount this story, if with different emphases.
35 Stephen Broadberry, 'Historical national accounting and dating the Great Divergence', *JGH*, 16 (2021), 286–293.
36 Stephen Broadberry, Johan Custodis and Bishnupriya Gupta, 'India and the great divergence: an Anglo-Indian comparison of GDP per capita, 1600–1871', *EEH*, 55 (2015), 58–75.
37 Stephen Broadberry and Bishnupriya Gupta, 'The early modern divergence: wages, prices and economic development in Europe and Asia, 1500–1800', *EcHR*, 59 (2006), 2–31.
38 Cf. Prasannan Parthasarathi, *The Transition to a Colonial Economy: Weavers, Merchants and Kings in South India, 1720–1800* (Cambridge, 2001); idem, 'Rethinking wages and competitiveness in the eighteenth century: Britain and South India', *P&P*, 158 (1998), 79–109.
39 Kenneth Pomeranz, *The Great Divergence: Europe, China and the Making of the Modern World Economy* (Princeton, 2000) set the terms of the recent debate on the subject. Cf. Bishnupriya Gupta and Debin Ma, 'Europe in an Asian Mirror: the Great Divergence', in *CEHME*: I, 264–285. Christopher Isett, 'China: The Start of the Great Divergence', in *CEHMW*, I: 97–122 briefly surveys eighteenth- and nineteenth-century China's economic history.

38 per cent of English wages.[40] The same sorts of patterns emerge when one compares the real wages of China and Europe across the early modern period: Chinese real wages fell across the eighteenth century while those in Europe, particularly those in northwestern Europe, rose dramatically.[41]

Scholars have vigorously dated the timing of the Great Divergence, something which matters because its timing helps to explain why it happened.[42] Some reckon that it happened during the eighteenth century after the Industrial Revolution had begun and during the consolidation of European colonial empires, especially in South Asia.[43] Most scholars now, though, agree that sometime just before the Industrial Revolution, Britain and the Netherlands began to grow more quickly and in a more sustained way not just than the rest of the world but also than other parts of Europe.[44] In recent times, there has also been a significant gap in growth among East Asian countries, as countries like Japan, South Korea and Taiwan have grown more rapidly than their regional neighbours.[45] Explaining this intra-Asian Little Divergence has also been a scholarly imperative.

II

Modern economic growth, then, happened in some places – mostly Western places – beginning in the early modern period, but not in others. Why? Capitalism is the most common explanation. Precisely *what* it is and *why* it happened where it happened has been the source of intense debate from almost the moment it began to happen. The optimist's case has followed along the lines laid out during the late eighteenth century by Adam Smith (1723–1790), who

---

40 Broadberry and Gupta, 'The Early Modern Divergence'.
41 Robert C. Allen *et al.*, 'Wages, prices and living standards in China, 1738–1925: in comparison with Europe, Japan and India', *EcHR*, 64 (2011), 8–38.
42 Stephen Broadberry, Hanhui Guan and David Daokui Li, 'China, Europe and the Great Divergence: a study in historical national accounting, 980–1850', *JEcH*, 78 (2018), 955–1000.
43 Prasannan Parthasarathi and Kenneth Pomeranz, 'The Great Divergence Debate', in *Global Economic History*, eds. Roy and Riello, 19–37.
44 See Jack Goldstone, 'Dating the Great Divergence', *JGH*, 16 (2021), 266–285; idem, 'Data and Dating the Great Divergence', in *Global Economic History*, eds. Roy and Riello, 38–53.
45 Jean-Pascal Bassino *et al.*, 'Japan and the great divergence, 730–1874', *EEH*, 72 (2019), 1–22; Debin Ma, 'Economic Change in East Asia from the Seventeenth to the Twentieth Century', in *Global Economic History*, eds. Roy and Riello, 287–298; Masaki Nakabayashi, 'Tokugawa Japan and the Foundations of Modern Economic Growth in Asia', in *CEHMW*, I: 67–96; Mark Metzler, 'Japan: The Arc of Industrialization', in *The New Cambridge History of Japan. Volume 3: The Modern Japanese Nation and Empire, c.1868 to the Twenty-First Century*, ed. Laura Hein (Cambridge, 2023), 293–337.

lived in what some thought was one of capitalism's cradles.[46] Smith had a theory of commercial society, characterised by the division of labour.[47] That division, he argued, was 'the necessary, though very slow and gradual consequence of a certain propensity in human nature ... the propensity to truck, barter and exchange one thing for another'.[48] Commercial society, then, was grounded on natural sociable human instincts but emerged only in particular circumstances. Smith reckoned that the Fall of Rome had inaugurated '[t]he rapine and violence which the barbarians exercised over the antient inhabitants' and 'interrupted the commerce between the towns and the country'.[49] Thereafter land served not only as the means 'of subsistence merely, but of power and protection'.[50] The entire feudal order, with its laws of primogeniture and of entail, grew up to protect land. Under feudalism, though, neither landowners nor their various tenants, free and unfree, really improved the land. During the early modern period trading cities started to import 'improved manufactures and expensive luxuries of richer countries'.[51] As the taste for luxury goods became more general, merchants tried to figure out how to manufacture those goods domestically to save costs: division of labour made manufactures cheaper to produce. As commercial and manufacturing towns grew, they actually 'contributed to the improvement and cultivation of the countries', not least because 'commerce and manufactures gradually introduced order and good government, and with them, the liberty and security of individuals, among the inhabitants of the country, who had before lived in almost a continual state of war with their neighbours, and of servile dependency upon their superiors'.[52]

46 'Nowhere else in the world did the birth of capitalism come about in so curious a fashion as in Scotland. Nothing is more surprising than the suddenness of its appearance. It is as though a pistol shot had given the signal of the capitalist spirit, fully grown, to come into the land and dominate it. You cannot help thinking of Victoria Regina, which blooms overnight.' Werner Sombart, *Quintessence of Capitalism: A Study of the History and Psychology of the Modern Business Man*, trans. M. Epstein (New York, 1915), 148. We thank Philip Roessner and Julian Goodare for this reference.
47 Michael Sonenscher, *Capitalism: The Story Behind the Word* (Princeton, 2022), esp. 1–20 distinguishes between Smith's theory of commercial society and later theories of capitalism. Sonenscher reckons that most have errantly conflated the two. On commercial society, see also Istvan Hont, *Politics in Commercial Society: Jean-Jacques Rousseau and Adam Smith*, eds. Béla Kapossy and Michael Sonenscher (Cambridge, MA, 2015).
48 Adam Smith, *An Inquiry into the Nature and Causes of the Wealth of Nations*, eds. R.H. Campbell and A.S. Skinner (Oxford, 1979), I, 25. Cf. Robert Brenner, 'Property and Progress: Where Adam Smith Went Wrong', in *Marxist History-writing for the Twenty-First Century*, ed. Chris Wickham (Oxford, 2007), 49–111.
49 Smith, *An Inquiry ... Wealth of Nations*, 381.
50 Ibid., 383.
51 Ibid., 407.
52 Ibid., 412.

The unintended consequences of commercial society, then, were prosperity and peace.

> A revolution of the greatest importance to the publick happiness, was in this manner brought about by two different orders of people, who had not the least intention to serve the publick. To gratify the most childish vanity was the sole motive of the great proprietors. The merchants and artificers, much less ridiculous, acted merely from a view to their own interest, and in pursuit of their own pedlar principle of turning a penny wherever a penny was to be got. Neither of them had either knowledge or foresight of that great revolution which the folly of one, and the industry of the other, was gradually bringing about.[53]

This is a distilled version of the *doux-commerce* thesis.[54]

Karl Marx (1818–1883) acknowledged that Smith was a great economist, even as he disagreed with many of Smith's premises and conclusions.[55] Smith's was a theory of commercial society; Marx's was a theory of capitalism, which is to say it was a theory of property.[56] Marx's philosophy of history was straightforward: 'The history of all hitherto existing society is the history of class struggles'. History, put most reductively, pitted the 'oppressor' against 'the oppressed' – they 'stood in constant opposition to one another, carried on uninterrupted, now hidden, now open fight, a fight that each time ended, either in a revolutionary re-constitution of society at large, or in the common ruin of the contending classes'.[57] In ancient Rome and medieval Europe, multiple classes, each with 'subordinate gradations', struggled against each other. By the time Marx wrote in the mid nineteenth century, that old world had passed. Instead, he wrote from the vantage of what he called 'modern bourgeois society', which he reckoned had 'sprouted from the ruins of feudal society'.[58]

Marx's narrative, like Smith's, jumped off from the feudal Middle Ages. The modern bourgeoisie lineally descended from medieval burghers, who themselves emerged from the serfs. The West's incursion into the rest of the world from the late fifteenth century onwards opened new markets. As more and more markets

---

53 Ibid., 422.
54 Cf. Hirschman, 'Rival Views of Market Society', 216–218; idem, *The Passions and the Interests: Political Arguments for Capitalism before its Triumph* (Princeton, 2013), esp. 56–66.
55 Spencer J. Pack, 'Adam Smith and Marx', in *The Oxford Handbook of Adam Smith*, eds. Christopher J. Berry et al. (Oxford, 2013), 524–538.
56 Sonenscher, *Capitalism*, 77–95.
57 Marx, *Communist Manifesto*, 55. See also, Gareth Stedman Jones, 'Introduction', in Karl Marx and Friedrich Engels, *The Communist Manifesto*, ed. Gareth Stedman Jones (2002), 3–184.
58 Marx, *Communist Manifesto*, 56.

emerged, manufacturing supplanted the 'feudal system of industry', which 'no longer sufficed for the growing wants of the new markets'.[59] Eventually the system of manufacturing proved insufficient to satisfy the ever-growing demand of ever-widening markets and itself got displaced by 'Modern Industry'.[60] The bourgeoisie – what Marx's co-author Friedrich Engels (1820–1895) called 'the exploiting and ruling class' – were a relentlessly revolutionary class, destroying the feudal order: 'In a word, for exploitation, veiled by religious and political illusions, it has substituted naked, shameless, direct, brutal exploitation.'[61] To do this, the bourgeoisie 'keeps more and more doing away with the scattered state of the population, of the means of production, and of property. It has agglomerated population, centralised the means of production, and has concentrated property in a few hands'.[62] Capitalism, on Marx's reading, was a relentlessly destructive force both whose logic and means were exploitation.

As Peter Coclanis explains in Chapter 2, there have been endless variations on these competing Smithian and Marxian themes.[63] For most economists and economic historians, capitalism has been, at the very least, the lesser of other economic evils. Among other social scientists and humanities scholars, by contrast, capitalism has rarely enjoyed good press.[64] Particularly influential of late has been the so-called 'New History of Capitalism' (NHC). Neither Marxist nor neo-liberal nor identarian, the NHC aims to analyse the cold hard facts of economic life. Gaining steam after the financial crisis of 2007–2008, the historians working in the NHC tradition are united by a few basic tenets.[65] First, economic life is 'politically constituted', so that political economy and the operations of the state more generally are essential components of any study of economic life.[66] Secondly, the NHC focuses on 'capitalism in action'.[67] This is NHC's signal tenet – it means emphasising slavery's importance. Indeed, NHC's unified field theory is that chattel slavery is the foundation of modern economic growth in America, which, in turn, became the chief engine of capitalism's global spread. As Sven Beckert and Seth Rockman put it in their introduction to the NHC manifesto, *Slavery's Capitalism* (2016),

59   Ibid., 56.
60   Ibid.
61   Ibid., 56–57; Friedrich Engels, 'Preface to the English Edition of 1888', in ibid., 46.
62   Ibid., 59.
63   Cf. Jeffry Frieden and Ronald Rogowski, 'Modern Capitalism: Enthusiasts, Opponents and Reformers', in *CHC*, II: 384–425.
64   Cf. Joseph Schumpeter, *Capitalism, Socialism and Democracy* (New York, 1942), 145–155 ('Sociology of the Intellectual').
65   Sklansky, 'The Elusive Sovereign: New Intellectual and Social Histories of Capitalism' nicely contextualises the NHC.
66   Sven Beckert and Christine Desan, 'Introduction', in *American Capitalism: New Histories*, eds. Sven Beckert and Christine Desan (New York, 2018), 10.
67   Ibid., 11.

During the eighty years between the American Revolution and the Civil War, slavery was indispensable to the economic development of the United States. Such a claim is at once self-evidently true and empirically obscure. A scholarly revolution over the past two decades, which brought mainstream accounts into line with the long-standing positions in Africana and Black studies, has recognized slavery as the foundational American institution, organizing the nation's politics, legal structures and cultural practices with remarkable power to determine the life chances of those moving through society as black or white.[68]

It is not a stretch from there to argue that all that modern wealth owes everything to an institution which all now regard as an unmitigated human evil.[69] The third distinctive feature which the NHC self-identifies focuses on knowledge production. On this view, the discipline of economics reveals itself as a potentially suspect mode of analysis.[70] Finally, the NHC reckon that they have 'often taken a more global perspective', including focusing on the state's role in shaping international economic life.[71]

The NHC has been influential amongst American historians, particularly those who are not economic historians. Critics claim that the NHC story is mostly a morality tale.[72] Whether or not that it is the case, it is fair to say that the NHC historians are activist historians, eyes zeroed in on past (and present) iniquities and inequities. Theirs is as a self-conscious critique of the powerful on behalf of the powerless.[73] That is why they focus especially on

---

[68] Sven Beckert and Seth Rockman, 'Introduction', in *Slavery's Capitalism: A New History of American Economic Development*, eds. Sven Beckert and Seth Rockman (Philadelphia, 2016), 1.

[69] Eric Williams, *Capitalism and Slavery* (Chapel Hill, 1994 [1944]) had previously made an analogous argument. Barbara Solow and Stanley Engerman (eds.), *British Capitalism and Caribbean Slavery: The Legacy of Eric Williams* (Cambridge, 1988) introduces and assesses Williams's argument. More recently, Joseph Inikori, *Africans and the Industrial Revolution in England: A Study in International Trade and Economic Development* (Cambridge, 2002) adds more flesh to the bones of the Williams thesis, while idem, 'The First Capitalist Nation: The Development of Capitalism in England', in *Capitalisms: Towards a Global History*, eds. Kaveh Yazdani and Dilip M. Memon (Oxford, 2020), 251–276 refines it.

[70] Beckert and Desan, 'Introduction', 12–13.

[71] Ibid., 13.

[72] See, for instance, Gavin Wright, 'Slavery and Anglo-American capitalism revisited', *EcHR*, 73 (2020), 353–383; Trevor Burnard and Giorgio Riello, 'Slavery and the new history of capitalism', *JGH*, 15 (2020), 225–244; Alan L. Olmstead and Paul W. Rhode, 'Cotton, slavery, and the New History of Capitalism', *EEH*, 67 (2018), 1–17; Eric Hilt, 'Economic history, historical analysis and the "New History of Capitalism"', *JEcH*, 77 (2017), 511–536. Economic historians have proved particularly astringent critics of the NHC.

[73] See, for instance, Sven Beckert, *Empire of Cotton: A Global History* (New York, 2015); Edward E. Baptist, *Half Has Never Been Told: Slavery and the Making of American Capitalism* (New York, 2014); Sven Beckert, 'The History of American Capitalism', in

'the distribution of social power in society'. Beckert put it most succinctly: when studying capitalism, 'Power in all of its dimensions is crucial'.[74] This approach gives the NHC project contemporary relevance and confers moral urgency on its findings. It also presents itself as an explanation for everything. American historians increasingly take NHC conclusions to be axiomatic; and the mini-industry of capitalism courses, particularly in American universities, continues to grow.

The NHC steadfastly refuses a single definition of capitalism. Most scholarly studies of capitalism, by contrast, have tried to define the object of study. Some are precise or technical.[75] Others are more capacious. One of the editors of the recent *Cambridge History of Capitalism*, for instance, defined capitalism as being characterised by '(1) private property rights; (2) contracts enforceable by third parties; (3) markets with responsive prices; and (4) supportive governments'.[76] The NHC, by contrast, have made a virtue of *not* having a rigorous definition of capitalism. As Seth Rockman put it, the NHC 'has minimal investment in a fixed or theoretical definition of capitalism. Few works in the field begin with an explicit statement of what the author means by capitalism. If the goal is to figure out what capitalism is and how it has operated historically, scholars seem willing to let capitalism float as a placeholder while they look for ground-level evidence of a system in operation'.[77] If the authors in this collection occasionally question one or another NHC premise or conclusion, they embrace its refusal to offer a single, straitjacketed definition of capitalism. Instead, they reckon that capitalism has histories, not a single history, and that it needs to be considered in its various contexts to discern what constitutes it.[78]

American History Now, eds. Eric Foner and Lisa McGirr (Philadelphia, 2014), 314–335; Seth Rockman, 'What makes the history of capitalism newsworthy?', *Journal of the Early Republic*, 34 (2014), 439–466; Walter Johnson, *River of Dark Dreams: Slavery and Empire in the Cotton Kingdom* (Cambridge, MA, 2013).
74 'Interchange: the history of capitalism', *JAH*, 101 (2014), 525.
75 The literature is vast, but see, for instance, Trevor Aston (ed.), *Crisis in Europe, 1560–1660: Essays from Past and Present* (1969); Leszek Kolakowski, *Main Currents of Marxism*, 2 vols. (Oxford, 1981); T.H. Aston and C.H.E. Philpin (eds.), *The Brenner Debate: Agrarian Class Structure and Economic Development in Pre-Industrial Europe* (Cambridge, 1985); Immanuel Wallerstein, *World-Systems Analysis: An Introduction* (Durham, NC, 2004); Ellen Meiksins Wood, *The Origin of Capitalism: A Longer View* (New York, 2017 [1999]).
76 Larry Neal, 'Introduction', in *CHC*, I: 2.
77 Rockman, 'What Makes the History of Capitalism Newsworthy?', 442. The sceptic might argue that the NHC has an implicit definition of 'capitalism' – extraction based initially on slavery.
78 See Immanuel Wallerstein, *Historical Capitalism with Capitalist Civilization* (New York, 1996), 13.

III

The chapters in this book are written in light of the NHC's claims, as well as in light of other recent innovative work on capitalism's history. Peter Coclanis opens the volume by thinking concertedly about the NHC narrative.[79] Coclanis is an economic historian who has written extensively before on the economic history of the American South and on the ways the South fits into the international economic order. In Chapter 2 below, he conceives of capitalism as an economic and social system or, rather, as a metaphorical construct that describes how a system works that is bounded spatially and temporally.

While embracing the concerns Marc Bloch (1886–1944) expressed about constructing origin stories, Coclanis reckons that Carl Degler (1921–2014) was right that capitalism came on the first ships; and, on Coclanis's reading, it came not only early but violently.[80] This conviction that capitalism had 'early and strong purchase' in America is, indeed, one thing upon which he and the NHC agree. On Coclanis's reading, capitalism affected different groups in different places in different times. In some places like the Ohio River Valley or South Carolina, for instance, capitalism's emergence was a slow, halting, unclear process. Coclanis also agrees with the NHC that there was 'compatibility, even affinity early on, between capitalism and slavery'. Where he parts company with the NHC, though, is in thinking that capitalism in general and in America more specifically was inexorably, inescapably violent. Violence, he contends, was not inherent but, instead, was

> associated with [Western capitalism] under certain conditions, most notably, in its early phases, and in cases involving expansion into new geographic zones, especially zones dominated by others or organized in non-capitalist ways, most markedly when there are power asymmetries strongly favourable to Western capitalists'[81]

To explain why and where capitalism emerged in North America when and how it did, we need to account for a range of considerations, including *mentalités*, resources ('knowledge, infrastructure, capital') and institutions, including the state.

Though no cheerleader for capitalism, Coclanis reckons that over time capitalism expressed itself quite positively, especially when compared to the alternatives. When and how capitalism expressed itself, on his reading, depended on the institutional setting. Here Colcanis is an institutionalist in the

---

79 See Peter Coclanis, 'Slavery, capitalism and the problem of misprision', *JAS*, 52 (2018), E46.
80 Carl N. Degler, *Out of Our Past: The Forces that Shaped Modern America* (New York, 1959), 1.
81 There are echoes of this argument in Ralph Austen's chapter (Chapter 5), as well.

New Institutional Economics (NIE) tradition.[82] One of the NIE's progenitors, Douglass North (1920–2015), defined *institutions* as

> the rules of the game in a society or, more formally, ... the humanly devised constraints that shape human interaction. In consequence they structure incentives in human exchange, whether political, social or economic. Institutional change shapes the way societies evolve through time and hence is the key to understanding historical change.[83]

If institutions are the rules of the game, there are different sorts of institutional orders. North, John Joseph Wallis and Barry Weingast contrasted *open-access orders* with *limited-access orders*.[84] Many things distinguish these two orders, but a few are salient. First, open-access orders have political systems which allow for the predictable and mostly peaceful change of the rules of the game. Characteristics of open-access political regimes include 'widespread political participation, the use of elections to select governments, constitutional arrangements to limit and define the powers of government and unbiased application of the rule of law'.[85] Secondly, open-access political orders have distinctive economies, ones marked by 'the ability to create economic organisations at will, open entry and competition in many markets, and the free movement of goods and individuals over space and time'.[86] This North *et al.* call 'open-access economics', a system which mutually reinforces 'open-access politics'.

Recognising the differences between open- and limited-access orders, Coclanis insists, helps us to make sense of capitalism's emergence and expressions in the Americas. The West Indies, a thorough-going slave economy, was a limited-access order.[87] Coclanis concludes that capitalism failed there and that the results of its failure remain visible today. Otherwise, capitalism was a success for most people most of the time in British North America, even in the Lower and Upper South, which was mostly, but not totally, a limited-access order before the American Civil War. The North, though, was, on Coclanis's

---

82 Éric Brousseau and Jean-Michel Clachant (eds.), *New Institutional Economics: A Guidebook* (Cambridge, 2008).
83 Douglass C. North, *Institutions, Institutional Change and Economic Performance* (Cambridge, 1990), 3. Sebastian Galiani and Itai Sened (eds.), *Institutions, Property Rights and Economic Growth: The Legacy of Douglass North* (Cambridge, 2014) surveys North's work.
84 Douglass North, John Joseph Wallis and Barry R. Weingast, *Violence and Social Orders: A Conceptual Framework for Reinterpreting Recorded Human History* (Cambridge, 2009).
85 Douglass North, John Joseph Wallis and Barry R. Weingast, 'Violence and the rise of open-access orders', *Journal of Democracy*, 20 (2009), 56.
86 Ibid.
87 Victor Bulmer-Thomas, *The Economic History of the Caribbean since the Napoleonic Wars* (Cambridge, 2012) surveys the region's economic history.

reading, a full-on open-access order. Unsurprisingly to him, it was one of the 'hearths of capitalist development' and the nation's 'economic dynamo'.

It is not just his estimation of capitalism's long-term causes and effects which distinguishes Coclanis from the NHC. More fundamentally, he and the NHC understand institutions differently. The NHC has highlighted its own interest in the state, stressing that political choices shape economic activity. Coclanis would agree, but, like several other authors in his volume, would also insist that we think even more capaciously about institutions, taking into account not just political economy but a whole other set of institutions which together shape the rules of the game.

John Majewski, like Coclanis an American economic historian, takes as his subject in Chapter 3 one of the themes in Coclanis's chapter – the American North/South economic divide.[88] On Majewski's reading the American Civil War pitted 'two rival forms of capitalism' against one another. The Northern form 'focused on encouraging widespread economic creativity', while its Southern counterpart focused 'more narrowly on staple crops and enslaved labour'. Majewski dubs the Northern vision *creative capitalism* and argues that few have really paid attention to the role of creativity as an economic force, even though all economies and societies rely on creativity. Majewski defines *creativity* as '… imagination and insight that produces something that is at once novel and some combination of economically useful, aesthetically pleasing and emotionally moving'. Creativity is, put another way, 'the insight and imagination that precedes a literal act of creation'. Creativity is a quality that societies can encourage, and Majewski reckons that the early nineteenth-century North focused concertedly on encouraging creativity. Creative capitalism specialises in turning creativity into a commodity, as imagination and novelty are converted into goods and services with a market value. Patents, a particularly important vehicle in commodifying creativity, were 'surprisingly prominent in northern culture'. As Majewski notes, patenting increased five-fold between c.1840 and c.1860: crucially, 95 per cent of patents were held by Northerners. Majewski illustrates how capitalism took root both in the urban and rural North, not only through new institutions but also through the northern support of public education and encouragement of widespread literacy. Creative capitalism, as Majewski shows, had a political valence. It was particularly strong in the anti-slavery movement and the political party which represented it. 'In the 1850s, the Republican Party took antislavery economic critiques and turned them into a successful policy agenda that successfully broadened the appeal of creative capitalism', he insists. But that Republican vision could only work if the federal

---

88 Cf. John Majewski, *Modernizing a Slave Economy: The Economic Vision of the Confederate Nation* (Chapel Hill, 2009); idem, *A House Dividing: Economic Development in Pennsylvania and Virginia before the Civil War* (Cambridge, 2000).

government limited slavery's spread. Hence Majewski's argument that the American Civil War pitted two rival capitalisms against one another.

Joseph Schumpeter (1883–1950) famously identified relentless churn as one of capitalism's signal characteristics.[89] 'Capitalism … is by nature a form of economic change and not only never is but never can be stationary', he posited.[90] Capitalism has this character because it prioritises innovation, which is the engine of creative destruction.[91] The precondition to the innovation characteristic of capitalism is the sort of creativity about which John Majewski is so interested. Another characteristic feature of capitalism which Schumpeter identified was the business cycle, the subject of Chapter 4 by Mark Metzler.[92] Metzler, who has long written about Japanese economics and about global economic history, turns his attention here to Atlantic slavery and what it can tell us about the business cycle. Metzler's argument is that modern business cycles 'are an expression of fundamental capitalist processes' and, moreover, that those cycles 'emerged early and with special clarity in the British trans-Atlantic slave trade'. Metzler, then, is interested in locating business cycles in time, an issue of no small significance since it helps us to get closer to understanding both capitalism's origins and its signature features. As he pointedly puts it, 'The vital point here is the corollary hypothesis that when we see business cycles, we are seeing capitalism'. In the process of making his argument, Metzler puts paid to the notion that business cycles were a British phenomenon which then infected the rest of the world.

Metzler studies business cycles by way of trans-Atlantic slavery.[93] He is definitely of the school which views Atlantic slavery as a thoroughgoingly capitalistic activity, for it involved multi-sided credit-funded transactions and investments and all across a very wide geographical scope. Metzler identifies six Atlantic slave trade cycles between 1644 and 1694 and a further seven between 1752 and 1807. He also notes that the eighteenth-century ones were 'temporally continuous with industrial-era business cycles'. While acknowledging that much work remains to be done both on the nature of cycles and on cycles within various industries, Metzler presents evidence which strongly suggests the presence of modern business cycles – and, hence, capitalism – across the Atlantic world by at least the mid seventeenth century.

---

89 See Joyce Appleby, *The Relentless Revolution: A History of Capitalism* (New York, 2010), which offers a Schumpeterian history of its subject.
90 Schumpeter, *Capitalism, Socialism and Democracy*, 82.
91 Ibid., 81–86.
92 Joseph Schumpeter, *Business Cycles: A Theoretical, Historical and Statistical Analysis of the Capitalist Process*, 2 vols. (New York, 1939).
93 See Mark Metzler, 'The interactive emergence of capitalist trade-cycle dynamics in maritime Asia, 1640s–1760s: overview and prospectus', *Asian Review of World Histories*, 10 (2022), 222–238.

Slavery, of course, sits at the heart of the NHC narrative of capitalism. Though NHC historians do not say explicitly that slavery was the means of 'primitive accumulation', they do assert that slavery made possible modern capitalism's existence.[94] In his chapter, Ralph Austen, an African historian particularly interested in political economy, considers the connection between violence and primitive accumulation. In *Capital* (1867), Marx famously argued,

> We have seen how money is transformed into capital; how surplus-value is made through capital, and how capital is made from surplus-value. But the accumulation of capital presupposes surplus-value; surplus-value presupposes capitalist production; capitalist production presupposes the availability of considerable masses of capital and labour-power in the hands of commodity producers. The whole movement, therefore, seems to turn around in a never-ending circle, which we can only get out of by assuming a primitive accumulation (the 'previous accumulation' of Adam Smith) which precedes capitalist accumulation; an accumulation which is not the result of the capitalist mode of production but its point of departure.[95]

As Austen rightly notes, Marx goes on to identify European colonisation and the violence associated with it – including 'the conversion of Africa into a preserve for the commercial hunting of blackskins' – as the origins of primitive accumulation.[96] Yet, Austen contends, while violence was central to European overseas expansion, it was mostly violence focused on displacing other European nations from expanding their colonies rather than on accumulating capital. Austen concludes that during early modern overseas expansion violence was ubiquitous, if not profitable or even militarily successful. Certainly he does not believe that the wealth produced by European overseas expansion – including the wealth produced by chattel slavery – was the foundation upon which modern capitalism was built. Rather, in his pithy formulation, 'The bottom line is a liberal one: violence does not (usually) pay!' Violence can be part of capitalism, but it is 'not a necessary condition or outcome of capitalist development'.

Where Ralph Austen focuses on what Western capitalism might have gained from European colonisation in general and from Africa in particular, Gareth Austin, an African economic historian, considers in Chapter 6 the development of capitalism within sub-Saharan Africa itself. Two questions particularly

---

94 Beckert, *Empire of Cotton* recasts the early modern age of 'merchant capitalism' as the age of 'war capitalism', which, he argues 'was the foundation from which evolved the more familiar industrial capitalism' (xvi). Cf. Karl Marx, *Capital. Volume I*, trans. Ben Fowkes (1992), 873 (ch. 26): 'This primitive accumulation plays in Political Economy about the same part as original sin in theology.'
95 Marx, *Capital. Volume I*, 873 (ch. 26).
96 Ibid., 915 (ch. 31).

concern him. First, did capitalism emerge in Africa *before* colonial rule? And, second, how did imported capitalism become established? In a magisterial chapter which surveys the terrain from the mid seventeenth century straight the way through until the mid twentieth century, Austin focuses his gaze particularly on the sub-tropical Cape and on tropical West Africa, which, he reckons, provides 'a means of identifying features that may help us to make sense of the variety of other cases within this vast sub-continent'. The Cape experienced 'European settler-elite capitalism', while West Africa experienced 'African indigenous capitalism'. In the former, European settlers took the land from the indigenous people, while in West Africa, the land remained in the hands of indigenous Africans. West African capitalism, Austin reckons, 'generated the most favourable outcomes in terms of welfare advancement and poverty reduction among the population anywhere in white-ruled Africa, including South Africa'. In part, this was because indigenous institutions and already-existing attitudes could be adapted to the opportunities opened by Western industrialisation and mechanised transportation. Austin calls this 'the domestication of capitalism' in West Africa, a process which he insists is explicable by neither the exogenous nor endogenous Marxist models. South Africa, by contrast, remained poorer than West African nations like Ghana and Nigeria, where capitalism took root. In his chapter, Austin illustrates why the 'settler-elite' form of South African capitalism proved unable to generate the transition from 'extensive growth' to 'intensive growth'. Austin concludes that proletarianisation and the dependence of most households on the market 'took different routes in South and West Africa' and that, in the end, '[t]he type of colonialism and the type of capitalism mattered'. And part of what made South and West Africa different, on Austin's analysis, were decisive institutional interventions, first in 1804 with the establishment of the Sokoto Caliphate and in 1807, with the abolition of the British slave trade. Neither ended slavery in West Africa, but together they fundamentally changed the economic dynamics in West Africa to allow for capitalism's development.

Ralph Austen and Gareth Austin's narratives cut against the grain of NHC historical claims about the connection between capitalism and slavery. So too does Emma Griffin, an historian of the Industrial Revolution, who in Chapter 7 interrogates the NHC's claims regarding slavery and capitalism.[97] In particular, she aims to 'challenge how far an emphasis on slavery takes us in understanding the causes of industrialisation and economic divergence'. On her reading, it takes us not very far at all. Pre-industrial societies were small, stable, similar, subject to real scarcity based on local resources and with size linked to

97 See also Emma Griffin, *Bread Winner: An Intimate History of the Victorian Economy* (New Haven, 2020); idem, *Liberty's Dawn: A People's History of the Industrial Revolution* (New Haven, 2013); idem, *A Short History of the British Industrial Revolution* (Basingstoke, 2010).

population. Industrial societies, by contrast, are large, changing, unequal. In them the link to population is broken, as is the connection between population size and local resources. Industrial societies also require greater inputs and greater energy. Finally, industrial societies produce not just for local markets but for a global audience. Griffin wants to understand why this came about.

To do that she compares two European neighbours – England and France. Both were early to colonisation and to industrialisation. But why compare two like countries rather than compare Europe as a whole with, say, East Asia? This, after all, is the scholarly move made by historians of the Great Divergence. Griffin, however, thinks that this has limited explanatory value when it comes to understanding why, where, when and how European countries industrialised. Instead, we need to find the distinctions between things that might seem to look alike – two northwest European countries, in this instance – before we can think about aggregates. By Griffin's reckoning, Britain and France pursued markedly different approaches to colonies and to their natural resources. Far more concertedly than the French, the British focused 'on the possibility of exploiting natural resources in distant lands', a focus which distinguished them not just from their French competitors but from the Spanish and Portuguese as well. For one thing, to extract the resources the British wanted to get from their colonies required a much larger migration there: it was unsurprising, then, that on the eve of the American Revolution, the British North American colonies numbered 2 million people, while French Canada had only around 70,000 people. The primary takeaway from all this for Griffin is that most historians – and certainly the NHC – have confused North American industrialisation with the rise of capitalism. Industrialisation and capitalism may happen at the same time, but they are not the same thing. Moreover, Griffin reckons that we need to understand North American industrialisation within the context of British industrialisation. Neither Britain nor America industrialised because of slavery. As Griffin pointedly puts it, 'Britain did not industrialise because, by some stroke of good fortune, it was the lucky possessor of textile-fibre producing colonies. It possessed these colonies and was able to extract the resources it wanted from them precisely because it had been prowling the globe in single-minded pursuit of resources.' Cotton became King Cotton – whose reign lasted only around seven decades – because the British had long before prioritised resource extraction from their colonies, something which distinguished them from their European counterparts.

Emma Griffin's story is about how one institution – the British state – shaped economic outcomes. In Chapter 8, Tracy Dennison, a modern European economic historian with a particular interest in Russia, is also interested in institutions and economic outcomes. But whereas much institutionalist literature has focused on institutional *effects*, Dennison wants here to examine institutional *changes*. She does this by way of examining Russian serfdom, particularly as experienced on the Sheremetyev estates. The Sheremetyevs were likely the most powerful imperial Russian noble dynasty, who owned over fifty estates over seventeen provinces; more than 350,000 serfs lived on those estates.

Dennison rejects the Marxist notion that serfdom is necessarily a sign of feudalism. But she does reckon that serfdom, a form of extreme coerced labour outstripped only by chattel slavery, existed in different institutional environments and that those environments shaped what happened after serfdom was abolished, as eventually took place across all of Europe. The exceptionally rich archives of the Sheremetyev estates allow Dennison to look afresh at the question of why some western European countries – like England – experienced modern economic growth after serfdom's abolition while other central and east European ones – like Russia – did not after they had abolished serfdom.

Dennison's answer to the question regarding intra-European economic difference is that different parts of Europe had different institutional environments. In general, western European, and certainly English, serfs were better protected against arbitrary property expropriation than were Russian serfs. Part of that owed to the fact that they, unlike Russian serfs, were not proprietary serfs. That meant that western European serfs had a tenurial relationship with formal, contractual rights. So, when Russian serfs were emancipated in 1861, they, like freed Southern slaves after 1865, were freed into limited-access orders.

While the Sheremetyev estates had developed an ad hoc institutional system to address serf property concerns, this ad hoc nature made it unsustainable in the long run. 'The Sheremetyevs had created an institutional island – a state within a state', Dennison concludes. 'When their power as sovereign lords was abolished, it would have been difficult to sustain the accumulated gains or the growth momentum on their estates.' In England, by contrast, the various manors were not islands, but part of a coherent, systematic 'larger institutional setting'. By Dennison's reckoning, this had profound and positive long-term economic consequences for the English, just as the lack of a coherent, systematic 'larger institutional setting' had profound and negative long-term economic consequences for central and eastern Europe. Where one achieved modern economic growth early, the other achieved it much later and less robustly.

If Tracy Dennison's chapter illustrates that the state mattered in economic outcomes, so too do Chapters 9 and 10 by Tirthankar Roy and Anirban Karak. Both have as their subject South Asia: Roy views the scene from 30,000 feet to identify three different transitions to capitalism in Indian history, while Karak focuses on the relationship between caste and capitalism across three and a half centuries. Roy, a professor of global economic history with a particular interest in South Asia, identifies in Chapter 9 three critical transitions in the development of Indian capitalism. Transitions like these, Roy notes, are 'usually in response to a revolution in politics'; certainly that was the case in South

Asia. The first capitalist transition in India occurred during the eighteenth century. As the Mughal empire was weakening in the interior, the British East India company began to acquire the right to collect taxes on big swathes of the subcontinent. The result was the 'partial collapse of the land-based capitalist order, the exit and migration from there to port cities, and the Company's protection'. From this transition emerged the Raj. The second transition was a late nineteenth-century phenomenon, when the British 'concentrated power to a degree unprecedented in the region'. Along the way, the British imperial authority 'used its power to expose the interior to commercialization'. During this transition, the numbers employed in factories jumped from 100,000 in 1860 to over 2,000,000 in 1940. In this period, the family firm was a characteristic economic unit; it differed from American and European firms, which recruited managers and partners from non-family networks. The third capitalist transition which Roy identifies occurred during the four decades after independence in 1947. That transition did not represent further capitalist expansion but, rather, a retreat from the world market; it was an era of planned development and a dependence on the communist bloc. The post-independence era's economic hallmarks included 'import-substituting industrialization with an accent on the production of capital goods'. While Roy has been loath to follow the New Institutional Economists down their explanatory road, his story of Indian capitalist transitions highlights the decisive role of state institutions in shaping economic outcomes in capitalist societies.[98]

For his part, Anirban Karak focuses his sights, in Chapter 10, on a narrower, but highly consequential, issue regarding the ways capitalism expressed itself in South Asia – caste. The Indian caste system was a socially stratified, hierarchical system in which people slotted into one or another group. It aimed to distinguish the pure from the impure and to segregate the one from the other. It had many consequences, not the least of them economic.[99] On Karak's reading, capitalism was emancipatory, rather than just being colonialism by another name. There were a variety of local actors who had their own agency and who embraced capitalist norms to free themselves from the bonds of caste. Thus we have in Karak's analysis at least two sets of institutions – the colonial state and caste system – working, if not in concert, then at least not at cross-purposes to encourage the development of capitalism in India.

The final three chapters in this volume move north and east from the Indian subcontinent to East Asia. There, Kenneth Pomeranz, Horus T'an, Alexander Evans and Mark Ramseyer focus on the institutions which shaped East Asian capitalisms. In Chapter 11, which surveys Chinese capitalism from the early sixteenth until the mid nineteenth century, Pomeranz, doyen of the so-called

---

98 Cf. Tirthankar Roy, 'Capitalism in India in the Very Long Run', in *CHC*, I: 182–183.
99 Surinder S. Jodhka, *Caste* (Oxford, 2012).

California School, argues that Chinese capitalism in this period focused more on commerce and finance than on production.[100] This, Pomeranz reckons, 'was the norm everywhere before the industrial revolution'. There was, he argues, no real proletarianisation of the Chinese workers, owing mostly to the nature of Chinese agriculture and to the particular modes of production in China at the time. A few other things stood in the way of Chinese capitalism taking on Western capitalist features. Perhaps most notably, though the Ming-Qing imperial state was not anti-merchant, it was anti-monopoly, which meant, in turn, that there were fewer opportunities for merchants to amass significant amounts of capital that could be turned into investments in production. Moreover, the Ming-Qing state also invested less concertedly in infrastructure projects which might encourage trade. As Pomeranz concludes, 'late imperial Chinese capitalists sometimes gained from state projects, but probably less so than capitalists in some other places'. It was not just the Chinese state's stance regarding economic monopolies which shaped Chinese capitalism but also its particular vision of empire. For the Qing's attitudes towards non-Han peoples meant that the Qing imperial peripheries differed from Western imperial peripheries in that they 'were not re-organized in ways that benefitted capitalists to anything like the degree that overseas conquests benefitted capitalists from Eurasia's other end'.

Horus T'an's complementary chapter (Chapter 12) likewise focuses on why China did not develop Western-style capitalism. He is particularly interested in the absence of an institution – the so-called 'second serfdom' in Manchuria – something which Immanuel Wallerstein reckoned had happened in eastern Europe after 'unequal exchange' had been established with the Baltic trade routes.[101] T'an compares the Manchurian and Polish examples, noting that the Chinese empire, like the early modern Baltic, had a thriving trading system and, indeed, possessed some of the features of the world-system anatomised by Wallerstein. Why, then, did eighteenth-century Manchurian landlords not assert themselves in the ways their Polish counterparts had? Why no 'second serfdom'? T'an argues that there were some things which mitigated against that in Manchuria, including low grain prices, a high human-to-land ratio and lower wages for rural workers. So, where Pomeranz sees Chinese capitalism's features as being largely the product of state political economic decisions, T'an focuses on the peculiar social, economic and

---

100 Cf. Peer Vries, 'The California School and beyond: how to study the Great Divergence?', *History Compass*, 8/7 (2010), 730–751.
101 Immanuel Wallerstein, *World-Systems Analysis: An Introduction* (Durham, NC, 2005); idem, *The Modern World-System I: Capitalist Agriculture and the Origins of the European World-Economy in the Sixteenth Century* (Berkeley, 2011 [1974]); idem, *The Modern World-System II: Mercantilism and the Consolidation of the European World-Economy 1600–1750* (Berkeley, 2011 [1980]).

demographic features shaping Chinese capitalism. T'an reckons that his conclusions help to explain what really causes capitalism to emerge. As he puts it, 'The demands of the urban economy in the core, rather than the geographical labour division, drove the capitalist world-economy.'[102]

In the book's final chapter, Chapter 13, Mark Ramseyer and Alexander Evans turn their attention to the pre-eminent east Asian capitalist country – Japan – during its transition to modern economic growth. Both Ramseyer and Evans are law faculty with expertise in Japanese law. Here they focus on property rights, what most would agree is a central feature of capitalism, however defined. In particular, they are interested in the connections between law and economics. In their piece, they examine the *perpetual lease*. This form of lease gave some Japanese farmers the right to cultivate land in perpetuity, something which became difficult in an era of modern economic growth. The Japanese response was to change the law to place a fifty-year limit on perpetual leases. Moreover, the judiciary consistently presumed against perpetual lessees in judicial proceedings. Together these legislative changes and judicial presentiment led to the withering away of perpetual leases.

Ramseyer and Evans observe that economic growth puts stress on legal systems. Like Dennison, they are interested in how institutions change and how those changes affect economic growth. Their takeaway is that where Japan was concerned, '[f]ar from static background rules, the economy's rules-of-the-road changed markedly as society's needs changed. That, perhaps, is how it should be: law is created to serve society, and if it poorly matches the economy, it probably is not serving very well.' But, they counsel, we need to remember the law's 'dynamism' and should expect to see it being similarly dynamic in places that are transitioning from linear to exponential growth.

IV

This volume's essays confirm the importance of considering institutional frameworks of the areas in which capitalism emerged to understand both what capitalism is and why, how, when and where it emerged. Avner Greif has argued that 'Studying institutions sheds light on why some countries are rich and others are poor, why some enjoy a welfare-enhancing political order and others do not …. The quality of these institutional foundations of the economy and the polity is paramount in determining a society's welfare.'[103] This is an insight

---

102 Robert Brenner, 'The origins of capitalist development: a critique of neo-Smithian Marxism', *New Left Review*, 104 (1977), 25–92.
103 Avner Greif, *Institutions and the Path to the Modern Economy: Lessons from Medieval Trade* (Cambridge, 2006), 3–4.

which most of the chapters in this book confirm. Institutions are not an explanation of everything. But they do help to explain something – and something important – not just about the timing and geography of capitalism's origins but also about the nature of capitalism itself.

2

Origin Stories: Expressions and Presentations of Capitalism in Early British America

PETER A. COCLANIS

With a nod to a British fellow named Churchill, it seems appropriate to approach the question of the origins of capitalism as 'a riddle wrapped in a mystery inside an enigma'.¹ Indeed, when one attempts even to circle near the question, one finds, with another nod, this time to a German fellow named Marx, that 'all that is solid melts into air'. Our problems begin, but certainly do not end, with the word 'origins' itself. For example, as a French fellow named Bloch pointed out in a famous 1925 essay, ambiguity surrounds 'origins' from the get-go, for it can mean both beginnings and causes, two very different things.²

Then there is the 'minor' problem of defining capitalism. Such is the nature of this task that some have responded with Talmudic specification, while others, disinclined to take on the rigours of the chore, oversimplify, obfuscate, cut and run, or dodge it altogether. Marxist scholars have generally inclined toward the Talmudic end of the spectrum. From the age of the Second International right down to the present day, Marxist writers have agonized over capitalism, contesting fiercely over matters regarding its emergence, principal features, and characteristics, and how to periodize it not only in public battles between and among famous figures such as Kautsky, Bernstein, Luxembourg, Hilferding, Lenin, Trotsky, and the like, but also in academic dustups such as the so-called transition debate of the 1940s and 1950s sparked by the work of Maurice Dobb and Paul Sweezy, which debate reemerged in somewhat different form in the 1970s with different principals, most notably Immanuel Wallerstein and Robert Brenner. Extensions to this debate and others, which are often rather esoteric, and are inside baseball-like in nature, have appeared intermittently over the years – one thinks, for example, of the spirited response to Ellen Meiksins Wood's important 1999 book *The Origin of Capitalism* – and still

---

1   Winston Churchill, 'Russia: "A riddle, wrapped in a mystery", 1 October 1939', in idem, *Never Give In! Winston Churchill's Speeches* (2013), 163–164.
2   Karl Marx and Frederick Engels, *The Communist Manifesto: A Modern Edition* (1998), 38; Marc Bloch, *The Historian's Craft*, trans. Peter Putnam (New York, 1952 [1949]), 29–35.

appear today in the pages of *Monthly Review*, *Science & Society*, *International Socialist Review*, etc.[3]

Near the other end of the spectrum when it comes to defining capitalism are people operating under what might be labelled the mainstream, neoclassical metatheoretical umbrella.[4] That's a mouthful. Until recently, such people typically dealt infrequently, reluctantly, and usually not too explicitly with the problem of defining capitalism, let alone explaining how and why it originated. Often, they felt such problems were unnecessary, as capitalism was assumed to grow organically through some type of spontaneous order out of human beings' natural propensity to 'truck, barter, and exchange one thing for another' – Adam Smith's famous phrase.[5] What more do we need? To be sure, most introductory econ texts included brief mentions early on of certain vaguely Weberian attributes said to be characteristic of capitalism – private property (or, more specifically, the legal right to possess it), economic freedom, competition, the importance of trade and exchange, the price system as organizational/regulatory mechanism, etc. – before moving on to x and y axes, supply and demand curves, and the like.

More recently, however, some writers sheltering under this umbrella have attempted to add specification in their approaches to definition, while retaining the explanatory parsimony the mainstream privileges. For example, in the introduction to the two-volume *Cambridge History of Capitalism*, published in 2014, Larry Neal focuses on four 'elements' found in 'each variant of capitalism whatever the specific emphasis': (1) private property rights; (2) contracts enforceable by third parties; (3) markets with responsive prices; and (4) supportive governments.[6]

Neal might have mentioned another 'element' – something relating to a particular form or particular forms of self-interest, an identifiable *mentalité or mentalités* – as a driving force in capitalism, but why quibble? His is still a rather broad remit, especially since the *Cambridge History of Capitalism* begins its coverage in ancient Babylonia, moves on to classical Greece, and covers, albeit unevenly, the entire world down to the present, with a concluding chapter on capitalism's future.

---

3   Ellen Meiksins Wood, *The Origin of Capitalism: A Longer View* (New York, 1999). For a sample of such debates – in this case, focusing rather more on Robert Brenner's work – see Alexander Anievas and Kerem Nisancioglu, 'The Poverty of Political Marxism', *International Socialist Review*, 94 (2014), 114–133.
4   For a good discussion of the differences between and among these economic traditions, see Richard D. Wolff and Stephen A. Resnick, *Contending Economic Theories: Neoclassical, Keynesian, and Marxian* (Cambridge, MA, 2012).
5   Adam Smith, *An Inquiry into the Nature and Causes of the Wealth of Nations*, ed. Edwin Cannan (New York, 1937 [1776]), 13 (Book I, Chapter II).
6   Larry Neal, 'Introduction', in *CHC*, 1: 2.

So, according to the mainstream view, how did the capitalist system come about? Again, answering this question involves a lot of reading between the lines, because most mainstream economists, even today, focus on the West and are more concerned with capitalism in full flower or capitalism in theory than in locating it historically in time and space. To be sure, the *Cambridge History of Capitalism* makes the case for the system's appearance in antique times. Theodor Mommsen argued much earlier that agricultural capitalism existed in the Roman world, and Weber also saw capitalist features in Roman agriculture. That said, most mainstream writers today would likely not go that far.[7] Rather, they would likely agree with or at least accept a scenario that goes something like the following.

They would likely argue, first, that the 'seeds' of capitalism are trans-historical, presenting very early in human or even non-human evolution – some would likely date things back to *Homo erectus*, the first hominid purposively to employ fire for individual/group advance. This said, what they mean by seeds is often frustratingly vague – things such as self-interest, some desire to store/save/accumulate, etc. They would go on to say that humans also seem to have something of a 'natural' market orientation – a natural propensity to 'truck, barter, and exchange' – which mindset was tangibly expressed by some for millennia, but which, according to Pirenne, Braudel, Lopez, and many others, gradually become more widespread behaviourally, in the West at least, in the twelfth century AD.[8] Over the next few centuries, said mindset and said behaviours – undergirded increasingly by institutional supports – spread among more and more peoples in more and more places in more and more ways. Sometime around 1500 AD, the market or capitalist mindset – the adjectives are often used interchangeably – gained the ascendancy in parts of Europe, whence it spread over the next few centuries to other parts of Europe, indeed, to other parts of the world.

What were some of the behavioural (and institutional) manifestations of the mindset? The focus early on is generally on merchants, on the growth of trade and commerce and the commercial sector more generally, and on the emergence or increased importance of business practices and institutions that reflect a greater degree of commercialization and concern for order and regularity, if

---

7 On Mommsen's and Weber's views on agricultural capitalism in the Roman world, see G.H. Mueller, 'Weber and Mommsen: Non-Marxist Materialism', *British Journal of Sociology*, 37 (1986), 1–20; John Love, 'Max Weber and the Theory of Ancient Capitalism', *History and Theory*, 25 (1986), 152–172.

8 Henri Pirenne, 'The Stages in the Social History of Capitalism', *AHR*, 19 (1914), 494–515; Robert S. Lopez, *The Commercial Revolution of the Middle Ages, 950–1350* (Cambridge, 1976 [1971]); Fernand Braudel, *Capitalism and Material Life*, trans. Miriam Kochan (New York, 1973 [1967]); idem, *The Structures of Everyday Life: Civilization and Capitalism 15th–18th Century*, trans. Siân Reynolds, 3 vols. (New York, 1979).

not predictability, and a reduced importance placed on non-market or extra-market forces to structure economic and social life. More specifically, attention is paid to the growth and regularization of markets and fairs, the increasing relative importance of cities and towns, and within them of mercantile groups, and to the emergence or growth of more sophisticated business practices and institutions – banks, bills of exchange, promissory notes, double-entry bookkeeping, guilds, common-law partnerships, insurance and other risk-reduction mechanisms, etc.

Although moral and legal sanctions against practices such as regrating, forestalling, and engrossing by 'badgers' and others remained common, as well as residual medieval support for 'just' prices and for injunctions against usury, over time such support and sanctions were increasingly challenged and frequently overridden on the ground by market considerations, and were clearly losing sway during the so-called early modern period. In recent years, several scholars have suggested that competition between and among rival nation-states in Europe facilitated said processes as well as technological innovation and diffusion, which spurred economic dynamism as well.[9]

Finally, according to some of the most eminent social scientists of the first quarter of the twentieth century – Weber and Tawney, most notably – the increasing power of 'capitalism' to organize economic and social life in parts of Europe in the early modern period was due as well at least in part to what might be called a 'spiritual' turn, that is, a growing valorization of commerce and commercialized human behaviour – or what mainstream economists often refer to as economic rationality – associated in complicated ways with the rise of Protestantism (particularly Calvinism). Their work was subject to much criticism – how, for example, to explain the mindsets and behaviours of merchants and others in Venice and Florence in Catholic Italy well before the Reformation, the valorization of temperance in the thirteenth and fourteenth centuries, etc. – and later defenders of the overall thesis placed less interpretive weight on Calvinist theology in the rise of capitalism and more on attendants and concomitants of Protestantism such as the rise of individualism and literacy. But many, if not most writers on capitalism writing in Weber's wake acknowledged that certain values and behaviours associated with Protestantism hardly impeded capitalism's rise and, in helping to loosen 'feudal' restraints of various types, likely played some type of enabling role.[10]

Whatever combination of factors one chooses to emphasize, the mainstream view privileges the 'naturalness' of the market, and the fact that over time said naturalness was increasingly made manifest in more and more commercialized

---

9 See, for example, Joel Mokyr, 'How Europe Became So Rich', *Aeon* (15 February 2017).
10 Max Weber, *The Protestant Ethic and the Spirit of Capitalism*, trans. Talcott Parsons (New York, 1958 [1905]); R.H. Tawney, *Religion and the Rise of Capitalism* (New York, 1926).

human behaviour, starting in the mercantile world, but extending relatively rapidly to other economic sectors in parts of Europe during the early modern period. Evidence of 'capitalist' values and behaviour can be found in the growing relative importance of capitalist land markets and ground rents, waged labour, proto-industrialization (for which merchants provided necessary marketing services and direction for the so-called putting-out system), in the 'industrious revolution', and in the diminished role of backward-bending labour supply curves.

To say that most heterodox writers in the West, particularly those of a Marxist bent, have seen things differently, is an understatement. Indeed, their disagreement with the mainstream view is near total, *ab ovo usque ad mala*, from eggs to apples, that is, stretching from beginning to end. For starters, they do not view capitalism as an organic, natural, much less innate, phenomenon growing out of humans' propensity to 'truck, barter, and exchange', but rather as an acquired, culturally, temporally, and geographically specific socioeconomic order whose appearance and trajectory need to be documented empirically, analyzed rigorously, and contextualized properly. Similarly, they typically deny that humans' purportedly accumulationist *mentalité* is hardwired, viewing the primary consideration behind human work and production as 'use value' – the fulfilment of basic needs rather than the desire for accumulation and more accumulation. Exchange for purposes of accumulation is rather a desideratum of capitalistic men and women rather than of human beings from time immemorial, as heterodox writers such as Karl Polanyi famously argued in *The Great Transformation*.[11] Moreover, this transformation occurred rather late in the game, during the eighteenth century, according to many, after what some view as a 'transitional' period.

Just as Marxists view human nature differently than do non-Marxists writing on capitalism – or on the 'market economy', the term often preferred by non-Marxists – they have traditionally emphasized different features of capitalism when trying to define it. Rather than looking for a market *mentalité* and manifestations of increasingly commercialized human behaviour, they generally view capitalism as denoting a distinct mode of production and class structure wherein labour is severed from claims on the means of production and capital in various forms comes to hold sway. Capital, of course, is an elastic economic concept, which can refer to phenomena that on the surface seem quite distinct: physical goods, tools, implements made by humans; money or credit that can be used to purchase such objects as well as others, including labour power; the class of economic actors that possesses or has privileged access to the preponderance of a society's capital, as denoted in the first two senses discussed above. The above descriptors have been used ever since the time of Marx and Engels. More recently, writers have incorporated other forms of capital into the equation, *to wit*: human capital (the skills, education, and health of a given

---

11   Karl Polanyi, *The Great Transformation* (New York, 1944).

individual or group); social capital (networks and relationships), and cultural capital (knowledge and skills that individuals or groups can deploy to enhance, solidify, or signal class position). These forms of capital, too, are seen as being held predominantly by a particular group: the capitalist class.

As stated early in this essay, in defining capitalism Marxists generally expect – and exact – a lot.[12] In addition to the above considerations, they generally expect to find other features present for a given mode of production to be deemed capitalist, most importantly, production predominantly for sale on markets rather than for personal use, and widespread presence of a market where labour power – particularly agricultural labour power – is freely bought and sold via formal or implicit contract, for specific periods of time or for specified tasks. Many go further still, with expectations regarding the pervasiveness, indeed, indispensability of money and credit – and thus of bankers and creditors – both in mediating economic transactions and in guiding, if not determining, production decisions at the micro level and beyond.[13]

As one can see, then, there are considerable, even profound differences in the way in which mainstream and non-mainstream/heterodox/Marxist writers have approached capitalism. One final difference needs to be mentioned as well. Most mainstream writers on capitalism view its advent and historical development in positive terms. Regarding its advent: Mainstream writers generally view the emergence of capitalism in terms of volition and self-interest, with individuals freely, legally, and more-or-less peacefully entering an economic world that would be increasingly recognizable as capitalistic. To be sure, some – Jürgen Kocka, for example – like Marxists and other heterodox writers believe otherwise, emphasizing instead what they see as the force, coercion, and violence constitutive of capitalism's birth.[14] And

---

[12] Interestingly, unlike earlier generations of Marxist and *Marxisant* scholars, few scholars associated with the new history of capitalism movement spend much time on definitional questions. Jonathan Levy and Caitlin Rosenthal are among the exceptions. See Jonathan Levy, 'Capital as Process and the History of Capitalism', *BHR*, 91 (2017), 483–510; Caitlin Rosenthal, 'Capitalism when Labor was Capital: Slavery, Power, and Price in Antebellum America', *Capitalism: A Journal of History and Economics*, 1 (2020), 296–337. On the relative lack of interest among new historians of capitalism in theorizing capitalism, see, for example, Sven Beckert and Seth Rockman, 'Introduction: Slavery's Capitalism', in *Slavery's Capitalism: A New History of American Economic Development*, ed. Sven Beckert and Seth Rockman (Philadelphia, 2016), 1–27, esp. 10.
[13] See, for example, Meghnad Desai, *Marxian Economics* (Oxford, 1979); Ernest Mandel, *Marxist Economic Theory*, trans. Brian Pearce, 2 vols. (New York, 1968–1970).
[14] Jürgen Kocka, *Capitalism: A Short History*, trans. Jeremiah Riemer (Princeton, 2016), 54–58. Sven Beckert also emphasizes the violence inherent in early capitalism ('war capitalism') in *The Empire of Cotton: A Global History* (New York, 2014), 29–97. For a recent Marxist study highlighting the violence, coercion, and dispossession characteristic of capitalism and capitalist development (and the resistance thereto), see Ian Angus, *The*

assessing capitalism's trajectory? While many mainstream writers readily acknowledge capitalism's deficiencies – a troubling tendency to promote or at least tolerate inequalities of one sort of another, for example – they nonetheless believe that, on balance, the dynamism and growth associated with capitalism produced very positive long-term social returns. Contrarily, most Marxists and other non-mainstream writers on capitalism view the economic system much more warily – indeed, generally negatively – although, as in the case with classical Marxists, they often have a grudging respect for capitalism's animation, and its ability both to propel technological change and to transform what Marx and Engels famously called the relations of production. 'The bourgeoisie, historically, has played a revolutionary part', and all that.[15]

Clearly, the discussion above is centred on developments in the Western world and efforts, mostly by Westerners, to explain said developments. Perhaps the most important breakthrough in the study of capitalism over the past half century or so relates to the publication – or 'discovery' – of work embedding Western capitalism in broader and deeper contexts. Scholars interested in the 'non-West', of course, had long been writing on the economic histories of various areas, and the ways in which these areas interacted and articulated with Westerners and Western economies over time. These scholars came from diverse fields – economic anthropology, sociology, history, political science, etc. – and were equally diverse ideologically and methodologically. That said, the hold of Western theory and praxis was sufficiently strong that until relatively recently most of those writing on capitalism, whether from mainstream or heterodox traditions, accepted or resigned themselves to Western categories, frames, and conventions in discussing and analyzing the economic histories of non-Western areas.

Ironically, change can be dated with the emergence, spread, and powerful influence of a Western analytical frame – world-systems analysis – beginning in the late 1960s and 1970s, and associated most closely early on with Immanuel Wallerstein and Andre Gunder Frank, both 'Western' writers. This is not the time or place for close examination of this hugely influential approach, much less with its conceptual architecture and claims. Suffice it to say that it soon occasioned a vast critical literature supporting or opposing it, extending and elaborating upon it, and in some cases posing alternatives to it.[16]

It is this last development, the posing of alternatives to early world-systems analysis, that concerns us here, for such alternatives – the existence of 'world

---

War against the Commons: Dispossession and Resistance in the Making of Capitalism (New York, 2023).
15 Marx and Engels, *Communist Manifesto*, 37.
16 See, for example, Immanuel Wallerstein, *The Modern World-System*, 4 vols. (1974–2011); Andre Gunder Frank, *World Accumulation 1492–1789* (New York, 1978).

systems' other than or earlier than the West-dominated 'world capitalist system', different periodization schemes, the existence of large-scale economic networks that worked entirely differently, the nature of global power dynamics, etc. – led scholars and the entire scholarly community down exciting new paths. In functional terms, such theories succeeded to varying degrees in decentring, even provincializing the West, allowing more space for both other interpretive formulations regarding the origins, drivers, and overall trajectory of capitalism, and about the conceptual efficacy of thinking and writing instead about different *capitalisms* in various locales.[17]

Perhaps the two most important results of this florescence relate to the reconsideration and subsequent revaluation upward of Asia in pre-modern economic history – what Frank famously called the 'reOrienting' of our understanding of early modern economic history – and as a concomitant, the emergence of the rich scholarly debate surrounding the timing and causes of the 'great divergence', that is, the period in which the West (belatedly) pulled decisively ahead of the most economically advanced parts of Asia, particularly the lower Yangzi delta, but other parts of Asia as well.[18] These two developments perforce required scholars all over the world to rethink various aspects of pre-modern economic history, including the definition and hallmark features of capitalism, its place(s) of origins and subsequent role(s) – particularly *vis-à-vis* other ways of organizing economic life – the relative importance and power of the West in early stages of capitalism, and the degree to which what were formerly viewed as Western developments/achievements were actually predicated on interactions and exchanges of various kinds, whether equal or unequal, with non-Western peoples and non-Western parts of the world. One major consequence of the above developments was that it has become increasingly difficult for Western scholars to hive off the West from other parts of the world, which point even specialists in 'Atlantic history', including people studying the economic history of British America, are at long last beginning to appreciate.

Capitalism may or may not have come to America 'in the first ships' as Carl Degler famously put it many decades ago – and I believe it did – but it seems impossible to deny that it was well along by the late sixteenth/early seventeenth century and that at the very least it provided much of the impetus propelling

---

17 See Kaveh Yazdani and Dilip M. Menon (eds.), *Capitalisms: Towards a Global History* (Oxford, 2020).
18 Frank, *ReOrient: Global Economy in an Asian Age* (Berkeley, 1998); R. Bin Wong, *China Transformed: Historical Change and the Limits of European Experience* (Ithaca, 1997); Kenneth Pomeranz, *The Great Divergence: China, Europe, and the Making of the Modern World Economy* (Princeton, 2000); Prasannan Parthasarathi, *Why Europe Grew Rich and Asia Did Not: Global Economic Divergence, 1600–1850* (Cambridge, 2011). For more on my own take on the debate, see Peter A. Coclanis, 'Ten Years After: Reflections on Kenneth Pomeranz's *The Great Divergence*', *Historically Speaking*, 12 (2011), 10–12.

those ships across (and around) the Atlantic and other oceans.[19] Before going any further, it seems appropriate, indeed, incumbent for the author to specify more precisely what he believes 'it' – capitalism – to be. Here, as in much of my scholarly work in economic history, I take an eclectic approach, drawing from both mainstream and heterodox traditions. At the end of the day, I am more comfortable in the mainstream camp, though I appreciate the general rigour of the heterodox critique and many specific points raised by heterodox scholars, particularly regarding the violence associated with capitalism's early days in the Americas. Moreover, I see myself less as a cheerleader for capitalism than as someone extremely respectful of its productive power and the manner in which in time capitalism, when buttressed by sufficient institutional support, is able, via incentives of one sort or another, to channel basic – some would prefer the word base – human instincts and tendencies in directions promotive of the greater good. And to do these things at scale and more efficiently than any other social scheme yet devised by Homo sapiens.

Despite the above nod to our species, I do not believe, as some apparently do, that capitalism is encoded in our DNA, or that it has been around since the time of the Babylonians, much less since time immemorial.[20] Rather, in one of several major concessions to heterodox scholars, I view capitalism as an economic and social system – or, more accurately, a metaphorical construct intended to capture how a given economy roughly works – that has a history or histories that must be bounded temporally, spatially, and culturally.

For the area most germane to this essay – British America – *Western* capitalism is the operative construct, which construct, I believe, is most usefully considered in evolutionary terms, entailing a long-term process marked by the progressive loosening of long-established constraints on what we now call the factors of production – land, labour, capital, and, yes, entrepreneurship – and the gradual, piecemeal demarcation, individuation, and commercialization of the same. To try to date the precise 'beginning' of the process seems a fool's errand, but it was increasingly visible by the late medieval period – the demographic decline associated with the Black Death of the middle of the fourteenth century AD certainly played a role – and continued apace in the early modern period. The process expressed and presented at different rates in different parts of Europe, with northwestern reaches of the continent (or of the Eurasian landmass) – the United Provinces/Dutch Republic, England, parts of Scotland, areas in France – gradually overtaking northern Italy, parts of the Iberian Peninsula, the cities of the Hanseatic League, and even Flanders

---

19   Carl N. Degler, *Out of Our Past: The Forces that Shaped Modern America* (New York, 1959), 1.
20   See, for example, Peter Temin, 'Price Behavior in Ancient Babylon', *EEH*, 39 (2002), 49–60; Michael Jursa, 'Babylonia in the First Millennium BCE – Economic Growth in Times of Empire', in *CHC*, 1: 24–42.

in their embrace of procedures, practices, protocols, and policies associated with early capitalism.

The determination that what we are observing is in fact an emerging capitalism cannot in my view be made by demanding the presence or absence of any one characteristic – free labour and wage relations as the dominant means of organizing and directing production, for example. Such a fixation raises difficult questions and creates thorny problems, particularly regarding agriculture, which even in the modern era has often been very slow to rely on, and is often resistant to wage labour all over the world, as mainstream and heterodox writers on capitalism have long acknowledged.[21] Such questions and problems can be reduced by broadening the analytical context in which we embed capitalism so as to include other relevant, even vital features as well. At the risk of overdetermination, we can start, but not necessarily end with the degree of commercialization of the other factors of production, land, and capital, most notably; the manner in which producers acquire their inputs, organize production, and dispose of their output; the relative importance of money as a medium of exchange and measure of value; commodity production and the significance of long-distance trade; the degree of competition; the degree to which land is alienable and property transferable (including intergenerationally); the movement toward more 'modern' commercial institutions and the employment of increasingly sophisticated commercial practices and tools; rationality of spirit/market *mentalité;* values/behaviours regarding capital accumulation and conducive to future capital accumulation; and the degree and credibility of state commitments to enforce contracts and protect property rights. The rising economic and political power of a particular group or class amassing disproportionate stocks of capital, the capitalist class, as it were, is a noteworthy part of our assessment – audit? – as well. Our approach is hardly tidy, much less marked by parsimony – the economist's holy grail – but it seems nonetheless a reasonable menu from which to find the entrée we crave: capitalism *al dente*, as it were.[22]

In any case, many writers denying the early role of capitalism in British America – or even in the early history of the United States – pass over or elide the issues raised above. To be sure, the history of any topic has to start somewhere, even in the middle, and long ago Marc Bloch famously called

---

21 Susan Archer Mann, *Agrarian Capitalism in Theory and Practice* (Chapel Hill, 1990), 1–27.
22 As illustrated by the rise of behavioural economics in recent decades, many economists have moved away from overly parsimonious, not to say overly simplistic approaches to explanation. For an early critique of the narrowness of mainstream economics, see Albert O. Hirschman, 'Against Parsimony: Three Easy Ways of Complicating Some Categories of Economic Discourse', *Bulletin of the American Academy of Arts and Sciences*, 37 (1984), 11–28.

attention to what he referred to as the 'idol of origins', which often moves scholars to fixate on establishing the 'beginning' of things rather than studying such things when they actually become important. Points taken. But scholars of British America and the early U.S. err in denying, for example, that slavery and capitalism can co-exist comfortably and durably. They err, too, in writing about the widespread existence, even prevalence of populations with non-market/pre-market *mentalités*, and/or about a 'market revolution' in the nineteenth century – in Jonathan Levy's case, a series of 'market revolutions' – without properly contextualizing and analyzing whence and why said populations found themselves doing what they did where they did in particular ways and for specific purposes at particular times.[23] Such errors in the interpretation of values and behaviour are akin in tenor – and consequences – to mistaking a twitch for a wink, to use Clifford Geertz's (and Gilbert Ryle's) venerable image.[24] Indeed, to foreground just a bit: For all of my disagreements with proponents of the new history of capitalism, two of the areas in which we do in fact often agree relate to capitalism's early and strong purchase, so to speak, in America and to the compatibility, even affinity early on between capitalism and slavery.

At the margin one can argue about the forces responsible for the European and African encounter with the Americas during the early modern period, for there were many. But, stepping back a bit, it is clear that all such forces were related in one way or another – whether as direct impetus or indirect enabler – to the growing dynamism of the economies in parts of Europe. Without such dynamism there would not have been the inspiration, much less the capacity or capability for Europeans – working under the auspices of rising nation-states or at least in ways broadly concordant with such states' interests – to conceptualize, operationalize, and sustain extra-European expansion of such magnitude. Indeed, it was difficult enough to do these things even in a time of dynamism. That is to say, failure seems to have been the default option for many attempts at expansion, whether intended for religious freedom, religious proselytization, scientific inquiry, trade and exchange, or settlement/territorial acquisition, and this option perforce had to be overridden.

Western economic dynamism, let me be clear, manifested itself primarily *within* Europe itself – in increased output and trade, in changing social relations of production, in urbanization, state formation, and enhanced war-making capacity. That said, such dynamism was also made manifest – more dramatically, if less important quantitatively – in state-sponsored or state-condoned thrusts beyond Europe, into and around the Atlantic, our principal interest here,

23 Jonathan Levy, *Ages of American Capitalism: A History of the United States* (New York, 2021), 63–64.
24 Clifford Geertz, 'Thick Description: Toward an Interpretive Theory of Culture', in idem, *The Interpretation of Cultures: Selected Essays* (New York, 1973), 3–30.

but, not coincidentally, much less unrelatedly into and around other oceans as well. In the Eastern Hemisphere, European merchants, merchant capital, states, and state-affiliated or 'state-adjacent' trading companies entered – or forced their way into and in some cases tried to redirect – different, autonomous trade networks and orbits previously disconnected or little connected to Europe.[25] In the Western Hemisphere, they did some of that, but over time also got involved in establishing altogether new production sites and trade networks, organized under their own auspices. The diverse portfolio of English/British colonies established in the Americas, considered *in toto*, should be seen in this context. To be sure, each of the colonies established followed its own trajectory and the initial motivation for each differed, but, stepping back, each in time – usually not *that much* time – found its place in imperial production/trade orbits, whether regional or international, that were recognizably capitalistic according to the criteria articulated just above. This was so even in 'outlier' colonies such as Plymouth and Massachusetts Bay wherein early settlement patterns on the surface might have suggested otherwise, and in other areas whose early economic order and activities on the surface seemed decidedly retrograde or even atavistic in developmental terms. Once a British colony or region in British America became part of broader economic orbits, doing so created a greater possibility – though no certainty – of growth and development along capitalist lines. Although different paths were taken, and although capitalism presented and expressed itself in different ways, most parts of British America – and in time growing proportions of the populations living therein – benefited from the path taken, with the white population benefiting a great deal.

One of my principal objections to those making the case that early English/British America should not be embedded in a capitalist frame is related to the fact that they do not adequately approach colonization in processual, much less sequential terms. If they did, they would understand that the importance early on of the subsistence sector in many parts of English/British colonies, the rudeness of productive activities, the relative unimportance of trade in such places, particularly long-distance trade, the slow pace of growth, etc., were largely functions of necessity, of material realities, of facts on the ground rather than reflections of economic ideology, let alone a self-conscious rejection of market principles. Although in my view it is certainly true that capitalism was progressive, it must be remembered that in its early days it created or, less insistently, countenanced and co-existed with what on the surface seem like economically regressive anomalies: the second serfdom in eastern Europe and slavery in the Western Hemisphere, most notably, but also at various times and various

---

25 Some have argued that such interactions were, in fact, vital to the rise of capitalism in the West. Alexander Anievas and Kerem Nisancioglu, employing Trotsky's theory of unequal and combined development, make such a case. See Alexander Anievas and Kerem Nisancioglu, *How the West Came to Rule: The Geopolitical Origins of Capitalism* (London, 2015).

places in the Americas settlements whose economies initially seemed to be backpedalling, moving in reverse toward more rudimentary forms. In English/British America this was often the case of colonies in the initial 'pioneering' phase of settlement and, later, on various 'frontiers' further west.[26]

Much has traditionally been made of the purported indifference, even aversion of colonists in some settlements to markets and market culture, etc., especially in early New England, which indifference/aversion is said to have been reflected in the way in which the rough beast, capitalism, slouched along before finally making it to Boston sometime in the late seventeenth century and to other parts of Massachusetts in the eighteenth century or even later. There are several problems with this line of arguing. First of all, as suggested above, all of the English/British colonies established in the Western Hemisphere – whether we refer to the early Puritan colony of Providence Island in the West Indies or those in 'Atlantic Canada' – were in one way or another outgrowths (some would likely prefer the word excrescences) of emerging English/British capitalism. Secondly, as a number of careful economic historians have demonstrated, it is difficult to find convincing evidence of economic behaviour, even in Massachusetts, that is inexplicable in market terms, particularly in light of the underdeveloped state of market structures and channels, inadequate transportation and communications infrastructure, the time needed to discover, assemble, and process useful economic information, and to develop credible state commitments for the protection of property rights, the problem of opportunity costs, the dearth of capital of all kinds, etc.[27] In this regard, it should

---

26 For an excellent recent discussion of the reasons for the inception and resiliency of the second serfdom, see Tom Raster, 'Serfs and the Market: Second Serfdom and the East–West Goods Exchange, 1579–1857' (Paris School of Economics M.A. thesis, 2019). For classic treatments of the rise of the 'second serfdom' in Poland and eastern Europe, see Marian Malowist, 'Poland, Russia and Western Trade in the 15th and 16th Centuries', *P&P*, 13 (1958), 26–41; Witold Kula, *An Economic Theory of the Feudal System: Towards a Model of the Polish Economy*, trans. Lawrence Garner (1976). Note that in recent decades scholars have increasingly viewed the second serfdom in a more nuanced manner, arguing that it was not necessarily a legally binding system, but 'a set of legal restraints on labor mobility' that grew out of power asymmetries between landlords and small-scale agriculturalists. See, for example, Alessandro Stanziani, 'Revisiting Russian Serfdom: Bonded Peasants and Market Dynamics, 1600–1800s', *International Labor and Working-Class History*, 78 (2010), 212–227.

27 Bettye Hobbs Pruitt, 'Self-Sufficiency and the Agricultural Economy of Eighteenth-Century Massachusetts', *WMQ*, 41 (1984), 333–364; Winifred B. Rothenberg, 'The Market and Massachusetts farmers, 1750–1855', *JEcH*, 41 (1981), 283–314. For a respectful Marxist critique of Rothenberg's interpretation of 'the market', see Rona S. Weiss, 'The Market and Massachusetts Farmers, 1750–1850: Comment', *JEcH*, 43 (1983), 475–478. Although our interpretations differ – he sees capitalism arriving in the U.S. much later than do I – Allan Kulikoff over the years has made major contributions to the debates on the 'market' question and farmers in early America, see Allan Kulikoff, *The Agrarian Origins*

be noted that even in export-oriented, slave plantation colonies in the British West Indies and South Carolina on the mainland – colonies that few today doubt were organized along capitalist lines – it took decades of effort, trials and errors, still-born projects, travel down blind alleys, etc., before the production systems and marketing channels typically associated with capitalist orders were firmly in place.

Well after initial settlement, much the same phenomenon – the appearance of economic retrogression masking underlying capitalist dynamism – can be seen on 'frontiers' in various parts of British America. In the Lower South, for example, we find apparent economic retreat in 'backcountry' areas such as the midlands and upcountry of the Carolinas once settlers began to move into these regions in the period between the 1730s and 1750s. Early on, these areas were largely out of the reach of markets and it showed. The careful estimates of GDP per capita in the Lower South made by Mancall, Rosenbloom, and Weiss, which show very little upward trend over the eighteenth century because of the rising proportion of the population in relatively isolated backcountry areas, bear out this point.[28] But by 1770 slaves comprised 20 per cent of the backcountry population in South Carolina, and over the next thirty years a planter class came into existence, slave-based plantation agriculture was established, and the area was emerging as the epicentre of the U.S. South's first cotton boom.[29] Moreover, capitalism and capitalist processes underlay and informed what is generally considered the most remote part of the colonial South, the southern Appalachians, as Wilma A. Dunaway demonstrated convincingly long ago.[30]

And the point made above regarding frontiers holds true elsewhere as well. The economic trajectory of the Ohio Valley constitutes another case in point. There are many fine historical studies documenting both the violence on this frontier and the rudimentary nature of economic life in this region in the early decades of settlement by Euro-Americans in the last quarter of the eighteenth century. Similarly, numerous studies detail the region's backbreaking, but rapid transformation into a dynamic site of capitalist agriculture, trade, and

---

of American Capitalism (Charlottesville, 1990), 13–33; idem, From British Peasants to Colonial American Farmers (Chapel Hill, 2000), 203–254. In this regard, also see Charles Post, 'Agrarian Class Structure and Economic Development in Colonial British North America: The Place of the American Revolution in the Origins of U.S. Capitalism', Journal of Agrarian Change, 9 (2009), 453–483.

28   Peter C. Mancall, Joshua L. Rosenbloom, and Thomas Weiss, 'Exports and the Economy of the Lower South Region, 1720–1770', Research in Economic History (2008), 1–68.

29   Peter A. Coclanis, The Shadow of a Dream: Economic Life and Death in the South Carolina Low Country, 1670–1920 (Oxford, 1989), 64–67; Rachel N. Klein, Unification of a Slave State: The Rise of the Planter Class in the South Carolina Backcountry, 1760–1808 (Chapel Hill, 1990).

30   Wilma A. Dunaway, The First American Frontier: Transition to Capitalism in Southern Appalachia, 1700–1860 (Chapel Hill, 1996).

commerce (a transformation aided in no small part by an institutional development, the Northwest Ordinance of 1787). Indeed, the fact that the Ohio Valley ultimately became an important part of what was perhaps the most impressive expression of sustained economic development in the entire world between 1800 and 1950 or 1960 – the agro-industrial complex of the American Midwest – suggests that the efforts of the early Euro/Euro-American settlers of the region, frontier farmer, frontier speculator, and frontier merchant alike, were from a capitalist perspective not in vain.[31]

Jonathan Levy has recently resurrected William Parker's old suggestion that early American households possessed 'split personalities', combining the values of 'peasants' and 'gamblers' to varying degrees.[32] Parker's formulation has always struck me as interesting as a heuristic, but not particularly helpful to understanding American capitalism. The behaviours Parker and Levy associate with 'peasants' – pursuit of landed property with secure legal titles, land improvements, food security, and 'safety first' market participation – can just as easily be read as market strategies appropriate to underdeveloped market settings. In this regard, it is important to note that land clearing was either the largest or second largest source of capital formation in the U.S. in the nineteenth century.[33] Moreover, it is also important to note that capitalist behaviour is not

---

[31] See, for example, R. Douglas Hurt, *Agriculture in the Midwest, 1815–1900* (Lincoln, NE, 2023); Malcolm J. Rohrbough, *The Trans-Appalachian Frontier: People, Societies, and Institutions, 1775–1850*, 3rd ed. (Bloomington, 2008); Eric A. Hinderaker, *Elusive Empires: Constructing Colonialism in the Ohio Valley, 1675–1800* (Cambridge, 1997); Brian Page and Richard Walker, 'From Settlement to Fordism: The Agro-Industrial Revolution in the American Midwest', *Economic Geography*, 67 (1991), 281–315. Regarding the early Ohio frontier, no scholarly study is more vivid than David McCullough's *The Pioneers* (New York, 2019) or Conrad Richter's exceptional, still underappreciated 'Awakening Land' trilogy of historical novels published between 1940 and 1950, the last of which, *The Town*, won the Pulitzer Prize for fiction in 1951. The first volume in the trilogy, *The Trees*, is particularly harrowing, depicting, as it does, the dark, dangerous, claustrophobic forest lands that had to be cleared before market agriculture could commence and develop. To be sure, some distinguished scholars have argued that both McCullough and Richter, in downplaying the violent dispossession of Native Americans from their land in the Ohio Valley, romanticized white settlement in the region. See, for example, Joyce E. Chaplin, 'Westward Ho!', *New York Times* (9 May 2019), 14.

[32] Levy, *Ages of American Capitalism*, 60–61. On Parker's distinction, see William N. Parker, 'From Northwest to Midwest: Social Bases of a Regional Economy', in *Essays in Nineteenth Century Economic History: The Old Northwest*, eds. David C. Klingaman and Richard K. Vedder (Athens, OH, 1975), 3–34.

[33] Martin Primack, 'Farm-Formed Capital in American Agriculture, 1850–1910' (University of North Carolina at Chapel Hill Ph.D. dissertation, 1962); idem, 'Land Clearing under Nineteenth-Century Techniques: Some Preliminary Considerations', *JEcH*, 22 (1962), 484–497; Robert E. Gallman, 'American Economic Growth before the Civil War: The Testimony of the Capital Stock Estimates', in *American Economic Growth and Standards*

synonymous with 'gambling' nor with speculation. Gambling is often used pejoratively, connoting high risk and reckless or hazardous uncertainty, and speculation is a particular practice relating to the purchase or selling of assets in the hope of gain from changes in their prices. Although gambling certainly occurs in capitalist economies and although speculation and speculators play roles – which roles, by the way, I view, *ceteris paribus*, as useful – neither is constitutive of the economic system.

As the above section suggests, several considerations must be factored into discussions regarding the existence, nature, and role of capitalism in early modern British America. Not surprisingly, the characteristic *mentalité* of the dominant European/Euro-American (male) population is one consideration, particularly the rationality of its responses to market signals and signs, its time preferences and horizons, attitudes/behaviours regarding saving/investment/accumulation, etc.

The resource environment, broadly conceived, matters a great deal too. By resources, we mean not only 'natural' resources, but the resources – knowledge, infrastructure, capital – needed to render 'land' into products and goods vendible in market settings, whether local, regional, or long-distance/international. In this regard, it is useful, if only as a reminder, to note that the ability to transform 'natural' resources – or human resources for that matter – into *economic* resources is a function of technology, culture, values, etc., at any given time. For example, uranium has been around forever, but became a valuable economic resource only after people developed the technological capability necessary to exploit nuclear energy via reactors, use uranium for medical diagnoses and therapies, etc., and then opt to exercise that capability. Culture and values, of course, can also lead peoples in the other direction as well, closing off possible options. For example, decisions in many countries in recent decades to reject the use of nuclear power in electricity generation have reduced the economic role of uranium, although it is likely that we have not heard the last word on this subject, or on others such as supersonic aircraft and GMOs. Similarly, while Noel Perrin overstated things in claiming that the Japanese reverted from guns back to the sword in the early modern period for social and cultural reasons – it seems more accurate to say that they closely managed guns and tightly controlled their distribution – no one would claim that they maximized their usage.[34]

In the case of humans, it was once both common and acceptable to buy and sell people – as we know all too well – and even children and young people were once viewed as viable labour inputs or resources. Although slavery in a variety of 'new' forms still exists today – as Kevin Bales among others

---

of Living before the Civil War, eds. Robert E. Gallman and Joseph J. Wallis (Chicago, 1992), 79–115.
34   Noel Perrin, *Giving up the Gun: Japan's Reversion to the Sword, 1545–1879* (Boston, 1979).

has documented – and child labour still exists in many parts of the world, widespread changes in culture and values have transformed the moral context in which slavery and child labour are embedded, narrowing and restricting, when not delegitimizing such labour configurations.[35]

Even where market *mentalités* are the norm and where economic resources are abundant, in capitalist economies decisions about what to produce, how to produce, and whether and where to sell whatever is produced also depend on considerations relating to supply and demand at any given time, with the price system and competition acting as organizing and regulatory/control mechanisms, assisted and sometimes even directed in the real world by the state. Referencing the state leads us toward yet another set of considerations, this one relating to the role of institutions in economic life, capitalist or otherwise. And this set of considerations may be the most important of them all, impeding or even preventing growth in otherwise favourable circumstances, or, conversely, rendering it possible in unfavourable market settings.[36]

Speaking broadly, institutions comprise the rules of the game, so to speak, the formal and informal mechanisms that shape and structure individual and community expectations as well as social transactions and interactions. Institutions take many shapes and forms, but they consist of *human-made* standards and norms, ranging from the family to the system of governance, from laws regarding property rights to the degree of support for civil society, from the availability/expectation of neutral, third-party conflict resolution to mechanisms designed to limit internal violence and promote social order. The way such mechanisms are designed and function goes a long way to explaining if and to what degree a population with a capitalist mindset, a favourable bundle of economic resources, and discernible, even robust market possibilities succeeds in translating such assets into growth and development and the time frame it takes to do so.

The manner in which these elements came together in British America during the early modern period resulted in institutional schemes, policies, processes, patterns, and behaviours that in formal terms are best represented under the rubric of capitalism, albeit a capitalism, subject to limits and constraints, that

---

35 Kevin Bales, *Disposable People: New Slavery in the Global Economy* (Berkeley, 2012). On the 'new slavery', also see the Global Slavery Index curated by Bales on the 'Walk Free' website [https://www.walkfree.org/global-slavery-index/ (accessed 19/06/2024)] and the 'Free the Slaves' website [https://freetheslaves.net/ (accessed 19/06/2024)]. According to Bales, there are currently about 50 million people worldwide caught up in the 'new slavery'.
36 Douglass C. North, *Institutions, Institutional Change and Economic Performance* (Cambridge, 1990); Daron Acemoglu, Simon Johnson, and James A. Robinson, 'Institutions as the Fundamental Cause of Long-Run Growth', in *Handbook of Economic Growth* 1A, eds. P. Aghion and S. Durlauf (Amsterdam, 2005), 386–472; Daron Acemoglu and James A. Robinson, *Why Nations Fail: The Origins of Power, Prosperity, and Poverty* (New York, 2012).

expressed and presented in different ways in different parts of British America over time. Other writers have attempted to situate some of these expressions and presentations under other interpretive heads altogether, such as frontier economy, non-market economy, household mode of production, independent commodity production, local-exchange economy, etc.[37] With all due respect, both the weight of the historical evidence and the correspondence and consistency of such evidence with the suppositions and principles associated with capitalism as discussed in this essay suggest à la Occam's razor that it is needlessly obfuscating, even unwise to employ these other classification schemes.

If capitalism expressed and presented in diverse ways in British America, initially English/British settlements everywhere in the Western Hemisphere faced common kinds of problems that had to be addressed, if not solved completely, before discrete development pathways began to emerge. Questions relating to basic subsidence had to be attended to – not always easy tasks – rough-and-ready governing structures put into place, and social orders, however rudimentary, established. Such tasks took varying amounts of time and proved problematic to varying degrees in different settlement areas, but, once attended to, the dominant settlement group, Euro-American males, was able, among other things, to begin the process of finding a viable strategy or viable strategies – often identifiable only in retrospect – intended not merely to sustain subsistence but hopefully to engender surpluses to enhance the material position of the dominant population groups and the settlements over which such groups reigned. This generally entailed exchanging such surpluses over long distances in ways sanctioned by the nation-state overseeing such groups in the various colonies.

The early strategies devised often involved highly circumstantial, even desperate agreements, arrangements, and deals of some sort with outside parties – whether Native Americans or government officials, company bigwigs, and investors in the mother country – that at the very least bought time for settler groups to begin the accumulation process. This sometimes protracted process entailed matters such as knowledge discovery, bio-prospecting, incipient capital formation, and the development of rudimentary 'production' sites and complexes and trading

---

37 See, for example, Michael Merrill, 'Cash is Good to Eat: Self-Sufficiency and Exchange in the Rural Economy of the United States', *RHR*, 3 (1977), 42–71; James A. Henretta, 'Families and Farms: *Mentalité* in Pre-Industrial America', *WMQ*, 35 (1978), 3–32; Christopher Clark, 'The Household Economy: Market Exchange and the Rise of Capitalism in the Connecticut Valley, 1800–1860', *Journal of Social History*, 13 (1979), 169–189; Gary Kulik, 'Dams, Fish, and Farmers: Defense of Public Rights in Eighteenth-Century Rhode Island', in *The Countryside in the Age of Capitalist Transition: Essays in the Social History of Rural America*, eds. Steven Hahn and Jonathan Prude (Chapel Hill, 1985), 25–50; Gregory Nobles, 'Capitalism in the Countryside: The Transformation of Rural Society in the United States', *RHR*, 41 (1988), 163–177; Michael Merrill, 'The Anticapitalist Origins of the United States', *Review*, 13 (1990), 465–497; Post, 'Agrarian Class Structure and Economic Development in Colonial British North America'.

relationships and networks. On the ground, the strategies attempted ranged widely. In New England and Atlantic Canada, the pull, if not the preference was toward the acquisition/extraction of natural resources or raw materials – by various means – for sale on markets after only minimal processing. In the southern mainland colonies and the West Indies, the route taken can be described with considerable accuracy as one of plunder and primitive accumulation. How better would one describe activities – common in South Carolina – such as piracy and making war on Native Americans to acquire land and property, as well as captives to sell as slaves in the British West Indies? Relatively early on, these same colonies, of course, deployed sizable contingents of dependent African labour whether as indentured servants or slaves, who either accompanied the first whites to these colonies or were acquired shortly after white settlers arrived. When viewed in this light, it is hardly surprising, indeed, it is apropos that a recent book by John J. Navin on life in South Carolina during the first half century of the colony's existence is entitled *The Grim Years*, for grim they certainly were.[38] Indeed, the early years of settlement – and thus of capitalism – *everywhere* in British America were harsh and rough, and often vicious, to which the title of one of Bernard Bailyn's last books, *The Barbarous Years* – on the violent, chaotic, and sometimes horrifying seventeenth century in British North America as a whole – powerfully attests.[39]

To expand upon a point touched upon earlier, the early days of (Western) capitalism in the Americas, including British America, were marked by a good deal of violence, coercion, and miscellaneous acts of villainy, whether attributable to the rapacity unleashed by, and arguably inherent in, this economic system, or to the 'conflict of civilizations', as Bailyn put it, or the repellent, but often unplanned or ad hoc savagery triggered in remote and seemingly wild and feral frontiers. To me, there is something to say for each of these possibilities. That said, however, I would not go as far as many heterodox scholars, including new historians of capitalism, go in concluding that violence, brutality, and inhumanity are inherent in Western capitalism. Rather, I view them as expressions associated with it under certain conditions, most notably in its early phases, and in cases involving its expansion into new geographic zones, especially zones dominated by others or organized in non-capitalist ways, most markedly when there are power asymmetries strongly favourable to Western capitalists. The early days of capitalist expansion in British America represented a perfect storm, as it were, unleashing in some areas at least, a tsunami of violent depredations by European colonizers against others of various types as well as against some of their own, But over time, as capitalism in the West

---

38 John J. Navin, *The Grim Years: Settling South Carolina, 1670–1720* (Columbia, SC, 2019).
39 Bernard Bailyn, *The Barbarous Years: The Conflict of Civilizations, 1600–1675* (New York, 2012).

matured, it unleashed other things as well, as Albert O. Hirschman brilliantly suggested long ago: New values promotive of stricter bounds on anti-social 'passions', a more capacious and socially benign sense of self-interest, and ultimately, broader moral sympathies allowing for the gradual amelioration in both material conditions and what Eugene D. Genovese referred to as the 'conditions of life' for members of various subordinate classes, races, and groups.[40] As we shall see, this was the case both in British America and in the United States thereafter.

There are different contexts and conceptual schemes in which to embed British America in the early modern period, some broader than others. It's been a long time since writers focused solely on the 'thirteen colonies', but disagreement still exists regarding how far to extend our gaze. 'Atlantic Canada' – Newfoundland, Nova Scotia, and, late in the colonial period, Quebec – and the British West Indies are often brought into the picture these days, while some prefer more capacious schemes still, embedding British America into one of another Atlanticist formulation, into 'hemispheric' and/or 'continentalist' schemes, and increasingly into a global frame. There is merit in each of these possibilities. Given our focus on the origins of capitalism in British America, however, it seems prudent to take an intermediate position and use as a heuristic or economic stylization the typology employed in McCusker and Menard's classic 1985 work, *The Economy of British America, 1607–1789*. In so doing, we shall focus on the ways in which early capitalism took root and expressed or presented in five discrete zones: New England and Atlantic Canada, the Middle Colonies, the Upper South, the Lower South, and the British West Indies.[41] That said, it is, of course, impossible to hive off these regions from one another completely. For example, the economies of New England, the Middle Colonies, and the British West Indies were quite closely linked, a point of renewed emphasis by new historians of capitalism.[42] Nor is it possible to view these five regions without due consideration of Europe, West Africa, the circum-Caribbean basin as a whole, transmontane sections of North

---

40 Albert O. Hirschman, *The Passions and the Interests: Political Arguments for Capitalism before Its Triumph* (Princeton, 1977); Eugene D. Genovese, 'The Treatment of Slaves in Different Countries: Problems in the Application of the Comparative Method', in *Slavery in the New World: A Reader in Comparative History*, eds. Laura A. Foner and Eugene D. Genovese (Englewood Cliffs, NJ, 1969), 202–210.
41 John J. McCusker and Russell R. Menard, *The Economy of British America, 1607–1789* (Chapel Hill, 1985). For a more complete elaboration of my view of this work, see Peter A. Coclanis, 'In Retrospect: McCusker and Menard's *Economy of British America*', *Reviews in American History*, 30 (2002), 183–197. For a recent, complementary attempt to interpret the economy of British America during the colonial period, see Joshua L. Rosenbloom, 'Colonial America', in the *Handbook of Cliometrics*, eds. Claude Diebolt and Michael Haupert (Cham, 2019), 785–810.
42 See, for example, Eric Kimball, 'What have we to do with Slavery?': New Englanders and the Slave Economies of the West Indies', in *Slavery's Capitalism*, eds. Beckert and Rothman, 181–194.

America, Asia, etc., the relevance of which areas is readily acknowledged and subject to intermittent attention below.

As is well known, in *The Economy of British America*, McCusker and Menard explicitly and self-consciously focus on the 'foreign' (export/import) sector, believing that the British colonies' involvement in international factor and product markets created the scale necessary to incentivize these colonies to specialize to varying degrees in what sold best in order to reap the benefits of their involvement. With each region specializing in its comparative advantage or advantages, the result was greater production and productive efficiency. In a time of strong demand for many goods/services exported by the colonies, such specialization provided the spark that led to significant income generation in the colonies, concomitant capital accumulation, and over time to robust extensive and intensive growth and to the precocious beginnings of the broader process of economic development.[43] McCusker and Menard are quite respectful of the achievements resulting from the foreign-trade sector, which in their view was organized and operated along capitalist lines. They note that for the white population the results of export-led growth were exceptional: By the time of the American Revolution, this was arguably the wealthiest population group in the entire world.[44] Such respect notwithstanding, neither McCusker nor Menard is a Pollyanna, and they are quick to point out that the income/wealth generated via export-led growth was not shared equally by the free population, and are clear about the fact that 'black slaves and native American groups ... paid a frightful price for white society's well-being'.[45]

For the better part of a generation, scholars studying the early American economy pretty much toed the line marked out by McCusker and Menard. Over the past few decades, though, many scholars have shifted their attention to other sectors, issues, themes, problems, etc. Some have moved away from measurement questions regarding the export trade and/or the relationship between exports and growth to focus on the reconstruction of trade circuits and business networks (including sophisticated efforts to visualize such circuits and networks graphically). Others have concentrated on various 'breaches' in

---

43   McCusker and Menard, *Economy of British America*, 17–50. See also, Edwin J. Perkins, *The Economy of Colonial America* (New York, 1988), 19–46.
44   McCusker and Menard, *Economy of British America*, 51–70. For a more recent econometric analysis that corroborates the fact that wealth *and income* per free inhabitant were extremely high (and distributed reasonably widely by the standards of the day) in British America prior to the American Revolution, see Peter H. Lindert and Jeffrey G. Williamson, 'American Incomes Before and After the Revolution', *JEcH*, 73 (2013), 725–765. Employing a different approach, economists Robert Allen, Tommy Murphy, and Eric Schneider have demonstrated that wages were also very high in colonial British America. See Allen, Murphy, and Schneider, 'The Colonial Origins of the Divergence in the Americas: A Labor Market Approach', *JEcH*, 72 (2012), 863–894.
45   McCusker and Menard, *Economy of British America*, 51.

officially sanctioned foreign trade – on problems such as piracy, smuggling, and other forms of extra-legal or clandestine exchange (often involving sailors, slaves, dockworkers, etc.). Still others have moved away from the export trade and large-scale trade altogether, studying instead the domestic sector: retailing, urban markets, exchanges, legal or illegal, involving various subaltern groups in the colonies. And still other scholars, influenced by anthropology and literary/cultural theory have focused on cultural practices, symbols, and signs shedding light on matters economic. To top things off, with the maturation of the field of environmental history we find more and more scholars investigating the relationship between the economy and the environment – topics such as the effects of the 'little ice age' on economic development, the beginnings of what John Bellamy Foster, drawing from Marx, has referred to as the 'metabolic rift' between humans and nature that began with the rise of capitalist agriculture, etc.[46] Much excellent work has been produced as a result of these shifts, but, at the end of the day, I nonetheless continue to believe that 'foreign' trade, exports/imports, and international product and factor markets remain crucial, *primi inter pares* among factors shaping the economy of British America and shall proceed accordingly.

British America encompassed a large area with a diverse array of environmental zones, resources, and production possibilities. This being the case, it is not surprising that comparative advantage and regional specialization – given prevailing technologies, the level of demand, alternative supply sources, the degree of market integration, etc. – came in various forms and shifted over time. Speaking very broadly, the export focus in the more southerly parts of British America – colonies in the West Indies, the Lower South, and the Upper South – was on agricultural staples produced, to a greater or lesser degree, by African/African-American slave labour: sugar in the West Indies; rice and indigo in the Lower South; tobacco, supplemented by wheat after about 1750, in the Upper South. There were always other exports from these areas, but the above-named crops were by far the most important of them. Why the outsized role of African/African American slave labour? Here, a variety of considerations factored in: Africans' prior experience with routinized agricultural labour; epidemiological concerns (their degree of inherited and acquired resistances to certain highly lethal mosquito-borne diseases); the availability of such labour at

---

46   See, for example, Geoffrey Parker, *Global Crisis: War, Climate Change and the Catastrophe of the Seventeenth Century* (New Haven, 2013); Philipp Blom, *Nature's Mutiny: How the Little Ice Age of the Long Seventeenth Century Transformed the West and Shaped the Present* (New York, 2019); Sam White, *A Cold Welcome: The Little Ice Age and Europe's Encounter with North America* (Cambridge, MA, 2017); John Bellamy Foster, 'Marx's Theory of Metabolic Rift: Classical Foundations for Environmental Sociology', *American Journal of Sociology*, 105 (1999), 366–405; idem, 'The Dialectics of Ecology: An Introduction', *Monthly Review*, 75 (January 2024), 1–26.

scale; the need to ensure that a labour force engaged in rigorous work in difficult environments could be secured and retained; and the belief that African/African American labourers lacked claims even to the relatively small bundle of rights and privileges according European/Euro-American labourers at the time.

What about Native Americans and their place in the economy? How do we treat them? Good questions, both. In the British West Indies, Native American populations were largely wiped out early on whether through depredations, dislocations, or diseases associated with contact with Old World populations. The situation on the mainland was more complicated. Generally speaking, Native Americans did not play major roles in the agricultural sector of the settlers' economy. They did, however, play a significant role in the export economy of the Lower South and to a lesser degree in the Upper South via the deerskin trade and via the fur trade in regions further north. Because at the time these populations by and large were not considered fully integrated members of the colonies in the Lower or Upper South – or really in any of the colonies of British America – it makes sense to take note of their economic roles but to focus primarily on the white and African/African American populations in the statistical analysis below.

Let us run through McCusker and Menard's five regions seriatim.[47] In the West Indies, almost all the labour in sugar/sugar processing was provided by African/African American slaves, with the tiny white populations on the islands – the wealthiest free population in British America – garnering the economic gains. Conditions were much the same in the agricultural export sector of the Lower South, where almost all the labour in rice and indigo was performed by slaves, with whites, again, capturing the economic gains. Export/output ratios were extraordinarily high in the British West Indies and quite high in the Lower South as well, particularly in coastal areas of South Carolina and Georgia, the centres of rice and indigo production. It should be noted, however, that the economies in the Lower South as a whole were more diverse than in the British West Indies, and the ratio between the free and slave populations less skewed. Whereas whites constituted less than 10 per cent of the total population of the British West Indies in 1770, in the Lower South at the same time about 55 per cent of the population was comprised of whites, and only in South Carolina did African/African American slaves constitute most of the population. The enslaved proportion of the population was smaller still in the Upper South, where free whites by 1770 comprised around 60 per cent of the total population. Not surprisingly, the export/output ratio and per capita wealth per free inhabitant were also lower in this region than in the British colonies in the West Indies and the Lower South.[48]

---

47   McCusker and Menard, *Economy of British America*, 91–208.
48   Ibid., 117–188; Alice Hanson Jones, *Wealth of a Nation to Be: The American Colonies on the Eve of the Revolution* (New York, 1978), 50–85; Perkins, *The Economy of Colonial*

In economic terms, the more northerly regions in British America possessed different comparative advantages and, as a result, specialized along different lines. Atlantic Canada's comparative advantage at the time was clearly not in agriculture, but in fishing and in the acquisition by one means or another of furs and animal skins. The population of the region found export markets for these products, but none sufficiently profitable to justify the cost of purchasing slaves as labourers. Relatively few labourers were needed in these 'land-extensive' extractive activities in any case.[49]

New England and the Middle Colonies possessed some natural-resource advantages to build around, but I would contend, along with others, that their real comparative and competitive advantages laid elsewhere. Like Atlantic Canada, New England exported fish and furs, supplemented by forest products of various kinds, and the Middle Colonies, particularly Pennsylvania, with good soils, produced and exported often sizable amounts of wheat. But the greatest advantages of these two regions resided elsewhere, related less to natural resources than to the regions' business cultures and to the populations' entrepreneurial zeal. Both regions were adept in matters of marketing and marketing organization – in the shipping industry, and in provisioning, commerce, and financial services, most notably. Moreover, they both found profitable niches in the processing of raw materials and agricultural products, as well as in handicraft manufacturing. Their greatest market advantages, however, related to the economic flexibility and entrepreneurial energy of their populations, people who, driven by necessity, constantly searched for market services to provide and profitable niches to fill, and ended up doing so with considerable aplomb. Although New York City had a considerable population of African/African American slaves and although slaves were present in small numbers elsewhere, in the aggregate, the population of New England and the Middle Colonies, like that of Atlantic Canada, was comprised overwhelmingly of free whites.[50]

The results of the various development paths pursued were, on balance, exceptionally impressive by early modern standards, if morally compromised by the standards of our own era. The free population of British America, as suggested above, was likely the wealthiest population in the world at the time of the American Revolution. About 80 per cent of the population in the mainland colonies (including Atlantic Canada) was free, and, even when including the British West Indies, where less than 10 per cent of the population was comprised

---

America, 212–238; Peter Lindert and Jeffrey G. Williamson, 'American Incomes Before and After the Revolution', *JEcH*, 73 (2013), 725–765. Trevor Burnard, *Planters, Merchants, and Slaves: Plantation Societies in British America, 1650–1820* (Chicago, 2015) offers an excellent synthesis of the histories of these three 'plantation' regions.

49 McCusker and Menard, *The Economy of British America*, 111–116.
50 Ibid., 91–111, 189–208, Thomas M. Doerflinger, *A Vigorous Spirit of Enterprise: Merchants and Economic Development in Revolutionary Philadelphia* (Chapel Hill, 1986),

of free whites, we find that just under 70 per cent of the total population of British America was free.[51] And by contemporary standards, the free population on average did very well indeed.[52] To be sure, there was considerable inequality in the distribution of income and wealth amongst the free population in British America, and such inequality should be noted. That said, it is still difficult to gainsay the fact that the market-oriented free population of British America, working assiduously in a favourable resource environment in a time of generally strong demand for the products and services it placed on offer, and doing so in an institutional environment with strong property rights and protections, was able to accumulate capital of all kinds and generate income flows and wealth stocks unusually large for the time. Nor were their economic accomplishments limited to gains in income and wealth: A rich body of research in historical anthropometrics demonstrates that the white population on the mainland was exceptionally tall on the eve of the Revolution, suggesting that the material gains registered carried over to biological well-being as well.[53] And the beat went on, as it were: Research by Angus Maddison, the leading authority on the subject, reveals that in 1820 North America and Western Europe – the centres of Western capitalism – were the two wealthiest regions in the world by a wide margin.[54] Although questions remain about the timing of (and reasons for) the divergence between these economies and those in other advanced areas in China and India, most scholars now agree that North America and Western Europe had moved ahead of the most developed parts of China and India by 1750 at the latest. And Western capitalism, science, institutions, and culture – aided, according to some, by relaxed resource constraints in the West provided by the location of coal in England and 'ghost acres' in the Americas – are frequently cited as the reasons why.[55]

---

51 The percentages in the text were calculated from population estimates in McCusker and Menard, *Economy of British America*, 103, 112, 136, 154, 172, 203.
52 Ibid., 117–188; Jones, *Wealth of a Nation to Be*, esp. 50–85; Perkins, *Economy of Colonial America*, 212–238; Lindert and Williamson, 'American Incomes Before and After the Revolution'.
53 Kenneth L. Sokoloff and Georgia C. Villaflor, 'The Early Achievement of Modern Heights in America', *Social Science History*, 6 (1982), 453–481; John Komlos, 'On the Biological Standard of Living of Eighteenth-Century Americans: Taller, Richer, Healthier', *Research in Economic History*, 20 (2001), 223–248.
54 Angus Maddison, *The World Economy: Historical Statistics*, OECD, Development Centre Studies (Paris, 2003), 262; Angus Maddison, *Contours of the World Economy, 1–2030 AD: Essays in Macro-Economic History* (Oxford, 2007), 69–71; Jutta Bolt and Jan Luiten van Zanden, *Maddison Project Database 2020* (Groningen, 2020) [https://www.rug.nl/ggdc/historicaldevelopment/maddison/publications/wp15.pdf (accessed 19/06/2024)].
55 For a recent sense of where the 'Great Divergence' debate now stands, see Victor Court, 'A Reassessment of the Great Divergence Debate: Towards a Reconciliation of Apparently Distinct Determinants', *EREH*, 24 (2020), 633–674; Kenneth Pomeranz and

Before moving on, a word or two about the primary drivers of capitalist development in British America and the early United States, which perforce means a few words on the tricky and controversial concept of human agency. On one level, of course, all historical actors had agency, but, playing off Orwell, some of these actors had more agency than others. Especially *economic* agency. For better or worse, likely better *and* worse, free white men by and large were responsible for blazing the capitalist development paths followed in British America and in the early republic. Obviously, others were involved in various capacities: free white women, sometimes in instrumental ways (*feme sole* traders, widows of planters and merchants, etc.); enslaved African/African Americans, particularly on sites of production; and Native Americans. Regarding the last: Native Americans clearly influenced development in important ways on the mainland, often setting ground rules, facilitating economic activity in many cases, setting limits in others, etc. But at the end of the day, time, technology, and demography were not on their side, and their power to shape economic life gradually declined sharply in most of the eastern half of the United States in the first half of the nineteenth century. In fine, then, free white men bear an inordinate share of the credit or of the blame, as the case may be, for the direction early capitalism took in British America and the United States. This being the case, it seems fair to ask what had capitalist man wrought?

This is a tricky question to pose currently, laden, as it is, with heavy moral freight. As we have just seen above, British America qua geopolitical unit was extraordinarily wealthy at the time of the American Revolution. But only about 70 per cent of the population was free at the time, and the unfree endured often brutal economic exploitation among other enormities and indignities. Moreover, portions of the free population fared poorly under early American capitalism, and Native Americans, in but not of the capitalist economy, generally speaking, lacked many of the rights and protections accruing to more privileged participants in the system, and were often treated shabbily to boot.[56]

Prasannan Parthasarathi, 'The Great Divergence Debate', in *Global Economic History*, eds. Tirthankar Roy and Giorgio Riello (2018), 19–37. Note that coal and 'ghost acres' – areas, such as the Americas, functioning as platforms to produce goods and products to be consumed elsewhere (in this case, England/Great Britain and Europe) – are emphasized by Pomeranz in *The Great Divergence*.

56 On poor whites in early America see, for example, Billy G. Smith, *The 'Lower Sort': Philadelphia's Laboring People, 1750–1800* (Ithaca, 1990); Smith, ed., *Down and Out in Early America* (University Park, PA, 2004); Billy G. Smith and Simon Middleton (eds.), *Class Matters: British North America and the Atlantic World* (Philadelphia, 2008); Tim Lockley, 'Rural Poor Relief in Colonial South Carolina', *HJ*, 48 (2005), 955–976; Seth Rockman, *Scraping By: Wage Labor, Slavery, and Survival in Early Baltimore* (Baltimore, 2009); Laura Panza, Jeffrey G. Williamson, and Trevor Burnard, 'The Social Implications of Sugar: Living Costs, Real Incomes, and Inequality in Jamaica, c1774', NBER Working Paper, No. 23897, October 2017, National Bureau of Economic Research, Cambridge, MA [https://www.nber.

I shall not try to minimize these very legitimate concerns, but rather attempt to broaden the context in which these concerns are assessed, first, by making a distinction with a difference, then by asking a question of my own. First, the distinction, an analytical one, between positive economics and normative economics. The former is concerned with empirical facts and relationships among them, including those of cause and effect. What is or what was, what happened or did not happen, and why. Normative economics is instead concerned with moral or value judgments about such phenomena, often with prescriptions for change thrown in. Both are valid approaches – here, I have focused primarily on the former – but to those evaluating capitalism in British America through a normative lens, it is useful as a guard against ahistorical or anachronistic thinking always to keep another question or consideration close to mind, almost as a mantra: Compared to what?

Although our focus here is on British America and the populations generally considered rights-holding constituent members thereof, it seems clear that certain areas and peoples central to early capitalism in British America – West Africa/West Africans and Native American territories/Native Americans – did not benefit from their early engagement with capitalism. This is so whether speaking in terms of positive or normative economics. In each case, economies and societies were disrupted, peoples exploited and abused, and in the case of Native Americans, territories seized by various means. On the other hand, Great Britain, the most important source of the free population of British America, gained in many ways from the production/exchange complexes established in the Western Hemisphere, as did individual Britons, sometimes extravagantly. Indeed, according to some schools of thought, the capital garnered and accumulated from economic engagement with British America – particularly from providing the export complexes of the West Indies, Lower South, and Upper South with slave labour and importing/processing/reexporting the agricultural output produced in these areas – proved important, even decisive in Britain's industrialization.[57] To be sure, many (including myself) believe that

---

org/papers/w23897 (accessed 19/06/2024)]; Panza, Williamson, and Burnard, 'Sugar and Slaves: Wealth, Poverty, and Inequality in Jamaica', *VoxEU COLUMN*, Centre for Economic Policy Research, December 6, 2017 [https://cepr.org/voxeu/columns/sugar-and-slaves-wealth-poverty-and-inequality-colonial-jamaica (accessed 19/06/2024)].

57 The most notable example of this line of reasoning concerns the famous Williams thesis on the relationship between the Atlantic slave trade – and, often, slavery more broadly in the Americas – and British industrialization (and sometimes European industrialization in general). This interpretation has gained purchase in recent decades and is generally accepted by people working from 'new history of capitalism' and 'racial capitalism' perspectives. The historian Gerald Horne fuses these approaches in two recent works. See Horne, *The Apocalypse of Settler Colonialism: The Roots of Slavery, White Supremacy, and Capitalism in Seventeenth-Century North America and the Caribbean* (New York, 2018); Horne, *The Dawning of the Apocalypse: The Roots of Slavery, White Supremacy, Settler Colonialism,*

such views overstate the importance of both the slave trade and the American trade for Britain's development, but capitalist development in British America clearly impacted Great Britain positively, unlike the cases in West Africa or in 'Indian country'.

And for the free population or populations in British America itself? We know that in the resource setting and market context in which they lived, most of the free population was served well by capitalist development, particularly compared to the experiences of populations living virtually anywhere else in the world at the time. But what if we assess things more broadly in terms of social and political development as well. How do the various regions in British America stack up?

Such an assessment requires calibration because the types of sociopolitical regimes differed in British America, with said differences due largely to the way environmental factors, available resources and market opportunities shaped the institutional structures developed under capitalism in various parts of British America, and how those institutions in turn influenced and even informed other dimensions of social life. Indeed, over the past three or four decades a rich body of literature has grown up regarding the key role of institutions in economic, social and political life, which literature has proven highly influential not only in history and economics, but in sociology and political science as well.

In economics the work often goes under the rubric of new institutional economics.[58] Such work was pioneered by an all-star cast of scholars that includes a quartet of Nobel laureates: Ronald Coase, Douglass North, Elinor Ostrom, and Oliver Williamson. Armen Alchian, Steven N.S. Cheung and Harold Demsetz are other luminaries associated with the early development of this field, and several younger (though not young) economists such as John J. Wallis, Avner Greif, and Daron Acemoglu, and various and sundry well-known collaborators from other disciplines such as political scientists Barry Weingast and James A. Robinson added important insights of their own.

Some of the figures named above – North, Wallis, Weingast, Acemoglu, and Robinson most notably – have focused attention on the differential roles of institutions in areas in the Americas colonized by the European powers

---

and *Capitalism in the Long Sixteenth Century* (New York, 2020). Note that in a recent work two mainstream economic historians – Maxine Berg and Pat Hudson – also have made the case that slavery was central to the British Industrial Revolution: Maxine Berg and Pat Hudson, *Slavery, Capitalism and the Industrial Revolution* (New York, 2023).

58 For good introductions/assessments, see Erik G. Furobotn and Rudolf Richter, *Institutions and Economic Theory: The Contribution of the New Institutional Economics*, 2nd ed. (Ann Arbor, 2005 [1998]); Oliver E. Williamson, 'The New Institutional Economics: Taking Stock, Looking Ahead', *Journal of Economic Literature*, 38 (2000), 595–613; Claude Ménard and Mary M. Shirley, 'The Future of New Institutional Economics: From Early Intuitions to a New Paradigm?' *Journal of Institutional Economics*, 10 (2014), 541–565.

specifically. Their work, and that of others such as Stanley L. Engerman, Kenneth Sokoloff, Robert C. Allen, Simon Johnson, Robert Raul Thomas, Matthew Lange, and James Mahoney – can help us to explain the complex interactions between and among *mentalités*, environment, resources, economic opportunities/activities, transaction costs, and institutions in various parts of British America. To be sure, these writers have their interpretive differences, emphasize different variables, and employ different terminology. It is unlikely, however, that any of these scholars would raise serious objections to the general argument made below, which is not particularly surprising, as the argument draws appreciatively and heavily from their own. In making my argument, I shall follow North, Wallis, and Weingast, who have attempted to develop a general theory of institutions, and make a distinction between what they refer to as 'open-access orders' and 'limited-access orders'.[59]

In stylized terms, 'open-access orders' are inclusive rather than 'extractive' and are characterized by institutional environments offering broad economic and political rights to large segments of a given area's population. These rights include, but are not limited to, credible state commitments to property rights and the rule of law; broad, impartially defined constitutional arrangements designed to 'limit and define the powers of government', including its use of violence; extensive access to economic opportunities and political participation; acceptance of the legitimacy of civil-society organizations; governmental power that is 'contestable' and 'subject to clear and well-understood rules'.[60]

As the term suggests, a 'limited-access order', is very different, and in many ways the obverse of an 'open-access order'. A 'limited-access order' is narrowly based, and characterized by extractive, often highly corrupt institutions offering only a small segment of the population access to economic and political opportunity. Property rights and the rule of law more generally are precarious in such orders, economic and political competition severely constrained, and violence controlled mainly through mechanisms designed by the government and privileged economic and political groups to protect monopolies and other forms of economic and political 'rents' under their control. Civil-society

---

59 Douglass C. North, John Joseph Wallis, and Barry R. Weingast, 'Violence and the Rise of Open-Access Orders', *Journal of Democracy*, 20 (2009), 55–68; idem, *Violence and Social Orders: A Conceptual Framework for Interpreting Recorded Human History* (Cambridge, 2009); Stanley L. Engerman and Kenneth L. Sokoloff, 'Institutions, Factor Endowments, and Paths of Development in the New World', *Journal of Economic Perspectives*, 14 (2000), 217–232; idem, *Economic Development in the Americas since 1500: Endowments and Institutions* (Cambridge, 2012)
60 North, Wallis, and Weingast, 'Violence and the Rise of Open-Access Orders', 56; North, Wallis, and Weingast, *Violence and Social Orders*, 1–29, 110–147.

organizations are often left unprotected, if not harassed or outlawed, and governmental authority arbitrary and often uncontestable.[61]

'Open-access orders' and 'limited-access orders' are not fixed categories and in the real world these orders exist on continua, with some blurring between forms possible. Moreover, examples of each can be found anywhere. This said, a number of scholars working in this vein have found strong correlations in the Western Hemisphere and elsewhere between certain 'strategies' and patterns of economic development and tendencies toward one or the other of these orders. To cut to the chase, areas whose early development focused heavily around slavery, plantation agriculture or mining, and exports were far more likely to partake of characteristics consistent with 'limited-access orders' than was the case in areas where slavery, plantations, and/or mining were less important.[62] In the latter areas, furthermore, 'open-access orders' arose earlier and far more easily and fully than in the regions where slavery, plantations, mining, and exports played lead roles. Given the burden of this essay – the origins and development of capitalism in British America – and the central argument made therein, one key implication of the open-access, limited-access order literature seems to be that capitalism expressed and presented in differential ways institutionally.

In retrospect, the British West Indies seems a clear-cut case of a 'limited-access' institutional order. Indeed, it is difficult to see how a society wherein 90 per cent of the population was enslaved c.1770 could be deemed otherwise, particularly since wealth, opportunity, and power were highly skewed even among the small free minority.[63] If the British West Indies did not differ across the board from British regions on the North American mainland – its free population shared much the same *mentalité* and culture as their brethren on the mainland – the environmental/resource setting and market opportunities in the West Indies took early capitalist development there down a particularly 'extractive' – and, indeed, pernicious – institutional path, one distinguishable even from the paths followed by regions on the British American mainland wherein slavery, plantation agriculture, and exports played powerful roles. The West Indian path vis-à-vis other regions on the mainland has been analyzed in detail in studies by Engerman and Sokoloff among others, so we will not

---

61 North, Wallis, and Weingast, 'Violence and the Rise of Open-Access Orders'; North, Wallis, and Weingast, *Violence and Social Orders*, 1–29, 30–109.
62 Engerman and Sokoloff, 'Institutions, Factor Endowments, and Paths of Development in the New World'; Engerman and Sokoloff, *Economic Development in the Americas since 1500*; Daron Acemoglu, Simon Johnson, and James A. Robinson, 'Reversal of Fortune: Geography and Institutions in the Making of the Modern World Income Distribution', QJE, 117 (2002), 1231–1294.
63 McCusker and Menard, *Economy of British America*, 154.

tarry.⁶⁴ Hold on to the word 'path', though, for I use it with intentionality, given my belief that future possibilities are influenced profoundly – and in the West Indian case were narrowly constricted by – paths established early on. That the West Indian colonies were in economic terms by far the most valuable of Britain's possessions in the early modern period, only to lapse later into long-term stagnation and decline in the modern period is often seen as powerful empirical proof of several well-known theses in the development literature – the 'resource curse' and Acemoglu, Johnson, and Robinson's 'reversal of fortune' argument come immediately to mind in this regard. But the fate of the West Indies testifies not only to developmental impedimenta associated with 'limited-access' orders, but also to the variation in outcomes associated with early capitalism.

The Lower South and the Upper South displayed many of the characteristics of extractive, 'limited-access' orders, but such characteristics 'presented' in less complete and constricted ways than was the case in the British colonies in the West Indies. The economies in the colonies comprising the Lower South and the Upper South were more diverse than were those in the British possessions in the West Indies; the enslaved proportions of the labour forces smaller; the free populations more variegated; absentee property and wealth holdings far less prominent. Higher proportions of the free (white male) population were eligible to vote for candidates for elected offices, and, overall, there was more economic opportunity for non-elites, not least because of the more favourable human/land ratio on the southern mainland. To be sure, by modern standards, opportunity in the southern mainland colonies, with their large enslaved populations and the status of free women severely circumscribed, seems narrow and repressive, but in 1770 almost 60 per cent of the population of the two regions was comprised of free whites as opposed to about 10 per cent in the British West Indies, and the demographic differentials alone made a difference in the structure and degree of opportunity available.⁶⁵

The parts of the mainland further north differed dramatically from the export platforms based on plantation slavery on the southern part of the mainland and in the West Indies. On the eve of the American Revolution, New England and the Middle Colonies were well on the way toward developing flourishing 'open-access' orders, characterized by 'inclusive' institutions,

---

64 See the works cited in note 62. That path led after slavery to what the influential Jamaican scholar George L. Beckford long ago referred to as 'persistent poverty' – via the 'development of underdevelopment', as it were. See Beckford, *Persistent Poverty: Underdevelopment in Plantation Economies in the Third World* (1972).
65 McCusker and Menard, *Economy of British America*, 136, 172. For a recent attempt to view colonial South Carolina as a 'limited-access order', see Peter A. Coclanis and Tomoko Yagyu, 'Mercantile Concentration in Eighteenth-Century Charleston, 1735–1775', *Historical Methods: A Journal of Quantitative and Interdisciplinary History*, 56 (2023), 1–17.

widespread economic opportunity and political rights, including suffrage. The population of these two regions was comprised overwhelmingly of free men and women – 96 or 97 per cent of the 1.137 million inhabitants c.1770 – and wealth and power were much more widely diffused than in the areas further south.[66] Though much smaller and less developed, Atlantic Canada – Nova Scotia and Newfoundland in particular – shared many of these features with New England and the Middle Colonies. As McCusker and Menard point out, for many purposes they can be seen as adjuncts of New England, which had increasingly incorporated these colonies, especially Nova Scotia and Newfoundland, into its economic orbit. Quebec, with its large French population, is more difficult to place, especially since it had only come under British control in 1763.[67] Clearly, though, all three of the regions comprising Atlantic Canada differed dramatically from the orders in the West Indies, the Lower South, and Upper South, and increasingly took on the features of open-access orders in the late eighteenth and nineteenth centuries. In Atlantic Canada, as in the Middle Colonies and New England, capitalist development, it seems, correlated with, and was almost certainly a causal factor in the promotion of increasingly wealthy, secure, open societies with considerable economic opportunity available for the populations living therein.

In the nineteenth century these 'open-access' areas, which retained their economic connections after the American Revolution, were the hearths of capitalist development in the U.S. and Canada. In the U.S., the northeastern quadrant of the country – north of the Ohio River and east of the Mississippi – proved the economic dynamo. The region was home to the nation's largest cities, most vibrant commercial and financial institutions, and the vast majority of the country's manufacturing output. As time passed, moreover, it gave rise to the aforementioned agro-industrial complex of the Midwest, arguably the most impressive expression of balanced capitalist growth and development in history. Eastern Canada – the Maritime Provinces, Quebec, and Ontario – developed apace, and in the nineteenth century the region became the 'manufacturing belt' of Canada and was increasingly integrated into the larger industrial economy of the northeastern quadrant of the United States via railway connections and canals.[68]

66 McCusker and Menard, *Economy of British America*, 103–203.
67 Ibid., 111–116.
68 Page and Walker, 'From Settlement to Fordism'; David Ward, *Cities and Immigrants: A Geography of Change in Nineteenth Century America* (Oxford, 1971), 11–47; Fred Bateman and Thomas Weiss, *A Deplorable Scarcity: The Failure of Industrialization in the Slave Economy* (Chapel Hill, 1981), 3–69, 157–163. Note, however, that the South's manufacturing sector during the antebellum period was not as small or underdeveloped as sometimes depicted. As Robert William Fogel and Stanley L. Engerman pointed out long ago, the South was one of the leading manufacturing regions in the world in 1860: Robert W. Fogel and Stanley L. Engerman, *Time on the Cross: The Economics of American Negro Slavery* (Boston, 1974), 1: 254–257. On the growth of manufacturing in the South during the

Alas, economic progress proved slower and more fitful in the Lower South and Upper South – and in the 'deeper' parts of the South populated largely by migrants from these regions. Although the South grew during the early national and antebellum periods, primarily because of labour exploitation made possible by slavery and robust demand for slave-produced agricultural export staples, after 1861 wartime destruction, supply-side changes arising from the Civil War, emancipation, and a slowdown in the growth rate of world demand for cotton, by far the region's leading market staple, dramatically changed the structure of economic opportunity in the region. Such changes had particularly pernicious effects because, lacking the capital needed to modernize the massive agricultural sector, the region rebuilt the sector in a decidedly retrograde manner, limiting its growth possibilities even after the region began its modern industrialization process in the 1880s. By then, the South had become the poorest region in the country, with the seaboard southern states in particularly parlous states.[69]

But even the South, with an extractive institutional order early on and with escape difficult because of the slavery/plantation development path it pursued, saw some change over time. The institutional order became more open and inclusive for whites in the first half of the nineteenth century via what some have labelled the move toward *herrenvolk* democracy. During the same period, the South itself became more diverse, with the hold of slavery lessening in various parts of the region, as distinguished scholars such as William H. Freehling and Lacy K. Ford have shown.[70] And as the capitalist North, with its open-access order, became wealthier, more developed, and more powerful in the antebellum

---

antebellum region, also see Tom Downey, *Planting a Capitalist South: Masters, Merchants, and Manufacturers in the Southern Interior, 1790–1860* (Baton Rouge, 2006); Michael J. Gagnon, *Transition to an Industrial South: Athens, Georgia 1830–1870* (Baton Rouge, 2012).
69 Fogel and Engerman, *Time on the Cross*, I: 247–257; Gavin Wright, *The Political Economy of the Cotton South: Households, Markets, and Wealth in the Nineteenth Century* (New York, 1978), 89–127; idem, *Old South, New South: Revolutions in the Southern Economy since the Civil War* (New York, 1986), 17–123; idem, *Slavery and American Economic Development* (Baton Rouge, 2006), 14–127; Roger Ransom and Richard Sutch, *One Kind of Freedom: The Economic Consequences of Emancipation* (Cambridge, 1977); Coclanis, *The Shadow of a Dream*, 111–158; John Majewski, 'Why Did Northerners Oppose the Expansion of Slavery? Economic Development and Education in the Limestone Stone', in *Slavery's Capitalism*, eds. Beckert and Rockman, 277–298, 382–384. For a provocative Marxist analysis of the role played by surplus-value extraction from slaves in the South's antebellum South's growth, see John Clegg and Duncan Foley, 'A Classical-Marxian Model of Antebellum Slavery', *Cambridge Journal of Economics*, 43 (2019), 107–138. For data on the yawning gap between per capita income in the South and other regions in the U.S. between 1860 and 1950, see Richard A. Easterlin, 'Regional Income Trends, 1840–1960', in *American Economic History*, ed. Seymour E. Harris (New York, 1961), 525–547, esp. Table I (p. 528).
70 William H. Freehling, *The Road to Disunion* (Oxford, 1990), I: 9–36; Lacy K. Ford, *Deliver Us from Evil: The Slavery Question in the Old South* (Oxford, 2009), 3–16 and *passim*.

period, its population was increasingly receptive to and often embracive of what Tomas L. Haskell has famously called a humanitarian sensibility, which among other things meant opposition to slavery and support for its abolition. That is to say, rising income and wealth in expanding bourgeois precincts in the North seem to have shrunk 'the realm of necessity' sufficiently to get significant and influential elements of the northern population to mobilize in one way or another against slavery.[71] This is not to say that this sensibility in and of itself led to emancipation, but it raised the issue in importance, kept it on the front burner, and inflamed regional temperatures sufficiently to help bring about a war that led through a complex and convoluted process to slavery's demise in the U.S.[72] Emancipation, however ad hoc, and 'freedom' for the emancipated, however arid, were steps forward, and it should be noted that the abolition of slavery came earlier in the U.S. than it did in many other parts of the world.

This said, we in the United States are still waiting – eight score and four years after the beginning of the Civil War – for the economic opportunities and economic benefits associated with, if not integral to, capitalism to be extended to all Americans, in so doing, enabling the entire population to partake in what Deirdre McCloskey has variously called the 'great enrichment' and 'human flourishing'.[73] Two cheers, then, rather than three for this human construct, a construct, however brilliant, with limits and flaws.

We began by playing off a quote by Churchill and so shall we end: 'No one pretends that capitalism is perfect or all-wise. Indeed, it has been said capitalism is the worst economic system except for all those other systems that have been tried from time to time.'[74] Amen.

---

71 Thomas L. Haskell, 'Capitalism and the Rise of the Humanitarian Sensibility', *AHR*, 90 (1985), 339–361, 547–566. For an excellent recent survey of abolition in the U.S., see Manisha Sinha, *The Slave's Cause: A History of Abolition* (New Haven, 2016).
72 On the complex way in which slavery ended in the United States, see James Oakes, *Freedom National: The Destruction of Slavery in the United States, 1861–1865* (New York, 2012). On its destruction in the Lower Mississippi Valley in particular, see John C. Rodrigue, *Freedom's Crescent: The Civil War and the Destruction of Slavery in the Lower Mississippi Valley* (Cambridge, 2023).
73 Deirdre Nansen McCloskey and Art Carden, *Leave Me Alone and I'll Make You Rich: How the Bourgeois Deal Enriched the World* (Chicago, 2020). The McCloskey–Carden book distils the major points made in McCloskey's 'Bourgeois Era' trilogy.
74 Winston Churchill, Parliament Bill, 11 November 1947.

3

Creativity and Capitalism in the Nineteenth-Century United States

JOHN MAJEWSKI

On 1 August 1838, the abolitionist William Lloyd Garrison addressed a predominantly Black audience at New York City's Broadway Tabernacle to mark the emancipation of 600,000 slaves in the British West Indies. Garrison used the occasion to relentlessly mock proslavery arguments that 'bloodshed and ruin must be the inevitable consequence of letting the oppressed go at once'. He argued at length that the experience of Antigua, where full emancipation had occurred in 1834, proved that freed slaves worked industriously without a hint of violence. At the end of his speech, Garrison predicted that emancipation in the United States would similarly lead to prosperity, though he did not focus on the link between free labour and hard work. Garrison instead highlighted entrepreneurship, invention and education, predicting that emancipation would 'wake up the entombed genius of invention and the dormant spirit of enterprise – open to them new sources of affluence – multiply their branches of industry – erect manufactories, build rail-roads, dig canals – establish schools, academies, colleges and all beneficent institutions – extend their commerce to the ends of the earth and to an unimagined amount'.[1] Contributors to *The Liberator* – Garrison's well-known abolitionist newspaper – similarly understood that economic progress depended on the discoveries, insights and imagination of a well-educated population. Noting that northerners patented 95 per cent of the nation's inventions, the contributor 'Anti-Slavery' argued in 1839 that slavery gave neither enslavers nor the enslaved the incentive and experience to invent and innovate. Southern enslavers, with little reason to encourage labour-saving machinery, looked down on inventors and innovators. 'The laborious and ingenious mechanic, in a slave state, ranks little higher in society, than though he were a slave!' wrote Anti-Slavery. 'His industry is despised, his skill unrewarded,

---

1 William Lloyd Garrison, 'Address', *The Liberator*, 8 (17 August 1838), 1.

his inventions unpatronised. What a field for mechanical skill and enterprise would abolition open at the south!'[2]

Garrison and his fellow abolitionists described the growing importance of what we in the twenty-first century might call economic creativity. Insight and imagination were increasingly turned into profitable and potentially transformative inventions and innovations. Creativity, in other words, became a commodity. In this chapter, I argue that the commodification of creativity became especially prominent in the U.S. North in the two decades before the Civil War in ways that profoundly influenced the antislavery movement as well as the broader culture and politics of the North. The proliferation of inventions – ranging from the steam engine to the sewing machine – contributed to accelerating industrial growth and marked the beginning of a transformative structural change. The same inventions became important cultural artifacts prominently displayed at industrial exhibitions and frequently featured in print culture. Economic creativity was important for the countryside as well, as a dense network of agricultural societies and periodicals encouraged experimentation with new implements, new cultivation techniques and new crop varieties. I label northern capitalism in the 1840s and 1850s 'creative capitalism' to denote the growing cultural and political significance of economic creativity. The cultural and economic importance of creativity made it an important political value as well. A broad swathe of the middle-class voters supported the expansion of public education, government investment in research and subsidies for transportation improvements. The Republican Party made these policies a key part of its economic agenda in the 1850s.

While Republican writers and politicians enthusiastically supported creative capitalism, many other northerners did not. A large group of wage workers and small farmers, often identified with the Democratic Party, believed that the commodification of creativity would invariably lead to the commodification of labour. In the face of competition from labour-saving inventions, these pessimists believed that a large class of workers would suffer a loss of income, status and independence. Even Republicans who celebrated economic creativity shared these fears; they had little interest in creating an economy of large-scale factories and permanent wage labourers. They instead sought to foster economic creativity within a society largely composed of educated and entrepreneurial farmers and mechanics, mixed with prosperous middle-class professionals. Large-scale enterprises, such as railroads and textile mills, would be the exception, not the norm, making wage work a temporary waystation instead of a permanent condition. To put it in Schumpeterian terms of creative destruction, Republicans wanted widespread creativity without the destruction of independent small producers such as farmers, retailers and mechanics. To realize this vision, Republicans supported giving settlers free homesteads from

---

2 Anti-Slavery, 'Inprofitableness of Slavery', *The Liberator* (13 September 1839), 1.

public lands in the West. Offering free land, though, required restricting the spread of slavery. Republicans, like Garrison and the abolitionists, saw slavery as an existential threat to creative capitalism. They frequently highlighted the low rates of schooling, literacy and invention in the slave states. If enslavers monopolized the best lands in the West, Republicans argued, creative enterprise would invariably falter. These Republican critiques rang true. Southern slavery was a highly profitable form of capitalism, though one that self-consciously limited economic creativity to a relatively small group of enslavers. The U.S. Civil War was thus a conflict of two rival forms of capitalism, one focused on encouraging widespread economic creativity, the other more narrowly focused on staple crops and enslaved labour.

I. Defining Creative Capitalism

Scholars have written extensively about technology, invention and innovation in the nineteenth-century U.S., but for a variety of reasons they have mostly eschewed creativity as a category of historical analysis. The word 'creativity' is of relatively recent vintage and was not widely used until the middle of the twentieth century.[3] Scholars therefore do not encounter the word 'creativity' in the primary sources; no nineteenth-century observers, intellectuals or leaders used the term. Even now, the meaning of creativity is often imprecise and unclear. Modern usage sometimes associates creativity exclusively with the arts and literature. The phrase 'creative writing', for example, mistakenly implies that only the writing of fiction and poetry requires creativity.[4] Such definitions cast creativity too narrowly to explain large-scale economic and political change. In other contexts, 'creativity' has become a promotional buzzword to sell the latest laptops, tables and smartphones or is used in contexts where knowledge workers are forced to do more with less, as when university administrators extol 'creative solutions' in response to staff layoffs and budget cuts.[5] Economists and other social scientists have sought to explain and measure creativity in more critical ways, devising methods to classify and explain the emergence of creative industries, creative cities and creative economies. This literature, however, largely focuses on the present, leaving one with the sense that creativity is a recent development.[6] There is little analysis of how creativity emerged as a powerful economic force.

---

3   See, for example, the word 'creativity' in the Google ngram program at https://books.google.com/ngrams
4   Wendy Bishop and David Starkey, *Keywords in Creative Writing* (Boulder, 2006), 70–75.
5   Oli Mould, *Against Creativity* New York, (2018).
6   Irina Surkova, 'Towards a Creativity Framework', *Society and Economy*, 34 (2012), 115–138; Richard Florida, *The Rise of the Creative Class* (New York, 2002); Daniel Araya

To make creativity a viable analytical category for historians, the first step is to more precisely define it. The working definition of creativity that I will use is *imagination and insight that produces something that is at once novel and some combination of economically useful, aesthetically pleasing and emotionally moving*. Imagination and insight consist of the ability to visualize positive change, whether it is a painter working with different brush techniques, an entrepreneur developing a profitable new business, a scientist making an important discovery or an inventor solving an important technical problem. The term creativity, in other words, denotes the insight and imagination that precedes a literal act of creation. As the economist Daniel B. Klein writes, 'Creativity is imagination made material'.[7] Imagination, though, must result in something that is some combination of useful, pleasing and moving. What is considered useful, pleasing and moving is inherently a social process often subjected to debate, controversy and contestation. A new musical composition, however novel, is not creative if it offends the ears of its listeners; an invention, however original, is not creative if it fails to solve a problem or make some improvement. That creativity is necessarily mediated by a wider culture and society helps account for why creativity rarely results in something that is entirely new or completely unprecedented. Creativity, in fact, often consists of revising and recombining older traditions or building on previous discoveries and insights.

All economies and societies rely on creativity, whether in the form of creative adaptations to the environment, the production of creative artistic productions or the emergence of creative familial and social arrangements. If creativity in art, music and storytelling are inherent in all societies and cultures, it is the lifeblood of capitalism, which depends on the commodification of creativity – the act of turning creativity into goods and services to sell, rent, licence or otherwise use in the pursuit of profit. Capitalism uses the lure of profits to systematically encourage economic creativity among market participants; a new invention, an appealing product design or an innovative service offers the potential to reap rich rewards. The commodification of creativity in capitalism fosters an economic environment of constant innovation embodied in Joseph Schumpeter's famous phrase 'creative destruction'. Schumpeter defined capitalism as an economic system that 'incessantly revolutionizes the economic structure *from within*'.[8] The ability of firms and entrepreneurs to profit from inventions, innovations and new forms of enterprise generates Schumpeter's revolutionary change in capitalist

---

and Michael A. Peters, *Education in the Creative Economy: Knowledge and Learning in the Age of Innovation* (New York, 2010). Notice Araya and Peters' subtitle, 'The Age of Innovation', as if widespread innovation is of recent vintage.
7 Daniel B. Klein, *Knowledge and Coordination: A Liberal Interpretation* (Oxford, 2012), 139.
8 Joseph A. Schumpeter, *Capitalism, Socialism and Democracy* (New York, 1942), 83.

economies. Sometimes the commodification of creativity occurs directly, such as when an inventor sells a patent or an author publishes a best-selling novel. In these two examples, the patent and the novel are products marketed and sold in the marketplace. At other times, the process of commodifying creativity is more indirect. The farmer who develops a new crop rotation or the engineer who improves an assembly line typically cannot sell their innovations in a commercial market, but they can use their innovations to increase output and hence, one presumes, profits.

The commodification of creativity is important for all forms of capitalism, but even among capitalist economies it can vary greatly according to the extent of markets, the availability of financing, the level of institutional support for innovation and a variety of other factors. At the dawn of the nineteenth century, the United States was a fundamentally capitalist economy geared toward the export of agricultural staples such as wheat and tobacco. It was not, though, the same type of capitalism that Schumpeter envisioned in which new technologies and industries lead to transformative changes. Instead, productivity slowly grew through the greater division of labour and modest technological change in much the same way that Adam Smith outlined in his *Wealth of Nations* (1776). Several factors accounted for the prevalence of slow and incremental Smithian growth. High transportation and communication costs impeded the size of markets, which limited the incentive to dramatically increase manufacturing output. The banking system was relatively underdeveloped and oriented towards short-term loans to substantial merchants rather than new manufacturing enterprises. Communities and institutions to support widespread invention and innovation had yet to fully develop. Creativity was important – producers, merchants and retailers made incremental improvements that required insight and imagination – but it was not a dominant economic, cultural or political value. By the 1840s, the northern economy was clearly moving toward a new form of growth that economists call Schumpeterian growth, which is characterized by rapid technological change and the dramatic rise of firms and industries. Schumpeterian growth is associated with high levels of economic creativity as new technologies, new industries and new firms frequently emerge to challenge older rivals.[9] The beginnings of Schumpeterian growth – and the increasing importance of economic creativity in northern culture and politics – gave rise to northern creative capitalism in the 1840s and 1850s.

---

9 Philippe Aghion, Ufuk Akcigit and Peter Howitt, 'The Schumpeterian Growth Paradigm', *Annual Review of Economics*, 7 (2015), 557–575.

II. Creative Capitalism and the Northern Economy

One sign of the arrival of Schumpeterian growth and creative capitalism was the acceleration of northern industrialization. Adjusted for inflation, the value of industrial production increased more than five-fold between 1830 and 1860.[10] Industrial production and employment grew especially rapidly in the 1850s; just over 1.3 million Americans worked in manufacturing in 1860, an increase of 37 per cent from 1850.[11] Many of these industries, it should be clear, grew through traditional Smithian growth – firms often remained small, capital investment was still modest and new technology was introduced unevenly.[12] Yet it was clear that technological change was accelerating across a variety of sectors while new industries began to emerge. In 1830, railroads, sewing machines, telegraphy and mechanical reapers were either in their infancy or did not exist. By 1860, they had become well established. Many older industries – including textiles, pharmaceuticals, publishing and machine tools – were undergoing transformative changes. Scholars have connected the growth of northern industry with the growth of markets, as a growing population and improvements in transportation and communication encouraged manufacturers to increase output and adopt new technologies, while banks and other financial institutions provided new sources of credit and capital. Scholars, in fact, have frequently subsumed northern industrialization under the rubric of 'market revolution'.[13]

Industrial growth and technological dynamism, however, required far more than growing markets; they also required institutions that could encourage creativity. The U.S. patenting system was one such institution. At root, a patent is a property right to a new technology. In exchange for disseminating information about an invention, a government grants patentees a monopoly for its use for a specified period. Patents thus turn creativity into a commodity that could be bought, sold, licensed or used as its holder saw fit. In the nineteenth century, the U.S. patent system was open, but not so open that applicants could easily submit frivolous applications for pre-existing inventions. The federal government charged a relatively modest filing fee of $30 so that many middling

---

10 Calculated from Joseph H. Davis, 'An Annual Index of U.S. Industrial Production, 1790–1915', *QJE*, 119 (2004), 1189.
11 Calculated from *Manufacturers of the United States in 1860* (Washington, DC, 1865), 729–30.
12 Kenneth L. Sokoloff, 'Productivity Growth in Manufacturing during Early Industrialization: Evidence from the American Northeast, 1820–1860', in *Long-Term Factors in American Economic Growth*, eds. Stanley L. Engerman and Robert E. Gallman (Chicago, 1986), 679–729.
13 Charles Sellers, *The Market Revolution: Jacksonian America, 1815–1846* (Oxford, 1994); Harry L. Watson, *Liberty and Power: The Politics of Jacksonian America*, rev. edn (New York, 2006).

artisans and mechanics could patent new inventions, but after 1836 it also required that applicants submit a description, engraving and model to prove the originality of their invention. A network of lawyers and patent agencies stood ready to broker agreements to sell or license patents, which allowed inventors to more easily sell or license their work to others.[14] In exchange for this property right, patentees had to disclose precisely how their inventions worked. In this respect, a patent was a speech act as well as a commodity, thus facilitating the flow of technical information to encourage more invention and innovation.

As a key form of commodified creativity, patents became critically important to U.S. industrialization. Before the Civil War, Americans patented nearly 41,000 inventions, making the United States a world leader.[15] U.S. patenting rates increased dramatically in the 1850s, when patenting rates increased five-fold from the early 1840s to the late 1850s.[16] Patenting before the Civil War was remarkably broad-based, with most inventors (69 per cent) patenting only one invention over their careers. The number of inventors holding multiple patents increased in the 1850s – foreshadowing the post-war era when invention became a far more specialized activity – but even these inventors averaged only 3.3 patents apiece. As antislavery activists frequently pointed out, northerners took out 95 per cent of all patents. Patenting rates were highest in New England and major metropolitan areas such as New York City, Boston and Philadelphia.[17] Inventors patented across a range of industries, including textiles, iron working, steam engines, sewing machines, agricultural implements, railroads, machine tools, printing and musical instruments. With widespread patenting diffused across many different industries, northern creative capitalism did not rest on the shoulders of a handful of great inventors and discoveries but relied instead on the widespread diffusion of creativity. As economic historian Ross Thomson argues, 'hundreds of major innovators contributed to technological change, thousands of inventors made them practical and tens of thousands diffused them'.[18]

Patents not only were critical to the northern economy, but they also played a surprisingly prominent role in northern culture. The Patent Office regularly published detailed reports on new patents, which were printed in great numbers. Patent agencies, eager to encourage new applications, published periodicals

---

14 Steven Lubar, 'The Transformation of Antebellum Patent Law', *Technology and Culture*, 32 (1991), 932–959.
15 B. Zorina Khan, *The Democratization of Invention: Patents and Copyrights in American Economic Development, 1790–1920* (Cambridge, 2005), 28–65.
16 Thompson, *Structures of Change*, 104–105.
17 Kenneth L. Sokoloff and Naomi R. Lamoreaux, 'Inventive Activity and the Market for Technology in the United States, 1840–1920', Working Paper 7107, National Bureau of Economic Research (May 1999), 39 (Table 1).
18 Thompson, *Structures of Change*, 101.

such as *Scientific American*, *American Artisan* and *American Inventor* that were filled with information about new patents. Publications aimed at a more mainstream, middle-class audience – such as *Frank Leslie's Illustrated Weekly*, *Harper's Weekly* and *The Saturday Evening Post* – also frequently report on new patented inventions. *New York Daily Tribune*, the nation's largest newspaper in the 1850s, published more than 300 articles, features and editorials containing both the words 'patent' and 'invention' between 1853 and 1860. Inventions and innovations became ubiquitous objects of display at industrial fairs held in several northern cities. From July 1853 to November 1854, tens of thousands of visitors attended the 'Exhibition of the Industry of All Nations' in New York City, which was designed to emulate the stunning success of London's 1851 Crystal Palace Exhibition.[19] One of the most impressive buildings in Washington, DC was the Patent Office, which was completed in 1842. The legislation that authorized the building – which was part of the 1836 overhaul of the patent system – required the display of patent models 'for public inspection'. The top floor of the three-storey building contained a vaulted exhibition space that soon became known as the National Gallery. By 1852, even the spacious National Gallery could not accommodate the Patent Office's 25,000 models, which necessitated continued expansion. Observers estimated that 100,000 visitors viewed the exhibits, making the Patent Office one of Washington's most significant attractions.[20]

Technological, engineering and organizational creativity was obviously critical for northern industrialization, but so was creativity expressed through fashion, art and design. Some industries, of course, involved little in the way of art and design. Increasing the productivity of processing industries – more efficiently turning wheat into grain or trees into lumber – was a technological and organizational challenge rather than an artistic one. The same was generally true for steam engines, machine tools and many other capital goods. On the other hand, a range of consumer goods incorporated fashion, art and design as a crucial element of production. The rise of middle-class parlour culture highlighted the conjunction of industrialization, consumer culture and artistic creativity. The creative domain of middle-class women, the parlour was a critical conduit between the outside world and domestic life. Through their choice of carpet, drapes, wallpaper, furniture, art, images, musical instruments and decorative objects, the parlour signalled refinement and respectability, while simultaneously projecting individual identity and values and aesthetic choices

---

19 Rachel N. Klein, *Art Wars: The Politics of Taste in Nineteenth-Century New York* (Philadelphia, 2020), 99–104.
20 Kenneth W. Dobyns, *The Patent Office Pony: A History of the Early Patent Industry* (Boston, 1994), 138–139.

regarding design, colour and layout.[21] The parlour also became a space for the performance of commercialized creativity, whether it was reading aloud a novel or performing with musical instruments and published sheet music. For firms and entrepreneurs, the parlour represented a rich market which encouraged them to simultaneously reduce prices while meeting the aesthetic demands of middle-class consumers. Northerner observers – especially those with an antislavery bent – celebrated the confluence of mechanical creativity and artistic creativity. Through both 'our discoveries in science' and the 'the enormous increase of mechanical power consequent upon mechanical invention', the antislavery newspaper editor Horace Greeley declared in 1853, 'we have democratized the means and appliance of a higher life; that we have spread, far and wide, the civilizing influence of Art'.[22]

The piano embodied the interdisciplinary creativity of early industrialization. As pianos became an important part of middle-class culture, the piano trade grew substantially. By 1860, piano output was larger in terms of value added than the production of mechanical reapers or firearms. A combination of lumber yard, iron works and craft workshop, piano factories embodied nineteenth-century industrialization. Piano factories sometimes took up an entire city block in buildings with multiple storeys; observers believed that the Chickering piano factory in Boston, for example, was the second largest building in the United States.[23] Such factories used highly advanced machinery, including large steam engines that heated lumber sheds to season the wood, precision drills that bore hundreds of holes into each piano's iron frame and sophisticated saws and planers that could carefully and efficiently cut wood veneers. In the midst of this profusion of industrial machinery, skilled craft workers made highly polished steel wire, which they carefully connected to the ivory keys and the piano's hammers. To ensure a high-quality sound, the heads of the hammers themselves had to be carefully constructed from prepared basswood and covered with speciality felt or buckskin. Putting together the 6,000 different parts in each piano, in the words of one journalist, required 'great skill, long experience and thorough workmanship'.[24] Artistry was at a premium, as pianos had to have both a precise sound and an attractive design, yet manufacturers succeeded in significantly lowering prices and expanding

---

21 Katherine C. Grier, *Culture and Comfort: Parlor Making and Middle-Class Identity, 1850–1930* (Washington, DC, 1988), 13–21.
22 Horace Greeley, *Art and Industry, as Represented in the Exhibition at the Crystal Palace, New York, 1853–54* (New York, 1853), 28, 45, 52–53.
23 Crawford, *America's Musical Life*, 235. See also 'Chickering & Son's Piano Forte Manufactory', *Ballou's Pictorial Drawing-Room Companion* 17 (23 July 1859), 56.
24 'The Piano Forte: Its Origin, History and Manufacture', *Graham's American Monthly Magazine of Literature, Art and Fashion* (May 1857), 417–425, quote on p. 423.

access.²⁵ At the same time, the piano trade offered a variety of designs and improvements to satisfy different tastes and preferences, ranging from virtuoso performers to middle-class families seeking to provide their children with musical education.

Perhaps the industry that relied most on the combination of engineering and artistic creativity – and the one that had the greatest cultural impact – was publishing and printing. Writing and editing are intellectual and artistic activities, but printed matter is a surprisingly complex physical commodity when produced on a mass scale. New machinery allowed foundries in the 1840s to produce 6,000 pieces of type in an hour, whereas traditional hand casting might produce 4,000 pieces per day. The development of stereotype and electrotype plates gave printers more choices in the use of fonts and symbols and allowed them to more easily store the plates of books, pamphlets and other printed material for future print runs. By the late 1850s, new typesetting machines made it easier to compose type and printing plates. Inventors developed rotary systems and applied steam power to dramatically increase the speed of the printing press. Papermakers similarly embraced mechanization, which resulted in lower prices, higher quality and greater uniformity. Not surprisingly, the number of newspapers and periodicals increased dramatically, while book prices plummeted so that inexpensive paperbacks sold for as little as 12 cents.²⁶ As print matter become less expensive, it simultaneously contained far more illustrations. Improvements in engraving and lithography led publishers to compete for middle-class readers with richly illustrated periodicals, while firms such as Currier and Ives became highly successful, selling inexpensive single-print reproductions.²⁷ The cultural influence of the rapidly expanding publishing industry was enormous, as information, literature and art became accessible to a growing number of households.

Creative capitalism had obvious appeal to the North's urban middle class, but for it to succeed both economically and politically, it had to take root in the countryside as well. While farm families constituted a smaller percentage of the North's overall population, in absolute terms the farm population continued to grow, rising from 4.8 million in 1820 to 9 million in 1860.²⁸ These farm

---

25   'Godey's Arm-Chair: A List of Articles We Can Supply. Piano-Fortes for $150', *Godey's Lady's Book and Magazine* (December 1859), 59.
26   Ronald J. Zboray, 'Antebellum Reading and the Ironies of Technological Innovation', *American Quarterly*, 40 (1988), 65–82; Jeffery D. Groves, 'Periodicals and Serial Publication', in *A History of the Book in America*, eds. Scott E. Casper *et al.* (Chapel Hill, 2007), III: 226–227; Louise Stevenson, 'Homes, Books and Reading', in ibid., III: 319–321.
27   Erika Piola, 'The Rise of Early American Lithography and Antebellum Visual Culture', *Winterthur Portfolio*, 48 (2014), 125–138; Cynthia Lee Patterson, *Art for the Middle Classes: America's Illustrated Magazines of the 1840s* (Jackson, MS, 2010), 128, 160–167.
28   Jeremy Atack and Fred Bateman, *To Their Own Soil: Agriculture in the Antebellum North* (Ames, IA, 1987), 298.

families purchased an array of consumer goods and agricultural implements while supplying the food, fodder, draught animals and other essential raw materials. Given the expansion of northern farming across the Midwest, it is easy to assume that northern agriculture could supply these inputs simply through the cultivation of more land. Creativity in agriculture, however, was just as important as creativity in manufacturing. Depleted soils, new pests and new diseases could cause crop yields to decline, potentially offsetting the production of newly settled lands. Economists Alan Olmsted and Paul Rhode have described the difficulties in maintaining yields as the 'Red Queen' problem. Like Alice in *Through the Looking-Glass*, farmers had to run faster just to remain in place.[29] Remaining in place – keeping crop yields and per acre output at least stable – required adaptation and creativity.

Part of creative adaptation of northern agriculture was diversification, which was especially prominent in northeastern states such as Massachusetts and New York. Many northeastern farms became highly diversified enterprises that grew fodder crops, cultivated fruits and vegetables and produced leather, wool, leather, dairy products and other goods from cattle, sheep, horses and livestock. Southern enslavers often sneered at the cold and rocky soils of New England, but farmland in Massachusetts was far more valuable than the rich cotton lands of Alabama and Mississippi because small family farms could profitably market an array of agricultural products to urban consumers.[30] In the Midwest, farmers developed a different strategy that focused on a greater degree of specialization in wheat, corn and hogs that could be marketed through their region's developing transportation network. That greater degree of specialization meant potentially higher rewards for improved agricultural implements such as steel ploughs, threshing machines and mechanical reapers. Northerners took great pride in the wide variety of innovative farm implements their region produced. The 1860 Census proudly reported that 'The general excellence of American ploughs, reapers, churns, scythes, axes, forks and other implements, was acknowledged by the public admission of disinterested judges from all parts of the world.'[31] Northern farmers also breed new varieties of wheat and other crops that could better resist insects and grow under different climatic conditions; they successfully introduced new breeds of cattle and swine; and they learned new crop rotations that maximized the value of nitrogen-fixing legumes.

To encourage agricultural experimentation and the dissemination of new information, northerners developed an array of institutions to encourage and

---

29 Alan L. Olmstead and Paul W. Rhode, *Creating Abundance: Biological Innovation and American Agricultural Development* (Cambridge, 2008), 13–15.
30 For a more general contrast of the value of real estate and farmland in the North and South, see Gavin Wright, *Slavery and American Economic Development* (Baton Rouge, 2006), 55–62.
31 *Agriculture of the United States in 1860*, xiv.

disseminate agricultural research. Agricultural societies at both the local and at the state level sponsored fairs, meetings and competitions that not only publicized new agricultural implements but also promoted discussion of new livestock breeds, new seeds and new crops, different crop rotations, new irrigation techniques and a host of other topics. In 1858, nearly 700 agricultural organizations in the Northeast and Midwest promoted forms of agricultural research.[32] The agricultural associations often organized fairs that offered prizes and premiums to stimulate experimentation and best practices. Thousands of visitors attended these fairs, which helped further disseminate best practice and new knowledge. Agricultural research also benefited from the growth of the publishing industry. In the 1850s, northerners published thirty agricultural periodicals, many of which had impressive numbers of subscribers. The *American Agriculturalist*, published in New York City, had as many as 100,000 subscribers, while many state-level publications reached more than 20,000 subscribers.[33]

The northern agricultural press – and the rest of the northern publishing industry – could not have flourished on such a massive scale without widespread literacy. Northerners willingly taxed themselves to ensure widespread public education. In the first half of the nineteenth century, parents typically had to pay tuition (called a rate bill) for public schools. Northern states and school districts used state and local subsidies to keep rate bills low – the average cost of rate bills in 1850 was 26 cents per term – but many northern states in the 1850s reduced the rate bill to zero. The continued expansion of public education signalled a strong political commitment to creative capitalism. Widespread literacy and numeracy provided large markets for northern publishers while allowing inventive mechanics and farmers to enhance their expertise, learn about new opportunities and make connections with like-minded individuals. In a popular textbook on political economy, Francis Wayland wrote that 'Nations are, at present, principally enriched by the result of discovery and invention; and in consequence of the general diffusion of knowledge and intelligence.'[34]

III. The Politics of Creative Capitalism

While industrial entrepreneurs, middle-class professionals and prosperous farmers embraced creative capitalism, its appeal was hardly universal. Many northerners feared that creative capitalism not only commodified creativity, but also commodified labour in new and damaging ways. As industrialization

---

32 Ariel Ron, *Grassroots Leviathan: Agricultural Reform and the Rural North in a Slaveholding Republic* (Baltimore, 2020), 67.
33 Ibid.
34 Francis Wayland, *The Elements of Political Economy* (Boston, 1864, 1837), 400.

grew, so too did wage labour and economic inequality, which challenged traditional conceptions of polity composed mostly of small producers such as modest farmers and mechanics. A variety of radical movements – ranging from workingmen's parties to utopian communitarian experiments to anti-rent movements – protested that the combination of new technology and capitalist imperatives imperilled republican values of economic independence while corrupting the nation's politics.[35] These critics of capitalism did not necessarily oppose technological progress. In his influential *Rights of Man to Property*, labour leader Thomas Skidmore sounded the common refrain that 'The discoveries, that yet remain to be made in every department of human knowledge, are inexhaustible, as will be the wealth which they will afford to the generations that make them and to those that shall succeed them.' Skidmore nevertheless believed that under capitalism, the poor rightly opposed labour-saving improvements because they diminished the demand for labour, allowing employers to cut wages. Common ownership of new industries and new improvements was the only solution. 'If, then, it is seen that the Steam-Engine, for example, is likely to greatly impoverish or destroy the poor, what have they to do, but TO LAY HOLD OF IT and MAKE IT THEIR OWN?'[36] Workingmen's parties and other radical movements made little headway in party politics, but many of the immigrants, factory workers and small farmers who shared their economic pessimism found a home in the Democratic Party. Some Northern Democrats loudly critiqued the rise of 'wage slavery' of the North and claimed that the enslaved workers of the South received far better treatment and care than the exploited factory workers of the North. Orestes Brownson – a prominent Catholic and Democratic intellectual – told abolitionists that 'You have enough work for all your philanthropy north of Mason and Dixon's line.'[37]

That Brownson critiqued the abolitionist movement is hardly accidental. As the most radical opponents of slavery, the abolitionists frequently compared the accomplishments of northern creative capitalism with the violence and backwardness of southern slavery. Abolitionists highlighted the lack of even basic schooling for both the enslaved and poor whites, which stood in striking contrast to the widespread literacy in the North. The lack of education in the slave states contributed to the absence of enterprise. Often citing census statistics, abolitionists highlighted how the slave states generated little manufacturing, constructed fewer railroads and produced little in the way of art, science and literature. Garrison's *Liberator*, for example, reprinted an article from the *Cleveland Leader* that mocked southern attempts to limit the census of 1860 to a simple enumeration of the population instead of the more complete

---

35 Daniel R. Mandell, *The Lost Tradition of Economic Equality in America, 1600–1870* (Baltimore, 2020).
36 Thomas Skidmore, *The Rights of Man to Property!* (New York, 1829), 381, 384.
37 Quoted in Howe, *What Hath God Wrought*, 545.

collection of social and economic statistics collected in 1850: 'The census is not a gratifying document to the Slaveholder. He reads there that the Free States are thrifty and prosperous. He reads that his own acres are barren. His harbors deserted. His Colleges feeble. His Factories scanty and poor. His Shipping nowhere. His paupers abundant.'[38] Abolitionists also frequently cited the annual reports of the Patent Office, which showed that invention in the slave states fell dramatically far behind that of the free states. The *National Era*, an antislavery paper published in Washington, DC, highlighted the 1852 annual report, which showed that residents in the free states took out 990 patents, while residents in the slave states took out 79. 'And so it has always been', wrote Gamaliel Bailey, the publication's editor. 'Had it not been for the mental power and activity, the spirit of progress and the genius of invention, developed by free labour institutions, this country would have been unknown, unfelt'.[39]

Harriet Beecher Stowe's *Uncle Tom's Cabin* – the most popular novel of the nineteenth century – dramatized these arguments. *Uncle Tom's Cabin*, of course, was a product of creative capitalism. The novel's tremendous sales – reaching 300,000 in a single year – reflected the growing economic power and cultural influence of the northern publishing industry. Entrepreneurs, including P.T. Barnum, took every opportunity to further commodify Stowe's work through theatrical productions, sheet music, lithographic images and even children's toys.[40] The highly sentimental novel did not focus on economic themes, but abolitionist economic arguments were readily apparent. Stowe presented southern enslavers as either dissipated aristocrats who lacked enterprise and ambition or cruel taskmasters who irrationally abused and ultimately murdered enslaved workers to satisfy their lust for power. Crude, lazy and ignorant, Stowe's poor southern whites reflected the region's lack of schooling and poor work ethic. Stowe showed the suppression of creativity among the enslaved through the character of George Harris. George's enslaver hired him out to a Kentucky bag factory, where he invented a machine for cleaning hemp that 'displayed quite as much mechanical genius as Whitney's cotton gin'. George's owner, however, seethed with rage that his 'intelligent chattel' was 'marching around the country, inventing machines and holding up his head among gentlemen' and relegated George to 'the meanest drudgery of the farm'.[41] Creativity, though, ultimately allowed George to prevail. With the help of make-up and a disguise, George passed himself off as a Spanish gentleman, going so far as to publicly enter a tavern where he procured the assistance of the factory owner. Stowe's portrayal of George reflected a common

---

38 'The Next Census', *Liberator* (14 January 1859).
39 'Report of the Commissioner of Patents for 1852', *National Era*, 7 (27 October 1853), 170.
40 John L. Brooke, *'There is a North': Fugitive Slaves, Political Crisis and Cultural Transformation in the Coming of the Civil War* (Amherst, 2019), 159–201.
41 Harriet Beecher Stowe, *Uncle Tom's Cabin* (Boston, 1852), 27–29.

abolitionist refrain that the enslaved, however exploited, constituted the most creative class in the South. The abolitionist newspaper *The Philanthropist*, once again citing the wide gap in regional patenting rates, declared in 1843 that 'Slavery and the Genius of Invention hold no co-partnership ... The principal inventive class in the South, is that of runaways and it is the hope of *Liberty* that quickens their wits.'[42]

In the 1850s, the Republican Party took antislavery economic critiques and turned them into a successful policy agenda that broadened the appeal of creative capitalism. Republicans advocated a homestead policy that would offer settlers free land in the western territories (which would be ruthlessly expropriated from American Indians) while simultaneously restricting the spread of slavery. Free western land, Republicans argued, would allow most (White) families to become propertied small producers. The West would become populated with numerous small farms, with networks for artisans and modest manufacturers to support them. The small producers of the West, Republicans made clear, would be incorporated into creative capitalism. Republicans advocated extending public education through a system of land-grant colleges that would offer subsidized scientific and engineering training for the children of farmers and mechanics. A new Department of Agriculture would provide support for additional research to add to the nation's network of agricultural societies and fairs. The federal government would also build a railroad to the Pacific to help ensure that new western lands had connections to the national market, while a protective tariff would shield new industries from foreign competition, thus allowing new centres of creativity to emerge.[43] The Republican economic agenda promised to extend creative capitalism in ways that appealed to its core constituency of middle-class professionals, prosperous retailers, successful artisans, entrepreneurial manufactures and commercially minded farmers, while the promise of free land and free education attracted wage workers and small farmers who traditionally gravitated toward the Democratic Party. Republicans, in essence, argued that creativity could be commodified without widespread and persistent wage labour.

The Republican vision could only work if the federal government restricted the spread of slavery in the West. Republicans believed that if slavery expanded westward, southern enslavers would monopolize the best lands, degrade the value of hard work and dominate the region's politics. Historians have labelled these powerful and influential arguments 'free labour ideology', and persuasively argue that such attitudes helped Republicans form a broad coalition

---

42 'Slavery and Invention', *The Philanthropist* (15 June 1843), 3.
43 Republicans such as Horace Greeley argued that higher tariffs would allow new domestic industries to emerge, thus increasing opportunities for invention. 'Why Change the Tariff', *New York Daily Tribune* (24 April 1852), 4.

of northerners to stop the expansion of slavery.⁴⁴ Historians, though, have underrated the role of education, invention and creativity in free-labour critiques of slavery. Horace Mann, the noted educational reformer, foreshadowed Republican critiques when he served in Congress in 1848 as a member of the Free-Soil Party, which called for the expansion of slavery. Mann argued that widespread education was impossible under slavery because 'the slave must be kept in ignorance'. Mann connected education to creativity, arguing that a 'cultivated intellect' had produced inventions such as the steam engine, the power loom and the printing press. The enslaver, on the other, 'abolishes this mighty power of the intellect'.⁴⁵

Republicans would use the same themes to formulate a searing economic critique of slavery. Hinton Rowan Helper's *The Impending Crisis*, one of the most influential Republican critiques of slavery, included several statistical tables to show the superiority of the North in schooling, literacy and patents. The North was 'the glorious land of free soil, free labour, free speech, free presses and free schools' that harness the productive and creative power of ordinary citizens. In the slave states, on the other hand, 'The common school-House, the poor man's college, is hardly known, showing how little interest is felt in the chief treasures of the State, the immortal minds of the multitude who are not born to wealth.'⁴⁶ In an 1860 speech opposing the admission of Kansas as a slave state, Republican senator Charles Sumner gave a lengthy recitation of census statistics to demonstrate northern superiority in the number of common schools, colleges, libraries, lyceums, writers, poets and, of course, patents. 'Thus, at every point is the character of Slavery more and more manifest, rising and dilating into an overshadowing Barbarism, darkening the whole land', Sumner argued. 'Through its influence, populations, values of all kind, manufactures, commerce, railroads, canals, charities, the post-office, colleges, professional schools, academies, public schools, newspapers, periodicals, books, authorship, inventions, are all stunted.'⁴⁷

Abraham Lincoln, in both his lived experiences and political ideology, exemplified the Republican vision of creative capitalism. In the 1860 presidential campaign, Lincoln emphasized his humble origins as the son of a small farmer and emphasized his early embrace of manual labour and hard work through the frequent invocation of the 'rail splitter' image. Lincoln combined this populist appeal with an enthusiastic embrace of creative capitalism. Although he was largely self-taught, Lincoln declared his support for public education in his very

---

44 Eric Foner, *Free Soil, Free Labor, Free Men: The Ideology of the Republican Party before the Civil War* (Oxford, 1995 [1970]).
45 'Speech of Hon. Horace Mann', *The Boston Daily Atlas* (2 August 1848), 1.
46 Hinton Rowan Helper, *The Impending Crisis of the South: How to Meet It* (New York, 1857), 83, 89.
47 Charles Sumner, *The Barbarism of Slavery* [Speech on 4 June 1860], (New York, 1863).

first political campaign for a seat in the Illinois legislature. A successful lawyer, he read widely not only in law, but in history, literature, mathematics and engineering. He delighted in all things mechanical, which made him particularly effective in patent cases. Lincoln took out his own patent in 1848, on a system of inflatable buoys that would allow steamboats to pass through shoals and shallow water.[48] Lincoln's version of free labour ideology stressed the importance of education, literacy and creativity. 'I know of nothing so pleasant to the mind, as the discovery of anything which is at once *new* and *valuable* – nothing which so lightens and sweetens toil, as the hopeful pursuit of such discovery', he told the Wisconsin Agricultural Society in 1859.[49] Lincoln's campaign imagery emphasized education, literacy and upward mobility. After giving a highly successful speech at New York City's Cooper Union in 1859, Lincoln posed at Mathew Brady's famed photography studio, which was itself emblematic of new technologies and creative capitalism. Dressed in an elegant three-piece suit, Lincoln's image emanated middle-class respectability. Significantly, Lincoln's hand rests on two untitled books, simultaneously symbolizing his status as an accomplished professional and his commitment to literacy and education. The photograph appeared in prominent magazines such as *Harper's Weekly* and *Leslie's Weekly*, which affirmed Lincoln's national status. Lincoln believed that Brady's daguerreotype helped win him the presidency. 'Brady and the Cooper Institute made me President', Lincoln later declared.[50]

The Republican economic platform – unleashing the power of ordinary citizens as discoverers, inventors and innovators while avoiding large numbers of permanent wage labourers – helped mobilize a powerful antislavery coalition in the 1850s. The aftermath of Civil War and emancipation, however, laid bare several faulty assumptions that ultimately derailed this vision. Even in its heyday in the 1850s, economic creativity was heavily circumscribed by gender and race. The North's rapidly expanding print culture and profusion of consumer goods offered middle-class women more opportunities to engage in creative activities. The expansion of schooling offered women more opportunities to teach and a handful of northern women even became popular writers and speakers. Yet the rise of creative capitalism often served to strengthen domestic ideals which celebrated women's role as homemaker, leaving most women far removed from the world of business and enterprise. In similar fashion, a small number of Black men and women achieved striking success as anti-slavery orators and

---

48 Jason Emerson, *Lincoln the Inventor* (Carbondale, IL, 2009).
49 Abraham Lincoln, 'Address before the Wisconsin State Agricultural Society, Milwaukee, Wisconsin', *The Collected Works of Abraham Lincoln*, ed. Roy P. Basler (New Brunswick, NJ, 1953), 480.
50 Harold Holzer, *Lincoln at Cooper Union: The Speech That Made Abraham Lincoln President* (New York, 2004).

authors, but racism limited opportunities for economic and social advancement for most Black families. As the Civil War era transformed into the Gilded Age, the rise of national industrial corporations and the accompanying increase in wage labour dashed Republican hopes that free land, free schooling and the end of slavery would result in an economy filled with prosperous, enterprising and creative small producers. To be clear, economic creativity continued to grow faster in the late nineteenth century than in the 1840s and 1850s – the patenting rate continued to accelerate, educational levels continued to increase and new technologies and new industries continued to emerge. The increasing rate of economic creativity, though, took place within an environment of growing inequality. The ideal of a creative citizenry of small producers lost much of its political and cultural salience. Industrial capitalism – with intense and sometimes violent conflict centred on wages, working conditions, unions, monetary policy, political corruption and corporate regulation – replaced creative capitalism as the operative framework of political economy. In many respects, the pre-Civil War critics of creative capitalism such as Skidmore were right – the commodification of creativity could not take place without a vast increase in wage labour and the economic and political upheavals that such a transformation entailed.

The rise and decline of creative capitalism can offer potential insights into how historians might think about capitalism or rather capitalisms. We can define capitalism in a general sense as the expansion of markets, credit and production. Yet as the essays in this volume aptly demonstrate, the expansion of markets, credit and production varies widely, with particular contexts generating particular values, justifications and appeals. Northern creative capitalism in the 1840s and 1850s was hardly the only form of capitalist development, even within the United States. Slavery, its arch enemy, was equally capitalistic. Slavery discouraged widespread creativity, but southern enslavers were still very much capitalists: they grew profitable crops for world markets and the slave trade ruthlessly shifted enslaved workers to the most productive soils. Within their own narrow sphere, enslavers engaged in considerable economic creativity: they supported railroads and other improvements that would make their plantations more profitable; they bred improved cotton plants and experimented with biological innovations; and they carefully measured the efficiency of their enslaved workers.[51] From a purely economic standpoint, northern creative capitalism and southern enslaver capitalism could flourish, each benefiting from the exchange of northern manufactured goods for southern raw materials. Each region's form of capitalism, though, generated sharply different cultural sensibilities and policy regimes that made

---

51 Olmstead and Rhode, *Creating Abundance*, 98–123; Caitlin Rosenthal, *Accounting for Slavery: Masters and Management* (Cambridge, 2018).

it increasingly difficult to coexist within one nation-state. By the 1850s, two rival forms of capitalism vied control for the national government, with the western territories potentially tipping the political balance between them.

4

The Trans-Atlantic Slave Trade and the Birth of the Business Cycle

MARK METZLER

This chapter argues that business cycles of the modern type are an expression of fundamental capitalist processes and that such cycles emerged early and with special clarity in the British trans-Atlantic slave trade. This unexplored nexus has implications for how we understand the basic dynamics of capitalism and slavery in the period when capitalism emerged as a dominant international system. The chapter begins by laying out the questions of capitalism, business cycles, and the slave trade in relation to each other. It then posits a chronology of trade cycles in the trans-Atlantic slave trade and, as a first step in a larger project, concludes with suggestions for connecting this level of analysis to theories of long-term structural change.[1]

To sharpen the research questions, I present strong forms of the arguments. One starting point is Joseph Schumpeter's thesis that business cycles are not incidental to the capitalist process but rather are the very mechanism through which capitalist development happens. In Schumpeter's schema, production and trade develop in synchronized waves, funded and guided by the creation of new means of payment, which in a capitalistic system means the creation of credit. This credit-funded process has its most 'developmental' effects (that is, is most productive of historical change) when it involves the innovative creation or colonization of '*new economic space*'. Newly created credit-capital in the hands of entrepreneurs gives those entrepreneurs the ability to bid for labour and productive resources in competitive markets. When they do this, they also bid up the price of labour and resources, creating an inflationary

---

[1] See also Mark Metzler, 'The Interactive Emergence of Capitalist Trade-Cycle Dynamics in Maritime Asia, 1640s–1760s: Overview and Prospectus', *Asian Review of World Histories*, 10 (2022), 222–238. This chapter has benefitted from comments by participants at the 2022 seminar hosted by Robert Ingram and James Vaughn at Ohio University; the 2022 'Temporalities of Capitalism' conference hosted by Christof Dejung and Moritz von Brescius at the University of Bern; and the 2022 Global Economic History seminar hosted by Masato Shizume at Waseda University. Special thanks to Kazuo Kobayashi, Patrick Manning and Prasannan Parthasarathi for their critical comments and suggestions.

impulse. Credit-funded investment tends to bunch in time, creating inflationary booms across multiple fields of enterprise. The result of this new enterprise will be to enlarge production and commerce, frequently also to speed it up and make it more efficient in providing returns on capital. The resulting enlargement and enhancement of production and commerce in turn creates new downward pressures on the prices of the goods or services. Hence the two-stage inflationary→deflationary process of business cycles. Falling prices create recessionary pressures and may cause business failures, shakeout, and consolidation. These recessionary phases are also, Schumpeter emphasized, *times of harvest* of the results of foregoing credit-funded investment.[2] In short, the characteristic temporality of capitalist development is both developmental and cyclic. Schumpeter did not say it, but these developmental enhancements to production and trade – enhancements from the standpoint of the efficient augmentation of capital – may also make enterprises more extravagantly wasteful of natural resources and destructive of people's lives, as seen in the history surveyed here.

A second starting point comes from the side of the trans-Atlantic slave trade. Here a strong form of the argument is offered by Joseph Inikori's thesis that production by enslaved African workers in the Americas was one of the most purely capitalistic and commodity-oriented economic sectors during the era when the industrial-capitalist system was emerging. The new, unprecedentedly extensive trans-oceanic division of labour and bulk staple trade 'depended on the forced specialization of enslaved Africans and their descendants in large-scale production of commodities for Atlantic commerce in the Americas at a time when demographic, socio-economic, and political conditions generally favoured small-scale subsistence production by independent, uncoerced producers'. Inikori did not emphasize capitalism as such, but his view has affinities with Fernand Braudel's image of capitalism emerging as a network or archipelago of enclaves within a sea of non-capitalist social relations.[3] Inikori and other writers on the trans-Atlantic slave trade and its counterpart bulk staple trades also emphasize the exceptionally high credit intensity of these trades and the long duration of the credit cycles involved. This 'wheel of commerce' was thus 'kept in motion by the supply of credit', as Nicholas

---

2   Joseph A. Schumpeter, *The Theory of Economic Development: An Inquiry into Profits, Capital, Credit, Interest, and the Business Cycle*, trans. Redvers Opie (Cambridge, MA, 1934 [1926]) and for a fuller summary explication, Mark Metzler, *Capital as Will and Imagination: Schumpeter's Guide to the Postwar Japanese Miracle* (Ithaca, 2013), 36–52.
3   Joseph Inikori, *Africans and the Industrial Revolution in England: A Study in International Trade and Economic Development* (Cambridge, 2002), 157; idem, 'Africa and the Globalization Process: Western Africa, 1450–1850', *JGH*, 2 (2007), 63–86.

Radburn put it.⁴ These wheels of commerce and credit were composed of a sequence of one-way voyages of commodities and of enslaved people, and they produced a kind of wheel in time also.

I. Capitalism Defined: Temporalities of Capitalist Development

For present purposes, Schumpeter's 'developmental' definition of capitalism will serve as a heuristic tool. Capitalism, in Schumpeter's view, is 'that form of private property economy in which innovations are carried out by means of borrowed money, which in general, though not by logical necessity, implies credit creation'. Consequently, owing to the dynamics of credit creation, 'the economic process of capitalist society is identical with the sequence of events that gives rise to the business cycle'.⁵ This seemingly idiosyncratic definition has two essential virtues. First, capitalism is indeed about the creation and accumulation of *capital*, and this is a capital-centred definition. The labour regimes utilized in these capitalist processes have varied tremendously. Second, it identifies *newly created credit* (which means newly created purchasing power) as the most developmentally potent form of capital. Schumpeter tailored this definition to his own theory, and the inclusion of *innovation* in particular might seem to presuppose too much. Pursuing this idea, however, leads one to focus on how the capitalist process generates economic revolutions, an essential point emphasized by Marx, Schumpeter, and many others. This definition focuses on the core processes of credit creation, capital investment and its realization in profits without attempting to define capitalism as a total system with its various governing political, legal, and ideological structures. My use of it is also provisional and heuristic – it is a searching tool rather than a once-and-for-all claim. The vital point here is the corollary hypothesis that when we see business cycles, we are seeing capitalism. When and where this characteristic temporality emerged is a question of great significance.

As early as the 1840s, the regular recurrence of major international commercial and financial crises was identified as a distinctive feature of the new industrial economy, and analyses of recurrent crises broadened into theories of generalized economic cycles.⁶ For nineteenth-century Britain, Rostow and

---

4 Nicholas Radburn, 'Keeping "the wheel in motion": Trans-Atlantic Credit Terms, Slave Prices, and the Geography of Slavery in the British Americas, 1755–1807', *JEcH*, 75 (2015), 686.
5 Joseph A. Schumpeter, *Business Cycles: A Theoretical, Historical, and Statistical Analysis of the Capitalist Process*, 2 vols. (New York, 1939), I: 223–224.
6 Daniele Besomi, 'The Periodicity of Crises: A Survey of the Literature before 1850', *Journal of the History of Economic Thought*, 32 (2010), 85–132; idem, 'Clément Juglar and his Contemporaries on the Causes of Commercial Crises', *Revue européenne des sciences sociales*, 47 (2009), 17–47.

Gayer, Rostow, and Schwartz can be taken as representative 'classic' accounts. Like Schumpeter, they identified major cycles with a typical duration of 7 to 11 years and dated them similarly, seeing peaks of major expansions marked by 'substantial long-term investment' as follows:[7]

1792 1802 1810 1818 1825 1836 1845 1854 1866 1873 1883 1890

Contrasting with this picture of nineteenth-century regularity, efforts to identify business cycles in the eighteenth-century British economy have given highly various results and altogether do not suggest a picture of cyclic regularity before the late decades of the century.[8] It is unclear whether economy-wide business cycles existed in England earlier in the century, and the question of the 'birth of the business cycle' remains open. In his own history of business cycles, Schumpeter traced the British process only back as far as the cycle that peaked in February 1793, noting more tentatively a previous cycle peaking in 1783. He also suggested that 'the schema of the cyclical process' could serve 'as a heuristic hypothesis' for searching back in time, in principle as far back as the early Renaissance.[9]

The approach taken here is to survey a single line of trade – in this case, the trans-Atlantic slave trade – on the idea that capitalist-type business-cyclic dynamics might emerge first in only a few sectors or lines of trade. Practically speaking, this is also an easier method of approach. For convenience, I have called these movements *trade cycles*, meaning *cycles in particular lines of trade* (as opposed to the older British usage in which *trade cycle* was synonymous with the American term *business cycle*).[10] A *cycle* is defined here as a distinct multi-year expansion in trade followed by a multi-year phase of contraction or levelling off. (In a trade involving multi-year transaction and credit cycles,

---

[7] W.W. Rostow, *British Economy of the Nineteenth Century* (Oxford, 1948), 28–39; Arthur Guyer, W.W. Rostow, and Anna Jacobson Schwartz, *The Growth and Fluctuation of the British Economy, 1790–1850: An Historical, Statistical and Theoretical Study of Britain's Economic Development* (Oxford, 1953), 356. Although the peaks of these expansions were frequently marked by crises, the connection between downturns and crises was variable.

[8] T.S. Ashton, *Economic Fluctuations in England, 1700–1800* (Oxford, 1959); J.H. Wilson, 'Industrial Activity in the Eighteenth Century', *Economica*, New Series, 7 (1940), 150–160; Philip Mirkowski, *The Birth of the Business Cycle* (1985); Julian Hoppit, *Risk and Failure in English Business 1700–1800* (Cambridge, 1987), esp. 116–121; N.F.R. Crafts *et al.*, 'Trends and Cycles in British Industrial Production, 1700–1913', *Journal of the Royal Statistical Society*, 152 (1989), 43–60; Stephen Broadberry and Bas van Leeuwen, 'British Economic Growth and the Business Cycle, 1700–1870: Annual Estimates', Working Paper no. 20, Department of Economics, University of Warwick (CAGE Working Paper Series) (2010).

[9] Schumpeter, *Business Cycles*, I: 296–297, 224.

[10] This paragraph is drawn from Metzler, 'The Interactive Emergence of Capitalist Trade-Cycle Dynamics', which applies this idea to maritime East Asia in the 1600s and 1700s.

it would make no sense to count fluctuations on a one- or two-year timescale as cycles.)[11] We can recognize these movements as cycles when several of them happen in succession – rather than mere responses to external events, these are recognizably continuous sequences in which an expansionary movement reinforces itself for a time but ultimately generates its own limits, typically in the form of over-indebtedness and oversupply of markets. Expansion then gives way to a counter-movement of consolidation or contraction, which creates in turn the conditions for a new expansion. In the stronger form of the definition used here, the expansions are funded by credit and the contractions are associated with excess debt. To understand economic cycles according to this stronger form of the definition will require actual cycle-by-cycle narrative historical analysis.

A single slave-trading voyage involved a series of multi-sided credit-funded transactions on several widely separated geographical stages. British slave traders' initial organization of the voyage in England involved diverse kinds of investments and credits, and their procurement of trade goods for Africa typically involved credit extended by the makers or sellers of those goods. At the second stage, on the West African coast, slave traders' purchases of enslaved people typically depended on their extension of trade goods on credit to African dealers who purchased slaves in local or inland slave markets that had their own credit/debt systems. Enslaved people may already have been bound by debt, often due to transactions on the part of people other than themselves. At the third stage, in the Americas, slave traders sold these 'bonded' people, typically on credit, to colonial slave dealers and planters. All of this was preparatory to the stage of actual production by enslaved plantation workers of commodities to be shipped and sold in Britain, often for reexport to other countries. The serial physical transactions of the slave trade itself, not including the follow-on plantation production cycles, might take twelve to eighteen months from start to finish. The settlement of the corresponding credit/debt transactions took still longer. For the people transported, these serial transactions were serial acts of violence, and it was their own lifetimes that were being transacted. This violent

---

11 Mechanistic analyses that do not differentiate major and minor movements will give different results. Broadberry and Leeuwen, 'British Economic Growth and the Business Cycle, 1700–1870', Table 19, for instance, treat every interim fluctuation as a cycle, counting 27 cycles between 1792 and 1868, where a Schumpeter- or Rostow-type approach that combines statistics with narrative analysis would instead count 9 major cycles. This result might almost seem to accord with Schumpeter's original idea that each major 7- to 11-year cycle (or 'Juglar cycle') was composed of three short-term inventory cycles ('Kitchin cycles'). Schumpeter's idea that we are dealing with an interaction of different types of cycles with different periodicities seems to me correct, but shorter-term cycles also seem to be more variable and more local than his schema suggests.

trade was one of the eighteenth-century world's longest and most multi-sided commodity chains with some of the most complex credit demands.[12]

The slave trade also raises questions left out of Schumpeter's account. *Economic development* is ordinarily assumed to be good, booms are taken as good, and slumps are taken as bad. But what is the meaning of economic *good times* in a trade where booming business meant more African victims? *Innovation* and *entrepreneurship* are also positive words, with Schumpeter presenting the entrepreneur as the hero in the drama of capitalist development. He also thought that the role of industrial owner-entrepreneur offered the closest approach to feudal lordship possible in modern times. He did not discuss the slave plantation system.

II. Cycles in the British Slave Trade: A First View

For reasons of do-ability, this chapter deals only with the British trade. For data, it draws primarily on the Trans-Atlantic Slave Trade Database (hereafter TASTD), which is a monumental scholarly achievement and resource.[13] Many scholars have used the data compiled there but none, so far as I know, have

---

12 Stephen D. Behrendt, 'Markets, Transaction Cycles, and Profits: Merchant Decision Making in the British Slave Trade', *WMQ*, 58 (2001), 171–204; Kenneth Morgan, 'Remittance Procedures in the Eighteenth-Century British Slave Trade', *BHR*, 79 (2005), 715–749; Radburn, 'Keeping "the wheel in motion"'; Paul E. Lovejoy and David Richardson, 'The Business of Slaving: Pawnship in Western Africa, c.1600–1810', *JAfH*, 42 (2001), 67–8; Judith Spicksley, 'Pawns on the Gold Coast: The Rise of Asante and Shifts in Security for Debt, 1680–1750', *JAfH*, 54 (2013), 147–175; Paul E. Lovejoy, 'Pawnship, Debt, and 'Freedom' in Atlantic Africa During the Era of the Slave Trade: A Reassessment', *JAfH*, 55 (2014), 55–78; Lorena S. Walsh, 'Mercantile Strategies, Credit Networks, and Labor Supply in the Colonial Chesapeake in Trans-Atlantic Perspective', in *Slavery in the Development of the Americas*, eds. David Eltis *et al.* (Cambridge, 2004), 89–119; Gregory E. O'Malley, *Final Passages: The Intercolonial Slave Trade of British America, 1619–1807* (Chapel Hill, 2014); Markus A. Denzel, 'The Transatlantic Cashless Payment System in the Northern Atlantic Zone from the 17th Century to c.1840', *Veröffentlichung der Joachim-Jungius-Gesellschaft der Wissenschaften*, 94 (2002), 263–277.
13 Available at www.slavevoyages.org. See also David Eltis and David Richardson, *Atlas of the Transatlantic Slave Trade* (New Haven, 2010); David Eltis and David Richardson, 'A New Assessment of the Transatlantic Slave Trade', in *Extending the Frontiers: Essays on the New Transatlantic Slave Trade Database*, eds. David Eltis and David Richardson (New Haven, 2008), 1–62; Stephen Behrendt, 'The Annual Volume and Regional Distribution of the British Slave Trade, 1780–1807', *JAfH*, 38 (1997), 187–211; Patrick Manning and Yu Liu, 'Routes of Atlantic Slave Voyages: Revised Framework and New Insights', Journal of World-Systems Research, 25 (2019), 449–466; idem, 'Research Note on Captive Atlantic Flows: Eliminating Missing Data by Slave-Voyage Routes', Journal of World-Systems Research, 26 (2020), 103–125.

connected it directly to the question of business cycles. From the 1510s, there was a regular Spanish and Portuguese trans-Atlantic slave trade running at a scale of hundreds of people transported per year. (Unless indicated, all numbers for the slave trade are from TASTD 'Estimates' database and refer to those put aboard ship, rounded to the nearest hundred people; ship numbers are also from TASTD.) The British slave trade remained occasional and episodic until 1641, after which it became a regular annual trade, at first almost entirely to the island of Barbados. A regular Dutch trade had begun four years before that, in 1637, which was the year the Dutch captured the Portuguese seaside fort at Elmina in present Ghana, which they made their local headquarters. The Dutch and British slave trades thus arose as part of a common movement.

From the 1680s, British slave traders were regularly transporting more than 10,000 people per year. From the 1710s to the 1750s, they transported around 20,000 to 30,000 people per year, and in the final phase of the British slave trade, from the 1760s to 1807, around 30,000 to 40,000 people per year. This trade belonged essentially to the three cities of London, Bristol, and Liverpool, which took the lead in succession. It will convey another sense of the scale of this forced migration to note that Bristol in the mid eighteenth century was England's second-largest city by a good margin, with a population of more than 40,000. Liverpool grew from a few thousand at the beginning of the century to 20,000 at mid-century to about 80,000 at the beginning of the nineteenth century. Thus, in two or three years of normal trade, slave traders from Bristol or those from Liverpool transported a population equivalent to that of their entire home city.

Altogether, the British handled close to 40 per cent of the total trans-Atlantic slave trade during the eighteenth century. The Portuguese–Brazilian trade was similar in volume. The Spanish trade became inactive from the 1660s to the end of the eighteenth century and became extremely active again after 1810. The Dutch and especially the French slave trades were very active in the eighteenth century though more intermittently so than the British. They were particularly affected by naval wars with the British, whose own trade frequently gained by war, with the major exception of the war of the American revolution. In total, according to TASTD estimates, in all the years up to 1810 British slave traders took 3.2 million people from Africa. Some 2.7 million survived the voyage, and 500,000 perished en route.[14]

Tables 4.1 through 4.3 posit a chronology of major trade cycles covering the entire period of regular annual slave trading by British dealers.

---

14 For a close account, see Stephanie E. Smallwood, *Saltwater Slavery: A Middle Passage from African to American Diaspora* (Cambridge, MA, 2008), esp. ch. 5.

Table 4.1. Major cycles in the British trans-Atlantic slave trade, by number of people embarked in Africa, 1640s–1690s.

Phases of major increases / high trade	Peak year (and number transported)	Recession phases
1644–47	1646 (<u>9,400</u> people) – 12 years –	Recession: 1650–53
1656–58	1658 (9,100 people) – 6 years –	Recession: 1659–60
1664–69	1664 (<u>11,500</u> people) – 14 years –	Recession: 1670–73
1675–78	1678 (11,400 people) – 5 years –	(No real recession)
1680–87	1683 (<u>17,300</u> people) [*Ramping up to new level; then some decline from the very high levels of the early 1680s.*] – 9 years –	Recession: 1689–90
1692–94	1692 (11,700 people) – 9 years –	Recession: 1695–96

Data for Tables 4.1–4.3: TASTD estimates of number embarked, rounded to the nearest hundred people. Thousands of people died every year aboard ship, so many fewer disembarked.

<u>Underlined text</u> = new historic high, – *Number of years between peaks* –.

There is no record of English slave trading from Africa in the years 1630–1640 except for 1633, when fewer than 400 people were transported. In 1644 England's slave trade exploded to a high level with over 5,000 people being put aboard ships in West Africa, and the first well-marked peak in the trade came in 1646. This was also the beginning of the 'sugar revolution' on Barbados, the micro-environment where England's overseas plantation economy first developed. The key innovation associated with this boom was the system of the sugar plantation itself, an integrated agro-industrial operation involving cane growing, milling, boiling and reducing the cane juice to crystallized sugar, packing it, and often also, by the 1660s, distilling the residual molasses into rum. The plantation was the basic unit of a new production regime with its own distinctive, hyper-exploitative legal forms, forms of labour, technologies, ideologies, and geographies. This transformation involved (1) a shift from diversified agriculture to sugar monoculture; (2) a shift from small farms to large plantations; (3) a shift from free or indentured English and Irish labour to enslaved West African labour; (4) a shift from sparse to dense settlement; and (5) a shift from low to high value of production per worker.[15] Despite its heavy labour and technical demands and its high start-up costs, the sugar economy in Barbados achieved quick success in the late 1640s. It was stimulated by a price boom caused by the revolt of Portuguese sugar planters against the Dutch occupation of northeastern Brazil, which was then the main supplier of sugar to London and other European markets.[16] The new system was itself based on Portuguese techniques transmitted in part by Netherlanders who had learned them during their occupation of northeastern Brazil.[17] This 'Barbadian model' was then carried by British planters to other parts of the Caribbean and was influential also in the extension of the slave plantation system in mainland North America.[18]

In the first surge in the English slave trade, from 1644 to 1649, an estimated 30,500 people were taken from Africa on British ships. An estimated 23,700 arrived alive. This was indeed a brutal and explosive beginning to a new trade and a new industry. Much of the early work involved clearing forests and building new farms, and mortality in the slave-labour camps was terribly high, with only a fraction of those who survived the crossing being able to survive for more than a few years. High planters' profits combined with high slave and servant mortality created the conditions for an ongoing high level of credit-funded investment in 'human capital' with a short average working life.[19]

---

15   B.W. Higman, 'The Sugar Revolution', *EcHR*, 53 (2000), 213–236. See also, William A. Green, 'Supply versus Demand in the Barbadian Sugar Revolution', *JIH*, 18 (1988), 403–418 and John McCusker and Russell Menard, 'The Sugar Industry in the Seventeenth Century: A New Perspective on the Barbadian 'Sugar Revolution', in *Tropical Babylons: Sugar and the Making of the Atlantic World, 1450–1680*, ed. Stuart B. Schwartz (Chapel Hill, 2004), 289–330.
16   Stuart B. Schwartz, 'A Commonwealth within Itself: The Early Brazilian Sugar Industry, 1550–1670', in *Tropical Babylons*, ed. Schwartz, 169–170.
17   For the Portuguese–Brazilian and Portuguese–African origins of the system, see ibid.; Arlindo Manuel Caldeira, 'Learning the Ropes in the Tropics: Slavery and the Plantation System on the Island of São Tomé', *AfEcH*, 39 (2011), 35–71; Jason Moore, 'Madeira, Sugar, and the Conquest of Nature in the 'First' Sixteenth Century: Part I: From 'Island of Timber' to Sugar Revolution, 1420–1506', *Review*, 32 (2003), 345–390; idem, 'Madeira, Sugar, and the Conquest of Nature in the 'First' Sixteenth Century, Part II: From Regional Crisis to Commodity Frontier, 1506–1530', *Review*, 33 (2010), 1–24.
18   Justin Roberts, 'Surrendering Surinam: The Barbadian Diaspora and the Expansion of the English Sugar Frontier, 1650–75', *WMQ* (2016), 225–256; Demetri D. Debe and Russell R. Menard, The Transition to African Slavery in Maryland: A Note on the Barbados Connection', *Slavery & Abolition*, 32 (2011), 129–141.
19   Richard S. Dunn, *Sugar and Slaves: The Rise of the Planter Class in the English West Indies, 1624–1713* (Chapel Hill, 2012), 300–334; and on sugar plantations as death camps and 'demographic sinks', Michael Tadman, 'The Demographic Cost of Sugar: Debates on Slave Societies and Natural Increase in the Americas', *AHR*, 105 (2000), 1534–1575.

The Barbados trade itself was markedly cyclic from the beginning. Reckoned by the number of ship voyages, the pattern looks especially regular, with peaks of slave ship arrivals coming in novennial or decennial intervals in 1646, 1654–55, 1664–65, 1674–75, and 1683. During the third boom in the mid 1660s, Jamaica emerged as a new market for selling enslaved workers. Toward the end of the fourth surge in the slave trade, in 1685–86, there were actually more voyages to Jamaica (16 per year) than to Barbados (14 per year). The Virginia slave trade also emerged on a larger scale during this boom. Unlike the first five surges in the trade, the higher trade of the early 1690s was a minor peak in both the Barbados and the Jamaica trade.

This increase in scale happened under a new governance regime imposed in 1660, directly following the restoration of the Stuart monarchy, when King Charles II declared the British trade to Africa the exclusive domain of the Company of Royal Adventurers into Africa, headed by his younger brother (and future ousted king) James, duke of York. This was the start of a 28-year monopoly. The company was reorganized in 1672 as the Royal African Company (RAC), and from then to 1688 it handled about three-quarters of the British slave trade. James Stuart became king in 1685 while also remaining governor of the RAC. The governor of Barbados served simultaneously as the RAC's trade factor there. The 'boom' years 1683–86 were also the period of most complete domination by the RAC, which then handled an estimated 86 per cent of the British slave trade.[20] James's eviction in the 'Glorious Revolution' of 1688 was a defeat for the RAC also, and in 1689 England's new chief justice John Holt annulled the company's authority to search and seize the ships of interlopers and to try them in its own admiralty courts, effectively ending its power to enforce monopoly claims. The campaign to deregulate the slave trade in the late 1600s was also a major issue in early debates over free trade.[21]

Table 4.2. Major cycles in the British trans-Atlantic slave trade, by number of people embarked in Africa, 1690s–1740s.

Phases of major increases / high trade	Peak year (and number transported)	Recession phases
1699–1702	1701 (26,800 people) – 7 years –	Recession: 1703, 1707

20 Matthew D. Mitchell, 'Joint-Stock Capitalism & the Atlantic Commercial Network: The Royal African Company, 1672–1752' (University of Pennsylvania PhD thesis, 2012), 8–9; K.G. Davies, *The Royal African Company* (New York, 1970); Pettigrew, *Freedom's Debt*, 30.
21 W. Darrell Stump, 'An Economic Consequence of 1688', *Albion*, 6 (1974), 26–35; William A. Pettigrew, *Freedom's Debt: The Royal African Company and the Politics of the Atlantic Slave Trade, 1675–1752* (Chapel Hill, 2014), 14–15.

1708–>	1708 (18,100 people) – 10 years –	(Decline in 1709; no real recession)
1717–19	1718 (22,900 people) – 11 years –	Recession: 1720–23
1724–32	1729 (<u>31,900</u> people) [Ramp up to new level; extremely high numbers transported 1729–32] – 8 years –	Recession: 1733–35
1736–40	1737 (<u>33,700</u> people) – 12 years –	Recession: 1742–43, 1745
1747–49	1749 (23,900 people) [Weakly marked peak] – 6 years –	(No real recession)

<u>Underlined text</u> = new historic high, – *Number of years between peaks –*

The Royal African Company's monopoly was terminated by law in 1697, with the provision that separate traders pay the company a duty of 10 per cent of the value of their trade to Africa to cover the costs of maintaining the company's coastal forts and trading posts. With this opening, the slave trade became effectively self-regulated by 'participants on the Atlantic periphery, rather than the British state',[22] and trade surged after 1699 to a level of more than 10,000 people routinely transported every year. In each of the years 1700, 1701, and 1702, more than 20,000 people were put aboard ship. This 'entrepreneurially organized' forced migration was probably the largest trans-oceanic movement of people that had yet been seen in human history. This was the first extended boom in the Chesapeake slave trade. Antigua also became a major market. The high levels of 1701–02 were rivalled in 1718, when the slave trade boomed simultaneously in Barbados, Jamaica, and Virginia, with South Carolina emerging as a new market. These levels were then surpassed in the late 1720s and early 1730s. Jamaica was now the predominant slave market, and St. Kitts joined Antigua as a large market.

The credit networks that supported this booming 'free trade' in slaves were local and diverse. British slaving ventures in the eighteenth century were typically organized by informal partnerships of two to eight merchants; and capital was supplied in a voyage-by-voyage way. The average total investment per voyage was about £3,000 in 1713. By 1790, in line with the secular increase in the price of slaves that began in the middle of the century, the average investment per

---

22 Pettigrew, *Freedom's Debt*, 15.

voyage had increased to about £8,000.²³ As much as half of this was the cost of the goods needed to trade to West Africa. Britain's slave trade was organized mainly out of London during its first eighty years but shifted after the 1720s more to the west coast ports of Bristol and Liverpool, both of which were small worlds where interested entrepreneurs knew each other and worked together in close networks. Liverpool compared to Bristol was more open to new entrants. The supply zones for purchasing slaves extended over thousands of miles of the African coast. Colonial slave markets in the Americas were likewise spread over vast distances. Slave ships usually sailed individually rather than in convoys.

The history of high-financial crises is often taken as a starting point in the history of business cycles, and the South Sea bubble of 1720 was the most conspicuous financial bubble during the entire period of the British slave trade. The bubble is also notable for its seeming lack of effect on the actual trade in slaves, even though the South Sea Company itself had originally been promoted as a slave-trading enterprise.²⁴ A connection that does stand out concerns the Royal African Company, whose share prices quintupled during the bubble to reach around £135 a share in July 1720. At that point the company launched a financial operation that resembled a modern share buy-back scheme. When the South Sea mania collapsed, RAC shares fell also, creating a financial crisis that induced the RAC to gamble on big new ventures in 1723 which then failed in 1724–25. In 1726 the company was selling off its ships and winding up various operations. It continued to operate Britain's forts along the African coast until 1752, supported by subsidies from Parliament, but it largely ceased to be a trading company.²⁵ Simultaneously the number of people transported into slavery increased after 1724 from around 15,000 people to more than 23,000 people per year. What Mirowski identified as the 'great depression' of the 1720s was not evident in the slave trade.²⁶ In the boom years from 1729 through 1732 over 30,000 people were transported a year. This is when slave trading out of Bristol reached its historic peak, surpassing slave trading out of London which was beginning to decline.

---

23   Robin Pearson and David Richardson, 'Social Capital, Institutional Innovation and Atlantic Trade before 1800', *Business History*, 50 (2008), 769–770; David Eltis and David Richardson, 'Prices of African Slaves Newly Arrived in the Americas, 1673–1865: New Evidence on Long-Run Trends and Regional Differentials', in *Slavery in the Development of the Americas*, eds. David Eltis et al. (Cambridge, 2004), 181–218; David Richardson, 'Prices of Slaves in West and West-Central Africa: Toward an Annual Series, 1698–1807', *Bulletin of Economic Research*, 43 (1991), 21–56.
24   Carl Wennerlind, *Casualties of Credit: The English Financial Revolution, 1620–1720* (Cambridge, MA, 2011), 197–234.
25   Mitchell, 'Joint-Stock Capitalism', 170–176.
26   Mirowski, *Birth of the Business Cycle*, 232.

Table 4.3. Major cycles in the British trans-Atlantic slave trade, by number of people embarked in Africa, 1750s–1800s.

Phases of major increases / high trade	Peak year (and number transported)	Recession phases
1752–55	1755 (31,200 people) – 11 years –	Recession: 1756–59
1760–66	1766 (42,400 people – 8 years –	Relative fallback: 1767–68
1770–75	1774 (46,700 people) [New major peak of slave trade 1770–76] – 10 years –	Recession: 1777–80
1782–88	1784 (40,500 people) – 9 years –	Relative low: 1790
1791–93	1793 (46,200 people) – 6 years –	Recession: 1794–95
1798–1803	1799 (49,900 people) [1799–1802: historic peak levels of slave trade] – 7 years –	Relative low: 1804–05
1806–07	1806 (38,200 people) [Parliament outlawed the slave trade in 1807]	

Underlined text = new historic high, – *Number of years between peaks* –.

The legal framework of the slave trade shifted again in 1752 when the rump Royal African Company was terminated and replaced by the Company of Merchants Trading to Africa. This was a 'regulated company' that separate traders joined by paying a fee, with those fees supporting Britain's West African forts. Otherwise the individual merchants' capitals and their trade ventures remained separate.[27] From the standpoint of slave traders this was in effect a lightly regulated 'free trade' system, meaning in this case the freedom to violently coerce captive workers into unpaid production. A new boom in the

---

27 Mitchell, 'Joint-Stock Capitalism', 178. A regulated company was an association of independent traders which provided some common services to members but was otherwise quite distinct from a joint-stock company, which involves a shared capital and a central authoritative managerial hierarchy: see W. Cunningham, *The Growth of English Industry and Commerce in Modern Times: The Mercantile System* (Cambridge, 1925), 214–223, 272–279; William A. Pettigrew and Tristan Stein, 'The Public Rivalry between Regulated and Joint Stock Corporations and the Development of Seventeenth-Century Corporate Constitutions', *Historical Research*, 90 (2017), 341–362.

slave trade simultaneously got under way. Cotton grown in the British West Indies now began to emerge as a significant factor.

Jamaica remained the greatest source of demand, though as Radburn explained, slave traders preferred the nearer markets in Barbados and other islands of the eastern Caribbean, not only because the voyage was shorter and the capital turnover time faster but also because the longer voyage to Jamaica meant that people were kept longer in shackles onboard ship and more of them took sick and died. Fluctuations in slave sales to Jamaica and other distant markets reflected the cyclicity of the trade as a whole but in a more exaggerated way (Table 4.4). At low points in the late eighteenth century, distant markets had 20 or 30 per cent of the total trade, and at high points, 70–80 per cent of the total. Radburn described a kind of overflow effect, with slave traders resorting to more distant markets when nearer markets were 'glutted'.[28] This suggests also the characteristically cyclic capitalist phenomena of 'over-trading' and 'over-production'. The credit extended by slave traders to slave purchasers also varied greatly in terms of months of credit extended, increasing during booms and being curtailed during slumps.[29]

Table 4.4. Peaks in the share of British slave sales to 'ultimate markets', 1750s–1807.

Peaks in the share of sales to more distant markets	Peaks in total British slave trade	Troughs (peaks in the share of sales to nearer markets)
1756	1755	1759–62 (mild trough)
1765	1766	1768
1773	1774	1777
1780 (secondary peak in 1784)	1784	1788
1790, 1793	1793	1798 (weakly marked)
1800 (weakly marked)	1799	1803
1807	1806	

Data: Radburn 2015; TASTD estimates.

28 Radburn, 'Keeping "the wheel in motion"'; see also Lorena S. Walsh, 'Mercantile Strategies, Credit Networks, and Labor Supply in the Colonial Chesapeake in Trans-Atlantic Perspective', in *Slavery in the Development of the Americas*, eds. David Eltis et al. (Cambridge, 2004), 89–119.
29 Radburn, 'Keeping "the wheel in motion"', 664–669.

These booms were now becoming connected to cotton as well as to sugar. This tended to happen first from the side of demand for cotton textiles in West Africa, driven by the boom in cotton–linen checked cloth sold in exchange for slaves. These shipments constituted close to half of British cotton cloth exports in this early phase of the trade, with stand-out peaks in 1753–54, 1763–67, and 1771–72. British imports of raw cotton accordingly traced two sharp boom–bust cycles in the 1750s and 1760s.[30] The larger part of the supply was now itself slave-grown cotton from the West Indies. That supply was relatively more constant from year to year while cotton from the Levant played the role of 'swing' production source with much greater cyclic ups and downs. Coming in the middle of the early 1770s boom, the trans-Atlantic credit crisis of 1772 was the greatest international financial bubble and bust since the South Sea bubble of 1720 but did not seem to slow the surge in the slave trade.[31] There were signs that the boom was reaching limits in terms of planter indebtedness by 1775.[32] At that point the American revolutionary war intervened to cause a sharp decline in the slave trade, from a level of 40,000 people transported a year in the first half of the 1770s to fewer than 8,000 people in the years 1779 and 1780. This depression of trade may have meant there were fewer new victims of the trade in Africa but it also led to poorer rations, more disease, and more early deaths for those already at work on the plantations.[33] Notably, West Indian cotton exports did not slump during the American revolutionary war. This was followed by an even greater boom in cotton shipments after the war ended, feeding the demands of the new mechanized cotton spinning industry. Economies of scale were central to the success of mechanized cotton spinning, a great intensification of industry that depended on a great extensification of cotton cultivation.[34]

From the early 1760s to the great peak of 1792, the volume of Britain's raw cotton imports from all sources increased by more than ten times, to 35 million tons. Supply continued to shift toward West Indies cotton, although cotton imports from the Levant increased substantially as well. The British

---

30   Inikori, *Africa and the Industrial Revolution*, 434–451 and Table 9.8; Prasannan Parthasarathi, *Why Europe Grew Rich and Asia Did Not: Global Economic Divergence, 1600–1850* (Cambridge, 2011), 134–137. For cotton imports, Alfred P. Wadsworth and Julia De Lacy Mann, *The Cotton Trade and Industrial Lancashire 1600–1780* (Manchester, 1965 [1931]), Appendix G; Barbara Gaye Jaquay, 'The Caribbean Cotton Production: An Historical Geography of the Region's Mystery Crop' (Texas A&M University PhD dissertation, 1997), ch. 3.
31   For the 1772 crisis, see Richard B. Sheridan, 'The British Credit Crisis of 1772 and the American Colonies', JEcH, 20 (1960), 161–186.
32   Radburn, 'Keeping "the wheel in motion"'.
33   Richard B. Sheridan, 'The Crisis of Slave Subsistence in the British West Indies during and after the American Revolution', WMQ, 33 (1976), 615–641; Eric Williams, *Capitalism and Slavery* (Chapel Hill, 1994 [1944]), 121.
34   Sven Beckert, *Empire of Cotton: A Global History* (New York, 2014), 40–42, 85–97.

slave trade thus approached its highest historic levels during the opening years of the industrial revolution.

The international credit crisis of 1793 was the first comprehensive business-cyclic crisis of Britain's new industrial-revolution system. As in 1772, it came at a point of tremendous increase in multiple branches of trade including both sugar and cotton, which experienced a severe temporary slump. The financial crisis focused on the fast-growing regional 'country' banks, and Liverpool's commercial and financial crisis was especially severe.[35] In 1799 the turning point in the cycle again coincided with an international crisis. Again this was a relatively comprehensive business cycle rather than a movement in only a few lines of trade.[36] The year 1799 also saw the all-time peak of the British slave trade, when some 50,000 people were transported.

Parliament outlawed the slave trade in 1807. Contradicting the warnings of slave-trade advocates, British trade in general continued to boom.[37] The surge of cotton imports continued, culminating in an explosive increase in the year 1810, when 132 million pounds of raw cotton was imported, most of it now grown by enslaved workers in the United States. A major slump followed in the 1810s. As for the wider trans-Atlantic slave trade, the Portuguese slave trade now surged to the highest levels yet seen – 63,000 people embarked from Africa in 1810, even more than the British trade at its peak.

III. Conclusions

The hypothesis of this chapter is that capitalistically organized trading networks generate their own characteristic conjunctural timescapes. Trade cycles of the modern type appear to be a specifically capitalist 'time signature' whose presence signifies a capitalistic style of system functioning. This question concerns the core capitalist processes by which credit-capital is created and invested into

---

[35] Francis E. Hyde, Bradbury B. Parkinson and Sheila Marriner, 'The Port of Liverpool and the Crisis of 1793', *Economica*, 18 (1951), 363–378; Radburn, 'Keeping "the wheel in motion"', 680–681; Behrendt, 'The Annual Volume and Regional Distribution of the British Slave Trade, 1780–1807', 173–174; Carolyn Sissoko and Mina Ishizu, 'How the West India Trade Fostered Last Resort Lending by the Bank of England', LSE Economic History Working Papers, No. 318 (2021), 9–10.

[36] Margrit Schulte Beerbühl, 'Tracing the Speculation Bubble of 1799 in Newspapers, Court Records and Other Sources', in *Understanding the Sources of Early Modern and Modern Commercial Law: Courts, Statutes, Contracts and Legal Scholarship*, eds. Heikki Pihlajamäki et al. (Leiden, 2018), 315–336; Radburn, 'Keeping "the wheel in motion"', 683–684; Sissoko and Ishizu, 'How the West India Trade Fostered Last Resort Lending by the Bank of England', 10–12, 14–15.

[37] Seymour Drescher, *Econocide: British Slavery in the Era of Abolition* (Chapel Hill, 2010), esp. 113–124.

trade and commodity production, then realized in commodity sales out of which debts are repaid and profits taken. This *investment→realization* process is itself a kind of cycle. One could say that it is Marx's *money→commodity→more money* loop, except that 'money' in its actual capitalistic operation must be understood to consist primarily of credit (debt), while commodities 'carry' debt claims throughout their voyages.[38] In the slave trade, where workers themselves were commodified, there were actually two interacting cycles, the first involving the trade in enslaved workers and the second involving the trade in the goods they made. This chapter has presented a preliminary time-schema of the first of these. A next step will be to incorporate an analysis of commodity cycles involving the major slave-produced goods of sugar, tobacco, and cotton.

When and how did business cycles develop? And how were cycles in particular lines of trade connected to the emergence of generalized business cycles across a range of trades? Already in 1940 an approach to this question was made by J.H. Wilson, whose first, negative finding was an important one: 'The most obvious feature is the lack of correspondence between the individual series. *The industries which show cyclical fluctuations reveal no simultaneity of booms or depressions.*' Eighteenth-century fluctuations 'were, in the main, localised to particular areas, or confined to individual industries'. Wilson did note the exceptional case of the wool trade, which showed 'the clearest tendency to a cyclical movement on the modern pattern'.[39] As for generalized economy-wide cycles, 'it is not until 1772 that we find anything approaching a modern trade cycle [i.e., business cycle] boom'. 1784 was a second case, making 1772 and 1784 'the first two peaks of the cycle'.[40] We can add that these movements were

---

38 Metzler, *Capital as Will and Imagination*, 37, 48.
39 Wilson, 'Industrial Activity', 153, my italics. Wilson's dating of cycles in woollen production were similar to the dates for cycles in the slave trade that I have posited here. However, a quick look at other data for the wool trade raises doubts, so I note it here as an open question: B. R. Mitchell with Phyllis Deane, *Abstract of British Historical Statistics* (Cambridge, 1962), 189; Elizabeth Boody Schumpeter, *English Overseas Trade Statistics 1697–1808* (Oxford, 1960), Tables 12 and 13.
40 Wilson, 'Industrial Activity', 153, 158, my italics. In harmony with the 'physical' approach taken in this chapter, Wilson followed Beveridge in using physical indices of production or trade rather than indices of value or prices. He also tried to subtract a growth trend from the data to reveal underlying cyclic dynamics, an inherently tricky operation that can subject the results to big changes if one alters an assumption or two. We will stay closer to the facts of the times if we simply look at the numbers on their face for interim peaks and lows. For more theoretical consideration of the question of physical indicators versus those based on value measured in money, see also Mark Metzler, 'Japan: The Arc of Industrialization', in *The New Cambridge History of Japan. Volume III: The Modern Japanese Nation and Empire, c.1868 to the Twenty-First Century*, ed. Laura Hein (Cambridge, 2023), 293–337.

evidently international, affecting several European countries.[41] The last several cyclic peaks of the British slave trade, in 1774, 1784, 1793, and 1799, thus seem to reflect generalized national and international business cycles.

What about other parts of the world? One assumption that should be set aside is the idea, prevalent in much of the English-language literature, that modern business cycles originated as a national-level English process and then spread out to the world. Data from maritime trade in East Asia, which was organized mainly by Chinese trading networks, suggests the existence of trade cycles in the late 1600s with a similar periodicity to those in the trans-Atlantic slave trade but with completely different peak years.[42] From the mid 1700s, there then seems to have been some synchronization of trade cycles in maritime East Asia and in the Atlantic. Again, one can hypothesize that when we see credit creation funding new enterprises, when we see that process generating decentralized entrepreneurial activity, and when we see trade cycles appearing in these processes, we are seeing capitalism in action. This may also be a case of capitalist *networks* operating in largely non-capitalist social and political environments. One would also suppose that a certain mass of activity would be required for these processes to appear.

This chapter has focused on a meso-level conjunctural timescale ranging from several years to several decades. Another set of questions involves the idea of 'regime' periods that extend across multiple trade cycles. In the case of the slave trade, successive new booms were often associated with the opening of new trading regions, new trade goods, and new modes of organizing trade and finance. The next step is to synthesize this material into a picture of multi-decade regime periods in order to build bridges from the early modern period to ideas of 'technical-economic paradigms', 'regulation regimes', and 'social structures of accumulation' developed as analyses of nineteenth- and twentieth-century history.[43] Bridging these two eras may in turn allow us to recast relatively time-bound ideas concerning modern industrial capitalism into a broader form.

One approach to this question is to consider the shifting of supply areas and markets. On the 'supply' side in West Africa, cycles in the Atlantic slave trade were connected to cycles of slave raiding and war in shifting locales that extended progressively further inland. Entire political–economic systems

---

41 Fernand Braudel, *The Perspective of the World*, Vol. 3 of *Civilization & Capitalism, 15th–18th Century*, trans. Siân Reynolds (New York, 1984 [1979]), 267–273.
42 Metzler, 'The Interactive Emergence of Capitalist Trade-Cycle Dynamics in Maritime Asia, 1640s–1760s: Overview and Prospectus'.
43 As in the work of neo-Schumpeterian analysts such as Christopher Freeman and Carlota Perez, 'Regulation School' theorists, such as Michel Aglietta, and 'social structures of accumulation' theorists, such as David M. Gordon.

were reorganized in the process.⁴⁴ Monetary transformations involve another complex set of questions. It is well known that the primary trade goods sold by European trading companies in Asia were silver and copper for monetary use. In a parallel way, cowries and diverse other kinds of metal and cloth monetary media were also staple trade goods in West Africa, which during this time developed one of the world's most complex and diverse monetary landscapes.⁴⁵

Ecological processes had their own time-dynamics. Soil depletion and deforestation for land clearing and to supply fuel for sugar boiling created resource limits that led to agricultural intensification in Barbados especially and to an aggressive extension of slave plantations into new territories. These considerations mesh with Jason Moore's analysis of successive commodity frontiers, as the plantation system used up people, fuel and farmland, and moved on. These extractive processes had their own kind of cyclicity, on multi-decadal timescales.⁴⁶ Understanding these dimensions of the entrepreneurial–developmental process helps us envision what is destroyed in the capitalist enterprise of 'creative destruction'.

44   Philip D. Curtin, *The Atlantic Slave Trade: A Census* (Madison, 1969), 205–230; Smallwood, *Saltwater Slavery*, 77–100; Gareth Austin, 'The 'Reversal of Fortune' Thesis and the Compression of History: Perspectives from African and Comparative Economic History', *Journal of International Development*, 20 (2008), 1003–1007; David Eltis, 'Africa, Slavery, and the Slave Trade, Mid-Seventeenth to Mid-Eighteenth Centuries', in *The Oxford Handbook of the Atlantic World: 1450–1850*, eds. Nicholas Canny and Philip Morgan (Oxford, 2012), 271–286; Kenneth Morgan, 'The Trans-Atlantic Slave Trade from the Bight of Biafra: An Overview', in *Igbo in the Atlantic World: African Origins and Diasporic Destinations*, eds. Ogbu U. Kalu et al. (Bloomington, IN, 2016), 82–98; Kazuo Kobayashi, *Indian Cotton Textiles in West Africa: African Agency, Consumer Demand and the Making of the Global Economy, 1750–1850* (Basingstoke, 2018), 33–37; R.A. Kea, 'Firearms and Warfare on the Gold and Slave Coasts from the Sixteenth to the Nineteenth Centuries', *JAfH*, 12 (1971), 185–213; Warren G. Whatley, 'The Gun-Slave Hypothesis and the 18th Century British Slave Trade', *EEH*, 67 (2018), 80–104.
45   Jan Hogendorn and Marion Johnson, *The Shell Money of the Slave Trade* (Cambridge, 1986); Jane I. Guyer, 'Introduction: The Currency Interface and Its Dynamics', in *Money Matters: Instability, Values and Social Payments in the Modern History of West African Communities*, ed. Jane I. Guyer (Heinemann, 1995), 1–33; Kobayashi, *Indian Cotton Textiles*, esp. 81–126; also Mark Metzler, 'Revisiting the General Crisis of the Late Nineteenth Century: West Africa and the World Depression', in *Africa, Imperialism, and Globalization*, eds. Toyin Falola and Emily Brownell (Durham, NC, 2014), 333–355 for a parallel synthesis of the rhythms of capitalist and imperialist development in Africa in the late nineteenth century.
46   Jason W. Moore, 'The Modern World-System as Environmental History? Ecology and the Rise of Capitalism', *Theory and Society*, 32 (2003), 307–377; idem, 'Madeira, Sugar, and the Conquest of Nature in the 'First' Sixteenth Century: Part I: From 'Island of Timber' to Sugar Revolution, 1420–1506'; idem, 'Madeira, Sugar, and the Conquest of Nature in the 'First' Sixteenth Century, Part II: From Regional Crisis to Commodity Frontier, 1506–1530'.

The present survey is preliminary and prospective, but the data is sufficient to allow the positing of a definite and detailed time-schema of the trade. One conclusion is that trade cycles similar to industrial-era general business cycles appeared early and distinctly in the British trans-Atlantic slave trade. This adds a dynamic temporal dimension to the argument launched by Eric Williams in 1944 concerning the hyper-capitalistic nature of the British slave trade. These trade cycles also appear to be temporally continuous with industrial-era business cycles, raising questions that will apply to other lines of trade. Pursuing a disaggregated 'trade-by-trade' approach may lead to findings of more and less systematically capitalist functioning in various lines of trade, with implications for understanding more about the dynamics of capitalist development as such. The work of understanding all of this will require approaches from multiple angles. To test whether these apparent cycles cohere or dissolve under closer examination, it will be necessary to build a period-by-period narrative analysis looking especially at credit creation and at what was new and 'innovatory' about each expansion or boom. The idea that business cycles indicate capitalist systemic functioning is both a hypothesis and a methodology. As a method, tracing capitalist 'development through cycles' at a meso-level timescale is a tool for systematically connecting 'event-level' histories to long-term structural changes.

5

Violence and Capitalism in Early Modern European Overseas Expansion

RALPH AUSTEN †

This chapter is a by-product of an ongoing project on the proto-colonial, colonial and postcolonial relationship between northwestern Europe and the Caribbean, South and Southeast Asia and tropical Africa from the mid-seventeenth through the early twenty-first centuries. In the early modern era, the Europeans' realm of hegemony was largely maritime and, in the regions of concern here, produced only what I call *proto-colonies* or, in the terms of the time, *factories* (coastal trading posts) and *plantations* (European-dominated settlements on islands or coasts producing export goods). The contradiction here was that Europe, with important inputs from but little coercive power over these overseas regions, moved towards an industrial–capitalist 'modernity' while the overseas partners subsequently experienced the humiliations of fuller 'colonial' subjugation and, for at least two centuries, a much more marginal role in the global capitalist system.

The present chapter will not offer anything like an adequate explanation of this 'great divergence' or the reasons for transition to a fuller territorial colonialism overseas. Instead it addresses a narrower issue at the immediate points of contact in the early modern global economy: violence. For one school, which I will roughly label 'Marxist', overt overseas violence is not characteristic of capitalism as an economic form but provides a necessary precondition for its development under the label of 'primitive' or 'original' accumulation. In Karl Marx's own words:

> The discovery of gold and silver in America, the extirpation, enslavement and entombment in mines of the aboriginal population, the beginning of the conquest and looting of the East Indies, the turning of Africa into a warren for the commercial hunting of black-skins, signalled the rosy dawn of the era of capitalist production. These idyllic proceedings are the chief moments of primitive [*ursprüngliches*/original] accumulation. On their heels treads the commercial war of the European nations, with the globe for a theatre.[1]

---

1 Karl Marx, *Capital*, trans. Ben Fowkes (1994), I: 914–926.

Marx himself did not do very much with this concept of primitive/original accumulation, nor have subsequent historians of capitalism and colonialism. A school of more market-based economic historians, beginning with Frederic Lane and culminating in Niels Steensgaard's work, has made colonial violence a central object of study but perceives it more as an obstacle to, rather than an instrument of, capitalist development.[2] States using force, or the threat of it, against other peoples were, at best, systematically commodifying violence as 'protection' and, at worst, establishing 'redistributive' regimes, concerned less with producing new wealth than redirecting already existing resources to the maintenance of European rulers and their immediate social allies.

For both Lane and Steensgaard, the Portuguese Indian ocean empire was a classic example of such a violence-based regime. Capitalist development would thus enter this part of Asia not via the wealth accumulated through Portuguese violence, but rather from the arrival in the Indian ocean of the allegedly more peaceful and entrepreneurial Dutch and English East India Companies. This chapter thus gives special attention to the Portuguese empire, not only in Asia but also in various regions of Africa as well as Brazil. It examines the Dutch and British mainly in Asia but also in northeastern Europe, the New World and Africa. For much of the time the objects of violence in all these arenas were rival European states rather than local populations.

I. Violent Accumulation vs. 'Protection': Plundering Spanish America

The greatest early modern European success in territorial conquest and local indigenous subjugation occurred in the southern portion of the New World, whose indigenous populations – in contrast to those of Africa and Asia – had neither the weaponry to resist Spanish invaders nor immunity to the diseases they brought from the 'Old World' of Eurasia. The various abuses committed by the Spanish against native American populations – including forced labour in the silver mines of Peru and Mexico – had become a matter of scandal (the Black Legend) throughout Europe. However, the bullion thus produced was essential to Western European trade in Asia, as well as the Baltic region of Europe itself, where there was little demand for European manufactures.

The Europeans of prime interest here are not, however, the Spanish but rather those nations that would become the centres of capitalist development (mainly the Netherlands and England). From the later sixteenth and earlier seventeenth

---

2 Frederic Chapin Lane, *Profits from Power: Readings in Protection Rent and Violence-Controlling Enterprises* (Albany, NY, 1979); Niels Steensgaard, *The Asian Trade Revolution: The East India Companies and the Decline of the Caravan Trade* (Chicago, 2017).

centuries (the same time as their more 'capitalist' incursions into the Indian ocean), the English, Dutch and French sought to acquire Spanish American silver by various attacks – both peaceful and violent – upon the Spanish-ruled territories in the Caribbean and the Central and South American mainland. Given the illicit nature of such enterprises, it is not possible to measure with any precision the proportion of accumulation based upon smuggling (illegal but consensual), market exchange and what was euphemistically called at the time 'forced trade' (the violent appropriation of silver and other commodities).

This mainly maritime violence took three forms: (1) 'piracy', the capture of merchant shipping and looting of coastal Spanish settlements purely for the personal enrichment of the perpetrators; (2) 'privateering', the licensing of the same activities by the English, Dutch, French and Spanish states, who saw them as an extension of wars based in Europe and were supposed to receive a share of the material proceeds; and (3) government-sponsored and even executed Dutch and English 'designs' for fully taking over large portions of Spanish and Portuguese Atlantic colonial territories.

In general, all these forms of aggression failed in their immediate goals although the case of Jamaica does, in unintended fashion, fit the Marxist paradigm of violent 'original appropriation'. Spain, here put into a position similar to that of an Asian empire confronting European assaults, was more than capable of achieving its key goal, defending the two annual silver shipments: primarily the heavily defended *flota* to Seville or Cadiz as well as the smaller convoy accompanying the 'Manila galleon' between Acapulco in Mexico and the Philippines.[3] The pirates and privateers, despite all the romance they generated in their own time and since, were not generally of great economic or political consequence.

The first effort by a burgeoning capitalist European power to take over a large portion of the Spanish overseas empire came in the form of the Dutch West India Company's 1624 'Grand Design'. The object of this venture was not Spanish territory as such but rather the Brazilian and West African holdings of Portugal, a state whose crown was forcibly united with that of Spain between 1580 and 1640. The Dutch quickly achieved political control over major sugar plantation zones in northern Brazil and two sources of that region's enslaved labour force, Luanda (Angola) and Elmina (Gold Coast/Ghana). However, the revenue from these conquests never covered their heavy costs and by 1654 all but Elmina were won back by the Portuguese.[4]

---

3 Kris Lane, *Pillaging the Empire: Global Piracy on the High Seas, 1500–1750* (New York, 2016); K.R. Andrews, 'The English in the Caribbean, 1560–1620', in *The Westward Enterprise: English Activities in Ireland, the Atlantic, and America, 1480–1650*, eds. K.R. Andrews *et al.* (Liverpool, 1978), 103–123.
4 Wim Klooster, *The Dutch Moment: War, Trade, and Settlement in the Seventeenth-Century Atlantic World* (Ithaca, 2016).

The years 1654–55 were when the English Lord Protector Oliver Cromwell launched his 'Western Design', an expedition of government forces comprising large numbers of warships, transport vessels and troops.[5] The goal of this project was to establish a base in the Caribbean from which all Spanish America could eventually be conquered. In its stated terms the Western Design was a near total failure. A combination of mismanagement, Spanish defences and tropical disease forced the expedition to abandon its original Caribbean target of Hispaniola (Dominican Republic and Haiti) and seek refuge in Jamaica, an island barely occupied by Spain and of no initial interest to the English.

In retrospect it is easy to see why a large island like Jamaica would provide optimal conditions for expanding a sugar plantation economy that English entrepreneurs (following Portuguese models) had already initiated very profitably in Barbados and several lesser Caribbean territories. However, the capital needed for such enterprises was difficult to raise because, from the 1660s through the 1680s, sugar prices in Europe dropped considerably, although plantations generally remained profitable.[6]

Given Jamaica's central geographical position in the Caribbean, what remained immediately most appealing to the survivors of the Western Design and many other seafarers and merchants who migrated to Jamaica's main city, Port Royal, was smuggling and piracy/privateering. As Nuala Zahedieh has convincingly documented, it was the very considerable profit from these illicit ventures that funded the Jamaican plantation system. Her conclusion neatly expresses one of this chapter's main points: 'the island provides a good example of imperialism as theft, albeit by one colonial power from another, rather than by a developed from a developing country'.[7]

The scale of wealth plundered by Jamaican privateers and its investment in local plantations rather than export to England did not, however, solve the larger goal of the attack on the Spanish empire, which was to accumulate silver for, among other uses, the purchase of Asian commodities such as spices, textiles, ceramics and tea.[8] Yet English merchants critical of the Western Design 'understood ... that they did not need to conquer the West Indies to secure trade to Spanish America, as "we still had the same benefit by a secondary way" by

---

5   Leslie Theibert Cooles, 'The Western Design and the Birth of an Imperial State', unpublished book chapter.
6   Richard S. Dunn, *Sugar and Slaves: The Rise of the Planter Class in the English West Indies, 1624–1713* (Chapel Hill, 1972), 205.
7   Nuala Zahedieh, 'Trade, Plunder and Economic Development in Jamaica, 1655–89', *EcHR*, 39 (1986), 205–222.
8   Nuala Zahedieh, '"A Frugal, Prudential and Hopeful Trade": Privateering in Jamaica, 1655–89', *JICH*, 18 (1990), 156.

shipping English goods to Cadiz and San Lucar, where they were exchanged for what the Spanish "brought from the Indies"'.[9]

For present purposes, England's accumulation of New World bullion is thus best understood in market economic terms as the peaceful exploitation of an economic advantage although (and as will be seen, typically) only at one remove from Marx's more violent picture of the Mexican and Peruvian mining systems. For modern neo-institutional economic historians, Spanish silver imports further constituted a 'resource curse' allowing the Iberian monarchy to pursue costly military policies (from which English entrepreneurs also profited) without consulting representatives of the commercial elite. Spain, in many respects a very rich country, thus failed to develop an economy that could trade with England and other European Atlantic states on a more egalitarian basis.[10]

II. The Portuguese Empire: Northwest Africa

During the same sixteenth century in which Spain first established and defended a New World overseas domain, the smaller Iberian monarchy of Portugal established its own global empire extending across both the Atlantic and Indian oceans.[11] This venture initially involved competition with the rival Iberian kingdom of Castile (later incorporated into the larger state of Spain). However, the expanding maritime Old and New Worlds were large enough to accommodate both European powers. Through the papacy's brokerage, Portugal and Castile signed the Treaty of Tordesillas (1494), which stipulated a division of all newly 'discovered' non-European lands along a meridian running just west of the Cape Verde islands. This agreement gave almost the entire 'West Indies' to Spain. Portugal received rights over one major New World territory – Brazil – but of more immediate significance, all the European-known portions of Africa and Asia.

The resulting Portuguese Asian and African empire flourished for a little over two centuries. Especially in the fifteenth and early sixteenth centuries, it was characterized by a great deal of violence, directed mainly against non-European populations, especially Muslims. The first wave of Portuguese overseas expansion was driven by a combination of economic, religious and social motivations. The interplay between these incentives can be seen most

---

9   Theibert, 'Western Design', 39.
10 Mauricio Drelichman and Hans Joachim Voth, 'Institutions and the Resource Curse in Early Modern Spain', in *Institutions and Economic Performance*, ed. Elhanan Helpman (Cambridge, MA, 2008), 120–147.
11 Unless otherwise indicated, the accounts of the Portuguese empire which follow are based upon A.R. Disney, *A History of Portugal and the Portuguese Empire: From Beginnings to 1807. Volume 2, The Portuguese Empire* (Cambridge, 2009).

clearly in Portugal's ventures – as well as catastrophic misadventures – in North and West Africa.

Portugal's first colonial undertaking was the 1415 conquest of Ceuta, a port city on the Moroccan side of the straits of Gibraltar. This enclave (which even today remains under Spanish rule) did not provide a base for further Portuguese territorial acquisition until 1458–74 when the neighbouring cities of Ksar es-Seghir and Tangier were taken over. Meanwhile Portuguese mariners systematically made their way down the Atlantic coast of Morocco, then along the uncharted Saharan littoral and finally into the even less known (to Europeans and North Africans) shores of 'Guinea' (West African savannah and forest zones). From there exploration continued to the Congo Basin of West Central Africa and finally, in 1488, to the Cape of Good Hope, where the Atlantic and Indian oceans converged. These last two locations would provide Portugal with access to very rich Asian markets and also a source of labour for its longer-term Brazilian plantation system. But for now I will focus upon the more limited circuits extending from Northern Morocco to what became known as the Gold Coast (present-day Ghana).

Although the establishment of a sea route to Asia was the most globally significant outcome of Portugal's maritime ventures, for most of the fifteenth century Lusitanian explorers sought to gain advantages over existing Muslim trans-Saharan caravan trade linking West Africa and the Mediterranean. The most sought-after commodity in this traffic was gold, whose major West African source lay in the Volta River basin, very close to the coastal zone named, in Portuguese, 'Mina' (the Mine). Despite their initial advantage in weaponry over the local Akan states and even the construction in 1482 of a massive fortress, Sao Jorge da Mina (mainly aimed at keeping out rival Europeans), the Portuguese could not use violence to access this precious metal. Iberia also produced few goods (other than the officially banned firearms and related military items) which were attractive to the Akan.

However, the Portuguese could exploit their establishments elsewhere on the African Atlantic coast to acquire two commodities that were exchangeable for Mina gold: slaves and woollen cloth. Slaves, from both Morocco and sub-Saharan Africa, were also of interest to the Portuguese themselves, although in the fifteenth century mainly for employment in elite households, a great variety of urban occupations and small-scale agriculture rather than in the plantation system – with its much greater scale of African enslavement – that would later develop in the Atlantic islands and Brazil.[12] From 1475 to 1535 the Portuguese also brought between 18,000 and 20,000 enslaved people from the Bight of Benin and West Central Africa into Mina, representing about

---

12 António de Almeida Mendes, 'Africaines esclaves au Portugal: dynamiques d'exclusion, d'intégration et d'assimilation à l'époque moderne (XVe–XVIe siècles)', *R&R*, 31 (2008), 45–65.

10 per cent of the goods exchanged there for gold. Another 40 per cent of Mina imports consisted of cloth, most prominently decorated woollen cloaks and mantels from the Portuguese-dominated enclaves on the southwestern Moroccan coast.[13]

In their mid-fifteenth-century explorations of the Saharan and Guinea littoral, the Portuguese mariners both traded with and attacked these towns.[14] The commercial society of a port like Safi could be described as cosmopolitan, with Muslim, Jewish and Christian (Portuguese and Genoese) merchants working together in the kind of *convivencia* often attributed to late medieval Iberia. The most valuable local export item, the woollen hanbals and burnouses, were not originally produced here but in Oran (western Algeria) so that their new work sites, looms and raw materials had to be provided by wealthy Jewish merchants in a kind of proto-industrial putting out system.[15]

Beginning in the 1480s, treaties were signed with the towns of Safi and Azammur recognizing a loose Portuguese sovereignty, which mainly allowed the Europeans to establish trading factories (without fortresses) in Moroccan territories. However, from 1505 onward the Portuguese launched a new offensive, imposing control (with and without fortresses and sizeable garrisons) over several key Moroccan towns.[16] In its more formal and militarized structure, this Luso-Moroccan empire did not last long. By 1550 only three enclaves (most importantly Ceuta and Tangier) were left. A new invasion from Iberia in 1578 concluded with the battle of al-Qasr al-Kabir, 'undoubtedly the greatest military disaster the Portuguese ever suffered in the course of their overseas expansion'.[17] Not only did the Lusitanians fail to regain any of their recently lost Moroccan territory but Sebastian, their childless young king, was killed in combat, leading, by 1580, to Portugal itself being annexed to Spain, a status that lasted sixty years.

From an economic perspective, the violent politics of the early sixteenth-century Portuguese presence in North Africa made only limited sense. The complex linkage between Moroccan textile production and Mina gold exports reached its height between 1491 and 1500 (as measured by Portuguese gold

---

13 Calculated from John L. Vogt, 'The Early São Tomé-Principe Slave Trade with Mina, 1500–1540', *IJAHS*, 6 (1973), 463–466; Ivana Elbl, 'The Volume of the Early Atlantic Slave Trade, 1450–1521', *JAfH*, 38 (1997), 47, 70–72.
14 Vincent J. Cornell, 'Socioeconomic Dimensions of Reconquista and Jihad in Morocco: Portuguese Dukkala and the Sadid Sus, 1450–1557', *IJMES*, 22 (1990), 379–418.
15 John Vogt, 'Notes on the Portuguese Cloth Trade in West Africa, 1480–1540', *IJAHS*, 8 (1975), 623–651.
16 Martin M. Elbl, 'Portuguese Urban Fortifications in Morocco: Borrowing, Adaptation, and Innovation along a Military Frontier', in *City Walls: The Urban Enceinte in Global Perspective*, ed. James Tracy (Cambridge, 2000), 350–352.
17 Disney, *History of Portugal*, II: 19.

imports).[18] During the supposed 'golden age' of Portuguese empire in the sixteenth century, imports of this precious metal steadily decreased, due in large part to the cutting off of textile exports from Safi and other southwest Moroccan ports, now under the control of the hostile local Saadian dynasty.[19] The one valuable commodity that the Portuguese hoped to gain by expanding their authority to the Dukalla hinterland of Safi was wheat, always in short supply within Iberia. However, collecting such grain as taxation (especially during the drought conditions of the early 1520s) further antagonized the local population, thus lending support to the Saadians.[20] To understand the penchant for violence even when it proved so costly, we need to examine the religious and social factors driving Portuguese overseas expansion.

For almost all participants in, and observers of, the initial Portuguese conquest of Ceuta, its religious motivation would have been obvious. The Gibraltar peninsula is the location from which, in 711 AD, the Berber Muslim freedman, Tariq ibn Ziyad, led an invading army that would produce some seven centuries of Muslim rule in *al-Andalus* (southern Iberia).[21] The kingdoms of Portugal and Castile/Spain took shape during the last centuries of this period and, although most of their wars were fought against one another and other Christian states, they identified themselves as leaders of the *reconquista*, a series of conflicts that, in 1492, finally removed the last enclave of Muslim sovereignty from the Iberian peninsula.[22]

But if Muslim regimes no longer represented a real threat within fifteenth-century Iberia, the concept of fighting them remained an important basis for the legitimacy of both the Portuguese and Castilian/Spanish monarchies. Moreover, in the Mediterranean (Ottomans) and Indian ocean (Mughals and Safavids) as well as in Atlantic Morocco, Islamic political forces were gaining new strength and territory in the form of what have been labelled 'Muslim gunpowder empires'.[23]

---

18   Vitorino Magalhães Godinho, *L'Économie de l'empire portugais aux XVe et XVIe siècles* (Paris, 1969), 214–243; John Vogt, *Portuguese Rule on the Gold Coast, 1469–1682* (Athens, GA, 1979), 77–79, 217–220. Godinho's monumental work is based mainly upon the archives of the Lisbon mint plus a few other sources, none of which go any farther back than 1504; he thus records a sustained decline only from 1522. Vogt claims to follow Godinho but does cite several documents from the Torre do Tombo (Portuguese National Archives) which give figures for 1494–96 that exceed any for the sixteenth century (2,800 marks p.a. vs. 2,025 in 1520).
19   Vogt, 'Portuguese Cloth Trade', 644, 650–651.
20   Cornell, 'Dukalla', 394–399.
21   The name 'Gibraltar' is a Spanish version of the Arabic *Jebal Tariq* (Mount Tariq).
22   Disney labels the fifteenth century as 'The Era of Neo-Reconquest'.
23   Weston F. Cook, *The Hundred Years War for Morocco: Gunpowder and the Military Revolution in the Early Modern Muslim World* (Boulder, 1994).

Historians of early modern Europe have credited the 'military revolution' in weapons, fortifications, tactics and the finances to support them with both the development of new state forms at home and the ability to dominate overseas regions. However, more recent research (along with postcolonial reflection) has recognized that European military advantages at this time (and this applies particularly to Portugal) were largely limited to maritime confrontations.[24] Thus as early as 1515 a Portuguese attempt to create a new fortified trading factory at the inland northern Morocco site of Mamora had to be abandoned when it was demolished by the artillery of the otherwise waning Wattasid dynasty based in Fez.[25]

The real winners in the Moroccan wars of the sixteenth century were the Saadians, a southern dynasty claiming Sharifian status (direct descent from the family of Prophet Muhammad), who fought the Portuguese invaders with gunpowder weapons. By 1578 the Saadians had seized control of the Moroccan interior, defeated the Portuguese at Qasr al-Kabir, and initiated a global position for their country that by-passed the Iberians in favour of direct ties with England, France and the Netherlands.

Although there were significant economic, political and religious grounds for the violent nature of the Portuguese presence in sixteenth-century Morocco, much of this behaviour must be attributed to the social base of the imperial regime. The *fidalgos* (second-tier nobility) who were sent out as 'captains' of the newly conquered posts in Morocco (but 'Governor' at Mina) saw themselves as a medieval-style hereditary military aristocracy although historians often describe them as a service class. They were dependent on state patronage rather than inherited landholdings for their support and were thus the beneficiaries of the redistributive empire created by the crown.

Even when they presided over thriving economies such as those of the Safi–Mina–Lisbon triangle (and most posts were far less prosperous), the *fidalgos* gained much of their wealth and status by carrying out raids into the Moroccan interior with the object of seizing wealth and enslaving local people, who could then be ransomed (if of high status) or sold into ready Portuguese markets, which favoured lighter-skinned Berber–Arab women, for domestic service.[26] Some *fidalgos* also took to seafaring, where they alternated between (and sometimes combined) roles as explorers, merchants and corsairs.[27]

---

24 J.C. Sharman, *Empires of the Weak: The Real Story of European Expansion and the Creation of the New World Order* (Princeton, 2019).
25 Cook, *Hundred Years War*, 148–149.
26 António de Almeida Mendes, 'Africaines esclaves au Portugal: dynamiques d'exclusion, d'intégration et d'assimilation à l'époque moderne (XVe–XVIe siècles)', *R&R*, 31 (2008), 45–65.
27 P.E. Russell, *Prince Henry 'the Navigator': A Life* (New Haven, 2000), 109–134.

Although they fought with gunpowder weapons, the *fidalgos* also maintained a 'traditional' hierarchy of knight and squire, thus requiring combat experience to (literally) earn their spurs as fully qualified warriors or state servants. Yet in the ideal combination of cavalry and musket firepower, Portuguese armies proved (at least at Qasr al-Kabir) far inferior to the Saadian 'carbineers'.[28]

In its most productive core, involving the purchase of gold in Mina, the Portuguese Morocco–Guinea sub-empire was not very violent and set a model for managing the subsequent Asian regime of the sixteenth century. When first arriving on the Saharan and Guinea coasts of Africa, the Portuguese did raid local populations but soon found that, even for the acquisition of slaves, it was more efficient to engage in market exchange rather than conquest or 'protection'. The threat of European interlopers in the gold trade did require fortifications such as Sao Jorge da Mina with at least a minimal garrison. However, real control of this trade rested upon its status as a royal monopoly, which required an elaborate civil service to monitor its operations in both Lisbon and West Africa. The trading goods from such far-flung places as Morocco and central Europe (copper) all had to pass first through the Casa da Mina in Lisbon before they were shipped to the Guinea coast. The apparatus worked well enough through the first quarter of the sixteenth century to provide 'about a quarter of all the [Portuguese] crown's revenue'.[29] But could such a system of 'monarchical capitalism' function effectively in the much richer world of the Indian ocean and would it provide the basis for further capitalist development in Iberia?

III. The Portuguese Empire: *Estado da India*

The most monumental achievement of Portuguese overseas expansion was the tracing of an all-water link between Europe and South, Southeast and East Asia followed by the establishment of political hegemony in the Indian ocean. This empire built upon earlier experiences in dominating northwestern Africa but differed in two important ways. First, little effort was made to extend European power beyond the sea routes and strategic port cities towards control over the interior of local territories and their populations. Second, this Asian empire lasted far longer than its Moroccan–Saharan–Guinean counterpart and was displaced mainly – but not exclusively – by the rival European powers of England and the Netherlands rather than by indigenous political forces. Finally, violence played a major role in the foundation and early defence of what the Portuguese came to call the *Estado da India* (the Indian State; hereafter Estado)

---

28 Cook, *Hundred Years War*, 251, 252, n. 49.
29 Disney, *History of Portugal*, 59.

during the first decades of the sixteenth century but receded somewhat into the background as rival empires (the Mamluks of Egypt and the Ottomans) abandoned the Indian ocean to Portugal. Once free of such imperial Muslim competitors, the Estado entered a kind of equilibrium with both Asian and private European trading partners.[30] But before examining how the Estado worked it is necessary to consider the stated goals of the Portuguese in this region and how they evolved in their own terms.

In 1498 when Vasco da Gama, the first Portuguese navigator to reach the sub-continent of India, was asked by his Calicut hosts what he sought there, his reply was 'Christians and spices'.[31] The Christians to whom da Gama referred were largely imaginary: East African subjects of a powerful kingdom ruled by 'Prester John' and non-Muslim Indians, only later to be understood as Hindus. In the Estado's following two decades, the idea of allying with these putative co-religionists in a new crusade against Islam significantly shaped Portuguese actions – particularly violent ones – in this region.[32]

'Spices' meant mainly peppers produced in the Malabar region of southwest India. Their import into European markets via the Cape of Good Hope route was a royal monopoly and a major source of revenue for the Portuguese crown. Within the Indian ocean economy, purchases of pepper – whose cultivation took place outside of their coastal enclaves – was a major cost for the Portuguese. Some of this expense could be met by Mina gold, but, as seen, this source of wealth diminished in the sixteenth century. The forced unification of the Portuguese and Castilian crowns in 1580 provided some new access to New World silver via Manila but, unlike in Morocco, the Portuguese could not generate enough goods to pay for the combination of exports, locally consumed supplies and administrative–military costs needed to maintain a hegemonic presence in this region.

To cover these expenses the Estado sought to control and tax the internal commerce of the Indian ocean and its surrounding waters. The form taken by this proto-colonial empire was thus not a contiguous landmass but rather a set of fortified customs centres, the most important being in southwestern India (Goa, Bassein and Diu), the [Persian] Gulf (Hormuz) and the Indonesian 'Spice Islands' (Malacca). The Portuguese used their bases to impose a more enduring form of violence upon the Indian ocean by demanding that all merchant ships passing near them purchase a *cartaz* (trading licence) as well as pay the customs duties at whatever fortress dominated their sailing routes.

---

30 The Mughals of northern India never sought a maritime dominion.
31 *A Journal of the First Voyage of Vasco Da Gama, 1497–1499*, trans. and ed. E.G. Ravenstein (1898), 48.
32 Filipe F.R. Thomaz, 'Factions, Interests and Messianism: The Politics of Portuguese Expansion in the East, 1500–1521', *IESHR*, 28 (1991), 97–109.

The *cartaz* system has been denounced as extortion and even piracy, thus reinforcing the Lane–Steensgaard view of the Estado as an unproductive protection racket or even a kind of piracy. However, placed in both its historical and immediate context, the system was as much a Portuguese adaptation to Indian ocean culture as a violent European incursion into this region. Before the sixteenth century, there had been a number of local maritime/mercantilist states that imposed themselves in very similar ways upon merchants, although none on as broad a geographical scale as the Estado. The sixteenth-century Indian ocean also contained many real pirates who sometimes partnered with local states but against whom the Estado also offered real protection to merchants in the form of armed escorts for their commercial and/or pilgrimage voyages.[33] Finally, the costs of Estado taxation were within the means of merchants even if – with good reason – not always appreciated.[34]

IV. The Portuguese Empire: Brazilian Plantations and Mines

Whether or not the Estado da India should be seen as contributing anything but augmented violence to the political economy of the Indian ocean, its end came violently during the first half of the seventeenth century, mainly at the hands of the Dutch and English East India Companies. The Netherlands and England (Great Britain after 1707) are the nation-states most closely linked to the emergence of European-centred global capitalism; the issues of colonial violence within these regimes will be dealt with in the following sections of this chapter.

For Portugal from the mid-seventeenth century onward, the main colonial project was in the Atlantic regions of West Central Africa and Brazil. In this zone the Portuguese created a new model of overseas enterprise with its own 'monstrous' form of capitalism: the slave plantation.[35] Violence within this regime took place at three levels: the capture of prospective workers in Africa; their transport in the horrendous 'middle passage' sea voyages to island and coastal colonies in the Caribbean and the American mainland; and their New

---

33 Sanjay Subrahmanyam, 'Of Imârat and Tijârat: Asian Merchants and State Power in the Western Indian Ocean, 1400–1750', *CSSH*, 37 (1995), 750–780; Sebastian R. Prange, 'The Contested Sea: Regimes of Maritime Violence in the Pre-Modern Indian Ocean', *JEMH*, 17 (2013), 9–33.
34 Michael N. Pearson, *Merchants and Rulers in Gujarat: The Response to the Portuguese in the Sixteenth Century* (Berkeley, 1976).
35 Ralph A. Austen, 'Monsters of Proto-Colonial Economic Enterprise: East India Companies and Slave Plantations', *Critical Historical Studies*, 4 (2017), 139–177. What follows on plantations, East India Companies and the Atlantic slave trade, unless otherwise indicated, draws from this article.

World employment under very harsh conditions as cultivators of sugar cane and other plantation crops.

The other major slave trading powers (mainly England/Britain, France and the Netherlands) engaged in this commerce as most of them had the Spanish American silver mines: at a distance, as peaceful maritime buyers or even piratical appropriators of a commodity whose violent 'original accumulation' took place at distant inland sites. The Portuguese also acquired most of their enslaved African labour in this way but in both West Central African Angola and (to a lesser extent) Indian ocean Mozambique, they established inland bases from which they themselves raided local people who would then be shipped to the New World plantations.[36]

The reputation of the Portuguese as inveterate (and often mixed-race) slave traders blinded many contemporaries as well as some scholars to their critical (in many senses) role in 'inventing' the early modern slave-powered sugar plantation. Both slavery and sugar cultivation could be found throughout the late medieval Mediterranean economy, but they were seldom, if ever, combined.[37] The Portuguese made this fatal match, first in the North Atlantic island of Madeira in the mid-fifteenth century, then transmitted it to the more tropical African island of São Thomé, and finally across the ocean to Brazil. Somewhere along this trajectory they also developed the vertical three-roller mill or *engheno*, a major improvement upon the olive mills and presses previously used for sugar and thus a key to the entire New World (and later Indian ocean) European plantation system.[38]

From the late sixteenth century Brazil became the major source of European sugar, transforming this erstwhile luxury spice into a bulk commodity for mass consumption. By the late seventeenth century, however, the Caribbean colonies of England and France had taken over most of the European sugar market. Brazilian plantations continued to be productive and import large numbers of slaves (ultimately accounting for 47 per cent of the total Atlantic traffic[39]) up until the 1850s, i.e., for decades after this commerce had been abolished by other European nations and the United States.

---

36 Mariana P. Candido, *An African Slaving Port and the Atlantic World: Benguela and Its Hinterland* (Cambridge, 2013), 17–21; M.D.D. Newitt, *A History of Mozambique* (Bloomington, 1995), 53–60, 86f.
37 Mohamed Ouerfelli, *Le sucre: production, commercialisation et usages dans la Méditerranée médiévale* (Leiden, 2008), esp. 149–228; J.H. Galloway, *The Sugar Cane Industry: An Historical Geography from its Origins to 1914* (Cambridge, 1989).
38 Anthony Stevens-Acevedo, 'The Machines that Milled the Sugar-canes. The Horizontal Double Roller Mills' (www.academia.edu/2349350, accessed 19/06/2024).
39 *Slavevoyages* (www.slavevoyages.org/voyage/database, accessed 19/06/2024).

V. The Portuguese Empire: Colonialism, Capitalism and Gold Mining

As much as their colonial empire fits Marx's evocation of 'the turning of Africa into a warren for the commercial hunting of black-skins', the Portuguese can hardly be labelled as exemplars of primitive/original accumulation. Their overseas ventures had deep roots in and continuing ties with Mediterranean merchant capitalism (especially Genoese and Jewish trading networks) as well as northern European merchants and entrepôts for their spice sales. However, the wealth gained from commerce in the Indian ocean and Atlantic basin was not invested in any very visible development of the Portuguese domestic economy which, by the modern era's dawn in the nineteenth century, appeared very backward in comparison to industrializing Western Europe. This 'backwardness' was criticized, from at least the mid-seventeenth century and in more recent historiography, as an outcome of the aristocratic social base and redistributive ethos of the Portuguese monarchy as well as of the pressure from the Inquisition against the most promising foundation for a more entrepreneurial middle class: Jewish converts to Christianity.[40]

In recent years a group of Portuguese scholars connected to the PWR (Prices, Wages and Rents in Portugal 1300–1910) Project have created a set of databases that allow for a more rigorous (if somewhat stylized) examination of their nation's economic history. The general result of their work has been to 'normalize' the Portuguese past. Thus the analysis of real wages indicates that, until the late eighteenth century, Portugal remained as prosperous as most other European countries, although less so than the Netherlands and England/Britain, and more so than Spain and France.[41] In response to the explanation of Britain's economic success by reference to the quality of its institutions (mainly restraints on monarchical power), Antonio Henriques and Nuno Palma find Portuguese performance to, again, rank very high among European states.[42]

Colonialism enters this argument as both a normalizing and a disruptive force. Some scholars note that the Portuguese standard of living was supported by the largest proportion of colonial-based income of any European country.[43]

---

40 Manuel Nunes Dias, *O Capitalismo Monárquico Português, 1415–1549: Contribuição Para O Estudo das Origens do Capitalismo Moderno* (Coimbra, 1963), II, 367–380; James C. Boyajian, *Portuguese Trade in Asia under the Habsburgs, 1580–1640* (Baltimore, 1993), 166–184.
41 N. Palma and J. Reis, 'From Convergence to Divergence: Portuguese Economic Growth, 1527–1850', *JEcH*, 79 (2019), 477–506.
42 Antonio Henriques and Nuno Palma, 'Comparative European Institutions and the Little Divergence, 1385–1800', *JEcH*, 28 (2023), 259–294.
43 L. Costa, N. Palma and J. Reis, 'The Great Escape? The Contribution of the Empire to Portugal's Economic Growth, 1500–1800', *EREH*, 19 (2015), 1–22.

However, others date the descent of Portugal into the ranks of the poorest European nations to the discovery of gold in early eighteenth-century Brazil. This windfall wealth produced, like Spanish silver imports in the sixteenth century, a 'resource curse/Dutch disease' phenomenon in which the prices of imported goods dropped sharply, reducing incentives for developing Portuguese manufacturing or more efficient agriculture.[44]

Not even the most positive views of the Portuguese economy credit it with any active role in the development of European capitalism. To the contrary, Portugal's heavy involvement in enslavement (of both Africans and Amerindians), slave-trading and slave plantations represents the kind of truly 'primitive' (i.e., violent) accumulation described by Marx. The scale of such violence increased during the eighteenth-century Brazilian gold rush, most obviously by the more than doubling of the number of slaves arriving during the 1700s, a period when Brazilian sugar production actually decreased or, at best, stagnated.[45] Most of the newly arrived African labourers were transported to the inland mining region of Minas Gerais, but due to the scattered and easily accessible nature of gold deposits in this area, control over the entire industry, including its workforce, proved very difficult to maintain by either mine owners or the colonial government. Violence, therefore, included not just the restraints placed upon the enslaved population but also a multilateral and ambiguous set of alliances, armed conflicts, contracts and market commerce between enslaved as well as free (manumitted or runaway) Blacks, mine owners and government officials.[46]

A link between what Brazilian authorities labelled the 'licentious liberty' of their mining frontier and the sufferings of the Portuguese domestic economy from the 'resource curse' of gold imports may only exist in the eye of the moralist beholder. However, the Dutch and especially the English did profit considerably from exchanging their products and third-party imports for Portuguese gold without much direct engagement in the disorderly world of Minas Gerais.[47] But what was the role of colonial violence in their own overseas ventures?

---

44 Davis Kedrosky and Nuno Palma, 'The Cross of Gold: Brazilian Treasure and the Decline of Portugal', Warwick: Competitive Advantage in the Global Economy (CAGE), Working Paper no. 574, July 2021.
45 Calculated from data in *Slavevoyages*.
46 Kathleen J. Higgins, *'Licentious Liberty' in a Brazilian Gold-mining Region: Slavery, Gender, and Social Control in Eighteenth-century Sabará, Minas Gerais* (University Park, 1999).
47 Charles R. Boxer, 'Brazilian Gold and British Traders in the First Half of the Eighteenth Century', *Hispanic American Historical Review*, 3 (1969), 454–472.

VI. Northern European Capitalist Empires: The Dutch Miracle and Violence

The most intensive early modern confrontation of capitalism, colonialism and violence occurred under the aegis of two monopoly trading companies representing the most economically advanced European nations of this era: the Dutch Vereenigde [United] Oostindische Compagnie (VOC) and the English East India Company (EIC).[48] Although both of these corporations were founded in the first decade of the 1600s, for the first hundred years of their existence, the VOC was clearly the most violent and prosperous of the two. The VOC hegemony in Asian waters was one aspect of Dutch domination of global commerce through most of the seventeenth century.[49] Is the violence of the VOC an aberration in this Dutch 'economic miracle' or, as claimed by Marx (who singled out the 'treachery, bribery, massacre and meanness' of the VOC in his chapter on primitive/original accumulation), a revelation of the true nature of capitalism?

Historians have argued more about whether the economy of the Dutch Republic represented full industrial capitalism and how vital the VOC was within it, rather than the extent to which it rested upon violence.[50] On this latter question they have thus left us with a split image. Dutch society is often represented as the anti-Portugal – a state with no hereditary monarchy and governed by a middle class more concerned with investing its wealth in further economic development than conspicuous consumption or military glory. Religious life included broad tolerance for various beliefs, thus allowing refugee Iberian Jews to play a major role in both the domestic and the overseas Dutch economy.[51]

The base of this economy rested upon a North Sea location that was simultaneously unfavourable – even hazardous – in the face of flooding and with limited cultivatable soil, but also favourable for establishing maritime commercial links between the Mediterranean and Baltic regions of Europe. The Dutch were dependent upon such sea traffic for their subsistence (grain and fisheries) but in the fifteenth and sixteenth centuries turned these necessities into virtues by pursuing them with new shipping and manufacturing technologies. These included a lighter and faster *fluyt* ship for Baltic trade; a herring bus that

---

48 Jan de Vries and A.M. van der Woude, *The First Modern Economy: Success, Failure, and Perseverance of the Dutch Economy, 1500–1815* (Cambridge, 1997); Els M. Jacobs, *Merchant in Asia: The Trade of the Dutch East India Company during the Eighteenth Century*, trans. Paul Hulsman (Leiden, 2006); Femme S. Gaastra, *The Dutch East India Company: Expansion and Decline* (Walburg Pers, 2003), 127–132.
49 Jonathan Israel, *Dutch Primacy in World Trade, 1585–1740* (Oxford, 1989).
50 Brandon, Pepijn, 'Marxism and the 'Dutch Miracle': The Dutch Republic and the Transition-Debate', *Historical Materialism*, 19 (2011), 106–146.
51 Jonathan Israel, *Empires and Entrepots: The Dutch, the Spanish Monarchy, and the Jews* (1990), 417–447.

could both catch and process its catch without frequent returns from distant fisheries; and mechanized, wind-powered saw mills for creating planks to build these and other ship types for both their own use (the Dutch had the world's largest merchant fleet) and as a capital goods export.

Yet, no matter what dates are chosen to define the 'Golden Age' of the early modern Dutch economy, they contain no decade in which the United Provinces of the Netherlands were not involved in a war with another European power. Before even considering the VOC, how do these conflicts (almost entirely fought on the soil or coastal waters of Europe) define the Dutch political economy?

Certainly the thriving commerce of the Dutch Republic (along with Italian city-state models of public finance) made it possible to raise the considerable loans and the taxes needed to pay for the 1568–1648 war for independence from Habsburg Spain.[52] The Netherlands also made a very direct and important contribution to the broader European 'military revolution' of this era, although it is not clear that such innovative gunpowder tactics had any influence on the ultimate victory over Spain.[53]

The limits of Dutch militarism can be seen in the failure of the Republic, so adept at ship construction and design, to participate in the early seventeenth-century 'Naval Revolution' by building dedicated warships suitable for 'line of battle' cannon duels rather than relying upon hired merchant ships and their older boarding tactics. The result of such negligence (in fact the entire Dutch navy had been allowed to shrink during a brief period of peace that followed the Thirty Years' War [1618–48]) was a Netherlands defeat (including expulsion from Brazil) in the first Anglo-Dutch War (1652–54).[54]

The Anglo-Dutch wars involved more than just these two nations but also restricted themselves to combat in European and Atlantic waters. The VOC initially behaved during wartime like other merchants by contributing ships to the Dutch naval fleet and lending money to the Republic. However, in time the Company and the Republic agreed to a division of labour, in which the VOC used its own resources to meet military and naval needs in Asia without taking any active responsibility for European warfare.

The largest Dutch seventeenth-century trade in terms of bulk rather than value was the commerce in grain, timber, codfish and naval stores with the countries bordering the Baltic Sea (most notably Poland and Norway). Some Marxist scholars claim this was also a violent enterprise because the Dutch

---

52 James D. Tracy, *A Financial Revolution in the Habsburg Netherlands: Renten and Renteniers in the County of Holland, 1515–1565* (Berkeley, 1985), 9–13; Michele U. Fratianni and Franco Spinelli, 'Italian City-States and Financial Evolution', *EREH*, 10 (2006), 257–278.
53 Geoffrey Parker, 'The Limits to Revolutions in Military Affairs: Maurice of Nassau, the Battle of Nieuwpoort (1600), and the Legacy', *Journal of Military History*, 71 (2007), 331–372.
54 Pepijn Brandon, *War, Capital, and the Dutch State (1588–1795)* (Leiden, 2015), 86–93.

had to force their way into the region against earlier established Hanseatic merchants and the Dutch navy periodically intervened against efforts by Denmark and especially the expansive but short-lived Swedish empire to regulate, excessively tax or otherwise interfere with Netherlands trade.[55] In comparisons with the VOC or the Dutch West India Company, these efforts involved only minimal and short-term violence and no fortified trading posts, to say nothing of broader territorial occupation and exercises of sovereignty over local populations. The key Dutch instrument for Baltic trade was the light *fluyt* ship, adapted to the shallow waters and bulky cargos of this region and, in contrast with the ponderous and heavily armed East Indiamen, carrying 'no guns (or only a few light ones)'.[56]

Because the Baltic commerce system was dominated by the Dutch, Jason Moore labels it as 'semi-colonial'.[57] However, apart from the owner–operators of the relatively small *fluyt* boats, there was little Dutch presence at the Baltic ports. As for trade goods, the Dutch and other more southern Europeans – as in Asia – could not provide enough of them to avoid paying for exports with New World bullion. Baltic merchants and landowners also began, during the later seventeenth century, to become active partners of Dutch firms, some of whom became their agents in the Amsterdam market. When, from 1651, the English navigation acts began to restrict Dutch participation in English commerce, Norwegian timber merchants sent cargoes directly to English ports, where they also established their own agencies.

The threats from Sweden and Denmark (which controlled the straits leading into the Baltic sea) as well as attacks from Spanish privateers based in Dunkirk required some Dutch naval protection.[58] However, little effort was made to limit the participation of merchants and ships from other European powers in Baltic trade and their percentages actually increased, as did the absolute total of Dutch commerce, during the 'golden' mid and late seventeenth century. If we are to choose a model of colonialism analogous to the Dutch presence in the Baltic, it would be Britain's 'free trade imperialism' in Africa, China and

---

55 Jaap R. Bruijn, 'The Timber Trade: The Case of Dutch-Norwegian relations in the 17th Century', in *The North Sea: A Highway of Economic and Cultural Exchange*, eds. Arne Bang-Anderson *et al.* (Oslo, 1985), 123–135; J. A. Faber, 'The Grain Trade, Grain Prices and Tariff Policy in the Netherlands in the Second Half of the Seventeenth Century', in *From Dunkirk to Danzig: Shipping and Trade in the North Sea and the Baltic, 1350–1850*, eds. W.G. Heeres and J.A. Faber (Hilversum, 1988), 33–41; Israel, *Dutch Primacy*, 140–149, 213–224.
56 Violet Barbour, 'Dutch and English Merchant Shipping in the Seventeenth Century', *EcHR*, 2 (1930), 281–282.
57 Jason W. Moore, '"Amsterdam is Standing on Norway", Part II: The Global North Atlantic in the Ecological Revolution of the Long Seventeenth Century', *Journal of Agrarian Change*, 10 (2010), 196.
58 R.A. Stradling, *The Armada of Flanders: Spanish Maritime Policy and European War, 1568–1668* (Cambridge, 1992).

Latin America during most of the nineteenth century as opposed to the far more violently mercantilist VOC Asian regime.[59]

VII. Northern European Capitalist Empires: East India Companies

At its founding in 1602, the VOC was designed as both a trading enterprise and the Asian agency in the Dutch Republic's war for independence from Spain. Thus, a major initial task was the removal of the Portuguese (under Spanish rule at the time) from their factories in the spice islands of Indonesia as well as Ceylon. However, Dutch commercial and political goals were linked by violence, as stated by the most famous of the VOC governors, Jan Pieterszoon Coen, 'we cannot carry on trade without war, nor war without trade'.[60] In its most extreme violent act the VOC, in the 1620s, secured the clove and nutmeg trade of the Banda islands by massacring or expelling virtually the entire indigenous population and replacing them with European planters and slave labour.[61] Elsewhere, the Company made monopolistic contracts with local producers (including restrictions of their output) through various combinations of force and political alliance.

The object of this violence was to control commerce, mainly in opposition to other Europeans, rather than to rule over Asian peoples and territories. However, in establishing the headquarters for such control at Jayakerta (a.k.a. Batavia/Jakarta) on the large island of Java in 1619, the VOC became involved in the equally violent politics of local states. Most immediately, the Company only took control of Batavia after fighting off first the English East India Company and then Banten (Bantam), the Java coastal state which was suzerain to (the now destroyed) Jayakerta.

In 1628 and 1629 Batavia was unsuccessfully besieged by Mataram, the dominant political force in Java at the time. Mataram was an interior state, not directly involved in global trade, but the VOC needed to maintain good relations with its rulers to assure access to rice (critical to victualling the Company's very large civil and military apparatus) as well as to timber (for maintaining the vital Dutch shipping fleet). From the last quarter of the seventeenth century, however, succession to the Mataram throne was violently contested so that,

---

59 John Gallagher and Ronald Robinson, 'The Imperialism of Free Trade', EcHR, 6 (1953), 1–15.
60 C.R. Boxer, *The Dutch Seaborne Empire, 1600–1800* (New York, 1965), 99.
61 Willard A. Hanna, *Indonesian Banda: Colonialism and Its Aftermath in the Nutmeg Islands* (Philadelphia, 1978).

between 1675 and 1757, the VOC became entangled in four full-scale Java wars, as well as many smaller power struggles.[62]

In these land contests the Dutch had little if any technological or disciplinary advantages over their Javanese opponents or allies and were not always militarily successful. But, whatever their political outcome, the Java succession wars proved to be a great financial burden on the VOC, thus contributing to the Company's loss of profitability in the eighteenth century. At the same time the Dutch expanded inward from Batavia and gained direct or tributary control over most of the northern Java coast (including Banten).

The resulting gains of territory and subject populations began, by the late seventeenth century, to shift the Dutch political presence from a proto-colonial to a 'colonial' form. In economic terms, it also allowed a move from exchange to production of such commodities as sugar and coffee. This last item is notable for being introduced from its Arabian–Ethiopian source to Southeast Asia by the VOC, which assigned its cultivation to peasant farmers on its Indonesian territories.[63] The ultimate failure of the Dutch East Indies as a proto-colony was thus precociously preparing the way for a new – and no less violent – future as a modern colony.

The English East India Company (EIC) would eventually follow a similar path to full colonialism but, up until the late 1750s, it remained far less violent than its Dutch rival. This behaviour did not arise from any essence of English character (see above on Spanish-American silver) but rather Asian circumstances. Over the seventeenth century, the Dutch succeeded in expelling the EIC from all the important trading sites in the spice islands. English Asian enterprise was thus forced to base itself in the Indian sub-continent, where it confronted the Mughal empire and its successor states, all more formidable than Mataram or Banten in Java.

The English equivalent of Coen's dictum on warfare and commerce was a 1616 dispatch by Sir Thomas Roe, the English and EIC ambassador to the Mughal court, in which he criticized both the Estado da India and the VOC for their aggressive and ultimately unprofitable actions and enjoined his countrymen to 'Let this be received as a rule that if you will profit, seek it at sea and in quiet trade; for without controversy it is an error to affect garrisons and land wars in Asia.'[64]

The EIC's two main trading and administrative centres, Bombay and Madras, were acquired without violence and, although fortified to some

---

62 M.C. Ricklefs, *War, Culture, and Economy in Java, 1677–1726: Asian and European Imperialism in the Early Kartasura Period* (Sydney, 1993).
63 Jacobs, *Merchant*, 260–275.
64 William Foster, *The Embassy of Sir Thomas Roe to the Court of the Great Mogul, 1615–1619: As Narrated in His Journal and Correspondence* (1899), 234.

degree, maintained only minimal military forces. But none of these areas were under Mughal control while, by the late seventeenth century, EIC commerce was growing fastest in Bengal, which did lie within the Mughal domains and contained no fortified English (or Dutch) bases.

In 1686 the Company shifted its pacific posture and declared war upon the Mughals with the support of army and naval forces sent from England. The result was a military fiasco, with decisive defeats on both the west and east coasts of India. Again, European firearms and tactics provided no advantage over Asian forces. But why undertake such violence in the first place?

The 1686–1690 Anglo-Mughal War was the project of Sir Josiah Child, Governor of the EIC. The Company was in this period an institutional ally of the would-be absolutist Stuart monarch, James II, who used it both to provide a source of income independent of Parliament and as the Asian sector of a nascent colonial empire that he wished to place under more centralized control.[65] Child shared James' absolutist vision but had his own concerns about Whig (liberal) parliamentary attacks upon the EIC's monopoly of Indian trade, competition for this trade with the VOC and the heightened tax demands of Indian rulers (especially in Mughal Bengal).

In the short term, the EIC's turn to violence failed in all of its objects. Yet, by the early 1700s, the Company entered its own golden age of commercial success with limited military–political entanglements. The 1688 'Glorious Revolution' replaced the Stuart monarchy with a parliamentary regime dominated by Whig politicians who quickly opened English–Indian trade to competition. However, as early as 1688 Parliament found itself in the first of a series of wars against France, financeable only by receiving very massive loans from the EIC, which effectively regained its monopoly charter in the early eighteenth century.[66]

In 1682 the VOC expelled the EIC from Banten, thus locking English merchants almost completely out of the Southeast Asian spice trade. Over the next few years, the correspondence of Child and other EIC figures was full of panic about the VOC taking over all Indian commerce. But Child also insisted that the only solution for the EIC was to imitate the Dutch and expand its own system of fortified factories with a local tax base.[67] The English do not appear to have been aware of the financial problems suffered by the VOC because of their wars in Java, to say nothing of efforts by the Dutch authorities to avoid

---

65 James M. Vaughn, 'John Company Armed: The English East India Company, the Anglo-Mughal War and Absolutist Imperialism, c.1675–1690', *Britain and the World*, 11 (2018), 101–137.
66 Michael Wagner, 'The East India Company and the Shift in Anglo-Indian Commercial Relations in the 1680s', in *The East India Company, 1600–1857: Essays on Anglo-Indian Connection*, eds. William A. Pettigrew and Mahesh Gopala (Abingdon, 2017), 60–72.
67 British Library, Add. MS. 41822, *passim*.

further costs by insisting that its factories now maintain strict neutrality in local politics.[68]

The EIC felt no such constraints and, in the context of the 1686–90 war, attempted to move its Bengal headquarters from the Mughal-supervised port of Hugli to the new and thinly populated riverine site of Calcutta. Following its defeat by Mughal forces, the EIC temporarily abandoned Bengal, returning to Calcutta only in 1690, under very straitened circumstances.[69]

The EIC finally gained its fortified factory in a somewhat ironic manner. In 1696 the Mughal regime in Bengal was threatened by a major revolt of local elites. The European companies trading there were asked to help defend the Mughal authorities and received, in return, permission to build temporary defensive walls around their trading posts. The EIC accepted the offer and began constructing what became Fort William in Calcutta but refused to take sides in the internal Bengali conflict. The VOC representatives – supposedly the model for armed factories – made a decisive military and naval intervention on the side of the Mughals but then, following the Company's new doctrine of political neutrality, dismantled the ramparts that had been put up during the rebellion.

On a broader Indian scale, the EIC's defeat in in the 1686–90 war left the Company (as in England) at the mercy of a hostile regime. However, the triumphant Mughal emperor, Aurangzeb, was also in need of revenue to fight regional wars and imposed no penalty upon the Company beyond a humiliating quest for forgiveness and a £15,000 indemnity. Within a few years the Mughal regime not only permitted the fortification of Calcutta but also granted the EIC very favourable customs payment conditions as well as taxing powers over the growing population in and around their factory. A half century later, under different circumstances, further British defensive construction in Calcutta would set in motion the violent conquest and full colonization of India; but in between the EIC enjoyed the most prosperous and tranquil phase of its history.

---

68 George D. Winius and Marcus P. M. Vink, *The Merchant-Warrior Pacified: The VOC (The Dutch East India Company) and Its Changing Political Economy in India* (Delhi, 1991), 83 fn. 53 *et passim*.

69 Susil Chaudhuri, *Trade and Commercial Organization in Bengal, 1650–1720* (Calcutta, 1975), 39–41; Om Prakash, *The Dutch East India Company and the Economy of Bengal, 1630–1720* (Princeton, 1985), 50; Winius and Vink, *Merchant Warrior*, 60–61.

VIII. Conclusion

Despite its title and several references to Marx, this chapter has little to offer on the history or definition of capitalism. What it provides instead is a descriptive account of the role played by violence in various early modern colonial (or 'proto-colonial') regimes and how such practices promoted or undermined the economic goals of these extra-European ventures. The bottom line is a liberal one: violence does not (usually) pay! Of the two East India Companies, the more violent VOC ultimately forced itself to invest so heavily into military forces and equipment that its Asian trade ran deficits for the entire eighteenth century.[70] The EIC's foray into violence in the 1680s failed on a military basis; it recovered economically because both its English and Mughal sovereigns needed a share of the Company's trading gains to finance wars that were not, for the most part, colonial projects.

This chapter has given what might seem like undue attention to the least powerful of the early modern colonial empires – Portugal. But in its various locations over long time periods, Portuguese overseas expansion provides an exemplary variety of relations between violence and economic projects. In their campaigns in North Africa the Portuguese seemed more motivated by 'medieval' notions of religious crusade and knightly honour than any kind of investment in sustainable material gains. At another extreme, their Lisbon–Mina–Safi trading and manufacturing system represents a more intense and peaceful set of enterprises even if it was both sustained and ultimately undermined by the enslavement of African people at its peripheries.

The Portuguese exploited slavery for very productive purposes in the Atlantic plantation system. When, in the eighteenth century, the object of this traffic in humans switched in large part from the disciplined cultivation of sugar and other crops to unsupervised harvesting of alluvial gold, the key Brazilian region of Minas Gerais became almost ungovernable, and the metropolitan economy experienced a 'resource curse/Dutch disease' crisis from which it did not recover for almost two centuries.

This chapter began not chronologically but analytically by treating anti-Spanish Caribbean piracy as something akin to Marx's notion of primitive/original accumulation. The privateer/pirate expeditions were not, however, operating in a pre-capitalist state of nature but rather an already existing, if not fully industrial, capitalist order. This economy allowed holders of surplus funds to openly invest in voyages of licensed plunder as well as to use the profits from such violent enterprises in even more legitimate and violent undertakings such as slave plantations.

---

70 Femme S. Gaastra, *The Dutch East India Company: Expansion and Decline* (Walburg Pers, 2003), 127–132.

Early modern colonialism itself is one of the institutions that made possible the transactions between violence, market exchanges and production innovations on a global basis. Violence is not a necessary condition or outcome of capitalist development, as suggested in the discussion of Dutch Baltic trade, so we should not assume its existence without evidence nor be either shocked or indifferent when it does appear.

6

Capitalism in Africa: Two Histories, 1650s–1940s[1]

GARETH AUSTIN

The economic historiography of Sub-Saharan Africa has focussed on why this sub-continent is relatively poor. From the late 1960s to the mid 1980s, the question was often framed as an inquiry into the nature of capitalist development in Africa. Dependency theory answered that capitalism had come late and in the wrong form.[2] This view was restated by rational-choice institutional economists in the 2000s, though they eschewed the word *capitalism*.[3] Of late there is a renewal of explicit interest in the history of capitalism, in Africa as elsewhere.[4] The origins and development of capitalisms in different parts of Africa have varied greatly. The purpose of this essay is to explore this variation through a comparison of two contrasting cases: European settler-elite capitalism at the Cape of Good Hope, which later extended into the interior of South Africa; and African indigenous capitalism in Ghana and Nigeria, before and during colonial rule. The defining feature of settler colonies was the appropriation of most of the land from the indigenous population. The defining feature of the so-called *peasant* (and *rural capitalist*) colonies of British West

---

1 I thank Robert Ingram and James Vaughn for the opportunity to participate in this project, and for the feedback I received in Athens, Ohio, in March 2022. I thank Saul Dubow for answering my questions on South African historiography when he had better things to do.
2 Samir Amin, *Unequal Development: An Essay on the Social Formations of Peripheral Capitalism*, trans. Brian Pearce (New York, 1976 [1973]).
3 Starting with Daron Acemoglu, Simon Johnson and James A. Robinson, 'The colonial origins of comparative development: an empirical investigation', *AmEcRev*, 91 (2001), 1369–1401. For a critique, see Gareth Austin, 'The "reversal of fortune" thesis and the compression of history: perspectives from African and comparative economic history', *JID*, 20 (2008), 996–1027.
4 Morten Jerven, 'The emergence of African capitalism', in *CHC*, I: 431–454; Frederick Cooper, 'Africa and capitalism', in Cooper, *Africa in the World: Capitalism, Empire, Nation-State* (Cambridge, MA, 2014), 11–37; Andreas Eckert, 'Capitalism and labour in Sub-Saharan Africa', in *Capitalism: The Reemergence of a Historical Concept*, eds. Jürgen Kocka and Marcel van der Linden (2016), 165–185; Gareth Austin, 'Capitalists and labour in Africa', in *General Labour History of Africa: Workers, Employers and Governments 20th–21st Centuries*, eds. Stefano Bellucci and Andreas Eckert (Woodbridge, 2019), 425–456.

Africa was that Africans retained control of most of the land. Donald Denoon coined the term 'settler capitalism', to include South Africa in a comparative framework.[5] In my view, comparison with the 'neo-Europes' exposes the need for a crucial distinction. Argentina, Australia or British North America are examples of 'settler-monopoly' colonies, where the European settlers secured not only ownership of most of the land but demographic dominance too. It was different in South Africa because the settlers remained a minority though they constituted a very powerful pressure group under colonial rule, and eventually became the sole rulers. South Africa is better considered specifically as a *settler-elite* colony that became a settler(-elite) state.[6]

For both South and West Africa, our comparison starts c.1650, on the eve of the Dutch arrival in Table Bay. The discussion is somewhat telescoped, in that it focusses on the economic transformations of the late nineteenth and early twentieth centuries and the implications for proletarianization. We will trace and compare the histories in parallel until the 1940s, a decade that marked a major change in both cases. In British West Africa, statutory marketing boards had been introduced as a wartime expedient in 1939 and were institutionalized when peace returned: a fundamental shift towards a larger state. In South Africa, the 1948 election and the shift from segregation to apartheid is important in the history of capitalism.

Defining capitalism itself is difficult: is it a thing, or a set of related things, the precise composition of which changes as *it* shape-shifts through the modern centuries in various parts of the world?[7] The approach here is to ask in what sense, if any, South and West Africa were capitalist in the mid-seventeenth century; to examine the changes over the following three centuries; and to assess in what ways 'capitalism' had become established by the mid-twentieth century. Capitalism's lack of a single defining feature may make it potentially richer as an agenda for research. We will discuss entrepreneurship and reinvestment, though bearing in mind that Karl Marx's notion of capitalists as having no choice but to reinvest is different in kind from the idea of capitalists as entrepreneurial in attitude, committed by choice to the long view and to reinvestment. As will be seen, a major theme of the comparison turns out to be differences in the extent and form of proletarianization: the appropriation of rights of access to land for most of the population, obliging them to sell their labour. It will be suggested that for imported capitalism (or elements of capitalism) to become

---

5 Donald Denoon, *Settler Capitalism: The Dynamics of Dependent Development in the Southern Hemisphere* (Oxford, 1983).
6 Gareth Austin, 'Capitalism and the colonies', in *CHC*, II: 301–347.
7 I discuss the problem in Gareth Austin, 'Comment: the return of capitalism as a concept', in *Capitalism: The Reemergence of a Historical Concept*, eds. Jürgen Kocka and Marcel van der Linden (2016), 207–234. See, further, Jürgen Kocka, *Capitalism: A Short History* (Princeton, 2016), 1–24.

established, it had to be *domesticated*: through complementary economic and political arrangements, an important aspect of which was supportive ideology.

This chapter has six main sections. Section I introduces the cases: elaborating the starting-point, that they cannot usefully be considered capitalist in 1650, and sketching their formal political histories. Section II discusses market production and entrepreneurship under settler-elite capitalism in South Africa, from 1652 to the eve of the mineral revolution; and West African market production and entrepreneurship, from the 1650s, during the Atlantic slave trade, through to 'legitimate commerce' and the Sokoto Caliphate in the nineteenth century. Section III examines the rise of slave economies at the Cape and in West Africa, and abolition in the former. Section IV explores the mineral revolution and the growth of manufacturing in South Africa, c.1870–1940s; and the export-crop revolution in British West Africa, from the late nineteenth century through to the interwar depression. Section V analyses the transition to wage labour in both cases, and asks how far proletarianization occurred. Section VI compares ideologies of the market and capitalism in South Africa and British West Africa. Finally, the Conclusion summarizes the main argument and suggests implications.

I. The Emergence of Two Capitalisms: Starting Points and Changing Political Settings

African market activity is a key element in the story of European settler capitalism, as is European merchant and industrial capital in that of indigenous West African capitalism. But for clarity, the focus here is on European capitalism in South Africa and African capitalism in West Africa. This section takes three initial steps. The first is to argue that none of the societies or economies in either region can usefully be labelled 'capitalist' as of 1650. The second is to outline the political economy of British lands policy in Ghana and Nigeria, to explain why this chapter's focus within West Africa is on those two countries in particular. The third step is to summarize the political frameworks within which – and in relation to which – capitalism was shaped in the two regions.

In 1650 West Africa had marketplaces and long-distance trade routes that were not confined to the Atlantic and Saharan slave trades. The goods exchanged in intra-regional trade included essentials such as salt, which was obtained at the coast and in desert oases, but also cloth, which was imported by societies which also exported it, suggesting that this part of trade was based on comparative rather than absolute advantage. Markets in factors of production were limited. Land was physically abundant and institutionally relatively easily accessible, so it is not surprising that there is no evidence of land being bought and sold in this period. There was a labour market, albeit in enslaved people.

Slave holding within the region was expanding as a joint product of the external slave trades: enslaved males tended to be embarked into the Atlantic trade at twice the rate of enslaved females, whereas within West Africa there seems to have been a larger demand for enslaved females than for enslaved males. As of 1650 the incidence of slaveholding and slave labour within the region was increasing from what is generally thought to have been much lower levels in the fifteenth and sixteenth centuries.[8] Money could be borrowed, including for investment, but capital markets were small and fragmented.[9]

We know more about West Africa than South Africa before 1650 because of the written sources arising from the growth of European trade with the former since the early fifteenth century. However, the archaeological evidence on South Africa, coupled with early European accounts, suggests a complex picture. The vicinity of Table Bay, where the Dutch were to land, was peopled by Khoekhoen pastoralists with a penumbra of San hunter-gatherers.[10] Most of the interior was occupied by societies, including states, practising a combination of arable and pastoral farming. Iron and copper ore were mined and processed where the ore was available, and, like salt, was traded with societies which lacked it. The surviving hunter-gatherers were also part of the trade networks. Labour was organized on gender and age lines, and in the arable-pastoral societies economic, social and political differentiation revolved to a great extent around control of cattle.[11] These were not 'pure' subsistence economies, but, perhaps more emphatically than for West Africa at the same time, no one suggests that they were capitalist.

Until about 1900 West Africans lived variously in a range of polities, including small independent chiefdoms and politically decentralized societies linked by defensive alliances (as among Ewe-speaking villages east of the Volta River) and/or a shared willingness to accept the authority of a particular shrine when they had disputes to settle (as in much of Igbo-speaking southeast Nigeria). But large states were created too. The century from 1650 saw the Oyo empire at its peak, uniting the Yoruba-speaking populations of southwestern Nigeria and extending into what is now the republic of Benin, before it broke up in the 1820s. The Asante (Ashanti) kingdom was formed about 1700, uniting the more northern of the various Akan-speaking states in the forest zone of what is today southern Ghana. Asante formed a tributary empire embracing most

---

8 Paul E. Lovejoy, *Transformations in Slavery: A History of Slavery in Africa* (Cambridge, 1983, 2012).
9 Gareth Austin, 'Factor markets in Nieboer conditions: pre-colonial West Africa, c.1500–c.1900', *Continuity and Change*, 24 (2009), 23–53.
10 *Khoesan* is a collective term for both peoples or their descendants.
11 Peter Mitchell, *The Archaeology of Southern Africa* (Cambridge, 2002), 355–369; Shula Marks and Anthony Atmore, 'Introduction' to *Economy and Society in Pre-Industrial South Africa*, eds. Shula Marks and Anthony Atmore (1980), 10, 20.

of what is now Ghana and extending into Côte d'Ivoire. After succeeding in conquering the coast in 1807, in the nineteenth century it generally adopted a more defensive posture, fighting several wars with Britain and its African coastal allies.[12] Far the most populous state in precolonial West Africa was the Sokoto Caliphate, a jihadist state formed in 1804 which expanded to control most of northwest and northcentral Nigeria, extending beyond that to the north, west and south. State policy mattered: the Caliphate, for example, established a vast single market with low taxes on trade, while its armies captured large numbers of 'pagans' in wars and raids, providing a steady supply of enslaved labour.[13] The auriferous Asante kingdom was unusual in controlling the money supply: by making gold dust the sole legal tender, and requiring all nuggets to be sent to Kumasi, the capital, for pulverizing into dust.[14] Merchants, however, were at least as important as states in their influence on economic change. They seem to have been responsible for the adoption of the cowrie, or a combination of cowries for low-value transactions and gold dust for high-value ones, over an increasing proportion of the region, especially from the seventeenth to early nineteenth centuries.[15] Again, except in mercantilist Asante, or in southeast Nigeria where Igbo traders such as the Aro dominated the export–import trade, long-distance trades within West Africa tended to be monopolized by members of one or other branch of two Muslim trading diasporas, the Juula in the west of the wider region and the Hausa in the east.[16]

Until the second half of the nineteenth century European control in what is now Ghana and Nigeria was confined to a scatter of slaving or ex-slaving forts along the Gold Coast, on sites for which they paid rent to the local rulers. In 1851 Britain declared a protectorate over Lagos and annexed it in 1861. In 1874, after a decisive military victory over Asante, Britain declared colonial rule over the polities of the Gold Coast proper that marked the border with Asante, i.e. on the south side of the Pra River. The real 'scramble' for Africa came later: in 1892–3 British forces (largely composed of Hausas) conquered southwest Nigeria. In 1896 Britain occupied the Asante kingdom and the northern savanna polities beyond it. By 1930 the Gold Coast Colony, Ashanti, the Northern Territories and British Mandated Togoland (part of the pre-1914 German colony of Togo) had been formally unified into the Gold Coast, which achieved

---

12 Ivor Wilks, *Asante in the Nineteenth Century: The Structure and Evolution of a Political Order* (1989 [1975]).
13 Paul E. Lovejoy, *Slavery, Commerce and Production in the Sokoto Caliphate of West Africa* (Trenton, NJ, 2006).
14 Gareth Austin, *Labour, Land and Capital in Ghana: From Slavery to Free Labour in Asante, 1807–1956* (Rochester, NY, 2005), 40, 466–467.
15 Paul E. Lovejoy, 'Interregional money flows in the precolonial trade of Nigeria', *JAfH*, 15 (1974), 563–585.
16 Philip D. Curtin, *Cross-Cultural Trade in World History* (Cambridge, 1984), 38–59.

independence as Ghana in 1957. The British government went on to consolidate the colonization of southeast Nigeria. This process had been initiated by a private company led by George Goldie, which had been making unequal treaties with local polities even before it was given a charter as the Royal Niger Company in 1886. In 1903 British forces occupied the Sokoto Caliphate and the Borno kingdom, which together became the colony of Northern Nigeria, though some armed resistance continued until 1906. In 1914, Southern Nigeria and Northern Nigeria were declared a single colony: a troubled union that became independent as Nigeria in 1960.

Successive colonial conquests of African societies established the political framework for the emergence and expansion of settler capitalism in South Africa. This began on a very small scale in 1652, with the establishment by the Dutch East India Company of a resupply stop on the sailing route between the Netherlands and the Dutch East Indies (Indonesia). European settlers, both Dutch and Huguenot (French Protestant refugees), enlarged the aims and territory of the Cape Colony. Following the second British conquest, in 1806, immigrants began to arrive from Britain. By the time of the 'Great Trek' of 1834–8, there was already an established tendency for 'Boer' farmers to migrate beyond the current colonial frontier to move deeper into the interior of South Africa. By 1840 about 10 per cent of Cape whites had moved out of the Colony.[17] This was partly in reaction to British 'interference' in emancipating the Khoesan in 1828 and then the slaves, but the Boertrekkers were anyway mostly relatively poor and hoping to find new land.[18] The Boer advance was helped, ironically or otherwise, by British wars of conquest against the Xhosa and Zulus. The eventual result of boertrekking was the formation of three independent Boer republics. Natalia was annexed by Britain in 1842 (effectively, in 1854). The outcome of the Anglo-Boer war of 1899–1902 was the forcible incorporation of the other two Boer states, Transvaal (the South African Republic) and the Orange Free State, into the British empire. However, in 1910 the former British and Boer territories were recognized as the Union of South Africa, with a prime minister responsible to a parliament elected very largely by the white population: at the time, about a fifth of the total population. The Union could impose its own taxes and even tariffs on trade and had 'dominion' status (the same as Canada) within the British empire.

---

17 Martin Legassick and Robert Ross, 'From slave economy to settler capitalism: the Cape Colony and its extensions, 1800–1854', in *Cambridge History of South Africa: I: From Early Times to 1885*, eds. Carolyn Hamilton et al. (Cambridge, 2010), 288.

18 Norman Etherington, *The Great Treks: The Transformation of Southern Africa, 1815–1854* (Harlow, 2001), 243–247, 268–269. Etherington brings together the 'Great Trek' and the '*mfecane*', the latter being the traditional term for the political upheavals and large-scale movements of black populations in southern Africa in the late eighteenth and especially the early nineteenth centuries.

Though the South African state did not declare itself a republic until 1961, it was already a 'settler state' from 1910, as some of its components had been from much earlier.[19]

II. Market Production and Entrepreneurship, c.1650–c.1900

The sub-tropical Cape and tropical West Africa differed not only in latitude but in the properties of their respective soils and local climates. The Europeans at the Cape could import technologies (wine growing and sheep rearing) and capital that together helped them put the land to profitable use, creating a demand for additional labour. The importance of technical knowledge is shown by the fact that Huguenot immigrants expelled from wine-making parts of France became richer in the Cape Colony than their fellow Huguenots from non-wine-making areas of their old country.[20] The large vineyards depended very strongly on slave labour.[21] The settler population grew undramatically, outnumbered by slaves for most of the eighteenth century. In 1795 the total population of the colony was about 50,000, almost half of them slaves, about 40 per cent whites, and 10 per cent Khoesan,[22] the latter often being forcibly indentured servants. Even within the white population income and wealth were very unequally distributed. But recent research has shown that, on average, the eighteenth-century settler population was as affluent as the inhabitants of prosperous parts of the Netherlands and Britain in the same period.[23]

In the second half of the nineteenth century, accelerated by the growth of mining from c.1870, urban markets for food expanded greatly. This demand was met to a very large extent by black farmers, especially in the Cape. They now had the market incentive to invest in ploughs and oxen to produce surpluses for sale. Other African entrepreneurs entered transport riding, carrying goods to market in ox-drawn wagons. The supply response from African farmers to market opportunity recalls the export-crop revolution in West Africa. It inspired

---

19 'Settler state', as distinct from colonial state, is the term used by William Beinart, *Twentieth-Century South Africa* (Oxford, 1994), 1–6.
20 Johan Fourie and Dieter Von Fintel, 'Settler skills and colonial development: the Huguenot wine-makers in eighteenth-century Dutch South Africa', *EcHR*, 67 (2014), 932–963.
21 Johan Fourie, 'Slaves as capital investment in the Dutch Cape Colony, 1652–1795', in *Agricultural Transformation in a Global History Perspective*, eds. Ellen Hillbom and Patrick Svensson (2013), 136–159. On slave resistance, see Robert Ross, *Cape of Torments: Slavery and Resistance in South Africa* (1983).
22 Johan Fourie and Jan Luiten van Zanden, 'GDP in the Dutch Cape Colony: the national accounts of a slave-based society', *South African Journal of Economics*, 81 (2013), 472.
23 Ibid.; Johan Fourie, 'The remarkable wealth of the Dutch Cape Colony: measurements from eighteenth-century probate inventories', *EcHR*, 66 (2013), 419–448.

an important historiography around the 1980s, refuting stereotypes about black agriculture in South Africa.[24] More recently, Clifton Crais has challenged aspects of this positive story, arguing with reference to the eastern Cape that the prosperous African farmers constituted only perhaps 3 per cent of the black population of that district, and that this period – following the violence of the colonial wars of conquest – also saw the embedding of systematic rural poverty.[25] If he is right, it was still the case that there was a category of rich African peasants and that African farmers produced much of the food that fed the expanding urban populations.

In West Africa, during the Atlantic slave trade, Europeans made a series of attempts to establish slave plantations on the coast to produce the same sorts of crops as were grown on plantations in the Caribbean. These were unsuccessful, in some cases because of insecure control over the land,[26] but also perhaps because of a lack of knowledge or readiness to adapt to local environmental circumstances: using excessively labour-intensive methods for labour-scarce West Africa. It was in the nineteenth century that industrialization in western Europe created markets for tropical crops produced using the land-extensive techniques that were profitable in West African conditions: that is, methods that used a high proportion of land (whether for cultivation or pasturage) relative to inputs of labour and capital, thus prioritizing returns to the scarce factors of production rather than yields per hectare.[27]

Palm oil, already produced for domestic consumption, was offered for export by African producers and traders from the Niger Delta to the Gold Coast in the early and middle nineteenth century.[28] In southeastern Nigeria oil palms grew so densely, on land lying fallow after food-crop cultivation, that there was no need to plant more.[29] This method of 'semi-cultivation', significantly less land-intensive than full cultivation, was also used in one of the major intra-regional trades, in kola nuts produced in the forests of the Asante kingdom and sold to Hausa traders for retailing in the Sokoto Caliphate (caffeine being a legitimate stimulant in Islam). Kola trees grew wild in the forests; producers would clear

---

24 Beginning with Colin Bundy, *The Rise and Fall of the South African Peasantry* (1979).
25 Clifton Crais, *Poverty, War, and Violence in South Africa* (Cambridge, 2011), 96–121.
26 Robin Law et al. (eds.), *Commercial Agriculture, the Slave Trade and Slavery in Atlantic Africa* (Oxford, 2013).
27 Long-term economic change in Sub-Saharan Africa, until well into the twentieth century, as a 'land-extensive path of development': Gareth Austin, 'Africa and the Anthropocene', in *Economic Development and Environmental History in the Anthropocene: Perspectives on Asia and Africa*, ed. Gareth Austin (2017), 95–118.
28 David Northrup, *Trade without Rulers: Pre-colonial Economic Development in South-Eastern Nigeria* (Oxford, 1978), 177–223; Martin Lynn, *Commerce and Economic Change in West Africa: The Palm Oil Trade in the Nineteenth Century* (Cambridge, 1997).
29 Northrup, *Trade without Rulers*, 188.

the plot surrounding a tree in order to harvest the nuts.[30] Palm products were joined as a major export from the Guinea coast of West Africa in the 1880s by the tapping of wild rubber trees in the forests of southwest Nigeria and southern Ghana. In contrast to the notoriously coercive mode of rubber extraction in equatorial Africa, in West Africa production was an African initiative and under African control.[31] In Ghana and Nigeria tapping wild rubber was successful, but – as might be expected given that intensive agriculture was relatively costly – attempts at rubber planting proved much less so.[32] After southeast Asian rubber came on the world market, for decades cultivated rubber in Ghana or Nigeria was profitable only during wartime shortages.[33]

III. The Rise of Slave Economies

Both the South and West African histories of capitalism involve slave trading and slave holding, before an eventual transition to certain sorts of wage labour. Let us start with slavery. Both regions fit the generalization about Sub-Saharan Africa in the seventeenth century that land was abundant relative to labour and capital.[34] In these conditions, the Nieboer-Domar hypothesis predicts that the coercion of labour would be profitable for would-be employers.[35] At the Cape, the colonists endeavoured to reduce the Khoesan population to dependent servants. But, already from the 1650s, they began importing slaves,[36] mainly from Madagascar, Dutch Ceylon, Indonesia and to some extent Mozambique. West African societies also imported captives; again, the unfortunate people concerned were usually foreigners, but they were obtained from within West Africa (often being sold and re-sold before reaching the final master) rather than from without.[37] Rising demand for labour to produce commodities for both the intra-regional markets (notably salt, cloth, kola) and the Atlantic one

---

30   Paul E. Lovejoy, *Caravans of Kola: The Hausa Kola Trade 1700–1900* (Zaria, 1980).
31   Raymond E. Dumett, 'The rubber trade of the Gold Coast and Asante in the nineteenth century', *JAfH*, 12 (1971), 79–101; Kwame Arhin, 'The economic and social significance of rubber production and exchange on the Gold and Ivory coasts, 1880–1900', *Cahiers d'études africaines*, 77/78 (1980), 49–62.
32   James Fenske, '"Rubber will not keep in this country": failed development in Benin, 1897–1921', *EEH*, 50 (2013), 316–333.
33   James Fenske, 'The battle for rubber in Benin', *EcHR*, 67 (2014), 1012–1034; William G. Clarence-Smith, 'Africa's "battle for rubber" in the Second World War', in *Africa and World War II*, eds. Judith A. Byfield et al. (Cambridge, 2015), 166–182.
34   Austin, 'Resources, techniques, and strategies'.
35   Austin, *Labour, Land and Capital*, 155–170, 495–498 discusses the properties of the hypothesis.
36   Robert Ross, *Cape of Torments: Slavery and Resistance in South Africa* (1983).
37   Lovejoy, *Transformations in Slavery*.

(palm oil, groundnuts, later also rubber) greatly stimulated demand for slaves. There were complications to this picture. Slave labour was not much needed in the palm-oil producing districts of the Niger Delta, where population was relatively dense. But in the nineteenth century, slaves were used in neighbouring districts to produce foodstuffs and cloth for trading into the palm oil districts.[38] Slavery was found in virtually all societies in eighteenth- and nineteenth-century Ghana and Nigeria, often on a large and increasing scale: Mohammed Salau estimates that by 1850 approaching half of the estimated eight million people in the population of the Sokoto Caliphate were enslaved.[39]

There were links between market production and trade in the precolonial nineteenth century and the further expansion of export agriculture in the early decades of colonial rule. This included links via the acquisition of slaves and pawns on the markets in coerced labour. Enslaved people were one source of labour on early cocoa farms in Nigeria.[40] In Ghana, such links via slave trading and pawning were probably quite important in the original planting boom in the Gold Coast Colony, but were stronger in the subsequent Asante cocoa-planting boom of 1901–16, which reinforced colonial Ghana's position as the world's leading producer. For the Gold Coast Colony, profits accumulated from earlier exports such as palm oil and rubber were reinvested in cocoa planting.[41] But perhaps because slavery was made illegal in 1874, a decade passed before cocoa-planting began to proliferate. By then, in the 1880s and 1890s, there was a tendency for slaves to be replaced by pawns, as the ban on the latter was less enforced.[42] In Asante, cocoa-planting had been spreading rapidly for several years by the time slavery and pawning were banned in 1908. In Asante, the larger cocoa farmers were those with command over additional labour. It is no coincidence that the first cocoa farm in a chieftaincy often belonged to the chief, making use of his right to summon subjects to help establish a farm. More widely, chiefs as well as many commoner households could use slaves, pawns and the children of free men and enslaved women, as part of the earliest cocoa labour forces. This in turn reflected Asantes' extra-subsistence earnings during the last decades before colonization, when the proceeds of kola and rubber production, and artisanal gold mining, had been invested in additional labour,

---

38 David Northrup, 'Nineteenth-century patterns of slavery and economic growth in southeastern Nigeria', *IJAHS*, 12 (1979), 1–16; Colleen E. Kriger, *Cloth in West African History* (Lanham, 2006), 49–51.
39 Mohammed Bashir Salau, *Plantation Slavery in the Sokoto Caliphate: A Historical and Comparative Study* (Rochester, NY, 2018), 161.
40 Gareth Austin, 'Cash crops and freedom: export agriculture and the decline of slavery in colonial West Africa', *International Review of Social History*, 54 (2009), 21–22.
41 Polly Hill, *The Migrant Cocoa-farmers of Southern Ghana* (Cambridge, 1963), 164–167.
42 Raymond Dumett and Marion Johnson, 'Britain and the suppression of slavery in the Gold Coast colony, Ashanti, and the Northern Territories', in *The End of Slavery in Africa*, eds. Suzanne Miers and Richard Roberts (Madison, 1988), 94–95.

brought in as slaves or pawns.[43] The inequality of access to such sources of coerced, or originally coerced, labour, meant that Polly Hill's view, expressed in 1960, is probably correct for both the Gold Coast Colony and Asante: 'the earliest farmers were among the largest in the whole history of the industry'.[44] Thus did the rise of slave economies in West Africa contribute directly to the beginnings of the export-crop revolution.

IV. Economic Revolutions, c.1900–c.1950

In the later-nineteenth century the economy of South Africa as a region was transformed by mineral discoveries. First, in the late 1860s and early 1870s the discovery of some spectacular diamonds triggered a rush in an area of Griqualand between the Orange Free State and the Cape Colony. In 1877 the area, now named Kimberley in honour of the British colonial secretary, was annexed to Cape Colony. Second, in 1886 large deposits of gold were found in the Witwatersrand hills in Transvaal. This was the cue for an even greater rush. By the late 1880s in Kimberley thousands of individual claims had been consolidated and thousands of independent diggers had been replaced by the joint stock companies, culminating in the monopolistic dominance of Cecil Rhodes' De Beers Consolidated Mines, which was investing in proper shafts and machinery.[45] The gold rush moved even more quickly from diggers to consolidated ownership and deep mining. Two new cities, Kimberley and Johannesburg, were growing rapidly. Demand for labour soared, both for mining – underground and overground – and for urban services. This included demand for skills of various kinds, but most obviously in mining: there was significant immigration of miners from Britain and other long-established mining countries. Opportunities for investment opened at a range of scales, from modest investments in new shops or other services to the large-scale investment that was required as the mines went deeper. Much of the latter capital came from overseas. Africa's first formal stock exchange was opened in Kimberley in 1880. This, and another in the gold-rush town of Barberton, were soon eclipsed by the Johannesburg stock exchange, founded in 1887. The latter was backed by leading Kimberley capitalists and competed also with London by offering minimal listing requirements: it became much easier to raise funds

---

43 Austin, *Labour, Land and Capital*.
44 Polly Hill, 'How large are Ghana cocoa farms (and farmers)?', *Economic Bulletin of Ghana*, 4 (1960), 6.
45 William H. Worger, *South Africa's City of Diamonds: Mine Workers and Monopoly Capitalism in Kimberley, 1867–1945* (New Haven, 1987).

in Johannesburg, including from British and continental European sources.[46] In the 1860s, South Africa's exports – all agricultural and pastoral – 'had only just reached' £2.5 million a year. In 1906–10, thanks to mining, they averaged £27 million a year.[47]

The economic expansion fuelled by the mineral revolution created opportunities for light manufacturing, where raw materials and energy were available relatively close to market: the proximity providing natural protection from imports. This was the case with beer and construction materials. In 1924, the newly elected Nationalist–Labour Pact government intervened to accelerate the expansion of manufacturing by introducing a programme of import-substitution industrialization behind a tariff wall. It is hard to imagine this happening had it not been for the combination of South Africa's high level of independence from then laissez-faire Britain, and the state's capacity and willingness to tax the mining industry. The systematic promotion of industrial development was taken further when Smuts returned to power, 1939–48, a period for which Bill Freund argued that South Africa could be considered a developmental state.[48] The foundation of the general industrialization programme was government investment in electrification, taking advantage not only of the revenues from the mines but also the availability of large quantities of high-grade coal.[49] This was also combined with equally high-quality iron ore from within the country to produce steel.[50] By contrast, in West Africa only eastern Nigeria had coal, at Enugu, and in more limited quantities and without substantial supplies of iron ore to complement it. Alongside the difference in mineral endowment, the role of the state must be underlined. Even before the Pact government, Smuts had instigated (1922–3) a state-owned electricity supply corporation, which enabled later manufacturing ventures. These included another fundamental state enterprise, the Iron and Steel Industrial Corporation (founded 1928, operational 1934). By 1948, when the National Party won the election and proceeded to introduce a formal policy of apartheid, manufacturing had overtaken agriculture and mining as the largest contributor to South African output (GDP). Mining remained by far the biggest export-earner, however, whereas much of the manufacturing output was not internationally competitive.

---

46 Marius Lucasiewicz, 'From diamonds to gold: the making of the Johannesburg Stock Exchange, 1880–1890', *JSAS*, 43 (2017), 715–732.
47 Charles H. Feinstein, *An Economic History of South Africa: Conquest, Discrimination and Development* (Cambridge, 2005), 100.
48 Bill Freund, *Twentieth-Century South Africa: A Developmental History* (Cambridge, 2019).
49 Ben Fine and Zavareh Rustomjee, *The Political Economy of South Africa: From Minerals-Energy Complex to Industrialisation* (1996) examines the industrialization drive.
50 Feinstein, *Economic History of South Africa*, 262 rightly emphasized 'geology's rich legacy' for South African economic development.

Colonial Ghana and Nigeria were the main sites of the British West Africa 'lands policy', under which the land remained almost entirely in African hands. This allowed some scope for the further evolution of African capitalism in agriculture and trade, within limits that will be discussed below. The adoption of this policy was not inevitable: it was the outcome of major controversy within and beyond the British government at imperial as well as colonial level.[51] The proposed alternative policy was to allow and support the establishment of plantations by European companies and individuals. W.H. Lever, the soap and margarine magnate, campaigned for nearly twenty years, until his death in 1925, to be allowed to acquire land in British West Africa for the purpose of producing his own raw material, palm oil, rather than having to buy it via intermediaries from small-scale African producers. His arguments were rejected by the Nigerian and Gold Coast administrations, but in the Gold Coast concessions were allowed to European planters. Several cocoa plantations were established by British planters in the early colonial period. They failed, however, in competition with African cocoa farmers; the last lingered into the 1930s and early 1940s.[52] Already in 1920, Sir Hugh Clifford, the governor of Nigeria, who had become the leading advocate of maintaining African ownership of West African agriculture, had been able to proclaim:

> Agricultural interests in tropical countries which are mainly, or exclusively, in the hands of the native peasantry ... (a) are self-supporting as regards labour, while European plantations can only be maintained by some system of organized immigration or by some form of compulsory labour; (b) Are incomparably the cheapest instrument for the production of agricultural produce on a large scale that have yet been devised; and (c) Are capable of a rapidity of expansion and a progressive increase of output that beggar every record of the past, and are altogether unparalleled in all the long history of European agricultural enterprises in the Tropics.[53]

Clifford was well aware from his previous post, governor of the Gold Coast, that the British cocoa planters there were struggling, having not had the advantage of assistance from the state to supply labour at below free-market cost. Underlying his peroration also were the statistics of the extraordinary growth of agricultural exports in both Nigeria and Ghana. What enabled Clifford's

---

51 A.G. Hopkins, *An Economic History of West Africa* (2020), 262–267; Anne Phillips, *The Enigma of Colonialism: British Policy in West Africa* (1989), 59–135.
52 Gareth Austin, 'Mode of production versus mode of cultivation', explaining the failure of European cocoa planters in competition with African farmers in colonial Ghana', in *Cocoa Pioneer Fronts since 1800*, ed. William Gervase Clarence-Smith (Basingstoke, 1996), 154–175.
53 Sir Hugh Clifford, Governor's Address to the Nigerian Legislative Council, 1920, quoted in Phillips, *Enigma of Colonialism*, 85.

side of the colonial policy argument to prevail was precisely the expansion of agricultural exports, which predated colonial rule, with the emergence of 'legitimate commerce' during the decades following British withdrawal from the Atlantic slave trade in 1807, and continued further after colonization, especially facilitated by the construction of railways.[54]

The cash-crop expansion of the early colonial period did indeed continue, and magnify, 'legitimate commerce', which we discussed above with reference to palm oil and wild rubber. Indeed, output of palm products soared in Nigeria: from 1900 to 1913, palm oil exports nearly doubled from 45,508 to 83,089 tonnes, while palm kernel exports doubled, from 85,624 to 174,719 tons.[55] Groundnuts (peanuts) had been introduced to West Africa in the Atlantic trade. They grow best in the savanna and were duly offered for export along the river valleys and coasts of Senegambia from the 1830s. In the region of West Africa with which this chapter is concerned, favourable soils and low transport costs were combined only when the railway reached the city of Kano, commercial capital of the Nigerian savanna, in 1911. In 1913, already, 16,553 tons of groundnuts were railed from Kano to the port.[56] Meanwhile, the production of another exotic crop, cocoa beans, had taken off in southwest Nigeria and the Gold Coast. The latter's cocoa exports jumped from zero in 1892 to about 40,000 tons in 1911, overtaking Brazil as the world's largest producer, and exceeding 200,000 tons for the first time in 1923.[57]

The adoption of cocoa cultivation is a particularly interesting case from the perspective of one of the attributes commonly associated with capitalism, namely entrepreneurial attitudes and reinvestment. Entrepreneurship means the role of bringing together factors of production, but entrepreneurial attitudes mean taking the long view and willingness to assume risk. Cocoa was exotic, and the plants take several years before they begin to bear, and several more before they reach full bearing; and then (in the case of Amelonado cocoa, the variety adopted in West Africa in this period) they may keep producing well for perhaps thirty years more. They very much fit the definition of a capital good. The risks lay in the long-term commitment and initially also in the unknown or little-known nature of the crop, as far as West Africans were concerned. Hill, from her pioneering research on the original cocoa-planting take-off in Akim Abuakwa district of Eastern Province of the Gold Coast Colony, highlighted the

---

54 Hopkins, *Economic History of West Africa*, 265–267.
55 Susan M. Martin, *Palm Oil and Protest: An Economic History of the Ngwa Region, South-Eastern Nigeria, 1800–1980* (Cambridge, 1988), 148, 151.
56 Jan S. Hogendorn, *Nigerian Groundnut Exports: Origins and Early Development* (Zaria, 1979).
57 Polly Hill, *The Migrant Cocoa-farmers of Southern Ghana* (Cambridge, 1963), 177; G.B. Kay, *The Political Economy of Colonialism in Ghana: Documents and Statistics, 1900–1960* (Cambridge, 1972), 336.

entrepreneurship involved. She characterized the migrant farming groups who bought land in neighbouring chieftaincies to plant cocoa, and were primarily responsible for the take-off, as capitalists in this sense. For Hill a 'capitalist' was someone whose 'primary concern has been the continued expansion' of their 'business'.[58] The adoption of cocoa was a major innovation, in that it entailed a new production function: a very different combination of land, labour and capital from the annual crops that farmers in what became 'the cocoa belt' had been used to planting for food.[59]

Very few of the first cocoa growers in West Africa had seen a bearing cocoa tree, while the first European agricultural officers and planters had no experience of producing cocoa beans under West African conditions. Experimentation was therefore necessary. African farmers soon worked out that the agricultural officers' advice to plant trees wide apart, in order to maximise yield per tree, made no economic sense when the farmers' priority was returns to labour. Instead, the West African approach to planting emerged as relatively close spacing, to accelerate the formation of a shade canopy, which eliminated weeds and therefore the need for weeding. Again, Ghanaian farmers worked out that the most economically efficient response to capsid infestation was temporarily to abandon the farm, allowing it to become overgrown; and then return to cut the trees from the overhanging vegetation, by which time the insects had disappeared.[60] This policy was helped by another feature of Ghanaian land-extensiveness: the practice of leap-frogging, by which farmers established a chain of cocoa farms as the frontier of cocoa farming spread outwards from its original centre in the Eastern Province.[61] Having multiple farms decreased the risk that all one's bearing trees would be infested at the same time.

This helps explain how Ghanaian cocoa farmers defeated European competition. Clifford's remark that the 'native peasantry ... are self-supporting as regards labour' could be read not only as referring to the absence of organized immigration and labour coercion, but also as a suggestion that reliance on family labour gave African cocoa farmers an advantage over European planters paying wages. Indeed, the evidence suggests that the weakness of the planters lay in their high labour costs. But this was not because they were reliant on wage labour. So were the larger African cocoa farmers. Rather, the difference lay in the intensity of techniques of production: in contrast to the land-extensive African approach, European planters – as if on ideological principle – put in additional labour to ensure that trees were arranged neatly and wide apart, and

---

58 Hill, *Migrant Cocoa-farmers*, 3. See also idem, *Studies in Rural Capitalism in West Africa* (Cambridge, 1970), 21–29.
59 Gareth Austin, 'Vent for surplus or productivity breakthrough? The Ghanaian cocoa take-off, c.1890–1936', *EcHR*, 67 (2014), 1035–1064.
60 Austin, 'Mode of production versus mode of cultivation'.
61 Hill, *Migrant Cocoa-farmers*.

assigned further labour and capital into spraying when the trees became infested with capsid, the most common insect problem of the period.[62]

Ghanaian cocoa thus fits into the general pattern of the export crop revolution in West Africa in that all these crops were grown using, as far as possible, land-extensive techniques: maximizing returns to the scarce factors (labour and capital) rather than to the abundant factor (land). But how were labour and capital mobilized? Cocoa trees were planted and nurtured by tool-aided labour. The food requirements were eased in the case of cocoa – not groundnuts or palm products – by the fact that tall food crops such as plantain were grown on young cocoa farms, both to shade the cocoa saplings and to feed the workers. This lasted only until the shade canopy formed, however; and there were cash requirements too, including to buy cloth and tools, and – in the case of the migrant farmers in Eastern Province – buy land, though the liquidity requirement was often eased by paying in instalments.[63]

Turning to Nigeria, the cocoa industry there was founded by large Lagosian merchants of Creole origin.[64] Originally, they invested in cocoa plantations in response to a trade recession. The subsequent spread of cocoa farming inland from Lagos owed something to reinvestment of gains from nineteenth-century market activity, but Sara Berry gave more emphasis to help, in providing credit and labour, from other members of the migrant farmers' lineages and ethnic communities.[65] The growth of palm-product production in southeast Nigeria continued while cocoa farming was taking off further west because soil and rainfall conditions mandated sticking with palm products rather than shifting to cocoa. This further expansion was achieved without dramatic new infusions of labour or capital in the palm oil-exporting districts themselves.[66] In the case of Kano groundnut exports, which appeared to erupt from nothing into a major trade, the opportunity cost was a reduced supply of millet to the Kano grain market, as peasants switched some of their land and labour-time to the export crop. Previously, they had produced a millet surplus which, sold for cowries, enabled them to pay their grain tax. The initiative for the groundnut take-off, however, came not from the peasants but from Hausa merchants. Their European counterparts, along with the Lancashire textile firms organized in the British Cotton Growing Association, plus the colonial administration,

---

62 Austin, 'Mode of production versus mode of cultivation'.
63 Hill, *Migrant Cocoa-farmers*; Austin, 'Vent for surplus or productivity breakthrough?'
64 A.G. Hopkins, 'Innovation in a colonial context: African origins of the Nigerian cocoa-farming industry, 1880–1920', in *The Imperial Impact*, eds. Clive Dewey and A.G. Hopkins (1978), 83–96, 341–342.
65 Sara S. Berry, *Cocoa, Custom and Socio-Economic Change in Rural Western Nigeria* (1975), 71–79.
66 Martin, *Palm Oil and Protest*, 45–55, 170–173; Chima J. Korieh, *The Land Has Changed: History, Society and Gender in Colonial Eastern Nigeria* (Calgary, 2010), 76–90.

had expected the arrival of the railway in Kano to induce a flood of exports of raw cotton. Farmers, however, were unwilling to expand their cotton output beyond that needed by local spinners and weavers, not least because to do so would imperil their own food security. So Hausa traders first secured confirmation from the British merchants that they were willing to buy groundnuts, and then made gifts of salt and cloth to peasants in return for promises to produce groundnuts. As with the Lagosian merchants and the larger Ghanaian cocoa pioneers, the group taking the lead in the export-crop revolution in Kano were reinvesting the wealth they had accumulated during the previous century. Specifically, some of them had run caravans in the Hausa trade with Asante, buying kola nuts and selling slaves.[67]

This account may suggest, so far, pure continuity in the fact of wealth accumulation by West African capitalists, many small but some large in the scale of their operations. The close relationship between merchant capitalists and export agriculture, with capital and management even moving from the former to the latter in the case of Lagos, is evidence of flexibility and resilience as well as innovation. But there were major sources of potential disruption too: growing competition in trade from increasingly monopolistic European companies, demonetization of African currencies, and the end of slavery and human pawning.

The beginning of steamship services between Europe and West Africa, starting from Liverpool in 1851, made it easier for relatively small merchants, European and African, to enter directly into the export–import trade. The result was increased competition and growing African participation.[68] It is generally argued that this period came to an end in the late nineteenth and early twentieth centuries, partly because of a growing concentration of ownership on the European side in response to falling terms of trade, and partly because colonial rule plus railways encouraged European firms to open branches 'up country' for the first time. The result was that independent African traders tended to be reduced to operating as brokers or shopkeepers for the European firms.[69] They also faced competition from an increasing number of Levantine traders, who established themselves in towns across British West Africa. This story of rise and decline for African merchant capital is well established but will

---

67 Hogendorn, *Nigerian Groundnut Exports*.
68 See especially Raymond E. Dumett, 'John Sarbah, the Elder, and African mercantile entrepreneurship in the late nineteenth century', *JAfH*, 14 (1973), 653–679; Dumett, 'African merchants of the Gold Coast, 1860–1905: dynamics of indigenous entrepreneurship', *CSSH*, 25 (1985), 661–693. These and related essays are collected in Dumett, *Imperialism, Economic Development and Social Change in West Africa* (Durham, NC, 2013).
69 Anthony Nwabughuogu, 'From wealthy entrepreneurs to petty traders: the decline of African middlemen in eastern Nigeria, 1900–1950', *JAfH*, 23 (1982), 365–379.

be modified by current research.[70] Indeed, it does not really work for Kano. In a major study of private enterprise in Nigeria published in 1994, Tom Forrest commented that 'many of the leading [Kano] businessmen of today descend from the long-distance traders of the pre-colonial period', some of whom were also owners of slave estates, producing for the market.[71]

Whatever the survival rate of African traders, there is no doubt that, whereas agriculture remained overwhelmingly in West African hands, vital service elements of the import–export economy such as shipping and banking not only emerged as British monopolies, but also became cartels.[72] In the export trade itself, bouts of intense competition between European buying firms alternated with moves towards monopsony, both in the form of some concentration of ownership (the formation of the United Africa Company from a merger of three trading firms in 1929) and periodic agreements between the firms to fix the prices they paid for commodities, especially in the hope of reducing the margins earned by African middlemen.[73]

The British administrations sooner or later introduced their own colonial currency and sought to demonetize the established ones. This caused a loss of wealth for people holding balances in commodity currencies such as cowries and (in southeast Nigeria) manillas.[74] This effect was much less severe where the precolonial currency was gold dust, as in southern Ghana including Asante, because of the intrinsic value of gold.

The most general threat to holders of wealth on the eve of colonization, however, was the prospect of the prohibition of slavery and pawning. We will examine this in Section V.

The emergence of a large manufacturing sector strongly differentiated the economy of mid-twentieth-century South Africa from that of Ghana or Nigeria. The economies of both South Africa and British West Africa expanded around specialization in the export of primary products. Agricultural exports led to expanded demand for consumer goods such as textiles, both because of the

---

70 A.G. Hopkins, *Capitalism in the Colonies: African Merchants in Lagos, 1851–1939* (Princeton, 2024).
71 Tom Forrest, *The Advance of African Capital: The Growth of Nigerian Private Enterprise* (Edinburgh, 1994), 197.
72 E.g. Ayodeji Olukoju, 'Elder Dempster and the shipping trade of Nigeria during the First World War', *JAfH*, 33 (1992), 255–271; Gareth Austin and Chibuike Ugochukwu Uche, 'Collusion and competition in colonial economies: banking in British West Africa, 1916–1960', *BHR*, 81 (2007), 1–26.
73 Roger J. Southall, 'Polarisation and dependence in the Gold Coast cocoa trade, 1897–1938', *Transactions of the Historical Society of Ghana*, 16 (1975), 93–115.
74 Walter I. Ofonogoro, 'From traditional to British currency in Southern Nigeria: an analysis of a currency revolution, 1880–1948', *JEcH*, 39 (1979), 623–654; Jan S. Hogendorn and H.A. Gemery, 'Continuity in West African monetary history? An outline of monetary development', *AfEcH*, 17 (1988), 138–139.

income that export crops generated but also because the income was relatively widely distributed among farmers, labourers and brokers. They also created opportunities to establish processing industries, to supply export and indeed domestic markets with finished products rather than raw materials. In 1923 Lever Brothers tested this by establishing a soap factory at Apapa in southeast Nigeria. The logic was to supply soap made from Nigerian palm oil to Nigerian consumers without the cost of shipping the raw material to England and the soap to Africa. But the experiment was deemed unsuccessful in the face of competition from a British-based factory, though the Apapa enterprise had the additional disadvantage of having to pay high prices for inputs from another Lever subsidiary.[75] More widely, in an increasing range of sectors Nigeria had a large enough market to absorb the produce of a local factory many years before such factories were established.[76] But that did not mean that the factory would necessarily be profitable against cheaper imports. When Britain abandoned its long-standing policy of free trade in 1931, in response to the Great Depression, the results included the imposition of tariffs against Japanese cloth entering British colonies, but not against British products competing with, or pre-empting, Ghanaian or Nigerian ones. According to the ILO, in the early 1950s the number of wage-workers employed in manufacturing was only 14,755 in the Gold Coast and 16,002 in Nigeria (1954 figures), in contrast to 641,775 in South Africa (1952-3).[77]

Table 6.1. Annual average exports (£ million, nominal prices) 1900-47.

Years	South Africa	Ghana	Nigeria	Combined Ghana & Nigeria
1900-1909	32,786	1,601	2,344	3,945
1910-1919	65,195	5,458	7,552	13,010
1920-1929	53,591	10,401	14,660	25,061
1930-1939	27,513	7,371	11,377	18,748
1940-1947	55,317	9,092	18,159	27,251

Source: Calculated from *African Commodity Trade Database, 1808-1939*, Version 1.3 (17 August 2017), compiled by Ewout Frankema, Jeffrey Williamson and Pieter Voltjer. See their 'An economic rationale for the West African Scramble? The commercial transition and the commodity price boom of 1835-1885', *JEcH*, 78 (2018), 231-267.

75 David Kenneth Fieldhouse, *Unilever Overseas: Anatomy of a Multinational, 1895-1965* (1978), 345-379.
76 Peter Kilby, 'Manufacturing in colonial Africa' in Peter Duignan and L.H. Gann, *Colonialism in Africa: IV. The Economics of Colonialism* (Cambridge, 1975), 495-496.
77 Andreas Eckert, 'Wage labour', in *General Labour History of Africa: Workers, Employers and Governments, 20th-21st Centuries*, eds. Stefano Bellucci and Andreas Eckert (Woodbridge, 2019), 38-39.

South Africa's primarily mining exports considerably exceeded in value the primarilyagricultural exports of British West Africa.[78] Despite the extreme inequality of the distribution of the income in the settler economy – between the shareholders, managers, white workers and black workers – they generated, directly and indirectly, a major growth of consumer purchasing power which provided markets for a whole range of manufactured goods. The greater scale (in value) of South Africa's primary product exports compared to West Africa's gave the former a major advantage when it came to the potential for industrialization. But this potential would not have been realized to the extent that it was without the above-emphasized commitment of the settler state to structural transformation of the economy, via protective tariffs and investment in industrial public goods, in the 1920s–40s. These combined to ensure that the South African market for manufactures would be to a large extent supplied from within the country. By the 1930s South African manufacturing included not only agricultural processing and textiles, but also heavy industry including metallurgy and chemicals, partly supplying the mines.

One huge difference between indigenous (and foreign) capitalism in British West Africa and capitalism in South Africa is in the scale of overseas (mainly British) investment in the respective cases. Herbert Frankel made an extremely useful quantitative study of foreign investment in Africa as of 1936. His figures are surely questionable in detail, but the general picture is consistent with what we know on various parts of it from other sources. Frankel estimated the amount of capital invested in Africa from abroad over the whole period 1870–1936 as follows: South Africa £523 million, Nigeria £75 million, Gold Coast (colonial Ghana) £35 million.[79] Per capita, Frankel gave a figure of £55.8 for South Africa (and South-West Africa, now Namibia) compared to £3.9 for Nigeria.[80] He did not give a separate number for the Gold Coast, but it would have been the main contributor to his higher estimate for British West Africa as a whole (including the Gambia and Sierra Leone), of £4.8. It is worth adding that, whereas South Africa had a series of stock-market foundations in the 1880s, the first stock markets in Nigeria and Ghana opened in 1960 and 1989 respectively.

The order-of-magnitude difference in the scale of foreign investment in South Africa and British West Africa is mainly accounted for by the mining industry: the Gold Coast had some mining including of course gold, Nigeria had tin

---

78 The gap would be greater on Feinstein's figures for South Africa, which include the premium on gold received because of currency devaluation, notably in 1933–1938. Feinstein's figure for the annual average of South African total exports in the 1930s comes to £94.25 million, an increase on the 1920s (£82.95 million): Feinstein, *Economic History of South Africa*, 102.
79 S. Herbert Frankel, *Capital Investment in Africa: Its Course and Effects* (1938), 158.
80 Ibid., 170.

mining on the Jos Plateau and a coal mine at Enugu, but the South African gold and diamond industries were on a different scale. As the last sentence illustrates, mining was far from specific to settler capitalism (and indeed was not necessary for it). In comparing the two large economies of British West Africa with South Africa, one has to remember the transformative effect of exceptionally valuable mineral discoveries in the latter case, without which it would surely not have come close to having a one-fifth share of manufacturing in GDP in 1960.

V. Abolition and Incomplete Proletarianization

In 1834 the Cape Colony was within the British empire, and the abolition of slavery across the empire (except India) therefore applied in the Cape. Except for pin-pricks on the coast of what is now Ghana, neither Nigeria nor Ghana were colonized until decades later. One might think that whenever somewhere was added to the British empire after 1834, abolition was automatically enacted. This was far from the case. Admittedly, slavery and human pawning were prohibited in the Gold Coast Colony in 1874, the year it was established. But north of the Pra River, in Ashanti and the Northern Territories, they were not banned until 1908, twelve years after colonial occupation had begun. In Nigeria abolition was an even longer story: the final category of slavery to be made illegal in British West Africa was concubinage in Muslim northern Nigeria, which was prohibited only in 1936.[81] Both in South Africa and British West Africa, the prohibition of slavery was dictated by decisions made in London and not in response to pressures from within the colonies concerned. There was one important difference: the slaveowners of the Cape, being Europeans, received compensation for the abolition of their human property; the slaveowners of West Africa, being Africans, did not. But in both cases, the economic conditions making labour coercion profitable for the coercers still existed. The market in enslaved people was abolished. But the market in the labour services of people free to choose whether to accept employment, was as yet very limited. The obvious way to generate a mass market in hired labour was to give prospective employees no alternative to accepting waged work. A very interesting aspect of comparing settler capitalism in South Africa and African capitalism in West Africa is that, under the common umbrella of British colonial rule, the path of all-out proletarianization – the British model – was followed in neither.

Within Cape Colony, in 1828 the government had already abolished the more severe restrictions on Khoisan workers, pass laws and compulsory service, and also encouraged Xhosa labour migration. These were small steps in the direction

---

81 Paul E. Lovejoy and Jan S. Hogendorn, *Slow Death for Slavery: The Course of Emancipation in Northern Nigeria, 1897–1936* (Cambridge, 1993).

of a free labour market,[82] but that would not solve the Nieboer-Domar problem, of the high cost of labour when land was abundant and labour and capital scarce. The government implicitly recognized this in agreeing to the four-year period of 'apprenticeship' for the people supposedly emancipated from slavery in 1834. Not long afterwards, in 1841, it tightened control of labour by making breach of an employment contract a criminal offence when committed by the worker, whereas it was only a civil offence when perpetrated by the employer.[83]

At the level of individual grain farmers facing high wage costs in the post-slavery Cape, a possible solution lay in mechanization. Some tried this from the 1850s onwards.[84] At the level of the white-ruled states in South Africa, an alternative approach was noted by a French missionary in the 1860s, who remarked that the Boers seemed to be trying:

> to force the natives against some impassable range or drive them back into arid deserts; to leave them no space in anticipation of the future and of the increase in population ... to live within such narrow limits that it becomes impossible to subsist on the produce of agriculture and livestock and to be compelled to offer their services to the [Boer] farmers in the capacity of domestic servants and labourers.[85]

Around the turn of the century Africans were emerging as sharecropping tenants on white-owned land, for example in the Orange Free State. Given that many Boer landowners were either relatively capital-poor even before the war, or had had their property destroyed during it, some African sharecroppers supplied not only their labour but also the capital needed to work the farm: especially in the form of a plough and ox.[86] Any form of tenancy was a step down for those who had owned their own farms, especially during the expansion of black farmers' production for the market in the later nineteenth century. But share tenancy did provide some scope for entrepreneurship and prosperity.[87]

The mineral discoveries meant that mineowners had a product so valuable that they could pay market rates to employees and still expect to make a profit:

---

82 Susan Newton-King, 'The labour market of the Cape Colony, 1807–28', in *Economy and Society in Pre-Industrial South Africa*, eds. Marks and Atmore (1980), 171–207.
83 See Legassick and Ross, 'From slave economy to settler capitalism', 294.
84 Wayne Dooling, *Slavery, Emancipation and Colonial Rule in South Africa* (Athens, OH, 2007), 159–187.
85 R.C. Germond (ed.), *Chronicles of Basutoland* (1967), 267, quoted in Feinstein, *Economic History of South Africa*, 34.
86 Timothy Keegan, *Rural Transformations in Industrializing South Africa: The Southern Highveld to 1914* (1987), 51–95.
87 Charles van Onselen, 'Race and class in the South African countryside: cultural osmosis and social relations in the sharecropping economy of the south-western Transvaal, 1900–1950', *AHR*, 95 (1990), 99–123.

provided they expanded output only modestly. In practice, from the moment that large companies took over the mines, they worked to drive down the real wages of black workers. To do so while still receiving enough workers required the cooperation of the state. Employers and government worked together to ratchet down black real wages from the high rates they commanded in the immediate aftermath of the gold finds on the Witwatersrand. For their part, the mining companies combined to establish monopsonistic agencies to recruit labour, respectively from inside and outside the borders of South Africa, and introduced the system of housing mineworkers in heavily controlled closed compounds.[88] The contribution of the state was to increase the pressure on Africans to sell their labour rather than their produce.

Francis Wilson constructed indexes of the annual real cash earnings of black and white workers in South African gold mining, and of labour productivity (measured by tons lifted per underground worker) from 1911 onwards (see Table 6.2).

Table 6.2. Average annual cash earnings and labour productivity in South African gold mining, 1911–46 (1936 = 100).

Year	Black workers' earnings	White workers' earnings	White earnings as a multiple of black earnings	Labour productivity
1911	100	102	11.7	85
1916	90	94	12.0	78
1921	69	90	15.0	79
1926	88	85	11.2	98
1931	92	90	11.3	94
1936	100	100	11.5	100
1941	89	94	12.1	110
1946	92	99	12.7	112

Source: Francis Wilson, *Labour in the South African Gold Mines 1911–1969* (Cambridge, 1972), 46–47, 190.

As the table shows, from an index level of 100 in 1911, black earnings were reduced to 69 in 1921. They recovered the 1911 level in 1936 but then slipped. This was not because 1911 was a peak; Wilson, while noting that there was no price index by which to adjust money wages before 1911, estimated that they

---

[88] Rob Turrell, 'Kimberley: labour and compounds, 1871–1888', in *Industrialisation and Social Change in South Africa*, eds. Shula Marks and Richard Rathbone (Harlow, 1982), 45–76.

had been reduced already, by more than 25 per cent between 1889 and 1911.[89] Thus the period 1889–1921 was characterized by the ratcheting down of black real wages. Meanwhile labour productivity, measured by Wilson's index of tons lifted per underground worker, stood at 85 in 1911, fell to 79 in 1921, then reached 100 in 1936. White wages were more resilient in the bad years: 102 in 1911, 90 in 1921, 100 in 1936, all on a much higher scale. The 1961 figures were: black wages 89; white earnings 99, labour productivity 124, while the ratio of white to black earnings was 17:1.[90] It was not until the early 1970s that black real earnings surpassed the 1911 level.[91]

The Natives Land Act of 1913, building on earlier laws such as Cecil Rhodes' Glen Gray Act in the Cape Colony in 1894, took to an extreme the policy of using land alienation as a means of driving Africans out of the produce market and into the labour market. It reserved 93 per cent of South Africa for whites; members of the black majority were not allowed to own or even rent 'white' land. Thus Africans could only be on white-owned land as wage workers, not tenants. That the purpose of the almost total alienation of land from the black population was to secure their labour even more than their land was confirmed, ironically, in 1936 when the proportion of land left for Africans was increased from 7 per cent to 13.5 per cent. Clearly, the 93 per cent figure had exceeded the area that the Europeans were actually going to farm. The government's aim was to force Africans to sell labour services to European employers, but to keep their subsistence farming going, Africans required more than 7 per cent of the area.

The same land legislation that forced more Africans to sell their labour worked by denying them enough access to land, whether owned or rented, to produce large marketable surpluses. The 'rise of the South African peasantry' was followed by their state-contrived fall. The ban on black tenancy, and therefore on sharecropping, hit the African population particularly hard, as that had been a major means by which they could access land beyond the meagre areas left under their ownership. It may also be seen as having a class dimension within the Afrikaner farming community: while it was welcome to capitalist farmers wanting to hire black labourers cheaply, it was bad for capital-poor white landlords. However, the ban was not immediately enforced everywhere; apparently for local political reasons, it was implemented much more rigorously in the Orange Free State than in southwest Transvaal, whose interwar economy was built on sharecropping. Charles van Onselen researched the careers and relationships of a number of black entrepreneurs in southwest Transvaal, such as Kas Maine. They became highly successful grain and livestock farmers in this period, owning the farming equipment and animals – everything but the land. It was not until the late 1940s, when light tractors were becoming much

---

89 Wilson, *Labour*, 46–47.
90 Ibid., 46–47, 190.
91 Lipton, *Capitalism and Apartheid*, 410.

more affordable to landowners with little capital, such that they no longer needed the black sharecroppers' plough teams, that sharecropping in southwest Transvaal really declined.[92]

At the same time, the state's aims stopped far short of proletarianizing the African population. It did not want large-scale movement of the black population to the towns; that would be politically risky and economically costly. Like the Chamber of Mines and the policy experts of the time, they were well aware that European employers would have to pay higher wages if there were no African labour reserves, where the household and subsistence farm bore part of the cost of maintaining the current workforce, as well as all the cost of rearing the next one, and looking after those too old to migrate to work. Meanwhile, more and more rural Afrikaners were being forced by debt to sell up. As Shula Marks commented, it is an irony of South African history that the first major population group to be fully proletarianized were not the Africans but the Afrikaners.[93]

In the protracted ending of slavery in West Africa, the likelihood of loss to the owners of human property because of emancipation was reduced by two trends. The first was that, after a rather militantly anti-slavery beginning to colonial rule in the interior of West Africa, the British adopted a distinctly gradualist approach. Therefore, for most slave owners, there was time to adjust before abolition even began to be enforced. The second trend was the export crop revolution itself. Where agricultural exports were sufficiently lucrative to enable masters to make the transition to becoming employers of free labourers, abolition might be expensive, but not prohibitively so. Cocoa farming was profitable enough for labourers to be hired rather than, through coercion, bought.[94] In Nigerian cocoa-farming, the transition from pawn to wage labour on annual contracts began on the plantation of J.K. Coker, the original champion of cocoa cultivation in the country.[95] But such a transition was not universal. Don Ohadike made the point that in parts of southeast Nigeria, abolition ended the market in coerced labour without, as yet, it being replaced by a market in free labour. The latter happened only with the emergence of

---

92 Van Onselen, 'Race and class'. See, further, idem, *The Seed is Mine: The Life of Kas Maine, a South African Sharecropper, 1894–1985* (Cape Town, 1996).
93 At a seminar in London in the 1980s, when Professor Marks was director of the Institute of Commonwealth Studies. The comment is not made in her co-authored 1980 essay, but one could say that the basis of it is set out there: Marks and Atmore, 'Introduction', 36 43n.
94 Austin, 'Cash crops and freedom'.
95 B.A. Agiri, 'The development of wage labour in agriculture in southern Yorubaland 1900–1940', *Journal of the Historical Society of Nigeria*, 12 (1983–84), 95–96.

a 'new generation of Igbo entrepreneurs' in the interwar period, 'many of [whom] were former slaves or their descendants.'[96]

The early twentieth century saw the emergence of hired labour as the main source of labour beyond self and family. Primarily, it took the form of seasonal migration from areas where export production was or would be absolutely or relatively unprofitable, to the cash-crop zones, mines and urban centres. By the mid-1940s about a third of cocoa farms in Asante (which was about to become the largest cocoa-producing region in colonial Ghana) were worked by hired labourers.[97] According to a large survey in 1956–7, the year before Ghana's independence, hired labourers (wage or sharecrop) outnumbered cocoa farm-owners in Asante by 1.89 to one.[98] Farmers tended to hire regular workers in small numbers. If they could not afford that, they might hire casual labour, often in the form of local youths, at particularly busy times of year. Hired labour was increasingly widespread, notably in the marketing and transport of exports as well as working for the government, including in public works. But most savanna areas – the exception was the groundnut belt around Kano and other northern Nigerian towns on the railway – still participated in the labour market primarily as exporters of seasonal labour, mainly though not exclusively male. If we combine the ILO's figures for the total number of wage-earners in 1953 or 1954 with the UN's estimates of the total populations in 1953,[99] we are comparing underestimates, for West Africa at least. Populations were underestimated in the colonial censuses, while the estimates for the number of wage workers in Nigerian and Ghanaian agriculture are nonsensically small.[100] But for what it is worth, wage-earners as a proportion of the total population (not just the workforce) come out for Nigeria at just under 1 per cent; for Ghana, just under 4 per cent; for South Africa, more than a fifth.

If proletarianization was the future, the cocoa economies of Ghana and southwest Nigeria took a detour. The timing varied, but in both cases an initial trend for slave and pawn labour to be succeeded and then exceeded by a

---

96 Don Ohadike, '"When the slaves left, owners wept": entrepreneurs and emancipation among the Igbo people', in *Slavery and Colonial Rule in Africa*, eds. Suzanne Miers and Martin A. Klein (1999), 204.
97 Austin, *Labour, Land and Capital*, 319.
98 Ibid., 319–320.
99 Eckert, 'Wage labour', 38–39; UN World Population Prospects 2022 (https://population.un.org/wpp/ (accessed 19/06/2024)).
100 Perhaps because it is easy to undercount migrant labourers, also if the sharecroppers were not included given that they do not earn wages. For Ghana 1954, the ILO figure for wage labourers in agriculture was 33,924. Given the 1.89 ratio of hired workers to farmers in Asante agriculture noted below, from a large and detailed survey in 1956–7, the number of hired workers, including sharecrop labourers, in Ghanaian agriculture in 1954 must have been several times the ILO number. That in turn would raise the percentage of hired workers in the population by perhaps 3 points or so.

proliferation of wage labour, gave way to a trend for annual wage contracts to be replaced by sharecrop labour.[101] In Asante, for example, wage labour multiplied from c.1918 until the mid-1930s, after which the migrant labourers, increasingly, would only accept sharecrop contracts. By mid-century, sharecropping was the main form of hired labour. Initially, the terms were that the worker got one third of the crop. Over the decades that followed, those contracts tended to become more favourable to the worker. As already implied, this move away from wage work towards sharecrop labour was not (as one might expect from economic theory) driven by farmers wanting to pass fluctuations in cocoa prices onto the workers. Rather, it was the latter who took the initiative; apparently partly to secure more autonomy from supervision, but also because, in most years, the sharecropper earned more than the wage worker.[102]

As in South Africa, the colonial administrations in British West Africa were keen to avoid proletarianization. Land sales in Akim Abuakwa had made possible the original cocoa take-off in the Gold Coast Colony. In the older cocoa-growing areas land was becoming scarce by the 1940s, and some individual cocoa farmers attempted privately to register their titles of ownership of their farms. The argument that 'the full development of any country' required unambiguous individual ownership was articulated by R.H. Rowe, surveyor-general of the Gold Coast and then of Nigeria, in the interwar years, and the issue was intensely debated by other British officials and intellectuals.[103] But the governors ultimately decided in favour of trying to shore up what they claimed to be the customary position: that land could not be sold to non-subjects of the chieftaincy in question, and ideally not to anyone. The economic logic was that the existing land tenure system, because it distinguished between ownership of the soil and ownership of property created on it (such as crops), provided sufficient security of tenure to encourage investment – and the remarkably rapid growth of cocoa-planting demonstrated they were correct on that. Politically, officials wanted to avoid poorer farmers selling up and crowding the towns. They were also acutely conscious that the African population tended to suspect any government proclamation on land of being a possible prelude to appropriation.[104] Evidently, what had happened in southern Africa was known to West Africans. The colonial government essentially accepted the land sales in pre-1914 Akim Abuakwa as a fait accompli, but sought to stop the trend there, reasserting what they claimed were the customary rules

---

101 Austin, *Labour, Land and Capital*, 423, 544. In southwest Nigeria the trend to sharecropping occurred much later, in the 1970s–80s: Ezekiel Ayodele Walker, 'The changing patterns of labor relations in the cocoa farming belt of southwestern Nigeria, 1950s to 1990s', *AfEcH*, 24 (2000), 123–140.
102 Austin, *Labour, Land and Capital*, chapters 16 and 19.
103 Ibid., quotation from Rowe, 341.
104 Ibid., 339–348, 531–533; Phillips, *Enigma of Colonialism*, 111–135.

against land alienation, especially to 'strangers' (non-subjects of the land-owning chief) but if possible to anyone.[105]

Let us now compare the evolution of real wages in the context of the different institutional settings of wage labour under settler-elite capitalism in South Africa and of African capitalism under colonial rule in British West Africa. In South Africa, black real wages shot up with the rapid growth of demand for mines labour, in the 1870s and 1880s. But they were then ratcheted downwards by a combination of moves from mining companies and the state.

Table 6.3. Real wages and infant mortality in Ghana and South Africa (Black population only), 1910s–1940s.

Decade	Ghana: infant mortality	Ghana: real wages	South Africa: infant mortality	South Africa: real wages
1911–20	295	84	254	100
1921–30	206	139	281	52
1931–40	110	148	302	64
1941–50	106	150	not available	73

Source: Sue Bowden, Blessing Chiripanura and Paul Mosley, 'Measuring and explaining poverty in six African countries: a long-period approach', *Journal of International Development*, 20 (2008), 1049–1079. The table is at 106.

Sue Bowden, Blessing Chiripanura and Paul Mosley have provided data for infant mortality in South Africa and colonial Ghana and also constructed real wage indexes (Table 6.3). They comment, rightly, that the absence of occupation of land by European settlers in 'peasant-export' economies, the term they apply to Ghana, and the consequent wide accessibility of land, put 'a floor under the labour market' and that real wages rose from relatively early in the period for which data are available and, when averaged over decades, did not fall back. In contrast, European occupation of most land in South Africa made African wages there very insecure: their figures show real wages as higher in South Africa at the beginning of the period but then falling drastically before beginning a gradual and partial recovery in the 1930s and 1940s.[106]

---

105 Austin, *Labour, Land and Capital*, 257–258, 516; further, Gareth Austin, '"More and more one cog in the world economic machine": globalization, development, and African agency in British West Africa', in *British Imperialism and Globalization*, ed. Joseph Inikori (Rochester, NY, 2022), 135–169.
106 Sue Bowden, Blessing Chiripanura and Paul Mosley, 'Measuring and explaining poverty in six African countries: a long-period approach', *Journal of International Development*, 20 (2008), 1049–1079.

VI. Ideology and Power

We should ask whether the capitalist trajectories of our cases enjoyed some sort of ideological support. In South Africa, where the settlers came from two of the original capitalist societies, it might seem a safe assumption that market institutions and private self-enrichment, for example, enjoyed broad assent from the white population. This needs qualification for Boer/African nationalism, but, to take the leading example, the disdain expressed by Paul Kruger, president of the South African Republic, was for international/metropolitan capital, rather than for the capitalist system as such. He himself helped set up a stock exchange in Pretoria in 1889, as an alternative to the Johannesburg one.[107] Between the wars, white miners fought – during the Rand Revolt of 1922, even literally – against the monopoly capitalism of the Chamber of Mines, but the Labour Party for which they voted at the next election promoted industrialization in a form which brought state and private capital together, albeit in the interests of manufacturing and at the expense of mining companies. In the 1930s and 1940s a movement of Afrikaner economic nationalism emerged, which one of its leaders termed *volkscapitalisme*: a movement seeking to extend Afrikaner ownership in the economy beyond its traditional base in agriculture, thereby making capitalism work for the Afrikaner people rather than their always having to adapt to it. The movement took concrete form with the establishment of cooperatives and private companies, notably finance companies in the Cape, with which Afrikaner farmers could be persuaded to entrust their savings. The companies went on to invest in other sectors, including manufacturing.[108] Some of the companies created then, notably in life assurance, thrived and diversified into other activities, perhaps especially since the end of white minority rule in 1994.[109] At state level, after 1948 the apartheid government specifically helped Afrikaner business where it could.[110] Liberal critics viewed apartheid and capitalism as contradictory, but successive apartheid leaders sought to make them at least compatible.[111]

Ideological support for, or even acquiescence in, capitalism might seem less likely in West Africa, where the first capitalist governments were the European colonial states, and in the case of Ghana though not Nigeria, the first

---

107 Lucasiewicz, 'From diamonds to gold', 726.
108 Dan O'Meara, *Volkskapitalisme: Class, Capital and Ideology in the Development of Afrikaner Nationalism, 1934–1948* (Cambridge, 1983).
109 Grietjie Verhoef, 'Savings for life to build the economy for the people: the emergence of Afrikaner corporate conglomerates in South Africa 1918–2000', *South African Journal of Economic History*, 24 (2009), 118–163.
110 O'Meara, *Volkskapitalisme*, 248–250.
111 For example, Martin Legassick, 'Legislation, ideology and economy in post-1948 South Africa', *JSAS*, 1 (1974), 5–35.

post-independence government was avowedly socialist rather than capitalist. Again, it has often been argued that indigenous African culture and institutions have been obstacles to capitalism.[112] There are major problems with the latter view, as a generalization; as with Hill's demonstration of the importance of indigenous systems of kinship and cooperation for the mobilization of finance and the organization of land-buying by the pioneer migrant cocoa farmers in the Gold Coast Colony.[113] Karin Barber has also highlighted a culture of support for the acquisition of wealth in Yoruba society, which has some parallels with Asante.[114] Again, in the nineteenth century private enterprise was encouraged in the Sokoto Caliphate, including with low taxes on trade, and also in the Asante kingdom, provided that big self-made fortunes were shared with the state.[115] In Asante there was also a group of militant capitalists who argued vitriolically against the death duties imposed under the independent kingdom, and who again opposed their reintroduction in Kumasi in 1930. They originated as a group of traders, and before the colonial occupation they were resident in British territory where they petitioned the British to overthrow the 'thief King' and make Asante a haven for tax-free accumulation of personal wealth.[116] Their hopes were partly realized, but some of the same individuals were among the renewed group which protested to the colonial regime against attempts by chiefs to levy death duties in the colonial era.[117] There is also clear evidence in Asante of what might be called a moral economy of accumulation: a widespread social consensus that a producer was entitled to participate in the market without confiscatory taxation by a state or monopsonistic profiteering by trading partners. The tax issue arose in 1883, when artisanal gold miners started the revolt that overthrew Asantehene Mensa Bonsu who,

---

112 Jean-Philippe Plateau, 'Institutional obstacles to African economic development: states, ethnicity, custom', *Journal of Economic Behavior & Organization*, 71 (2009), 669–689.
113 Hill, *Migrant Cocoa-Farmers*.
114 Karin Barber, 'Money, self-realization and the person in Yoruba texts', in *Money Matters: Instability, Values and Social Payments in the Modern History of West African Communities*, ed. Jane I. Guyer (Portsmouth, NH, 1995), 205–224; T.C. McCaskie, 'Accumulation, wealth and belief in Asante History: I. To the close of the nineteenth century', *Africa*, 53 (1983), 23–43; Gareth Austin, 'Reciprocal comparison and African history: tackling conceptual eurocentrism in the study of Africa's economic past', *African Studies Review*, 50 (2007), 14.
115 Lovejoy, *Slavery, Commerce and Production*; Gareth Austin, '"No elders were present": commoners and private ownership in Asante, 1807–96', *JAfH*, 37 (1996), 1–30.
116 Ivor Wilks, 'Dissidence in Asante Politics: two tracts from the late nineteenth century', in Wilks, *Forests of Gold: Essays on the Akan and the Kingdom of Asante* (Athens, OH, 1993), 169–188.
117 Kwame Arhin, 'Some Asante views of colonial rule: as seen in the controversy relating to death duties', *Transactions of the Historical Society of Ghana*, 15 (1974), 63–84; Arhin, 'A note on the Asante *akonkofo*: a non-literate sub-elite, 1900–1930', *Africa*, 56 (1986), 25–31.

desperate to restore revenues, had imposed un-customarily large demands on the miners.[118] The revulsion against monopsony was provoked by the actions of European cocoa-buying companies, who repeatedly formed price-fixing 'pools' to dictate the price at which they would buy. That was met, not only in Asante but even earlier in the Gold Coast Colony, by the formation of organized 'holdup' movements, which withheld the cocoa crop from the market. The same provocation in the cocoa belt of southwest Nigeria did not elicit the same organized response, the difference being probably that in Ghana chiefs were willing to put their authority behind the holdups.[119] Finally, an individual economic nationalist should be mentioned: Winfried Tete-Ansá, from the Gold Coast. He lambasted the European trade and banking monopolies, but argued in his self-published book *Africa at Work* (1930) that the solution lay in 'mutual organization' among Africans. He urged Africans to adopt Western business forms, especially joint-stock companies, and appealed to African Americans to participate.[120] He himself founded three joint-stock companies. These included a bank, which – presumably because of an old law that banned Africans from establishing banks on the Gold Coast – he set up in Nigeria. Though none of these ventures were particularly successful in commercial terms, his bank was the first manifestation of what became a major African banking movement in late colonial Nigeria.[121]

All these forms of protest and nationalist practice, in both South and West Africa, have in common that they were not against participation in the market. Rather, their struggles were over the terms of participation and, thereby, over the returns on doing so. This suggests that capitalism in some sense either was already, or was becoming, domesticated within local social and political culture.

VII. Conclusion

This chapter has explored two apparently opposite cases of the emergence of capitalism in Sub-Saharan Africa, as a means of identifying features that may

---

118   Austin, 'No elders were present', 24–26.
119   John Miles, 'Rural protest in the Gold Coast: the cocoa hold-ups, 1908–1938', in *The Imperial Impact: Studies in the Economic History of India and Africa*, eds. Clive Dewey and A.G. Hopkins (1978), 152–170, 353–357; Gareth Austin, 'Capitalists and chiefs in the cocoa hold-ups in South Asante, 1927–1938', *IJAHS*, 21 (1988), 63–95; Rod Alence, 'The 1937–38 Gold Coast cocoa crisis: the political economy of commercial stalemate', *AfEcH*, 19 (1990–1991), 77–104.
120   W. Tete-Ansá, *Africa at Work* (New York, 1930).
121   A.G. Hopkins, 'Economic aspects of political movements in Nigeria and the Gold Coast, 1918–39', *JAfH*, 7 (1966), 133–152; Chibuike Uche, 'Indigenous banks in colonial Nigeria', *IJAHS*, 43 (2010), 467–487.

help us make sense of the variety of other cases within this vast sub-continent. Accepting that the mere presence of markets and merchant capitalists is not sufficient for describing a society as capitalist, neither South nor West Africa was capitalist in 1650. By the 1940s colonial Ghana and Nigeria on one hand, and the Union of South Africa on the other, had some of the characteristics most strongly associated with capitalism. Regular hired labour, almost unknown in 1650, was now widespread in both, and virtually all households had become dependent on the market for their livelihoods, whether by selling labour or produce. These changes in social relations of production were driven by major advances in the productive forces, as Marxists would say, in the late nineteenth and early twentieth centuries.

Before focusing on the broad economic advances and proletarianization let us consider the sources and character of economic change, starting with an attribute which, like the existence of merchant capitalists, is not unique to capitalist societies but is often seen as capitalistic: entrepreneurial attitudes, in the sense of taking a long-sighted, risk-taking and innovative approach to economic life. Such attitudes were not conspicuously lacking in either West or South Africa during this era. Given the traditional tendency of many Europeans during the colonial period to disparage Africans as short-sighted and conservative, the above-cited work of Hill, Hogendorn and their contemporaries was important in documenting major historical examples of the opposite during the export-crop revolution in West Africa. The adoption of an exotic tree-crop, cocoa, was a particularly clear example of risk-taking, consolidated with sustained capital formation. There is a similarity with the 'rise of the South African peasantry' in the late nineteenth century, though the latter (like the continued growth of palm oil production in southeast Nigeria in the nineteenth and early twentieth century) perhaps fits the model of rational supply-response rather than the more demanding form of entrepreneurship required by the rapid adoption of cocoa planting.

There were differences in timing, but both Nigeria and Ghana on one hand, and South Africa on the other, experienced economic changes worthy of the term revolution. In the West African cases the process began in the aftermath of two political interventions: the declaration of the jihad, in 1804, that created the state and single market known to historians as the Sokoto Caliphate, and the British slave trade abolition act of 1807. They cleared the way, not for the end of slavery within West Africa – on the contrary – but for West African producers to find much larger – and eventually new – markets for agricultural commodities that could be produced using methods efficient for the specific environmental conditions and factor ratios that prevailed in the region. The expansion of cotton and indigo growing, and of Hausa textile production and trade in intra-regional markets, was accompanied on the coast by a vigorous supply response to the demands of markets in industrializing Europe. As A. G. Hopkins argued in 1973, the entry of small producers, in the latter case, into export production for overseas markets was a fundamental shift from centuries of the Atlantic trade being dominated by the sale of enslaved people, an activity requiring a larger scale of organization.[122] The export-crop expansion accelerated after the imposition of colonial rule, but again by African initiative, with groundnuts from northern Nigeria and cocoa in southern Ghana and southwest Nigeria. The adoption of cocoa represented a shift to a new and higher production function, a productivity advance. Export agriculture delivered opportunities for higher earnings for farmers and labourers, and higher nutrition both in the cocoa belt and in the area supplying migrant labour.[123] But, the advance in productivity proved a single shift, not the beginning of a series of such advances.[124] African rural capitalism in West Africa generated the most favourable outcomes in terms of welfare advances and poverty reduction among the general population anywhere in white-ruled Africa, including South Africa. In that regard it is consistent with the relatively optimistic view of capitalism in the colonies taken by John Sender and Sheila Smith, writing from the perspective of Marx's view of imperialism.[125] But there is a difference.

British West Africa was not a case of capitalist relations of production being imposed from the outside and displacing precapitalist ones. Land sales played a part at the start of the Gold Coast cocoa take-off, but not elsewhere, partly because the colonial government sought to pause what was an endogenous emergence of local land scarcity and a local land market, trying to stop it spreading beyond Akim Abuakwa district. Elsewhere, while land use was individual at the point of production, full individual land ownership remained for the future. Again, the spread of wage labour was eclipsed by a shift towards a managerial form of sharecropping. The cocoa take-off was primarily a story of African agency, and of a productive mixture of market and non-market institutions, all of indigenous origin. The history of capitalism in colonial Ghana and Nigeria does not fit well with either Marx's exogenous model of capitalism being imposed by imperialism, as he thought was happening in British India, nor his endogenous model of capitalism emerging from below, as had happened in Britain.[126] Rather, it is a story of the *domestication* of capitalism, because of a combination of indigenous institutions and attitudes being compatible with and adaptable to the opportunities for agricultural capitalism in West Africa

---

122 Hopkins, *Economic History of West Africa* (2020 [1973]), 173–217.
123 Alexander Moradi, Gareth Austin and Jörg Baten, 'Heights and Development in a Cash-Crop Colony: Living Standards in Ghana, 1870–1980', African Economic History Working Paper Series, 7 (Lund, 2013).
124 Austin, 'Vent for surplus or productivity breakthrough?'
125 John Sender and Sheila Smith, *The Development of Capitalism in Africa* (1986).
126 Karl Marx, 'The British rule in India' (1853), in *Marx and Engels on Colonialism* (1976), 35–41; idem, 'Preface' to *A Contribution to the Critique of Political Economy*, trans. Rodney Livingstone and Gregor Benton (1974 [1859]), 424–428.

offered by industrialization in the West and the introduction of the technologies of mechanized transport.

In South Africa the mineral discoveries from the late 1860s to mid-1880s offered international capital the opportunity to invest profitably on a scale not found elsewhere in colonial Africa. Private entrepreneurs and the state used the mining revolution as the basis for a general industrial expansion. Historians have often described this as an industrial revolution or industrialization.[127] The qualification is that most of the manufacturing sector, to the 1940s and indeed to the 1990s, remained dependent on tariff protection. It made a rapid start in the 1920s–40s, but its further development was constrained by the continued scarcity of human capital that was the result of apartheid obstacles to black education. A further problem was that opportunities for scale economies were restricted by the limited size of even the largest domestic market in Sub-Saharan Africa; limits that were in large part the result of institutional constraints on black wages.[128] Settler-elite capitalism, by definition, came to South Africa from outside. Taking advantage of the mineral endowment of the country, it mobilized massive resources of labour and realized major advances in economic growth and structural change. But as long as South African capitalism remained in the settler-elite form, it was unable to find more than a foothold for the next stage of structural development, based not on extensive growth (literally more of the same: with additional inputs of labour and capital rather than advances in total factor productivity) but on intensive growth (advances in total factor productivity).

Both the Dutch Cape Colony and West Africa had gone through large expansions in the use of enslaved labour. The proportion of slaves in the Cape population reached about half at its peak, while the proportions in the populations of the larger states of what became Ghana and Nigeria were probably not much less than that by the time of colonization at the end of the nineteenth century. In both cases enslaved labour was used primarily in market-oriented agriculture, in response to the opportunities faced by owners in distinctly different physical environments. In both the Cape and the West African cases slavery was eventually banned under British colonial rule – several decades apart – with compensation for the European slaveholders in South Africa but not for the West African ones. In both cases, the emancipation occurred when the economic conditions for profitable coercion of labour still existed: relative

---

127 For example, the classic article by Stanley Trapido, 'South Africa in a comparative study of industrialisation', *Journal of Development Studies*, 7 (1971), 309–320.

128 For excellent surveys of the evolving debate about the consequences of apartheid for economic growth and development see Nicoli Nattrass, 'Controversies about capitalism and apartheid: an economic perspective', *JSAS*, 17 (1991), 654–677, and Martine Mariotti and Johan Fourie, 'The economics of apartheid: an introduction', *Economic History of Developing Regions*, 29 (2014), 13–25.

scarcity of labour would give workers who could choose their employer high bargaining power. The transition to wage labour took different routes in South and West Africa.

In West Africa it was the export crop revolution that solved the Nieboer-Domar problem, because certain commodities – especially cocoa – were sufficiently profitable that masters could afford to make the transition to hiring labour. The slave trade was succeeded by a market in labour services, mainly supplied by male seasonal migrants from savanna areas too distant from the railway to make groundnut-farming a profitable alternative. Besides the proliferation of waged work in the towns and mines, in cocoa production hired labourers eventually outnumbered farmers.

In the Cape most of the rural population may have been proletarians after 1838, when the former slaves joined the former indentured servants as workers free from a master but also 'free' from land rights. At the end of the eighth Anglo-Xhosa frontier war, the Xhosa people of Ciskei were conquered and largely dispossessed: 'crowded onto insufficient land, [they] had become cheap labour for the Colony'.[129] Large numbers of Africans at least remained as independent farmers or went on to become sharecropping tenants on European-owned land. These latter categories were the victims when, especially with the Natives Land Act, the state stepped up the pressure on Africans to leave the produce market and sell their labour instead. But, as the Act made clear, the state and most settler capitalists were determined not to fully proletarianize the black population. The migrant labour system, based on most African households retaining some sort of access to small plots in the reserves, had the effect that, as Harold Wolpe put it, 'capital is able to pay the worker *below* the cost of his reproduction'.[130] The liberal critics of the segregated labour market were right that it had become a brake on economic growth by the 1980s, but it is crucial to remember that this was not the case during the mining revolution and the early growth of manufacturing. Charles Feinstein, who himself shared the liberal diagnosis of the inefficiency of the apartheid economy, argued that during its whole history before the devaluation of the rand in 1933, the gold mining industry would have been only a fraction of its size had it paid black workers even merely double what they actually received (see Table 6.2).[131]

The artificially low pay of African workers in South Africa enabled employers to pay white workers more than in an integrated free market, which was why white workers fought so hard to resist raising the colour bar in mining jobs. This illustrates the meaning of 'settler-elite' colonialism. Within the white population were many relatively poor people; but in law, and in economic practice, the white population as a whole was an elite.

129 Legassick and Ross, 'From slave economy to settler capitalism', 314.
130 Harold Wolpe, *The Articulation of Modes of Production* (1980), 298.
131 Feinstein, *Economic History of South Africa*, 109–112.

Finally, let us return to the relationship between capitalist and 'pre-capitalist' social relations of production, when they co-existed. An influential thesis is that the latter subsidized the former.[132] This fits the South African story, probably by 1900 and, at the latest, after the 1913 Act. African capitalism in West Africa presented an opposite case. The history of migrant labour in cocoa cultivation shows employers having to concede successively better contracts to retain their work forces, and workers and their children benefitting from correspondingly high purchasing power. The difference stems from the extent of access to land left to the migrant labourers and their households. In British West Africa, the fact that almost all the land – not just a small over-crowded fraction of it – remained in African hands strengthened the bargaining position of the workers, not the employers. The type of colonialism and the type of capitalism mattered.

It could be argued that in this respect British rule in West Africa, while allowing and even supporting small-scale African capitalism, especially in agriculture, set limits to its possible evolution. The profits of African capitalism were somewhat curtailed by the bargaining strength of un-proletarianized workers, just as they were by European cartels in the services sector. This helps to explain why, by the time of independence, African capitalists in West Africa, while flourishing compared to their counterparts subjugated by settler-elite capitalism in South Africa, were still mostly small-scale, and relatively weak in relation to the state.

---

132   Claude Meillassoux, 'From reproduction to production: a marxist approach to economic anthropology', *Economy and Society*, 1 (1972), 93–105.

7

European Empires and the Origins of Global Capitalism

EMMA GRIFFIN

The industrial revolution marks a turning point in world history. Starting in Britain in the late eighteenth century and spreading rapidly to other anglophone countries and a handful of Britain's European neighbours in the early nineteenth century, industrialisation marked the demise of the traditional, agrarian economy. Pushing up incomes and living standards, changing patterns of work, habitation, transportation and culture, industrial revolutions ushered in new lifestyles in those parts of the world in which they occurred and established a divergence between parts of Europe (and other regions inhabited by Europeans) and most of the rest of the world. It is little surprise that the causes and consequences of this pivotal global development have intrigued historians for several generations.[1]

Through most of the twentieth century, this topic was approached primarily as an item of British history. Scholarship was premised on British, or at least European, exceptionalism, and assumed that this exceptionalism lay at the root of the industrial revolutions that transformed certain nations from the late eighteenth century onwards. Consequently, the search was on for those features of early modern Europe – its scientific culture and its institutions, political, financial, commercial or legal – that set it apart from other parts of the world.[2]

In the 1990s, however, global historians began to argue that a wider perspective was both informative and necessary. After all, as they pointed out, on the eve of Britain's industrial revolution, the centre of the world economy

---

1 The literature is large but for some influential works, see N.F.R. Crafts, *British Economic Growth during the Industrial Revolution* (Oxford, 1985); Peter Stearns, *The Industrial Revolution in World History* (Boulder, 1993); David Landes, *The Wealth and Poverty of Nations: Why Some Are So Rich and Some So Poor* (New York, 1998); Joel Mokyr, *The Enlightened Economy: Britain and the Industrial Revolution, 1700–1850* (New Haven, 2011).
2 See especially Eric Jones, *European Miracle: Environment, Economies and Geopolitics in the History of Europe and Asia* (Cambridge, 2003); idem, *Growth Recurring: Economic Change in World History* (Oxford, 1988). See also, Ivan Berend, *An Economic History of Nineteenth-Century Europe: Diversity and Industrialisation* (Cambridge, 2013); François Crouzet, *History of the European Economy, 1000–2000* (2001).

had lain in the east – not in Europe, and certainly not in Britain. Perhaps the most influential proponent of this view was Kenneth Pomeranz, who argued that parts of China were as wealthy as Britain in the middle of the eighteenth century, and that China might have embarked on the pathway to industrialisation had it possessed some of the advantages enjoyed by Britain, namely its American colonies which supplied Britain with raw materials, and its rich, accessible coal deposits which supplied the British economy with a cheap source of power.[3] Pomeranz also coined the term the 'Great Divergence' to describe the gulf that opened between industrialising and non-industrialising nations from the eighteenth century onwards. But if Pomeranz was influential, he was certainly not alone, his arguments no doubt gaining traction through amplification by other scholars, looking at both China and other parts of the globe.[4] As a useful corrective to the eurocentrism of traditional accounts, these scholars drew attention to pockets of advanced development outside Europe and challenged the claim that longstanding structural differences made the great divergence inevitable.

Yet in the lively debate triggered by this provocation, scholars began to question these claims of similarity between China and India on the one hand, and Europe on the other, on the eve of Britain's industrial revolution. Critics not only argued that per capita wealth in India and China was considerably lower than it was in Britain and parts of Europe, they also pointed to profound differences in the social, cultural and political spheres.[5] Both lines of argument undermined the claims that the British economy was rather unexceptional

---

[3] Kenneth Pomeranz, *The Great Divergence: China, Europe, and the Making of the Modern World Economy* (Princeton, 2000).

[4] Roy Bin Wong, *China Transformed: Historical Change and the Limits of European Experience* (Ithaca, 1997); Andre Gunder Frank, *ReOrient: Global Economy in the Asian Age* (Berkeley, 1998); Peter C. Perdue, *China Marches West: The Qing Conquest of Central Eurasia* (Cambridge, MA, 2005); Prasannan Parthasarathi, *The Transition to a Colonial Economy: Weavers, Merchants and Kings in South India, 1720–1800* (Cambridge, 2001); idem, 'Rethinking Wages and Competitiveness in the Eighteenth Century: Britain and South India', *P&P*, 158 (1998), 79–109; Joseph Inikori, *Africans and the Industrial Revolution in England: a Study in International Trade and Economic Development* (Cambridge, 2002); Robert C. Allen, *The British Industrial Revolution in Global Perspective* (Cambridge, 2009).

[5] James Z. Lee and Feng Wang, *One Quarter of Humanity: Malthusian Mythology and Chinese Realities, 1700–2000* (Cambridge, MA, 1999); Peer Vries, *State, Economy and the Great Divergence: Great Britain and China, 1680s–1850s* (New York, 2015). Stephen Broadberry and Bishnupriya Gupta, 'Lancashire, India and Shifting Competitive Advantage in Cotton Textiles, 1700–1850: The Neglected Role of Factor Prices', *EcHR*, 62 (2009), 279–305; Carol Shiue and Wolfgang Keller, 'Markets in China and Europe on the Eve of the Industrial Revolution', *AmEcRev*, 97 (2007), 1189–1216; Robert Brenner and Christopher Isett, 'England's Divergence from China's Yangzi Delta: Property Relations, Microeconomics, and Patterns of Development', *JAsS*, 61 (2002), 609–662.

and only broke through to a modern pattern of economic growth thanks to fortuitous advantages such as coal reserves and cotton colonies.

Nonetheless, there was one element of Pomeranz et al.'s argument that was not so easily put to one side. This concerned the assertion that Britain's colonies and its exploitation of resources beyond its own borders served as the seed-corn for its own process of industrialisation. Indeed, these claims have arguably gained, rather than declined, in significance. In addition to the rise of global history, scholars from across a range of disciplines have drawn attention to the role of resource extraction in the rise of modern industrial capitalism, along with the serious environmental degradation that has occurred in tandem.[6] Alongside these arguments, the rise of the New History of Capitalism, which has recently dominated debates about the emergence of the modern, global economy, has forced attention on difficult and long neglected questions regarding the costs of industrialisation on places and peoples who served the industrialising nations' needs, yet failed to share in their gains.

The New History of Capitalism is a large literature concerned with the origin and place of capitalism in the modern world and goes beyond the parameters of the Great Divergence debate of the early 2000s.[7] Yet at its heart it shares a similar problematic: why did some nations grow rich during the nineteenth century, whilst others stagnated, even declined? In common with earlier writers looking at the Great Divergence, the New History of Capitalism shares an appreciation that the connections between industrialisers and other parts of the world makes a global framework necessary. Where it departs, however, is its switch in focus away from raw materials to human capital, more specifically to the significance of slavery. The New History of Capitalism has elevated the role of slavery as a foundational force in modern economic development. Thus Sven Beckert's hugely influential *Empire of Cotton* argued that slavery 'stood at the center of the most dynamic and far-reaching production complex in human history'.[8] More recent works have posited that slavery was the 'ultimate cause'

---

6 Alexander Etkind, *Nature's Evil: A Cultural History of Natural Resources* (Medford, MA, 2021); Sven Beckert et al., 'Commodity Frontiers and the Transformation of the Global Countryside: A Research Agenda', *JGH*, 16 (2021), 435–450; Jason W. Moore, ed., *Anthropocene or Capitalocene? Nature, History, and the Crisis of Capitalism* (Oakland, 2016); Ian Angus, *Facing the Anthropocene: Fossil Capitalism and the Crisis of the Earth System* (New York, 2016).
7 In addition to the references that follow, see 'Interchange: The History of Capitalism', *JAS*, 101 (2014), 503–536; Sven Beckert and Seth Rothman (eds.), *Slavery's Capitalism: A New History of American Economic Development* (Philadelphia, 2016).
8 Sven Beckert, *Empire of Cotton: A Global History* (New York, 2014), 244.

and 'crucial' to industrialisation;[9] the 'critical factor', a 'key input';[10] and that there was 'no nineteenth-century capitalism without slavery'.[11]

My purpose here is not to add to the growing body of work critiquing the new history of capitalism.[12] Nor do I wish to challenge their central argument that slavery played an active role in British, or North American, economic development. In terms of creating capital, which was subsequently reinvested in developing industrial economies, it clearly did. Instead, my aim here is to query the universalising claims implicit in this literature and to challenge how far an emphasis on slavery takes us in understanding the causes of industrialisation and economic divergence.

When historians first turned to global history to understand the roots of industrialisation, they looked primarily at China and India, and much of the criticism of Pomeranz and others came from scholars arguing that their claims of similarity between eastern and western nations were overstated. The New History of Capitalism (NHC) is also geographically specific – in this case, however, the locale is nineteenth-century America.[13] But if early modern India and China were very distinct from eighteenth-century Britain, the same cannot be said of the United States. There was, to be sure, a profound difference in scale: the extent and range of natural resources available in North America was of a wholly different order of magnitude to those of England, Scotland and Wales. Yet alongside this difference there were strong linguistic, cultural, economic, social and political similarities between Britain and the US. Indeed, the two nations were tied together in a colonial relationship down to 1782 – the year in which Britain for the first time formally recognised American Independence. Culturally they remained very close thereafter. It is perhaps significant that historians of American empire debate the degree of co-dependency between the two nations through to the end of the nineteenth century.[14] Certainly,

---

9 Edward E. Baptist, *The Half Has Never Been Told: Slavery and the Making of American Capitalism* (New York, 2014), 130, 141.
10 Anievas Alexander and Kerem Nişancioğlu, *How the West Came to Rule: The Geopolitical Origins of Capitalism* (2015), 122.
11 Walter Johnson, *River of Dark Dreams: Slavery and Empire in the Cotton Kingdom* (Boston, 2013), 254. Robin Blackburn, *The Making of New World Slavery: From the Baroque to the Modern, 1492–1800* (Oxford, 1997) is an earlier, influential account.
12 Peter Coclanis, 'Slavery, Capitalism, and the Problem of Misprision', *JAS*, 52 (2018), 8–9; Alan L. Olmstead and Paul W. Rhode, 'Cotton, Slavery, and the New History of Capitalism', *EEH*, 67 (2018), 1–17; Trevor Burnard and Giorgio Riello, 'Slavery and the New History of Capitalism', *JGH*, 15 (2020), 225–244.
13 Eric Hilt, 'Economic History, Historical Analysis, and the 'Nw History of Capitalism', *JEcH*, 77 (2017), 649–650.
14 A.G. Hopkins, *American Empire: A Global History* (2018); Zach Sell, *Trouble of the World: Slavery and Empire in the Age of Capital* (Chapel Hill, 2021).

however, it should come as no surprise that the industrial revolutions of two tightly bound nations might have many features in common.

Indeed, it is worth keeping in mind that the arguments about slavery that loom so large within the NHC were initially developed in the context of Britain. This thesis was put forward by Eric Williams in the 1940s, as an explanation for Britain's industrial revolution, and it has echoed throughout the literature ever since.[15] The resurgence and vitality of an argument developed in the context of eighteenth-century Britain in the writing about nineteenth-century America underscores the possibility that the connections between the two nations were meaningful and significant. We need to take care, however, to avoid universalising the experiences of two closely connected anglophone nations.

The reframing of Britain's industrial revolution as a subject of global, rather than purely British, history during the past twenty years has enriched our understanding in fundamental ways. Few scholars today would refute the central claim that the reorientation of Britain's economy at the end of the eighteenth century is best understood in a comparative framework or that the events in one small northern European country had causes and consequences that lay elsewhere. What is less certain, however, is that we have been looking in the right parts of the globe. This chapter argues that Europe is a more obvious, and more illuminating, point of comparison than China, India or the United States. Britain's nearest neighbour was France: a rich, large, populous European nation. France's national wealth, population density, climate, culture and resources were distinct (though arguably not hugely dissimilar) from those of Britain. On the other hand, the autocratic monarchy of *ancien régime* France produced a political framework that was decidedly different. Different too was France's position within global power networks, particularly following France's defeat in the Seven Years War, 1756–73.[16] This military defeat left France with a considerably diminished sphere of influence in Europe vis-à-vis Britain, as well as vastly depleting the extent of its empire and overseas possessions. And yet, these disadvantages notwithstanding, France was within the first wave of nations in continental Europe to industrialise, doing so, along with Belgium and Switzerland, around fifty years later than Britain. In all, then, France makes

---

15   Eric Williams, *Capitalism and Slavery* (Chapel Hill, 1944). See also, Barbara Solow, 'Caribbean Slavery and the Industrial Revolution', in *British Capitalism and Caribbean Slavery*, eds. Barbara Solow and Stanley L. Engerman (Cambridge, 1987); Blackburn, *The Making*; Inikori, *Africans*; Nuala Zahedieh, 'Regulation, Rent-seeking, and the Glorious Revolution in the English Atlantic Economy', *EcHR*, 63 (2010), 887; Stephen Mullen, *The Glasgow Sugar Aristocracy: Scotland and Caribbean Slavery, 1775–1838* (2022); Gareth Austin, 'Capitalism and the Colonies', in *CHC*, II: 301–347.
16   Daniel Baugh, *The Global Seven Years War 1754–1763: Britain and France in a Great Power Contest* (Harlow, 2011); James Pritchard, *Louis XV's Navy, 1748–1762: A Study of Organization and Administration* (Kingston, Ontario, 1987).

an extremely useful case-study, enabling us to unpick those elements of British and American society and economy that were present at the time of industrialisation from those which were necessary for industrialisation to occur.

It is helpful to begin by defining some terms. Before historians sought to explain the Great Divergence, and before the development of the approach we now call the 'New History of Capitalism', our vocabulary was that of the 'industrial revolution', and much of the scholarship was devoted to trying to understand what this thing we label the 'industrial revolution' actually was. At its simplest, it might be defined as a revolution in the process and purpose of manufacture. The word manufacture is of Latin (*manus*, hand) and French (*facture*, making) origin, and refers to the action of making goods. All societies engage in some form of manufacture. Simple manufacture involves taking local resources from the immediate environment and fashioning them, generally by hand, into something useful, necessary or desired – forms of housing, clothing, footwear, transport, adornment and so forth. In many parts of the early modern world, much more complex forms of manufacture already existed and the practice of producing goods that were for sale rather than for local consumption was widespread. Nonetheless, the industrial revolution involved the intensification of manufacture in several respects: the move away from local resources and local markets to more productive forms of manufacture, based on distant resources and sold on distant markets.

To expand manufacturing in this way, several other things follow: some form of new technology will be required; working patterns will change as people work with the new technology; and more power will be required to drive that technology. Furthermore, more intensive manufacturing will call for more raw materials to process. As a result, industrial revolutions are always, by nature, complex and multifaceted affairs simultaneously pushing forward change on multiple fronts at once. But it is important to keep in mind that the defining feature of the industrial revolution is an increase in the volume of manufacture – it does not specify the form of that manufacture or how the increase is obtained. In Britain, the leading product was textiles, the technology was spinning machines and steam engines, the power was coal, the outcome was the factory. But we do not want to place undue emphasis on these things, which are characteristic of Britain's industrial revolution but not necessary for all and every process of industrialisation.

This chapter concentrates on the role of natural resources. It is uncontroversial to state that cotton textiles lay at the heart of the British industrial revolution. And as cotton does not grow in Britain, the industrial revolution therefore involved more than the invention of new mechanised ways of producing cloth. It also involved the switch from Britain's indigenous fibres of flax, hemp and wool to a new, foreign fibre cultivated thousands of miles away. Making sense of how, and why, Britain made this switch from one set of fibres to another requires us to situate the British economy within a global nexus of trade and empire.[17] Not only does this require us to extend our gaze across the globe, but it also takes us much further back in time than the ordinary chronology of industrial revolutions.

Long before the industrial revolution, a complex and sophisticated system of global exchange and trade was already in place. The Portuguese discovered the sea route to India around the Cape of Good Hope in 1498. In the same decade, the Spanish sailed west across the Atlantic to find their own sea route to Asia; Christopher Columbus discovered the Americas instead. The two nations went on to reap considerable benefits from these breakthrough voyages.[18] In the Americas, they gained access to valuable natural resources, primarily silver and gold.[19] And in Asia, they gained control over trade in a range of luxury items – tea, spices, cotton fabrics, silks, porcelains – coveted items that had hitherto been delivered to European markets by Arab, Venetian and Turkish traders.[20] By the early sixteenth century, two more European nations had joined the battle for control of these lucrative Asian trade routes and Atlantic lands. Britain founded the East India Company in 1600 to establish eastern trade routes and seek to take a slice in the global trade in luxury goods in Asia. In its search for a northwest passage to India, it encountered the north coast of North America and established trading posts there. Around the same time, the Dutch chartered their East India Company (VOC) with the same ambition.

Clearly European exploration pre-dated industrialisation by several centuries. And though it had been motivated primarily by a desire to secure lucrative trade routes, it in fact resulted in the incursion of Europeans into foreign lands and resources in far more complex and far-reaching ways. The resources that European travellers encountered came in a variety of forms. There was of course the gold and silver that proved so profitable to the Spanish. But the Americas possessed other things too: some could be gathered or plundered (wood); some hunted (furs and skins) or fished; some cultivated (tobacco, sugar, other crops). Furthermore, the act of voyaging strengthened the nation's fleet,

---

17   Beckert, *Empire of Cotton*; Giorgio Riello, *Cotton: The Fabric that Made the Modern World* (Cambridge, 2013); Giorgio Riello, 'Counting Sheep: A Global Perspective on Wool, 1800–2000', in *Wool: Products and Markets, 13th–20th Century*, eds. Giovanni Luigi Fontana and Gérard Gayot (Padua, 2004), 103–131; Pat Hudson, 'The Limits of Wool and the Potential of Cotton in the Eighteenth and Early Nineteenth Centuries', in *The Spinning World: A Global History of Cotton Textiles, 1200–1850*, eds. Giorgio Riello and Prasannan Parthasarathi (Oxford, 2009), 327–350.
18   C.A. Bayly, *The Birth of the Modern World, 1780–1914* (Oxford, 2004); Jeffrey Sachs, *The Ages of Globalization: Geography, Technology, and Institutions* (New York, 2020), 95–128.
19   Nicholas Canny and Philip Morgan (eds.), *The Oxford Handbook of the Atlantic World, 1450–1850* (Oxford, 2011).
20   Philip J. Stern, *The Company-State: Corporate Sovereignty and the Early Modern Foundations of the British Empire in India* (Oxford, 2011), esp. 83–118.

sailing traditions, and its navy. And where Europeans settled overseas, the new communities potentially formed a market for European goods. So, whilst European exploration may have been largely inspired by a quest for control over trade routes and the search for gold, several other consequences followed. In subsequent years, different actors with different goals came to the fore, creating a complex kaleidoscope of competing colonial priorities.

For the historian of industrialisation, however, it is interesting to observe that from a very early date, the English were seeking to exploit the resources they found on their travels far more extensively than other Europeans. Let us start with the ideas of Richard Hakluyt as expressed in his *Discourse of Western Planting* – a long memorandum written for Elizabeth I in support of Walter Ralegh's plan for a settlement in Virginia.[21] Hakluyt was a writer, not a traveller (he never travelled further than France). He is often described as a 'promotor' owing to his commitment to promoting English overseas expeditions and settlements, and that perspective is clear in his descriptions of the lands he had never seen. Repeatedly, Hakluyt was keen to emphasise the extent of the resources they contained: timber, for shipbuilding, pitch, tar and soap; hemp for cordage; mines, for gold, silver, copper, lead and iron; fish and fish oil; fur and hides. Not only did the sailing fleets employ English workmen, he approvingly noted, but unemployed Englishmen could also migrate overseas and find work there. Hakluyt argued that the English should 'plant forts' between Florida and Nova Scotia to fully exploit the lands' potential. Hakluyt even clarified what form these forts should take. He was dismissive of the Spanish presence in America; they, he suggested, have planted 'thinly and slenderly'; in truth they are 'very weak'; they are but a 'hollow drum', all noise with no substance, or a donkey wrapped up in a lion's skin.[22] Hakluyt believed that a more substantial presence was required.

Richard Hakluyt was writing in the late sixteenth century, at least 200 years before Britain's industrial revolution, but his vision is instructive. Hakluyt imagined an English settlement in the Atlantic that differed from that of Spain, that indeed differed from prevailing models available. Of course, as an active

---

21 Richard Hakluyt, *A Particuler Discourse Concerninge the Greate Necessitie and Manifolde Commodyties that Are Like to Growe to this Realme of Englande by the Westerne Discoveries Lately Attempted, Written in the Yere 1584 [Discourse of Western Planting]*, eds. David B. Quinn and Alison M. Quinn (1993). For discussion, see David Harris Sacks, 'Discourses of Western Planting: Richard Hakluyt and the Making of the Atlantic World', in *The Atlantic World and Virginia, 1550–1625*, ed. Peter C. Mancall (Chapel Hill, 2007), 410–435; idem, 'The True Temper of Empire: Dominion, Friendship and Exchange in the English Atlantic, c.1575–1625', RS, 26 (2012), 531–558; Peter Mancall, *Hakluyt's Promise: An Elizabethan's Obsession for an English America* (New Haven, 2007), 237–243.

22 http://nationalhumanitiescenter.org/pds/amerbegin/exploration/text5/hakluyt.pdf; https://ia802704.us.archive.org/16/items/discourseonweste02hakl_0/discourseonweste02hakl_0.pdf (accessed 19/06/2024).

promotor of voyages, investment, settlements and plantation, Hakluyt was far from being a neutral observer.[23] Furthermore, there was a considerable gap between Hakluyt's smooth words about abundant resources and Spanish weakness. His *Discourse* has been described as a 'prose epic' by one historian, as distinct from an accurate representation of realities on the ground.[24] Nonetheless, there is a discernible focus on the possibility of exploiting natural resources in distant lands, and this marks out English behaviour in the Americas as distinct from those of its Spanish, Portuguese and French neighbours.[25]

The first half of the seventeenth century saw the enactment of this vision of English settlement in the part of North America now renamed 'Virginia'. And a significant body of writing was produced as part of this process of settlement. As much of this writing was intended to encourage settlement and investment, it inevitably contained a very positive account of all the riches that lay in wait. A series of *Declarations of the State of the Colony* averred that the land supplied vines, oranges, lemons, aniseed, almonds, rice, salt, sugar cane, dyestuffs and other luxury goods then imported from southern Europe and the East. The writers claimed there was an abundance of wood – oak, walnut, cedar, ash, fir – as well as mulberry trees for silk, and iron ore. Furthermore, the texts had a clear focus on how these resources could be exploited for manufacture: goods such as timber, wood oils, iron ore, 'a kind of hemp or flax', cotton and furs might be transformed into ships, ship sails, pitch, tar, soap, textiles and clothing.[26] In other words, these writers were not simply suggesting that the land provided fish, bird and fowl sufficient for a comfortable existence for whosoever might choose to settle there, but that there were commodities, a surplus, that might be exploited and exported back to the mother country too.

During this period, the first half of the seventeenth century, ever more attention was given to resources for exploitation. Cotton was increasingly likely to appear on lists of things that could be cultivated. The possibility of making

---

23 Nate Probasco, 'Cartography as a Tool of Colonization: Sir Humphrey Gilbert's 1583 voyage to North America', *Renaissance Quarterly*, 67 (2014), 425–472; William H. Sherman, 'Bringing the World to England: The Politics of Translation in the Age of Hakluyt', *TRHS*, 14 (2004), 199–207.
24 Peter C. Mancall, 'Before 1619', in *Virginia 1619: Slavery and Freedom in the Making of English America*, eds. Peter C. Mancall, Paul Musselwhite and James Horn (Chapel Hill, 2019), 22–24. Mary Fuller quoted in Harris Sacks, 'Discourse', 414.
25 J.H. Elliott, *Empires of the Atlantic World: Britain and Spain in America, 1492–1830* (New Haven, 2006).
26 For example, *A True Declaration of the Estate of the Colonie in Virginia* (1610); Virginia Company of London, *A Declaration of the State of the Colonie and Affaires in Virginia* (1620), 5; Raphe Hamor, *A True Discourse of the Present Estate of Virginia* (1615), 795–856, esp. 828–829; John Smith, *A Map of Virginia* (1612); John Josselyn, *An Account of Two Voyages to New-England* (Boston, 1865), 49–57; Sir William Berkeley, *A Discourse and View of Virginia* (1663).

wealth from silk cultivation was dangled in front of the reader in multiple texts.[27] There was repeated discussion of 'naturall kinde of Hempe, a species of Flagg in that Countrey', that was being exported to England and manufactured as cordage and linen, as well as a form of 'Silke-grasse' which promised 'admirable Returne and Profit'. This land, it was claimed, possessed resources sufficient not simply to 'furnish her owne people, but supply other Nations with Stuffes and Linnen'.[28] A letter, purporting to explain how silkworms might be raised in Virginia, closed breezily with a list of nine commodities, including cotton, by which new settlers might 'get gain and wealth' with ease.[29] Intellectual historians have rightly drawn attention to the ways in which this large and complex literature forged new ideas about empire, exploration and colonies.[30] At the same time, students of British settlement in early America have drawn attention to the very large gap between the rhetoric of these texts and the reality on the ground. As Jonathon Eacott reminds us, 'creating wealth and strength out of New England ... was slow and difficult'. [31] But for a historian with interests in British industrialisation there is something else that stands out. Across these texts, English writers were not only formulating a very particular vision of asset-stripping activities in distant lands for domestic manufacture, they also offered the reader with guidelines outlining how such asset-stripping might practically be achieved.

The particularity of these views emerges yet more clearly when contrasted with French exploration in the Americas. The French, like the English, had set about exploring the Americas in the sixteenth century in the hope of repeating the success of the Spanish with their discovery of silver and gold in Mexico and Peru. These hopes were to be disappointed and for the French too, this gave rise to new motivations and new agendas rather than the abandonment of exploration. But whereas the English quickly turned their attention from gold to the more mundane resources that they did find and the ways in which

---

27 Samuel Hartlib, *The Reformed Virginian Silk-Worm* (1655), 8–14.
28 *Virginia: More Especially the South Part Thereof, Richly and Truly Valued ... the Second Edition, with Addition of the Discovery of Silkworms, with their Benefit* (1650).
29 Hartlib, *Reformed Virginian Silk-Worm*, 16.
30 William A. Pettigrew, 'Political Economy', in *The Corporation as a Protagonist in Global History, c.1550–1750*, eds. William A. Pettigrew and David Veevers (Leiden, 2019), 43–67.
31 Jonathan Eacott, 'Leverage: Foreign Strength in British Economic Thinking and Policy, 1600–1763', *WMQ*, 77 (2020), 552. For the disastrous attempt of Scotland to establish its own Atlantic colony see: Sophie Jorrand, 'From "the Doors of the Seas" to a Watery Debacle: The Sea, Scottish Colonization, and the Darien Scheme, 1696–1700', *Études écossaises*, 19 (2017). The literature on British settlement in north America, and its many early setbacks is large. See, for example: L.H. Roper, 'Conceiving an Anglo-American Proprietorship: Early South Carolina History in Perspective', in *Constructing Early Modern Empires: Proprietary Ventures in the Atlantic World, 1500–1750*, eds. L.H. Roper and B. Van Ruymbeke (Leiden, 2007), 389–410.

they might be monetised, the French imagination wandered to a very different set of concerns.³²

Let us begin with Samuel de Champlain – a French explorer, navigator and chronicler. De Champlain is, of course, no more representative of French thought than Hakluyt is of English thought; he was, however, every bit as prolific and influential a writer and thinker about his nation's overseas expeditions. De Champlain made around two dozen trips across the Atlantic in the very early seventeenth century, serving in a variety of capacities on expeditions funded by the French crown, and producing maps and chronicles of his visits.³³ The narratives of his travels provided detailed descriptions of both the peoples of the new lands and of their various flora and fauna. De Champlain was certainly interested in the natural environment he encountered and the resources it contained, but this was primarily because he wanted to establish what could be consumed by those trying to settle there. Like the British, he encountered some magnificent woodlands on his expeditions, but when he surveyed the trees of north America he thought not of the timber, masts, planks, ships, pitch and tar of his British equivalents. Instead, he enquired what fruits or nuts it bore, whether they could be eaten, and what effect they might have upon the bowels.³⁴ His interest lay in how the life of French travellers could be sustained in this new, alien environment, rather than on what could extracted, exported or manufactured from it.

As French exploration and settlement developed in the seventeenth century, the associated literature branched along two distinct lines: missions and botany, each with its own, distinctive set of concerns. Much of the energy and funding for French exploration in the Americas came from the Catholic Church, and their missionaries were primarily interested in making contact with indigenous inhabitants as a prelude to conversions.³⁵ Like de Champlain, they tended to be concerned about the physical environment insofar as this was the would-be settlers' source of food and shelter. This interest rarely extended to exporting

---

32 Jacques Mathieu, *La Nouvelle-France: les Français en Amérique du Nord, XVIe–XVIIIe siècle* (Québec, 1991); Gilles Havard and Cécile Vidal, *Histoire de l'Amérique française* (Paris, 2003); James Pritchard, *In Search of Empire: the French in the Americas, 1670–1730* (Cambridge, 2004); Silvia Marzagalli, 'The French Atlantic World in the Seventeenth and Eighteenth Centuries', in *Oxford Handbook*, eds. Canny and Morgan, 234–251; Saliha Belmessous, 'Greatness and Decadence in French America', *RS*, 26 (2012), 559–579.

33 Lisa J. M. Poirier, *Religion, Gender, and Kinship in Colonial New France* (Syracuse, 2016), 18–72; David Buisseret, 'The Cartographic Technique of Samuel de Champlain', *Imago Mundi*, 61 (2009), 256–259.

34 Samuel de Champlain, *Narrative of a Voyage to the West Indies and Mexico in the Years 1599–1602*, ed. Norton Shaw, trans. Alice Wilmere (1859); David Hackett Fischer, *Champlain's Dream* (Toronto, 2008).

35 Dominique Deslandres, *Croire et faire croire: Les missions françaises au XVIIe siècle 1600–1650* (Paris, 2003).

commodities for France's manufacturing industries, and the Jesuit missionaries were largely silent on the question of resource exploitation.[36] On the rare occasions where they did address material resources, they did so in a partial and incomplete manner. For example, Jean-Baptiste Labat was a Jesuit missionary and settler of Martinique, where he managed the Fonds-Saint-Jacques estate and worked as an island engineer. His *Nouveau voyage aux isles de l'Amerique*, published some two decades after his return, was mostly devoted to describing the soil, trees, plants and fruits of the islands; however in the sixth and final volume he promised to discuss 'le commerce et les manufactures qui y sont établies, et les moyens de les augmenter'.[37] Yet he did not really deliver this promise. Most of this section was an extended discussion of cocoa preparation, to which a few notes on vanilla and cashew nuts were added. Like so many French travel writers, so far as Labat was interested in colonial resources (and he was not very interested at all), his interest veered towards culinary curiosity rather than the potential for resource extraction and manufacture.

Alongside the large literature in French concerning the voyages and encounters of the Jesuits, sits a smaller, yet nonetheless significant body of botanical works. The significance of the emerging fields of botany and natural history has long been recognised within French intellectual history.[38] What has not been remarked, though, is the stark difference between the agenda of French botanists and that of English settlers and travellers. Botanists, their work often funded by the French crown, took an interest in foreign plants, mammals, birds, fish, primarily as objects of study in their own right, rather than as resources to be exported and exploited. As their activities and expeditions were supported by the King, students of botany dutifully returned to France laden with novel plants and curiosities as gifts to the king and as emblems of his magnificence. Although works of botany sometimes discussed the same natural resources as

---

36 See, for example, Pierre Biard, *Rélation de la Nouvelle France, de ses terres, naturel du païs, & de ses habitans* (Paris, 1616); Gabriel Sagard, *Le grand voyage du pays des Hurons* (Paris, 1632).
37 Jean-Baptiste Labat, *Nouveau voyage aux isles de l'Amérique* (Paris, 1722).
38 Emma Spary, *Utopia's Garden: French Natural History from Old Regime to Revolution* (Chicago, 2000); Londa Schiebinger, *Plants and Empire: Colonial Bioprospecting in the Atlantic World* (Boston, 2004); Sarah Easterby-Smith, 'Botany as Useful Knowledge: French Global Plant Collecting at the End of the Old Regime', in *Re-Inventing the Economic History of Industrialisation*, eds. Kristine Bruland *et al.* (Montreal, 2020). See also, Richard H. Grove, *Green Imperialism: Colonial Expansion, Tropical Island Edens and the Origins of Environmentalism, 1600–1860* (Cambridge, 1995); Richard Drayton, *Nature's Government: Science, Imperial Britain, and the 'Improvement' of the World* (New Haven, 2000); James E. McClellan III and Francois Regourd, 'The Colonial Machine: French Science and Colonization in the Ancien Regime', *Osiris*, 15 (2000), 31–50.

many English works, they did so with a very different slant.[39] For the most part they were silent on the themes of manufacture and industry. Such topics were discussed in the conditional tense, with writers observing that exploitation of one plant or another might be possible, at the same time indicating that those possibilities were not, presently, being pursued. For example, the Dominican botanist, Jean-Baptiste du Tertre, remarked that the inhabitants of the French West Indies were studying how to cultivate the cocoa plant and considered that if they could master cocoa cultivation they 'might make a considerable profit' from it.[40] Like so many French travellers in the Americas, du Tertre was alive to the possibilities of resource exploitation, yet at the same time consistently implied that French settlers had not proceeded far with the work of extraction and commodification.

Of course, it is important to bear in mind that the themes that resonate within French literature around exploration map only loosely onto the reality of French exploits around the globe. The French could, and certainly did, supplement their research interests with the more workaday business of asset-stripping and money-making. France, like its British, Dutch, Spanish and Portuguese neighbours, had its monopoly-holding merchant companies with traditional mercantile goals.[41] French merchants established successful trading posts in furs, fish and other commodities, who doubtless had as little interest in plant classifications, languages and conversions as their English equivalents.[42] In other words, the history of French exploration in the Americas goes beyond the Jesuit missionaries and botanists.[43] Yet taken as a whole, the French trading companies occupied a minor place in the world of French exploration and failed to establish themselves in the style of the British. In most books, discussion around concepts such as manufacture, trade and commerce was missing. Over and again, relations with indigenous peoples and natural history formed the dominant themes.[44]

---

39 Jean-Baptiste du Tertre, *Histoire générale des Antilles habitées par les François* (Paris, 1667), II: 83–88, 90–96.
40 Ibid., 184.
41 Elizabeth Cross, 'The Last French East India Company in the Revolutionary Atlantic', *WMQ*, 77 (2020)
42 Catherine M. Desbarats, 'France in North America: The Net Burden of Empire during the First Half of the Eighteenth Century', *French History*, 11 (1997), 1–28; James S. Pritchard, *In Search of Empire: The French in the Americas, 1670–1730* (Cambridge, 2004); Christopher L. Pastore, *Between Land and Sea: The Atlantic Coast and the Transformation of New England* (Boston, 2014), 11–49.
43 Marzagalli, 'French Atlantic World', 236–239.
44 Pierre-François-Xavier de Charlevoix, *Histoire de l'isle espagnole, or de S. Domingue, écrite particulièrement sur des mémoires manuscrits du P. Jean-Baptiste le Pers* (Paris, 1730). See also idem, *Histoire et description générale de larNouvelle France, avec le journal historique d'un voyage fait par ordre du Roi dans l'Amérique septentrionnale* (Paris, 1744);

In drawing attention to the differences in the ways that French and British writers conceived of exploration, it should not be imagined that I am suggesting that the French were engaged in a benign or altruistic form of exploration, contrasted with the self-interested, exploitative activities of the British. As scholars of early modern botany have indicated, naming, classifying, and collecting the natural resources of distant places are not neutral acts. They may legitimately be understood to involve the exercise of imperial power.[45] And although historians have suggested that the French state was not sufficiently powerful usefully to exercise that power in colonial contexts, we should nonetheless keep in mind that the line between botany and economic exploitation was in reality rather fine.[46] In the pre-modern world, natural resources formed the basis of almost all manufacture. Exotic plants, shells and wildlife might be offered as a gift to the king, but they might also be exploited for medicinal, culinary or other manufacturing purposes. Foreign curiosities could be processed into luxury goods and monetised – exploited to 'get gain and wealth' – in much the same way that the British sought to do with the more mundane items they dealt in: hemp, flax, new 'species of Flagg', and so forth. Indeed, we should resist the temptation to dismiss the culinary as in some way tangential to the history of manufacture. The rise of the French sugar complex in the Antilles later in the eighteenth century demonstrates the economic potential of food processing.[47]

The inescapable truth is that European exploration in all its various forms was harmful, destructive and exploitative. French missionaries may not have sought to strip the environment of its natural resources as ruthlessly as British settlers, yet they nonetheless brought their diseases, to sometimes devastating effect.[48] Equally, the English-language literature was not monolithic and there was a small cohort of English botanists and missionaries with interests and priorities that were not wholly dissimilar to those of the French. The point, rather, is that taking the two literatures as a whole the difference is substantial and real. Throughout the eighteenth century, British settlers and explorers had a much sharper eye on how best to exploit the resources the new lands

---

Claude-Charles Le Roy de Bacqueville de la Potherie, *Histoire de l'Amérique septentrionale: divisée en quatre tomes* (Paris, 1753).
45 Charlotte de Castelnau-L'Estoile and François Regourd (eds.), *Connaissances et pouvoirs: les espaces impériaux (XVIe–XVIIIe siècles): France, Espagne, Portugal* (Bordeaux, 2005).
46 Loïc Charles and Paul Cheney, 'The Colonial Machine Dismantled: Knowledge and Empire in the French Atlantic', *P&P*, 219 (2013), 127–163.
47 Paul Butel, 'France, the Antilles, and Europe in the Seventeenth and Eighteenth Centuries: Renewals of Foreign Trade', in *The Rise of Merchant Empires: Long-Distance Trade in the Early Modern World, 1350–1750* ed. James Tracy (New York, 1990), 153–173.
48 Dean R. Snow and Kim M. Lanphear, 'European Contact and Indian Depopulation in the Northeast: The Timing of the First Epidemics', *Ethnohistory*, 35 (1988), 15–33.

contained than their French counterparts. Their writing leaves little doubt that British settlers were far more actively engaged in asset stripping and resource exploitation than their French equivalents.

This then is the context for understanding French territorial losses, most of them to the British, over the course of the eighteenth century. At the start of the century, New France was a vast territory spanning from Newfoundland in the north down to the Gulf of Mexico in the south, but France struggled to hold onto these extensive possessions in the years that followed. In 1714, much of France's northern territories were ceded to Britain; the rest were ceded to Britain and Spain at the conclusion of the Seven Years War in 1763 and were subsequently absorbed into Canada and the United States.[49] Clearly, this amounted to a substantial re-ordering of France's global empire and of France's position as a global power.

The reason for these losses were complex and no doubt connected in part to some of the features of French colonialisation already outlined here. British determination to extract resources from the American continent had required substantial migration to put in place the people and infrastructure necessary to cultivate and export commodities to Britain. The population of British North America stood at 2 million by the 1760s. The French Canadian population, by contrast, stood at a mere 70,000 at this time.[50] Throughout North America, French holdings were sparsely populated and consequently could only be weakly defended. They resembled, perhaps, the 'hollow drum' or the donkey wrapped up in a lion's skin that Hakluyt had warned Queen Elizabeth of almost two centuries previously – a fact that was recognised by many French commentators. Writing after the loss of colonies in north America, Nicolas-Louis Bourgeois offered an account of the state of Louisiana and Mississippi under French possession, admitting that they had never been effectively exploited, and drawing attention to the contrast with the British colonies.[51] Boston, for example, he described as a large, populous town, with beautiful houses, magnificent public buildings, several churches, skilled workers, cafes and newspapers. In Boston 'one could believe oneself in a good European town', where things were done 'as in London'.[52] Of course, as we know, strong settlement did not in the end mean that Britain could hold onto its north American colonies either, as large, confident, wealthy communities that resembled those of Europe posed problems of a different kind. That, however, is tangential to the concerns of this chapter, which is not about how to hold onto an empire, but rather, how to feed

---

49 François Crouzet, 'The Second Hundred Years War: Some Reflections', *French History*, 10 (1996), 432–450.
50 Marzagalli, 'French Atlantic World', 240.
51 Nicolas-Louis Bourgeois, *Voyages intéressants dans différentes colonies françaises, espagnoles, anglaises* (Paris, 1788), 265–272.
52 Ibid., 228–229, 233.

an industrial revolution – and the evidence here is unambiguous. Eighteenth-century Britain's access to a global resource base was not a lucky accident. It had very deep roots and was the consequence of at least two centuries of sustained activity dedicated to securing the resources required by Britain's manufacturing industries. The French evidence underscores the singularity of this course of action.

Following its losses in North America in the 1760s, France's empire was greatly reduced in size: all that remained were its colonies in the West Indies, and a few outposts in India and in the Indian Ocean. Yet despite this considerable change in the extent of the French empire, its character remained largely unchanged. French commentators frequently commented upon the possibilities for exploiting its colonial possessions, whilst indicating that these possibilities were yet to be properly explored. For example, Jean-François Charpentier de Cossigny, engineer, amateur botanist and settler of Mauritius, quoted a text from 1784 that had predicted that

> l'Isle de France [Mauritius] étonnera un jour l'Europe et l'Asie, par la richesse, la variété et l'abondance de ses productions, et par les ressources de sa nombreuse population. Je prédis qu'elle aura dans la suite des temps la plus grande influence sur le commerce que les Français feront dans les Indes, sur l'existence qu'ils y auront, sur le rôle qu'ils y joueront.

But a decade later, de Cossigny was still repeating much the same view – that Mauritius and Ile de la Réunion were ripe for development and 'have not yet reached that degree of prosperity they might'.[53] Jean-Baptiste Thibault de Chanvalon's comments on Martinique were in much the same strain.[54] St Domingue (modern day Haiti), alone amongst the French colonies, managed to escape the fate of failed development. By the eighteenth century, it had become the largest and most successful of Europe's sugar colonies and was regarded as the jewel in the crown of the French empire.[55]

I have been considering the different ways in which writers with an interest in travel and exploration evaluated the resources of the lands they encountered. Yet these were not the only writers with an interest in natural resources – or, as they were

---

53   Charpentier de Cossigny, *Voyage à Canton ... à la Chine, par Gorée, le cap de Bonne-Espérance et les îles de France et de la Réunion* (Paris, 1798), 39.
54   Jean-Baptiste Thibault de Chanvalon, *Voyage à la Martinique, contenant diverses observations sur la physique, l'histoire naturelle, l'agriculture, les mœurs et les usages de cette isle, faites en 1751 et dans les années suivantes* (Paris, 1763).
55   M.-R. Hilliard d'Auberteuil, *Considérations sur l'état présent de la colonie française de Saint-Domingue* (Paris, 1777), II: 31–32 ; Bourgeois, *Voyages intéressants* 70. See also, A.S. de Wimpffen, *Haïti au XVIIIe siècle: richesse et esclavage dans une colonie française* (Paris, 1797); idem, *Voyage à Saint-Domingue, pendant les années 1788, 1789, 1790* (Paris, 1997).

commonly called in both languages, 'first material'. In both Britain and France, a distinct body of writing that we can loosely describe as 'political economy' in which governing elites and the wider reading public addressed the means of economic improvement, provides a useful counterpoint to the perspective of those engaged in global exploration. Let us take a look at one such example. The *Journal de Commerce* was a relatively short-lived periodical published in Brussels between 1759 and 1762, and ran a series of articles, probably written by Jacques Accarias de Sérionne, about French trade and French colonies that concluded in 1762. The date is obviously significant as it was immediately prior to the loss of France's remaining north American territories. At the time of writing, that misfortune was of course unknown; what was recognised, however, and very clearly so, was that the development of Mississippi and Louisiana was limited.[56] In the familiar lament, de Sérionne observed that Louisiana would be a source of great riches 'if cultivated'.[57] Rice, tobacco, indigo, silk, cotton and leather might all be produced there, he believed, and if they were France might compete with English trade of these items with Europe. Owing to its immense extent and favourable climate, Louisiana might be considered an 'inexhaustable well' (*un fonds inépuisable*).[58] Echoing the views of a much earlier generation of British writers, de Sérionne recommended state funding for voyages and suggested parts of the world he considered ripe for exploration and exploitation – Australasia, a northern passage to Asia, north Japan, parts of north America, Africa, the Pacific. But this, of course, was a pipe dream. Scarcely had these essays been published, and France was retrenching rather than expanding its empire.

De Sérionne's perspective was not only out of step with the realities of French imperial control, it was also out of step with most French thought about the relationship of overseas territories and the domestic economy. In this decade, French political economy was dominated by the Physiocrats. Their arguments were, of course, not monolithic, yet the view that the soil formed the cornerstone of national wealth, rather than business, manufacturing, commerce or trade, was certainly widely held.[59] Even in its imperial heyday, France had had a far more complicated relationship with its empire, and fears that overseas materials posed a threat to domestic industry were taken seriously. Regulations surrounding what could be imported from abroad had always been far more severe than they were in Britain as the French crown sought to protect the interests of domestic

---

56 'Commerce d'Amérique', *Journal de commerce* (Décembre 1762), 10–30.
57 Ibid., 15.
58 Ibid., 17–18.
59 Jacob Soll, 'For a New Economic History of Early Modern Empire: Anglo-French Imperial Codevelopment beyond Mercantilism and Laissez-Faire', *WMQ*, 77 (2020).

manufacturers above those of overseas merchants and adventurers.⁶⁰ In consequence, French political economy looked primarily to domestic agriculture to widen the resource base of French manufacturing, and it was only at the tail end of the eighteenth century, as the superiority of British manufacturing became increasingly apparent, that this perspective began to change.⁶¹

I have been arguing that since the late sixteenth century, French writers, whether writing from the perspective of overseas exploration and settlement or from that of political economy, viewed French soil as the natural source of raw material for manufacture and displayed comparatively little concern for resources that could be obtained from abroad. As might be expected, the situation was different in Britain. In the late sixteenth and early seventeenth centuries, English political economists had also largely held to the view that a nation should develop industries based upon raw materials that were available domestically. Clearly, however, that traditional view ran counter to that of the new body of writing, discussed above, extolling the value and virtue of resources that could be easily and profitably obtained from overseas.⁶² By the eighteenth century, we find a convergence between those interested in the domestic economy and those interested in the colonies, with most writers now agreeing that the exploitation of overseas materials was a necessary (if perhaps unfortunate) expedience. A clear exposition of this view was offered in mid-century by Malachy Postlethwayt in his well-known two-volume *Universal Dictionary of Trade and Commerce*. This *Dictionary*, first published in 1757, was modelled upon the earlier *Dictionnaire universel de commerce* of Jacques Savary des Brûlons, published posthumously in 1723.⁶³ Postlethwayt shared some of Savary's faith in state support for, and regulation of, domestic manufacture, but he departed from the widespread faith of French commentators that domestic resources could sustain a nation's manufactures. He proposed that Britain should encourage her American colonies to produce first materials for her manufactures, for the production of 'such materials for British manufactures as can be raised there (North American colonies) by agriculture, husbandry, or planting in every respect'.⁶⁴ From this date, British writers were increasingly likely to concede that overseas resources were a requirement of domestic industry. For example, Thomas Mortimer, writing in the 1770s, echoed the earlier view that the manufacturer ideally works with materials that can be sourced at home as this affords stability in the case of war. Yet confidently

---

60 Felicia Gottmann, *Global Trade, Smuggling, and the Making of Economic Liberalism: Asian Textiles in France, 1680–1760* (Basingstoke, 2016).
61 [Jean-François de Tolozan], *Mémoire sur le commerce de la France et de ses colonies* (Paris, 1789).
62 See, for example, Charles Davenant, *An Essay on the East India Trade* (1696).
63 Soll, 'For a New Economic History of Early Modern Empire', 525–550.
64 Malachy Postlethwayt, *Universal Dictionary of Trade and Commerce* (1764), xxix.

added that 'it is well known that the small extent of the British Isles could never produce a sufficient quantity of raw silk, hemp, flax, iron, naval stores, &c. for her consumption'[65] and took for granted the role of the American colonies in making good this deficiency.

We also know it was not simply political economists who were thinking about the problem of first materials. The Society for the Encouragement of Arts, Manufactures, and Commerce was founded in London in 1754 by a group of scientists, industrialists and manufacturers with – as its name suggests – the goal of encouraging manufacturing and trade.[66] The pages of its journal have regularly been used to demonstrate British manufacturers' particular penchant for technology and invention, but they make clear that manufacturers were exercised by the search for suitable 'first materials' as well. For example, premiums awarded by the Society in 1762 included spinning technology, which (as we all know) went on to form such an integral part of the British industrial revolution, but they included much else besides: prizes for producing textiles from hop stalks and hemp; in addition acorns, bees, carrots, mangoes and all manner of other organic materials were being investigated as the basis of new manufactures. In 1785, as the prize for producing textiles from hop stalks had not been awarded, the call for entries was reissued.[67] Proposals for breeding silkworms in England;[68] growing mulberry trees;[69] for growing breeds of Chinese hemp;[70] and for making paper from twigs and treebark were published.[71] Indeed, the Society regarded the country's supply of hemp (a requirement for production of sail cloth, canvas and cordage) as more significant than improvements to spinning machinery. The Society offered a prize of £50 for improvement to the spinning wheel and £100 for an improvement to the spinning wheel that could spin six or more threads at one time.[72] On the other hand, they made available £700 for an innovation that would increase hemp supply.[73]

---

65 Thomas Mortimer, *The Elements of Commerce, Politics, and Finance* (1772), 66, 157. See also, Richard Rolt, *A New Dictionary of Trade and Commerce Compiled from the Information of the most Eminent Merchants* (1756); Julian Hoppit, 'The Contexts and Contours of British Economic Literature, 1660–1760', *HJ*, 49 (2006), 79–110.
66 Anton Howes, *Arts and Minds: How the Royal Society of Arts Changed a Nation* (Princeton, 2020).
67 *Transactions of the Society, Instituted at London, for the Encouragement of Arts, Manufactures, and Commerce*, 139–144.
68 Ibid., 1787.
69 Ibid., 1798.
70 Ibid., 1787.
71 Ibid., 1788.
72 *Premiums Offered by the Society Instituted at London for the Encouragement of Arts Manufactures and Commerce*, 4 (1761), 49–50.
73 Ibid., 13–16.

The interest displayed in eighteenth-century Britain on finding a suitably expansive resource base for domestic industries was also evident in the Society's interest in colonial produce. Here, there was a predictable focus on consumption goods for use in both the plantations and for sale on the home market – coffee,[74] cinnamon,[75] breadfruit trees,[76] mangoes and so forth.[77] As ever, however, those surveying the plants and resources of the colonies also displayed an interest in materials for manufacture. In this vein, a form of 'red earth' useful for the construction of cisterns and reservoirs, roofing, foundations and other building purposes was identified;[78] as were gum cashew for 'purposes in dying';[79] 'ché' also for dying;[80] and, as ever, the cultivation of mulberries for silk.[81]

There is clearly much more that could be said about eighteenth-century Britain, its approach to technology, raw materials, and manufacturing, and the consequences of that approach for the onset of industrialisation. In conclusion, however, let us turn away from these well-worn debates and instead situate this British approach within the global history framework that has recently shaped and influenced analysis of the development and spread (or not) of industrialisation.

Over the past twenty years, global historians have rightly challenged the view that the British industrial revolution relied upon British ingenuity and exceptionalism and drawn attention to the ways in which exploitative, colonial relationships provided Britain with advantages over other nations. My purpose here is not to deny the extent or significance of these possessions, but instead to suggest that these should not be understood as an explanation of British industrialisation, but instead as something that itself that needs to be explained. The evidence presented here suggests that it was no accident that Britain, at the end of the eighteenth century, ended up with the capacity to exploit resources in distant parts of the globe, sometimes within the context of colonies, sometimes within asymmetrical trading relationships. It was the outcome of a pattern of behaviour and thought spanning at least two centuries. Britain did not industrialise because, by some stroke of good fortune, it was the lucky possessor of textile-fibre producing colonies. It possessed these colonies and was able to extract the resources it wanted from them precisely because it had been prowling the globe in single-minded pursuit of resources. This was part of widespread, clear and conscious attempt by British elites to source material

---

74 *Transactions of the Society*, 1791.
75 Ibid., 1790, 1791, 1792, 1793.
76 Ibid., 1794, 1798, 1799.
77 Ibid., 1786.
78 Ibid., 1787.
79 Ibid., 1791, 172.
80 Ibid., 1793, 208.
81 Ibid., 1793, 222–223.

for domestic manufacturers, an attempt that was not matched, moreover, by any of its European neighbours.

Framing British industrialisation in this way also helps us to address a series of questions about the industrialisation of North America. Whilst this, as a historical phenomenon, is usually described as the rise of 'capitalism' rather than industrialisation, the different terminology should not distract from the fact that the New Historians of Capitalism are seeking to explain a phenomenon that is closely interlinked with the British industrial revolution. And although it has become historical commonplace to argue that the British industrialisation must be situated in a global context, the same is not the case for historical analysis of the growth of American capitalism, which continues to be considered in isolation not simply from events in India and China, but even from its very close partner and former coloniser, Britain. This will not do. Owing to the British influence, the North American economy had developed along the lines of a peculiarly British model of intensive resource extraction and exploitation. The New Historians of Capitalism would do well to take heed from the counsel of global historians. America, no less than Britain, was part of a much wider global economy, and it will be by widening our frame to consider America's place within this international context that the growth of American capitalism can be properly understood in all its complexity.

8

Capitalism in a Feudal Society?
Property Rights and Economic Development
in Russia under Serfdom[1]

TRACY DENNISON

Could a society characterized by serfdom be capitalist? The restrictions on peasant mobility and monopoly privileges of noble landlords observed in both medieval and early modern serf societies have been viewed, at least since Marx, as hallmarks of feudalism, a distinctly different economic system from capitalism. Detailed empirical studies of serfdom have complicated this story over the years, as sources have revealed lively rural factor markets, high rates of peasant (serf) land ownership, enforceable property rights for rural tenants, and significant capital accumulation among enserfed peasants, whether medieval or early modern. The difficulties arising from attempts to establish clear boundaries between 'feudal' economies and 'market' or 'capitalist' economies have prompted economic historians to think more in terms of economic development over the long run rather than identifiable transitions (if temporally heterogeneous) from one kind of economic system to another. This approach has several advantages for historical studies of development. For one thing, it makes it easier to accommodate the intermingling of market and non-market forces that have persisted across historical space and time. It also enables us to better account for the very different trajectories of societies with apparently similar superficial characteristics (such as 'serfdom').[2]

This long-run perspective has led economic historians to re-frame old questions. Much recent research is centred on the question of how and why western Europe – and northwest Europe, in particular – experienced early and rapid economic growth and sustained rises in living standards relative

---

[1] For helpful comments and criticisms, I am grateful to members of the Caltech Early Modern Group, participants in the Economic History Seminar at Universidad Carlos III de Madrid, and the editors of and participants in this project on comparative histories of capitalism.
[2] And to think about a historical version of 'Varieties of Capitalism': Peter A. Hall and David Soskice, *Varieties of Capitalism: The Institutional Foundations of Comparative Advantage* (Oxford, 2001).

to eastern Europe and other parts of the globe in the early modern period. And why did the end of serfdom not usher in an era of 'capitalism' in central and eastern European economies? Proposed explanations are various. Some researchers have emphasized the importance of geography (temperate climates) and resource endowments (such as coal or waterways) in sustained economic growth.[3] Others, including many of those who study the 'New History of Capitalism', see global empires and the extraction of colonial labor and raw materials as the key variables.[4] Still others view cultural factors as critical determinants: the culture of science, the ideas of the Enlightenment and the rise of 'bourgeois' norms.[5]

This research focuses on another set of explanations for divergence: those that emphasize property rights and institutions. Institutions and their role in long-term economic growth and development have garnered considerable attention in the social science literature over the past couple of decades. Clearly assigned property rights and robust mechanisms for their enforcement have been identified as key factors in contemporary development contexts, and there is now a large literature in both economics and political science devoted to evaluating their historical contribution to sustained long run growth, including, to put it in the terms of this volume, the development of 'capitalism'.[6] The origins and evolution of these institutions, however, remain unclear, making it difficult to derive policy recommendations of more universal applicability. There have been interesting attempts to theorize (formally and informally) the emergence of such systems, but very little of this work engages empirical evidence in the historical literature, especially qualitative evidence from administrative entities (such as courts or other sites of dispute resolution), which often reveal processes of change over time.[7]

---

3   For instance, Jeffrey Sachs, *The End of Poverty: Economic Possibilities for our Time* (2005); E.A. Wrigley, *Energy and the English Industrial Revolution* (Cambridge, 2010).
4   This field has generated a large literature in recent years. Works often cited include Edward Baptist, *The Half Has Never Been Told: Slavery and the Making of American Capitalism* (New York, 2014); Sven Beckert, *Empire of Cotton: A Global History* (2014); Sven Beckert and Seth Rockman (eds.), *Slavery's Capitalism: A New History of American Economic Development* (Philadelphia, 2018); Walter Johnson, *River of Dark Dreams: Slavery and Empire in the Cotton Kingdom* (Cambridge, MA, 2013).
5   On Enlightenment ideas, see Joel Mokyr, *The Enlightened Economy: An Economic History of Britain, 1700–1850* (New Haven, 2012); on bourgeois values, see Deirdre McCloskey, *Bourgeois Dignity: Why Economics Can't Explain the Modern World* (Chicago, 2012).
6   The 1997 volume devoted to the contributions of Douglass North offers illuminating examples of this research program: John N. Drobak and John V.C. Nye (eds.), *The Frontiers of the New Institutional Economics* (San Diego, 1997).
7   Most recently Joseph Henrich, *The Weirdest People in the World: How the West Became Psychologically Peculiar and Particularly Prosperous* (2021).

In contrast to the bird's eye view taken by Emma Griffin in the preceding chapter, this one takes a worm's eye view: a micro-level examination of institutional development on the ground in one locality. It employs an unlikely example to do so: the serf estates of one of Russia's wealthiest noble families. In imperial Russia, noble landlords had sovereign powers over their estates and the serfs who worked their land. Some of the larger magnates created what I have called elsewhere 'quasi-formal' legal frameworks within which serfs – who had few legal rights – could engage in economic transactions, such as land purchases and sales, that were otherwise off-limits to people of their status.[8] The estate archive of the wealthy Sheremetyev family shows us how a set of administrative practices designed to solve one problem (to make property transactions possible for serfs) was extended to a range of additional problems between the late eighteenth and the mid-nineteenth centuries. Once the administrative capacity had been created for land transactions, it could be applied – as a kind of fixed capital – in different contexts in ways that benefitted both the landlord and the serfs. The local archive allows us to observe, over a period of 50–70 years, the development of an entire set of institutions, which appears to have enabled much more extensive economic activity by the time of emancipation in 1861 than we observe when the archive begins in the early eighteenth century.

There is a substantial social science literature on property rights in Russia, most of it focused on the so-called 'transition' period after the collapse of the USSR in 1991. Historians, however, have so far paid little attention to these questions and their deep roots in the Russian past. The view that 'all property belonged to the tsar' has persisted,[9] as has the view that communally oriented Russian peasants had no notion of – or interest in – private property,[10] obviating, apparently, the need to examine the mechanics of property rights on the ground.[11] This is unfortunate, as a clearer picture is needed – not only to deepen our understanding of Russia but to cast new and better light on the long-run divergence in economic trajectories between western and eastern

---

8 Tracy Dennison, *The Institutional Framework of Russian Serfdom* (Cambridge, 2011).
9 Richard Pipes leaned heavily on this cliché in *Property and Freedom* (1999), which is unfortunate since the larger argument of the book is an important one. In fact, the same was said of land in every monarchy, but we have evidence for robust rights to individual property in European societies going back many centuries.
10 The legacy of Chayanov as observed in many existing twentieth-century studies of rural Russia. This is discussed in Dennison, *Institutional Framework*, 6–17.
11 Ekaterina Pravilova, *A Public Empire* (Princeton, 2014) makes clear that the notion of private property, in the political philosophical sense, gained ground in early modern Russia around the same time as in other parts of Europe. But in Europe there were sophisticated systems of private property (assignment and enforcement mechanisms) long before there were political ideologies centred on them, where in Russia property as a political philosophy seems to have come before established practices on the ground.

Europe before the twentieth century. Identifying the ways in which Russian development differed from that of western Europe can offer new angles from which to view European histories, as well as the history of Russia.

I. Institutions in Historical Context

In the literature on the assignment and enforcement of property rights, a distinction is usually made between formal systems of law issuing from central states to which all citizens have access and the private informal arrangements used by contracting parties in places where formal systems either do not exist or are viewed as unreliable. Research for a wide range of societies over time and space indicates that formal systems contribute more to greater long-term growth and stability.[12] It is still not clear, though, how such systems emerged or how to create such systems where they do not already exist. More recent attempts, such as those in post-Soviet eastern Europe, remind us that revising state laws and legal institutions and expanding access to state courts does not guarantee that people will turn to them to resolve disputes.[13] What makes these systems work in some places but not in others?

Some researchers have sought answers to this question in European history, looking for clues about the origins of these institutions in places where they are most deeply rooted. While this has yielded important insights about institutions and their relationship to economic growth, the history of their emergence and development is less clear. This is partly due to the nature of the sources, which are scant for the early iterations of the institutional systems we are trying to understand. By the time we have abundant written records, in the early modern period, these institutions were extensive and well established.[14] It is also due to the way history has been approached in the literature about institutions. Institutions, their forms and their effects, are a well-established research paradigm in quantitative social science, which, at its best, brings empirical data to bear on well-specified questions about institutional *effects*. But explaining institutional *change* over the long run has been a greater challenge. The tendency in empirical studies has been to focus on discrete events, treated as

---

12 Sheilagh Ogilvie and A.W. Carus, 'Institutions and Economic Growth in Historical Perspective', in *The Handbook of Economic Growth, Volume 2A*, eds. Steven Durlauf and Philippe Aghion (2014), 403–489.
13 Jordan Gans-Morse, *Property Rights in Post-Soviet Russia* (Cambridge, 2017); Kathryn Hendley, 'Rewriting the Rules of the Game in Russia: The Neglected Issue of Demand for Law', in *East European Constitutional Review* (1999), 89–95; Katharina Pistor, 'Supply and Demand for Law in Russia', *East European Constitutional Review* (1999), 104–108.
14 Indeed, the proliferation of written records was itself endogenous to the growth and development of formalized legal mechanisms.

institutional turning points – favourites include the Black Death, the Glorious Revolution, and the French Revolution – and their purported effects on some specific economic, demographic, or political outcome variable.[15] This account of change is built largely around exogenous determinants and has little to say about internal political processes or internal indicators of change in social or economic practices.

Internal processes are not as easy to identify or measure; getting at them often requires a willingness to dig deep into the qualitative documents in historical archives: to read decades of court records or other kinds of judicial or legislative documents, or even to study a single archive (for a specific court, or a manorial estate or some representative body) over a significant period of time. In fact, archives themselves can be valuable sources of evidence for change over time. Archives *as* evidence is not quite the same thing evidence *from* archives. The latter refers to the information, or data, we extract from documents *in* an archive, such as censuses, land tax registers, or marriage contracts. To use the archive as evidence means considering the kinds of documents that were generated and preserved, how (or whether) these changed over time, and what these changes imply about changes in social, economic, or legal practices.[16]

The story told in this chapter is based on changes observed in an existing archive: sometimes they are new kinds of documents detailing new transactions, and sometimes they are familiar forms of documents that begin to mention new practices or new populations. In most cases, they were not triggered by any specific event or decree (that we know of). These are important as they hint at real change in specific practices – unlike decrees or proclamations which tend to tell us what authorities *wanted* to happen rather than what actually did. Changes in forms of documentary evidence give us hints about those shifts in the distribution of power or wealth below the surface which could have given rise to the more visible conflicts that attract greater attention.

Russia seems an unlikely place to look for clues regarding the development of institutions to support property rights, not least because it has presented as an acute case of institutional dysfunction since well before the 1917 Revolution. But there were pockets of functionality in imperial Russia, at the local level, that generated better economic outcomes than is often assumed. How did such places come into existence? The archive studied here suggests a process of institutional innovations that was quite accidental; these innovations arose as ways to solve local problems, not as part of any plan to improve the local economy

---

15 Examples include Douglass C. North, J.J. Wallis, and Barry R. Weingast, *Violence and Social Orders* (Cambridge 2009); Daron Acemoglu, Davide Cantoni, Simon Johnson, and James A. Robinson, 'The Consequences of Radical Reform: The French Revolution', *AmEcRev* (2011) 3286–3307.
16 Warren C. Brown *et al.* (eds.), *Documentary Culture and the Laity in the Early Middle Ages* (Cambridge, 2013).

or raise standards of living. This case study raises interesting questions about the motivations for these changes and the implications of this example for our understanding of economic growth and development. Furthermore, that longer-term outcomes were different in Russia than they were in western Europe enables us to speculate a bit on what was different about European institutional frameworks and how this might have been relevant to long-run divergence between west and east. The existing literature on institutions in history focuses overwhelmingly on western Europe (and especially on England). The view from *outside* this region can offer a useful perspective on European development, as certain features come into better focus in comparative context.

II. Serfdom in Imperial Russia: Background

Serfdom in Russia was codified by tsarist decree in the seventeenth century. The Law Code of 1649 (called the 1649 *Ulozhenie*) formally restricted the already limited mobility rights of Russian peasants on noble estates, prohibiting them from ever leaving the lands they worked at the time of the decree. (Before 1649, they were free to seek new tenancies during one designated period each year.) The decree was supposed to deter competition among landholders for scarce labor by prohibiting the recruitment of other lords' serfs and the abandonment of estate lands by peasants themselves. The law gave noble landowners broad powers of enforcement – of both state decrees and landlords' own regulations – on their holdings, such that state authority was said to 'stop at the gates of the manor'.

The low fiscal and administrative capacity of the early modern Russian state made land an important tool; it became one of the main forms of compensation for loyalty and service to the crown. Most patrimonial holdings were relatively small and were worked by a labour force of under 100 serfs. The nobles who held such estates usually resided on them and were heavily involved in their management. These estates generated relatively few written records compared to the vast holdings of the noble grandees – the 1 percent of noble families who held more than 50 per cent of proprietary serfs. This group had multiple holdings – in some cases 40–50 estates – across the Russian empire and possessed tens – even hundreds – of thousands of serfs. Many of these were old princely families, whose loyalty to the tsar was secured with gifts of land and serfs, beginning with the reign of Alexei Romanov in the late seventeenth century. Their names appear frequently in accounts of imperial Russian history, and include, among others, the Gagarins, Golitsyns, Naryshkins, Orlovs, Sheremetyevs, and Stroganovs. These noble families resided at the imperial court in St Petersburg and were among the tsar's highest ranking military officers and counsellors.

These powerful magnates held multiple estates in different provinces of European Russia. Surviving archives indicate that somewhere around the early to mid-eighteenth century they began using centralized administrative systems to govern their disparate holdings from their chancery offices (канцелярия) in the capital. These administrative systems produced regular sets of 'Instructions' (инструкции) – the rules and regulations in accordance with which an absentee landlord's local holdings should be managed. Each individual estate in this larger system had a local administrative office (вотчинное правление), which was run by an estate manager, often referred to in the literature as a 'bailiff' (приказчик), and a host of other officials (selectmen, tax collectors, guards/police, scribes) who were either hired directly by the landlord or selected from among the serf population. These were the officials tasked with ensuring that the instructions issued by central chanceries were followed.

These sets of 'instructions' covered a range of topics from communal land distribution, the use of common pastures and wood, the collection of taxes, the regulation of marriage and household formation, and the specific punishments to be meted out for violations of estate policy. Many landlords issued updated versions at various points – every 15 or 20 years, on average.[17] While there were many similarities in the instructions of the wealthy noble estate owners, they were far from identical. In some cases, landlords issued region-specific versions: one set for their predominantly agrarian holdings in the Central Black Earth region, another for their proto-industrial, wage economy estates in the Central Industrial Region. Some issued only a basic set of instructions for all holdings, and gave local bailiffs greater leeway to make decisions on the ground. And while many of the same issues were addressed by landlords in their instructions, their approaches could be quite different. Some landlords (such as the Gagarins) took more explicitly coercive measures to ensure their rules were followed, ordering bailiffs to use corporal punishment and other harsh punitive measures (including banishment to far-off settlements) to ensure compliance.[18] Others (Baki estate) did without bailiffs and allowed the communal officers, chosen from among the resident serfs, to manage the day-to-day affairs of their estates.[19] Still others sought compliance through monetary fees and fines administered by hired estate managers. Most used some combination of these approaches.

---

17 Selected examples on various themes from a range of estates were published in the 1980s as part of a series called *Материалы по истории сельского хозяйства и крестьянства России*. See, for instance, *Сельскохозяйственные инструкции (первая половина XVIII в.)* (Москва, 1984) (ред. ...).
18 Dennison, *Institutional Framework*, xx.
19 Edgar Melton, 'The Magnate and her Trading Peasants: Countess Lieven and the Baki Estate 1800–1820', *Jahrbücher für Geschichte Osteuropas*, 47 (1999), 40–55.

For landlords who used them, the instructions served as a kind of ersatz legal framework, setting out the rules by which their serfs, who were effectively their subjects, should abide and the consequences for violating those rules. While the instructions varied in certain respects from landlord to landlord, they all give the impression that these wealthy magnates were the rulers of smaller states within a state. This hardly surprises when we consider that proprietary serfs in Russia were not legal persons like free peasants were. They had no access to civil institutions and were formally prohibited from engaging in economic transactions with free persons.

III. Governing Serf Estates: The Sheremetyev Example

The estate management practices established by the Sheremetyev family, one the most powerful noble dynasties in imperial Russia (if not *the* most powerful), are the focus of this study, as their approach appears to have been unique in some certain important respects.[20] The Sheremetyevs were among the wealthiest landholders in Russia, and their serfs were among the wealthiest, too. The standard of living on Sheremetyev estates was known by contemporaries to be above the average, and a remarkable number of Sheremetyev serfs ranked among the very well off; many were even better off than lesser nobles. A few, like the Ivanovo textile entrepreneur, Ivan Grachev, became millionaires. Others reported substantial earnings from smaller-scale manufacturing, trade, and crafts, with some buying their way into the merchantry over the course of the nineteenth century.[21]

It is widely acknowledged in the historical literature that serfs on the Sheremetyev estates enjoyed higher standards of living than other serfs. This is often attributed, vaguely, to the kind of 'enlightened seigneurialism' practiced by these magnates, or to the vast wealth of the Sheremetyevs themselves, which enabled them to underwrite serf enterprises on their estates or make loans to their more entrepreneurial serfs.[22] While there are a few scattered examples of this kind of assistance in the historical record, it cannot account for the differences we observe systematically between the estates of the Sheremetyev

---

20 There is no evidence to indicate that other wealthy landlords developed systems of formal mechanisms for assigning property rights and resolving disputes like the Sheremetyevs.
21 Dennison, *Institutional Framework*; Л.С. Прокофьева, *Крестьянская община в России* (Ленинград, 1981); К. Н. Щепетов, *Крепостное право во вотчинах Шереметьевых* (Москва, 1947).
22 Edgar Melton, 'Enlightened Seignorialism and its Dilemmas in Serf Russia: 1750–1830', *JMH*, 62 (1990), 675–708.

family (across successive generations) and those of other wealthy landlords.[23] It seems far more likely, as I have argued elsewhere, that it was the administrative system of the Sheremetyevs – the way their estates were governed – that gave rise to the extensive market activity and high standards of living we find on their estates. By providing a quasi-formal legal framework within which serfs – who were legally excluded from recourse to civil institutions – could engage in a variety of economic transactions, the Sheremetyevs reduced the risk to serfs of participation in land, labor, and credit transactions on their own estates, and well beyond, including transactions with outside serfs, with merchants and even with noble landlords.[24] But evidence from the Sheremetyev archive suggests that this outcome was not planned; their administrative infrastructure evolved over time in response to local demands and its stimulating effects on the local economy were incidental – and cumulative.

The Sheremetyevs held over 50 estates in 17 different Russian provinces, on which lived over 350,000 serfs. Since the Sheremetyevs – successive generations of them – were important figures at the court of the tsar, these far-flung estates were managed from a central office at their St Petersburg palace. The estate archives offer us clues about the evolution of administrative practices, and about the organization of local society and the serf economy. This chapter uses the archive for the Sheremetyev estate of Voshchazhnikovo, located in Yaroslavl' Province, some 300 kilometers northeast of Moscow. Voshchazhnikovo was home to roughly 3,500 serfs across the eighteenth and nineteenth centuries. It was neither the largest nor smallest of the Sheremetyev estates, nor was it the only one of their estates in Yaroslavl' Province. It had no economic specialism – unlike the textile manufacturing estates in neighboring provinces, from which so many of the examples of landlord support for enterprise are drawn. But like other Sheremetyev estates, Voshchazhnikovo had a lively local economy. By the mid-nineteenth century we observe extensive markets in land, labor, and credit, rural manufactories, and a burgeoning service industry. Serfs transacted with a wide range of people from outside the estate and across the broader central industrial region. The estate archive offers us suggestive hints about the process of economic development.

Looking across the whole set of surviving materials, we can observe a slow but steady growth in the number and type of documents generated between the years 1750 and 1860.[25] It seems that administrative officials were keeping more

---

23 Klaus Gestwa, *Protoindustrialisierung in Rußland: Wirtschaft, Herrschaft, und Kultur in Ivanovo und Pavlovo 1741–1932* (Göttingen, 1999) discusses the context of the prosperous textile industry located on the Sheremetyevs' Ivanovo estate.
24 Dennison, *Institutional Framework*.
25 This discussion is based on the documents found in RGADA, f. 1287, op. 3, archive of the Voshchazhnikovo Estate in Yaroslavl' Province. There are about 3,000 documents (*dela*) for Voshchazhnikovo over this period; they show considerable variation in length and level

records about more kinds of activities over this period. This is borne out by the records themselves, which, as we will see, on occasion make explicit reference to the adoption of new policies. The earliest documents, from the first half of the eighteenth century, are one-off 'instructions' and decrees related to things like: the carrying out of the state tax census (the so-called 'soul revisions'), the provision of travel documents for serfs who wished to work outside the estate boundaries, the collection of feudal levies, communal meeting decisions, donations to estate parishes, and the provision of legal documents enabling serfs to buy additional land (more will be said about this shortly). The range of activities covered grows gradually from the 1740s, and the first full set of estate instructions, detailed in 29 separate points over 30 pages, appears in 1796. This is a comprehensive set of administrative guidelines for the Sheremetyev estates, setting out the procedures for everything from tax collection to military conscription, the distribution of land, the election of communal officials, marriage, household policies, and much more. The instructions make explicit the rules and the consequences for breaking them (monetary fines, imprisonment, exile).

As a coherent set of governing procedures gradually emerged, the Sheremetyevs also expanded the services offered to serfs on their estates. The first services recorded were those offered by many of the large landholding magnates: a work-around that enabled serfs to buy land or to obtain a document that permitted travel and work beyond estate boundaries. The 1649 Law Code, which formally established serfdom, forbade enserfed peasants from selling, purchasing, or holding land in their own names. Some landlords helped serfs circumvent this obstacle by allowing them to purchase land in the landlord's name with a legal document, in which the landlord at the same time renounced all subsequent rights to the land.[26] Many serfs availed themselves of this service and the archives of wealthy landlords are full of contracts for land purchased by individual serfs, beginning in the early 1700s.[27] The other service offered early on was the provision of 'passports' to loosen mobility constraints. This was a legal document that permitted serfs, whose mobility was formally restricted, to be away from their estates for extended periods of time (months or years at a time), usually to engage in wage labor in towns.[28] Again, the archival record

---

of recorded detail. A detailed account of the social and economic life of this estate, based on this archive, is in Dennison, *Institutional Framework*. This chapter uses this same archive to examine the development of the thriving local economy.
26 Though it must be noted that this arrangement was not *entirely* without constraint; as part of the agreement, any subsequent plan to alienate the purchased land had to have the landlord's approval.
27 Dennison, *Institutional Framework*, 143–145.
28 Ibid., 158–160.

shows that many of these documents were issued, with numbers increasing steadily right up to emancipation in 1861.[29]

These services were not only of use to serfs, who were legally constrained in their economic transactions, but they benefitted the landlords, too. The land that serfs purchased in the landlord's name was owned by the serfs and acknowledged as such by landlords; but in official records, it counted as land owned by the lord, making estate holdings appear larger than they actually were.[30] They also benefitted from serfs' possession of land in that it contributed to an improvement in the serfs' economic position and made it possible to extract greater revenues from them. The same was true of the travel documents which enabled serfs to take advantage of wage labor opportunities elsewhere and increased their ability to pay their rents and dues in full and on time.[31] Moreover, in the short term, landlords benefitted by charging fees for these services, giving them extra revenues on top of existing rent streams.[32]

As noted, many of the wealthy landlords, the ones who managed and kept detailed records for multiple estates, offered these two services. The Sheremetyevs, however, appear to have gradually extended the range of administrative and legal services they offered to their serfs – well beyond what other absentee peers offered to theirs. Furthermore, this expansion of services does not seem to have been undertaken by design; there is no correspondence that hints at any kind of larger plan or at the notion that these services might bring greater economic returns to serfs and landlords alike.[33] Rather, we see a kind of piecemeal evolution that was largely a response to demand from serfs themselves. What started with the provision of two specific services to circumvent legal restrictions (land purchase and mobility) became, by the mid-nineteenth century, a complex administrative apparatus that offered a wide

---

29   The steady increase in migration to urban areas was not unique to Sheremetyev serfs. See Jeffrey Burds, *Peasant Dreams and Market Politics: Labor Migration and the Russian Village, 1861–1905* (Pittsburgh, 1998); Boris B. Gorshkov, 'Serfs on the Move: Peasant Seasonal Migration in Pre-reform Russia 1800–61', *Kritika: Explorations in Russian and Eurasian History*, 1 (2000), 627–656.

30   In official Sheremetyev reports on landholdings, they are careful to note that there are 'lands purchased by serfs themselves and in their possession, for which no payments are made to my treasury'. RGADA, f. 1287, op. 3, ed. khr. 555, l. 21 (Estate Instructions 1796/1800).

31   Many families at Voshchazhnikovo had members living and working in other areas, including Moscow, St Petersburg, Riga, Helsinki – as well as smaller cities closer to the estate (Rostov Veliki, Uglich, Borisoglebsk).

32   The fees ranged from a few kopecks to a few roubles, depending on the service. They cost considerably less than quitrent dues or state taxes and were clearly not so onerous as to prevent less well-off serfs from using them. See n. 36 below.

33   The lack of intention goes some way toward explaining why the Sheremetyevs remained unique in their approach to estate management. It was unplanned and, as far as one can tell, never acknowledged as critical to their estates' prosperity.

range of notarial, dispute resolution and contract enforcement services. Once the infrastructure for handling land purchases and travel documentation had been established, estate officials realized that they could adapt it for other uses.

The demand for legal services appears to have been strong. Even serfs who were not in the more prosperous strata of the estate population were willing to pay for notarial services and the extra-local forms of dispute resolution the administration offered.[34] The archive contains, for instance, documents registering credit transactions – even among family members. Brothers lent to brothers, who pledged land or trade inventory as collateral.[35] In the cases of default, it is noted in the sources that the collateral was seized in accordance with the terms of the contract. One especially detailed case shows the inner workings of the administration. A middling serf woman who earned a living as an itinerant peddler died in 1819 with numerous debts to a wide range of creditors from all strata of society across several provinces. Upon her death, the Sheremetyev administration collected registered evidence of her debts and organized the auction of her assets, including trade inventory, to pay off creditors.[36] This is especially illuminating as it demonstrates both the Sheremetyevs' commitment to their administrative obligations *and* the ways in which the services they provided enabled serfs to extend their economic activity beyond subsistence agriculture and well beyond the boundaries of their home estates.

Other services included the registration of pre-mortem contracts, such as the case in which a family patriarch turned his land over to his son, on the condition that he and his unmarried daughter (the heir's sister) would be provided for so long as they lived.[37] And complex transactions related to recruitment obligations appear, with the administration allowing serfs to purchase exemption certificates for themselves or their sons or to formally draw up terms under which a particular son would agree to be conscripted if the family's turn came up in the annual recruitment lottery. In fact, it is a conscription-related case that gives us some hints about the way in which the Sheremetyevs approached the provision of services and the expansion of their administrative system at the local level. In 1857, a Voshchazhnikovo serf who had purchased a conscription exemption certificate requested permission to sell his exemption to another serf. Local officials wrote to the Sheremetyevs' central office in St Petersburg to ask for guidance, since this

---

34   The Sheremetyevs used a progressive taxation system which required them to divide households into three tiers: prosperous, middling, and poor. For the Voshchazhnikovo estate, it was, in many cases, possible to link the serf names in registered transactions to socioeconomic tiers. We find representatives of all but the very poorest stratum in recorded transactions. See Dennison, *Institutional Framework*, 132–198.
35   RGADA, f. 1287, op. 3, ed. khr. 1155, l. 1 (Serf Contracts, 1832. The case of the Dolodanov brothers).
36   RGADA, f. 1287, op. 3, ed. khr. 729 (Petition Regarding Credit, 1819. The case of Anna Shatilova).
37   RGADA, f. 1287, op. 3, ed. khr. (Contracts).

was the first instance of such a request. The central administration responded that such transactions were not uncommon on other Sheremetyev estates and therefore ought to be permitted at Voshchazhnikovo as well.[38] This is one of the few explicit references in the archive to a conscious effort on the part of officials to coordinate policies across estates, as well as a willingness to respond to serfs' engagement in new kinds of economic transactions.

The Sheremetyev archive provides a window on the evolution of an estate administrative system over a century, shining interesting light on the interplay between the demand from serfs for more formalized mechanisms for dispute resolution and willingness of the landlord to supply them. The evidence for the Sheremetyev estates indicates that this system evolved in the following way. First, the Sheremetyevs began by offering a service that enabled the peasants on their estates to overcome the prohibition on serf ownership of land. Land transactions could be undertaken in the name of the landlord, who, at the time of purchase, would waive his right to the land or to the proceeds of a sale or rental arrangement, effectively giving the serf full ownership rights. The administration proved its credibility over time by consistently honoring serfs' rights to the lands they had purchased in the Count Sheremetyev's name. This must have gone some way toward bolstering demand for the additional services that started to appear later. After the system of registering land transactions with the estate administration had been well established – and had proven useful in cases of disputes – we begin to see evidence that other kinds of transactions were being formalized: contracts for land and real estate transactions among serfs; labor arrangements; various forms of credit; household divisions and the allocation of tax and conscription burdens; wills and pre-mortem inheritance contracts. The timeline appears as something like this: systematic records of land transactions and the registration of passports appear from about the 1750s; the first dispute resolution documents for credit and intra-estate land transactions appear in the 1790s; and by the 1810s/20s recorded instances of a much broader range of transactions fill the books.

At the same time, references to a wider range of economic activities begin to appear in the archive. In addition to serfs traveling far afield to engage in trade (St Petersburg, Helsinki, Odessa) and the establishment of rural industries (brick and paper manufactories), the archives indicate the rise of new services in the 1820s and 1830s (innkeeping, transportation and even tutoring children) as well as new forms of consumption (real estate, clothing, and household goods). There was also considerable capital accumulation among the serf population, which was acknowledged in the Sheremetyevs' progressive taxation scheme which levied different rates on those with capital worth under 500 roubles, those with capital valued between 500 and 1,000 roubles, and those with capital

---

38   RGADA, f. 1287, op. 3, ed. khr. 2312, l. 26 (Instructions and Decrees, 1857).

valued more than 1,000 roubles.[39] (For reference, the annual quitrent levies per household ranged from 15–60 roubles per year, so these are substantial assets!) Serfs built luxurious homes (over one-third of families had two-level houses of either stone or wood with glass windows, some of which were decorated in the 'merchant style'),[40] owned land far from the estate (in other districts or provinces),[41] held trade inventory and other assets – all of which they used as enforceable loan collateral for many of the credit transactions recorded in the archive.[42] In short, Russian serfs transacted in a remarkably sophisticated market economy.

It is reasonable to wonder why, if this system generated such benefits to the economy (and, as a result, to the Sheremetyevs' coffers), there were no documented attempts by other landlords to emulate it. But we cannot assume that the connection between greater security in property rights and the expansion of the local economy was obvious to contemporaries. (It is difficult to 'prove' even retrospectively, though the archival findings, in light of more recent social science research, are highly suggestive.) There is no indication in the sources that the Sheremetyevs saw this connection. They appear to have been focusing on solving real problems in the moment. Their serfs were clearly keen to formalize transactions and to expand their economic horizons, and the Sheremetyevs had an administrative apparatus that they could use to accommodate that – and charge fees for it along the way. But it should be noted that the administrative apparatus itself was not cheap; it was comprised of paid officials, from scribes to clerks to estate managers, who were charged with implementing the 'instructions' as well as the innovations on them. Not every Russian landlord had the same budget constraint; if there was no obvious connection at the time between the administrative infrastructure and the economic returns, then it is hard to imagine that other landlords would have willingly allocated scarce resources to building an expensive infrastructure like this.

That the Sheremetyevs' administrative system was originally designed to compensate for the lack of alternatives is important to understanding why it never developed into a more comprehensive system of formal property rights and legal mechanisms that extended across the whole society. In contrast to institutional equivalents in pre-modern Europe (where serfdom existed), the Sheremetyevs' system was not connected to any larger framework of practices and procedures to secure property or resolve disputes. It was more like a private system (services for a fee) for local residents without access to civil (or ecclesiastical or even other private) institutions. That said, it was not a private order

---

39   RGADA, f. 1287, op. 3, ed. khr. 555, ll. 49–50 (Estate Instructions, 1796/1800).
40   RGADA, f. 1287, op. 3, ed. khr. 1598 (Report on Serfs' Houses, 1843).
41   RGADA, f. 1287, op. 3, ed. khr. 2320, ll. 76–7 (Descriptions of Estates, 1858).
42   RGADA, f. 1287, op. 3, ed. khr. 1108 (Serf Contracts, 1831); RGADA, f. 1287, op. 3, ed. khr. 1155 (Serf Contracts, 1832).

system, but more like a state within a state; the system was, at least internally, formalized and transparent and open to all Sheremetyev subjects. And while this administrative apparatus expanded in scope and became quite sophisticated over time, it nonetheless remained an institutional island within European Russia, and this lack of larger integration limited the spillover effects.[43] When the formal rights of landlords over their serf subjects were abolished in 1861, the Sheremetyev system ceased operations. The last recorded transactions in the archive are for the years around 1859–61. From the 1860s on, the archive consists in a set of sporadic records related to land allocations and monies due/ received. There was no larger an interconnected system of property rights that took over the functions that the Sheremetyevs' administration performed. This feature is especially remarkable in the comparative context of serfdom and emancipation in western (and central) European societies.

IV. Serfdom, Property Rights, and Long-Run Development in Europe

Serfdom in medieval western Europe and early modern central Europe differed from serfdom in Russia in several key ways related to property. Serfdom in Europe was always a tenurial relationship. Although mobility was restricted and serfs were obliged to provide rents and services to landlords, they did have rights to the land they worked and the rents and services they provided were more formalized and contractual than in the Russian case. The system of property rights that had developed over centuries in Europe, and the mechanisms for enforcing those rights, meant that European serfs were better protected than Russian ones against arbitrary expropriation. This was true in medieval western Europe and early modern central/eastern Europe. Serfs' rights were not granted purely at the pleasure of the landlord, but acknowledged beyond the manor, and could, legally, be enforced using the local judicial system of secular authorities, or royal courts, including appellate courts, and even imperial courts (in the case of the Holy Roman Empire).

In practice, this meant that landlords throughout Europe were constrained in their ability arbitrarily to raise rents or to change the terms of customary arrangements or to confiscate productive land from their subjects. In times when grain prices were depressed and land lost value, landlords could not move serfs into other economic sectors to keep their rent streams intact. Existing evidence

---

43 For example, Sheremetyev serfs frequently borrowed from outsiders but did not lend, since the Sheremetyevs could not compel those who weren't their subjects to comply with terms of contracts. The Sheremetyevs' administration could enforce agreements among their own serfs, but had no jurisdiction over others. This is discussed in greater detail in Dennison, *Institutional Framework*, esp. 192–193.

indicates that when landlords tried to do these things (they were always everywhere trying!), serfs could file suit in higher courts and make life difficult – and very expensive – for their lords.[44] This is in stark contrast to the case in Russia, where serfs were effectively subjects of their landlords and had no recourse beyond the estate. We have copious examples of Russian landlords changing the terms of serfdom – raising rents, adding obligations and new taxes, moving serfs off the land in one place to other estates in other parts of the empire (even selling them without land), and reallocating their labor away from agriculture to migrant labor or factory labor if the returns to the landlord were higher in these sectors. Russian serfs had very few formalized property rights – in fact, in the case of proprietary serfs, they were themselves the property.

These differences had important implications for the end of serfdom in these societies. When serfdom ended in Europe, whether it did so gradually as in medieval western Europe, or by decree as in east-Elbian Europe, it was not necessary to create a whole new institutional system to accommodate a vast population that had been hitherto excluded. The enserfed population already possessed formal rights to property and access to civil institutions. The end of serfdom in Europe meant mainly the end to landlords' rights of extraction from the serf population. The Russian case was, of course, more complicated since the enserfed population had not only been exploited, but had also been excluded from a larger institutional and administrative system – a system that proved inadequate in the 1860s to accommodate the newly freed peasantry.[45] As a result, many features of the institutional framework of serfdom – in particular, communal land tenure and communal responsibility for taxes and redemption payments – remained in place after emancipation, perpetuating inequalities and hampering growth.

There were nonetheless interesting similarities in the development of European institutions and those found on the Sheremetyev estates in Russia. In particular, we can observe similar processes of incremental change as the

---

44 William Hagen details a very high-profile example on the estate of the Kleist family in the Duchy of Brandenburg. See William W. Hagen, 'The Junkers' Faithless Servants' in *The German Peasantry*, eds. Richard J. Evans and W.R. Lee (1986), 77–101. This is not meant to imply that it was easy for serfs to do this or that they did not face punitive measures from landlords for trying to go 'above their heads'. Nor is it the case that they were guaranteed to win such cases. But despite these costs, some serfs did use higher courts and we know that these avenues were open to them and this is very different from what we observe in Russia. See also Winfried Schulze, *Bäuerlicher Widerstand und feudale Herrschaft in der frühen Neuzeit* (Frommann-Holzboog, 1980).

45 A detailed discussion is beyond the scope of this chapter. For a sense of the larger argument about the inadequacies of state and administrative capacity and their implications for the shape of Russian land reform, see И. А. Христофоров, *Судьба Реформы* (2011). See also Tracy Dennison, 'Weak State, Strong Commune: Rural Authority in Imperial Russia', *Revista Storica Italiana*, 135 (2023), 623–654.

result of localized problem-solving; and these small changes similarly ended up having larger consequences over time. Medieval England offers a comparison. The Sheremetyevs' system of contract enforcement and dispute resolution was, for instance, the Russian version of the English manorial court: seigneurial institutions where the business of the estate was conducted. Surviving manorial court rolls indicate that this included things like the collection of rents, the administration of fees and fines, the processing of land transfers, and the resolution of disputes (such as those involving credit transactions). For a long time, seigneurs enjoyed certain juridical monopolies on their manors. The exceptions involved those transgressions regulated by church officials (bigamy, blasphemy, fornication, to name a few) and specific criminal charges that were the purview of the royal courts. But the day-to-day business of manorial life was regulated locally by manor courts. Seigneurs could and often did compel villeins (serfs) to use their courts – and only theirs – to register transactions and resolve disputes. Villeins had few options for recourse beyond the manor (especially against landlords).

From around the twelfth century certain changes become apparent in the archives – changes which, according to many legal historians, were largely responses to developments in the common law (and possibly canon law courts which were also emerging around this time).[46] In short, manorial court procedures very gradually began to converge with those of the royal courts. Customary law was formalized in documents that look more similar across localities and to those generated by the royal courts. The property rights of tenants (including villeins) and their obligations to the manor started to become explicitly specified in written contracts. It is not that the practices of manorial courts were *informal* in previous centuries, but that the increased contact between them and the royal courts created legibility issues that required written documentation. For instance, when a tenant sued a landholder for breach of custom in the Kings Courts, the landlord was often held responsible for producing evidence of the terms of the customary contract. The oral testimonies that had long sufficed in the manorial courts were no longer good enough.

These changes evolved at least in part because of demand from tenants for extra-local dispute resolution services, as was the case in Russia (though on the Sheremetyev estates, 'extra-local' meant beyond informal communal decisions). This can be gleaned already from the archives in the thirteenth and fourteenth centuries. Recent research on medieval Cambridgeshire, for example, indicates that it was not as unusual as previously assumed for villeins to use manorial courts other than their own lords'. The enforcement of seigneurial monopolies on local justice appeared to be upheld most often when both parties to a suit

46   See John S Beckerman, 'Procedural Innovation and Institutional Change in Medieval English Manorial Courts', *Law and History Review*, 10 (1992), 197–252; Paul Brand, *The Making of the Common Law* (1992).

were from the same lord's jurisdiction. While there are not enough studies to say how common it was to sue outside one's own jurisdiction, it is clear that at least some villeins did it – even unlawfully.[47] Furthermore, the archives indicate that attempts on the part of manorial lords to enforce their monopolies picked up significantly in the fifteenth century as the number of cases brought before them dropped off steeply, in contrast to the unprecedented rise in the number of cases appearing in ecclesiastical and royal courts. So, as in the Russian case, villagers sought decisions made by those outside their local manor (or commune); however, unlike in Russia, they had competing options. The sources for medieval England portray the existence of an increasingly dense network of dispute resolution venues at this time, among which rural inhabitants (including villeins) could choose.

Many medievalists now acknowledge that these gradual changes in the institutional underpinnings of society may have been more significant than the Black Death in undermining the institution of serfdom and altering the balance of bargaining power between peasants and lords.[48] These incremental changes in institutional arrangements, which occurred over centuries, made it possible for rural society in medieval England to settle into a new equilibrium after experiencing the exogenous shock of plague. Institutional change beneath the surface was *already* altering the economic and social landscape; the plague just accelerated this process.

This underlying process of change was evident for the Sheremetyev estates as well, but it was not connected to any larger institutional changes beyond the estate. There was no concurrent evolution in legal forms or court processes more broadly; the Sheremetyevs' serfs did not have the option of using other landlords' notarial services or court systems, nor centralized state-run versions. When serfdom was abolished in 1861, there was no possibility of a shift to a new institutional equilibrium, since the various parts of the institutional system had not been moving together beforehand. As a result, the post-1861 landscape looked all too similar to the previous one – and even worse for serfs like those on the Sheremetyev estates whose property rights probably became less secure and whose economic prospects became more limited. As a result, there was limited scope for the development of what we might think of as 'capitalism' in Russia. Without the widespread development of clearly assigned property rights, administrative infrastructure for recording them, and legal mechanisms

---

47 Chris Briggs, 'Seigneurial Control of Villagers' Litigation beyond the Manor', *Historical Research* (2008), 399–422.
48 Most recently, see Mark Bailey, *The Decline of Serfdom in Medieval England: From Bondage to Freedom* (Woodbridge, 2016).

for enforcing them, the incentives for investment and hence for large-scale capital accumulation remained too weak for self-sustaining growth.[49]

V. Conclusion

The Sheremetyev family, over a century, established an institutional framework across their many geographically dispersed estates that enabled an extraordinary amount of economic activity, with surprising levels of wealth accumulation and investment among serfs. This appears to have been largely unintentional. They started by offering two services – land purchase and the provision of travel documents – that were mutually beneficial to themselves and their serf subjects. They proved reliable in their willingness to allow serfs a certain freedom to travel and a certain degree of security in their real property, their business enterprises, and the debts owed them by others. The formal recording of property transactions proved useful to serfs in the case of disputes as documents could be produced as evidence. Gradually the estate administration began to respond to increased demand for notarial and dispute resolution services by providing serfs with the ability to formalize a wide variety of transactions, ranging from labor and credit agreements to marriage, household formation, and retirement contracts. Nowhere in the archive is there any indication of an intention to create 'a system', nor any awareness of the connection between this administrative system and the flourishing economy around the estate. (There are many qualitative reports in the archive about how to properly manage the estate and these issues never arise.)

There are hints in the archive about the limitations of this system well before 1861. (Transactions with outsiders were difficult for the Sheremetyevs to enforce; they only had jurisdictional authority over their own serfs.) But the 1861 abolition of serfdom makes clear the weaknesses. The Sheremetyevs had created an institutional island – a state within a state. When their power as sovereign lords was abolished, it would have been difficult to sustain the accumulated gains or the growth momentum on their estates.[50] The contrast with England (for example) is suggestive. There, we observe a similar incremental change over time in manorial institutions, but this was a kind of co-evolution with the institutional framework *within which* the manorial system evolved. Medieval manorial economies were not separate islands; they were integrated into a larger institutional setting, and serfs themselves increasingly

---

49   The importance of these features is further discussed, in the context of twentieth-century Japan, by C. Alexander Evans and J. Mark Ramseyer, Chapter 13 in this volume.
50   This is speculative since recordkeeping changed after 1861 and it is difficult to test hypotheses across the temporal divide: Dennison, 'Weak State, Strong Commune'.

had choices among different administrative systems. This appears to have been true to varying degrees throughout much of western and central Europe. This kind of integration was lacking in Russia, even as late as the nineteenth century, and it appears to have had significant implications for development.

9

Capitalism in South Asia: Three Transitions

TIRTHANKAR ROY

In the 1970s, historians of South Asia debated whether the economic system that emerged from British colonial rule in the region (roughly 1765–1947) could be called 'capitalist' or not. The mode of production debate, as it became known, is not live anymore. Inspired by Marxism–Leninism, then popular in many developing-world regions, it concentrated on the relationship between land and labour and explored how peasants fit concepts like class, consciousness and capitalism.[1] Urban firms, manufacturing industries, artisans and commerce were marginal themes in these debates.

Since then, capitalism has returned to academic and historical discourses, though not yet so prominently in India. Most contemporary uses focus more on large enterprises like industry or plantations than on peasant property. And most avoid defining *capitalism*, let alone describing it in the Marxist way as labour power turning into a commodity. Seth Rockman, a contributor to the movement called the new history of capitalism, would make only 'minimal investment in a fixed or theoretical definition of capitalism.'[2] Most contributions to this movement deal with North America. A recent comparative history project free of such a bias does start with a section titled 'definitions of capitalism' that, in the end, derives a use for the term as a signifier of patterns of 'entrepreneurship, finance, management, workers and political leaders.'[3] Capitalism is defined, if defined is the right word, by the context in which businesses evolve.

I use the term in this contextual way rather than to characterize an economic system at a point in time and I narrow the scope of that usage even more. The

---

[1] Utsa Patnaik (ed.), *Agrarian Relations and Accumulation: The 'Mode of Production' Debate in India* (Delhi, 1990).
[2] Cited in https://economic-historian.com/2020/09/a-comment-on-the-new-history-of-capitalism/ (accessed 19/06/2024).
[3] Catherine Casson and Philipp Robinson Rössner (eds.), *Evolutions of Capitalism: Historical Perspectives, 1200–2000* (Bristol, 2022), 2. See also the discussion on how the context of its usage changes the meaning of the word in Larry Neal, 'Introduction,' in *CHC*, I:3–5.

term demands attention to capital: investments and investors, the problems they solve, the means they use and the aids they receive from society or the state. Capitalist transformation draws attention to great movements in the business and economic history of a region involving all these dimensions and usually in response to a revolution in politics.

We can distinguish three such transitions in South Asia on which substantial evidence exists. One of these occurred during the passage of empires in the eighteenth century with the emergence of a state rooted in oceanic commerce, a first in the region and a revolutionary change in many ways. The second significant shift occurred in the late nineteenth century in the wake of the first globalization sustained in India's case with a colonial system that maintained minimal barriers to trade, cross-border capital flows and labour migration. The colonial system was more than this. It enabled the transplantation of the limited liability joint stock principle from Britain to India, enabling investment in large-scale industry. Paradoxically, the colonial system of laws also preserved indigenous religion-based codes in matters of succession and inheritance of property, which artificially preserved a role for Indian 'culture' in otherwise capitalistic businesses. The third movement happened in the middle decades of the twentieth century when economic nationalism led to a dismantling of the colonial-era openness and reshaped capitalism in its image.

I do not claim that these are uniquely South Asian phenomena. The historian Chris Bayly suggested that elements of the eighteenth-century transition were present in many regions of the world.[4] Indeed, the spread of European rule in Asia and Africa, though variable in timing, local processes and motivation, was distinguished by a drive to protect private profits that one would not find to the same degree in empires in an earlier era. During the second transition, there was considerable overlap between South Asia and the pattern of enterprise formation in the western world. In all regions, joint stock limited liability enabled industrialization while creating corporate governance issues and takeover risks that did not exist before. Twentieth-century economic nationalism was a universal ideology, though India, with its semi-industrial economy at the time of independence from British rule, could act on it with a resolve rarely seen elsewhere.

I. The Eighteenth-Century Transition

A convenient point to begin is the seventeenth century because business history sources become dense enough from then, thanks mainly to the records of European commercial firms operating in India. One of the most powerful

---

4 C.A. Bayly, *The Birth of the Modern World, 1780–1914* (2004).

empires of the world, the Mughals, ruled over the Indo-Gangetic Basin around 1700. During the Mughal era and for a considerable time after the empire started to decline, the revenue system sustained a great deal of trading and banking enterprise. There is hardly any account of capitalism in the Indo-Gangetic Basin in the early modern era that does not foreground politics.

The Basin had fertile land watered by easily accessible groundwater and rivers fed by snow melt from the Himalayan mountains. Rich soil and steady water supply were a scarcity in the tropical monsoon geography of South Asia. The core zone over which the Mughals claimed authority yielded substantial revenue from farmlands. The grain, however, needed to be converted into cash before the treasury could collect that tax. The income sustained a large aristocracy consisting of military commanders and provincial elites. Large-scale deployment of capital was needed to move the taxed and marketed grain to the markets, fund the bullock caravans and boats that carried the grain further inland, and lend to the elite to meet their consumption needs.

Most of this world remains faceless. It is hard to identify firms, let alone know how they operated. No doubt most Indian businesses of this time worked as 'family firms,' but that phrase probably hides many variations. We do know of deposit bankers of the imperial capitals in the seventeenth century, their main clients being the military–political elite of the same cities.[5] Although details of business organization and biographies remain missing, the 'great firms' of the imperial cities commanded considerable economic power, if not political power, and in one controversial claim, their exit from the imperial cities and move towards the emerging regional centres contributed to the quick collapse of the empire in the early eighteenth century.[6]

As the empire fell and cities in the heart of the Indo-Gangetic Basin depopulated, many merchants and bankers left for the capitals of the regional states or successor states. There was a consolidation of local military power and a weakening of imperial power. Bankers and financiers, who might have come to the aid of the bankrupt state, were more active in the newly emerging provincial centres of commerce and manufacturing than in the imperial cities. Some of these regional states actively promoted trade in their domain, hoping to earn more money from it.

In Awadh, one of the prosperous successor states to emerge in the eastern part of the Basin, commercial enterprise and networks connected the Gangetic plains from the eastern coastal regions to the western trans-Himalayan trading zones and gave rise to expanding and ambitious merchant and banker firms.[7]

---

5   Irfan Habib, 'Usury in Medieval India,' *CSSH*, 6 (1964), 393–419.
6   For a survey that reflects this weakness of the scholarship well, see Karen Leonard, 'The "Great Firm" Theory of the Decline of the Mughal Empire,' *CSSH*, 21 (1979), 151–167.
7   Muzaffar Alam, *The Crisis of Empire in Mughal North India: Awadh and the Punjab, 1707–48* (Oxford, 1986).

In Bengal, the firm of Jagatseths held the licence to carry on various monetary functions that ordinarily should be done by the state. They were big and powerful to the same extent that the Bengal Nawab's hold on the financial system was precarious. Yet, money was valuable in Bengal because Bengal had emerged as a node of Indo-European trade.

It would be a mistake to think that the eighteenth century was a golden age of capitalism because capitalists drew closer to the regional courts. As the eighteenth century progressed, frequent wars drained most of these states of money and increased pressure on bankers and wealthy merchants. Risks to capital would almost certainly have gone up in the aggregate in the second half of the eighteenth century and the scope of inter-regional investments shrunk. War finance made the Maratha state critically dependent on bankers in their realm. In Mysore, the late eighteenth-century warlord Hyder Ali and his son Tipu Sultan undertook measures to reform the fiscal system while also liberally using coercion and extortion.

In another way, the eighteenth century may have obstructed business growth. Fragmentation of power meant 'a network of customs barriers ... existence of innumerable systems of currencies ... and frequently fluctuating exchange rates.'[8] At the height of its power, the Mughal state gathered a substantial part of its gross revenue from inland trade duties and customs.[9] Local officers collected much of that tax and retained some for their upkeep, but the imperial court set the rates. During the collapse, the local warlords controlled the right to tax, potentially increasing uncertainty on the rates and the legitimacy of the right to collect.

Meanwhile, a different enterprise cluster was emerging on the seaboard. Indian merchants had been deeply involved in the Indian Ocean trade, especially across the Arabian Sea towards Africa and West Asia and across the Bay of Bengal towards Southeast Asia, for centuries. A wide variety of goods were traded. The ruling powers along the littoral depended on the seafaring merchants, even partnered with them.[10] Some of them were substantial ship-owning merchants.

The rise of European trade on the seaboard did not displace these indigenous groups. Arabian Sea trade remained in the hands of Gujarati merchants. But there were three types of change initiated by the Europeans. First, European business created an opportunity for local merchants with links to coastal and

---

8 Dwijendra Tripathi, 'Occupational Mobility and Industrial Entrepreneurship in India: A Historical Analysis,' *Developing Economies*, 19 (1981), 52–68.
9 Sumit Guha, 'Rethinking the Economy of Mughal India: Lateral Perspectives,' *Journal of the Economic and Social History of the Orient*, 58 (2015), 532–575.
10 See also C.A. Bayly and Sanjay Subrahmanyam, 'Portfolio Capitalists and the Political Economy of Early Modern India,' *Indian Economic and Social History Review*, 25 (1988), 401–424.

maritime trade to accumulate capital as agents, suppliers, brokers, or partners. Second, European enterprises involved large joint-stock companies, the like of which did not exist among the indigenous capitalist worlds. Some of the shipowning merchant firms of western India disappeared, but that process reflected the limited longevity of family firms rather than a broader crisis. Third, whereas most indigenous trades used auction-type sales, the Indo-European business expanded the scope of long-lasting contractual arrangements, which helped some new groups to join the exchange as agents in contract enforcement.

The British East India Company acquired the right to collect the taxes of a large chunk of eastern India in 1765. In the next decade, it acquired a few more territories. The emergence of British India was still far away and so was complete control over governance. The formation of a state by merchants, however, implied a kind of entanglement of capitalism and state power that was unprecedented in the political landscape of South Asia. The Company had never been a stranger to military or state power. It functioned with a Crown charter. It possessed coastal lands in India (Bombay, Calcutta, Madras) that it ruled. It made laws there and its police enforced these laws. Most European cargo ships were battle ready. Anglo-French warfare in Europe had pushed the Company and their French rival into joining succession battles in Indian states on opposing sides.

None of these factors explains why a merchant firm should succeed as a state power inside India, where the successor states had bigger and better-trained armies and many of these advantages would not count for much. Most answers to the puzzle start from the extensive collaborations between European and indigenous merchants, which brought the local officers of the Company in close touch with the regional state power. Peter Marshall, who did the most significant work on the passage of empires, writes, 'at every stage, accommodations between British and Indian interests were crucial to the rise of British ascendancy.'[11] Where merchants and bankers had the power to shape state policy, the rise of British power was based on secret or covert alliances, as in 1750s Bengal. Even when not, as in the Deccan Plateau, the Company forces were sufficiently strong to be seen by some indigenous states as a handy ally against a powerful enemy (often the Maratha forces). In all cases, land ceded under deals, not conquest, led to territorial possessions.

Alliance, however, did not mean friendship nor a one-sided extraction of advantage but the perception of shared benefit or threat. The shared advantage was partly economic and so was the threat. For example, the Company, a merchant firm, functioned without an effective third party to enforce business contracts or settle commercial disputes. State power would help businesses in

---

11 P.J. Marshall, 'Presidential Address: Britain and the World in the Eighteenth Century: III, Britain and India,' *TRHS*, 10 (2000), 6.

this sense. Further, alliances needed to be credible, more so than the alliances the rivals struck. In the Company's case, some of these alliances drew on legal tradition that might have made it more credible to both parties.[12]

The Company evolved from a militaristic to a governing power as it began thinking about public goods and institution-building. The transition happened from the 1820s and was again based on collaborations of a different sort. Chris Bayly wrote: 'incoming colonial power succeeded when they were able to entice intermediate groups.' States need skilled people to collect data, advise policy and influence taxpayers. The Indian middle class found the East India Company a more enlightened and useful employer than the indigenous states.

In this way, the change in the political landscape of the eighteenth century signified a capitalist transition. A way to capture the spirit of that transition is to say that the relationship between overland and overseas commerce, the land and the sea, had changed. The change signified the partial collapse of the land-based capitalist order, the exit and migration of capitalists from there to the port cities and the Company's protection. David Washbrook, in an article reflecting on the eighteenth century, stressed the growing rift between the internal state system and the seaboard.[13] The essay did not follow up the idea, staying with the seaboard to show India's enlarging role in the world economy. I have argued that the Company's tax policy aimed at demilitarizing the warlords, converting them into landowners, and that frequent wars in the eighteenth century weakened the old military system and the interior states, which made the interior–seaboard rift wider. Eventually, a seaboard power took control, thanks to superior fiscal capacity and by pulling Indian capitalists to its side. These two things, superior fiscal power and the support of indigenous merchants, saved the regime from extinction during the rebellion of 1857.[14]

British India, or the Raj, emerged from a fault line between the seaboard and the interior. In turn, colonialism used its superior fiscal, military and legislative powers to bridge that gap more than past regimes and to create an integrated market system. This was a key ingredient in the second transition.

---

12   Clara Kemme explores ideological roots, 'The History of European International Law from a Global Perspective: Entanglements in Eighteenth and Nineteenth Century India,' in *Entanglements in Legal History*, ed. Thomas Duve (Frankfurt am Main, 2014), 489–542. Mandar Oak and Anand Swamy, 'Myopia or Strategic Behavior? Indian Regimes and the East India Company in Late Eighteenth Century India,' *EEH*, 49 (2012), 352–366 explores credibility.
13   David Washbrook, 'India in the Early Modern World Economy: Modes of Production, Reproduction and Exchange,' *JGH*, 2 (2007), 87–111.
14   Tirthankar Roy, *The Economic History of India 1707–1857* (2021).

II. The Nineteenth-Century Transition

By the 1860s, British India concentrated power to a degree unprecedented in this region. It collected a far higher amount of tax per head than its predecessors. It neutralized the warlords who had a role in the fiscal system earlier. It had struck a deal with the 550-odd princely states, offering them protection against predatory threats from other princely states while extracting the right to trade or build railways on their lands with little fuss. In this way, the empire used its power to expose the interior to commercialization.

The first serious moves occurred in transit taxes. As it consolidated its rule, the East India Company reduced transit duties, abolishing them in 1838 and extended its authority over many local collectors. In 1840, the Company collected 7–10 per cent of its revenue from trade taxes, a massive decline from the 47 per cent that the Mughals hoped to get by taxing trade. From the 1850s, the focus shifted to infrastructure like the railways, just as industrialization in Britain greatly increased the demand for food and raw material from India. Multiple currencies were abolished and a single currency system came into existence (1835). That unification drive enabled the monetary authority to concentrate on a single-point policy – keep the exchange rate stable – thus eliminating some of the risks to trade, remittance and investment.

A developed commercial tradition had created a sizeable indigenous trading and banking system before the British colonial empire appeared in the region. However, colonialism and globalization changed the structure of trading and, in turn, trade financing. Unlike artisanal and high-valued goods traded in the past, agricultural commodity exports became the main item of trade from the mid-nineteenth century, sustained by the railways, the telegraphs, the port city infrastructure and indigenous banking. The entire financial system, including a nascent corporate banking segment, had to reorient to this new and vast field to deploy money.

The process encouraged the migration of merchants and bankers and the shift of wealth from the interior of India to the seaboard cities – Bombay, Calcutta, Madras and later Karachi – and a string of interior towns which emerged as nodes of agricultural trade after railways arrived. A similar movement was underway from Britain to India. After the Industrial Revolution, British manufacturing, capital and enterprise circulated more. India was one of the biggest markets for these goods and the fifth largest destination of British capital (1865–1914). Foreign trade carried a low tariff until World War I.

Company, contract and negotiable instrument laws were transplanted almost verbatim and made no discrimination based on the ethnicity of the enterprise. A labour contract law was introduced in 1859 to ensure the supply of plantation workers in Assam. The provisions of the law were harsh on defaulting workers, but it followed British precedent in the matter. One area where the state intervened directly was in making chunks of land available to plantation owners in tea and coffee by special laws. These lands were usually uninhabited forest lands.

In the port cities, the first half of the nineteenth century saw an efflorescence of trading firms under joint Indo-European enterprise. In the eighteenth century, fine Indian textiles were exported in large quantities. Even as the cotton textile export business declined after 1820 due to Manchester's competition, the port cities invested money in a range of agricultural commodities (indigo, opium, cotton) trade that grew in scale. From the 1860s or a little later, the railways contributed significantly to the growth of internal and external trade, broadening the commodity base from niche products like indigo or opium to mass-produced ones like wheat, cotton, rice and oilseeds.

After the monetary system and the military, the third area of state activism was law. Legislative activity accelerated after the mutiny (1857) and slowed after 1900. The average number of 'supreme government acts' passed every year was 0.6 in 1835–50, 1.8 in 1880–1900 and fell rapidly after that. The most frequently used among the new laws were those related to procedure in general and business procedure in particular. The Code of Civil Procedure (1908), the Indian Contract Act (1872), the Evidence Act (1872), Limitation Act (1908), Stamp Act (1899) and Registration Act (1877) accounted for 70 per cent of all High Court suits settled in 1900–10. The actual pattern of legal reference suggests also that the legislative process responded to problems of business transaction. India received a new company law within a few years of the framing of a company law in Britain. Stock trading began in the 1860s as commercial profits moved into factory investments and joint stock limited liability companies owned these factories.

The economic system these changes fostered stood upon the long-distance trade of agricultural goods and factories processing agricultural goods. In the first half of the twentieth century, trade and finance formed colonial India's third most important economic activity. Together, these activities generated 9–12 per cent of the gross domestic product (agriculture 45–59 per cent and industry 11–15 per cent).[15] The main articles of trade were agricultural commodities. A great deal of banking capital went to financing commodity trade. A part of the commercial profits was reinvested in factories like cotton textile mills.

Shipping tonnage handled at Bombay, Madras and Calcutta ports increased from one hundred thousand tons to over ten million tons between 1798 and 1940. Between 1860 and 1940, the railways cheapened cargo movement from inland to the seaports many times. The carrying capacity of the bullock caravans in peninsular India, the only pre-railway mode of long-distance cargo transport in the region, was ten thousand tons c.1800. A century later, goods carried by the main South Indian railway companies amounted to over five million tons. If

---

15 S. Sivasubramonian, *National Income of India in the Twentieth Century* (Delhi, 2000).

we add the Great Indian Peninsula Railway, which connected Bombay with the western part of the Deccan plateau, the figure rises to eight million tons. In all of India, the cargo carried by the railways increased from about three million tons to one hundred and twenty million between 1871 and 1929.

In this way, trade, banking and industry became parts of an integrated system. A closer look at industry and finance suggests that the integration process was not always smooth. Indeed, in one field, artisanal industries, it occurred differently.

III. Factories, Handicrafts and Bankers

By 1914, the fourth largest cotton textile mill industry in the world, financed and managed by Indians, had developed in Bombay and Ahmedabad. A large jute textile mill industry had emerged in Calcutta under European management. In the early twentieth century, the tropical world's largest metallurgical industry was in India. Between 1860 and 1940, factory employment increased from about 100,000 to 2,000,000.

This industrialization was a paradox. Its foundation was laid in the era of free trade. The largest extent of the growth occurred between 1870 and 1921 before tariff protection was available. Indians moved into cotton textiles, the industry in which Britain had dominated. In common with other parts of the colonized tropics, India did not possess well-developed capital and labour markets in the nineteenth century, nor was its indigenous artisanal tradition poised to experience a technological revolution. It had cheap labour, cotton and merchant capital, but transforming these 'advantages' into competitive factories would have been challenging. Interest rates were high, large-scale employment of wage labour was unknown, inland transport cost was large because of the limited reach of wheeled traffic and navigable rivers, the merchants were not familiar with machinery and there was no system of formal training of workers.

The empire provided some means to overcome these obstacles. The free trade regime increased market access. The railways brought down carriage costs. British capitalists and shareholders invested in India. Bombay's merchants found it easy to hire supervisors and buy machinery from cities with which they already had well-developed trading links. The reduction of costs was not universal. The benefits were confined to the port cities and merchant-banker communities already part of the overland trade network. But though confined in space, the scale of the process was by no means small. When the empire ended, the three port cities were among the most industrialized and wealthiest in the tropical world. They possessed large seaports, railway hubs, universities, hospitals, banks and multinational companies. Many of these institutions had been set up by the Indian capitalists who profited from foreign trade.

Factories did not dominate the industrial landscape. A much larger field of industrial activity was the handicrafts, especially handmade cloth. An industry integrated into Indian urban life, handloom weaving had a turbulent history in the nineteenth century. The emergence of power-looms and world trade was the more visible process affecting it. Less visible and gradual were changing dynamics of state power and the disappearance of patrons and consumers.

Until the 1980s, the commonly held view among historians was that the changes added up to a decline in the industry. A power loom that could move six times faster than the handloom or a spinning machine that could produce a hank of yarn using one-eighth the labour a hand-operated spinning wheel needed left the Indian spinner and weaver with little chance to compete. Technology and British colonial policies of free trade damaged handloom weaving and dislodged it from its place in Indian economic life. Crafts were banished from 'industrial capitalism.'

In 1963, Morris D. Morris published a paper on Indian economic history that offered a contrary case.[16] Morris pointed out that the story of decline could not be true because, according to the 1951 census, 10 million people were employed in traditional industries. Resilience was a key part of the story and remained overlooked. Later quantitative studies confirmed Morris' hunch. In 1900–1940, the market share of handmade cloth rose from 20 to 30 per cent and artisanal real wages rose in the same period. Weaving as a livelihood remained anchored in the economic base of many small towns and contributed to the economic and social processes that made modern India.

After Morris, economic historians calculated how many artisans lost jobs in the nineteenth century to show that Morris was wrong. Some interesting statistical studies followed. But the real challenge was ignored. If craft skills were resilient, how does the narrative about them change? If not obsolescence, then what was the core process? Can we re-insert the crafts in a story of 'industrial capitalism'?

Almost all recent studies of handloom history engage with these questions about capitalism. One of these says that nineteenth-century globalization had mixed effects on the artisan.[17] Even as it damaged the more generic type of weaving, it strengthened another more skill-intensive part. As designed cloths traded over larger areas, skills and the people embodying them circulated more than before and some handmade goods emerged as brand names. These businesses used another kind of capital together with the physical ones like looms and equipment: design capability. The machines tried to copy this

---

16 Morris D. Morris, 'Towards a Reinterpretation of Nineteenth Century Indian Economic History,' *JEcH*, 23 (1963), 607–618.
17 Tirthankar Roy, *The Crafts and Capitalism: Handloom Weaving Industry in Colonial India* (2020).

capability, sometimes with success, sometimes not. That redefinition of 'capital' invites the crafts back into 'capitalism.'

Douglas Haynes offers another take on these questions with a study of sites of craft production in western India. Craft towns, he suggests, had a different ecosystem from port cities: low cost of living, one core business, allied services in the same place and a community of employers with solid connections to local and municipal politics.[18] Karuna Dietrich Wielenga's more conventional mix of economic, social and technological history for South India shows that the production of craft textiles stabilized in the twentieth century. However, it continually struggled against material shortages and market access.[19] Santosh Kumar Rai's study of weaving fine cotton and silk in a part of northern India shows that weavers struggled to secure livelihoods by adjusting technology, industrial and business organization.[20] These recent works do not tell an unmixed positive story about the skilled crafts, but all draw attention to forms of adaptation.

Responding to a vast increase in demand for trade credit in moving agricultural goods, banking of all types expanded in colonial India. Banking laws regulated some firms, but most were not regulated. The ones that were not were often called indigenous bankers. It was a diverse set. Several large family firms carried considerable market reputations at one end of the set. The corporate banks accepted the bills they issued, which made for overlap between their operations. On the other end, local lenders operated with no legally recognized instrument and only based on their knowledge of the clients, who were farmers or urban groups of small means.

This spread worried the provincial governments in colonial India and later concerned the central bank and the government of the Indian Union. The cause of the worry was the very high interest rates charged as one went from the regional to the local. The call to regulate indigenous banking was old, partly driven by a fiscal motive and partly by the usurious nature of local lending. The pushback was strong too. Many officials felt that regulation would reduce the flow of credit. At stake was a dispute over why interest rates were high, the excessive power of the lender, or extreme risk. In 1918, the Usurious Loans Act empowered the courts to reduce interest rates. The law followed an English precedence. Few cases, however, came to court. Decades before, individual provinces had passed laws restricting land transfers in the event of a failure

---

18 Douglas Haynes, *Small Town Capitalism in Western India: Artisans, Merchants and the Making of the Informal Economy, 1870–1960* (Cambridge, 2012).
19 Karuna Dietrich Wielenga, *Weaving Histories: The Transformation of the Handloom Industry in South India, 1800–1960* (Oxford, 2020).
20 Santosh Kumar Rai, *Weaving Hierarchies: Handloom Weavers in Early Twentieth Century United Provinces* (New Delhi, 2021).

to repay mortgaged loans. Interestingly, most regions did not take that road, preferring alternative institutions like the credit cooperative.

These changes in the pattern of deployment of capital changed the capitalists. Strangely, the capitalists also represented indigenous tradition more emphatically than before. A helpful way to understand the transformation is to discuss the firm.

IV. The Firm

Business historians of Marxist persuasion suggested that colonialism mattered because the colonial state favoured European merchants and discriminated against the Indians. Indigenous merchant groups could carry on by having 'survived the onslaught of foreign conquest or [managing] to carve out a niche for themselves as collaborators of the metropolitan power.'[21] Since the law was ethnicity-neutral, these propositions must rely on anecdotal evidence and it is impossible to say how reliable that sort of evidence is.

Ethnicity, however, did matter. How ethnicity mattered depended on the kind of information ethnic networks exchanged. Nineteenth-century India did see the establishment of textile and other factories. But it was, in the main, a trading economy. The nineteenth-century globalization did not just stand on abstractions like free trade but on information exchange and contracts designed by firms operating overseas. All transactions involved much longer distances on average than before. Law did little to help mitigate the risk that a distant supplier or agent would default on a contract.

Business firms adapted to these risks by selecting partners and managers from the same social set as the owners. They also adapted by building new channels of information exchange. Modern solutions to agency problems were information-based. In these two senses – recruitment and information-sharing – 'networks' were essential to business organizations. It would be a mistake to think that the networks were necessarily ethnic. Many indigenous groups were part of the European commercial world in the empire, which led Stanley Chapman to suggest denationalizing the British overseas trading firm.[22] But selectivity existed too. While Europeans and the western coastal group Parsis or Calcutta's Bengali entrepreneurs exchanged information, Europeans and the migrant western Indian group Marwaris did not. Some shared social spaces that helped exchange information, others did not. Historians sometimes try to understand these selection biases through political power or terms like

---

21 A.K. Bagchi, 'Colonialism and the Nature of "Capitalist" Enterprise in India,' *Economic and Political Weekly*, 23 (1988), 38–50.
22 Stanley Chapman, 'British-Based Investment Groups before 1914,' *EcHR*, 38 (1985), 230–251.

'discrimination' and 'collaboration.' Politics had no apparent role in the formation of these networks.

A broad divide can be seen in the formation of these networks. Indo-European (and later Indo-Japanese) businesses continued to be in the hands of non-Indian groups because these firms had better knowledge of overseas markets, including reexport markets and had better access to the shipping, insurance and finance necessary in international marketing operations. A London partner of an Indo-British firm arranged to auction goods brought there, procure goods in Britain for trade in Asia and occasionally provide capital, managers and partners.

On the other hand, with a few exceptions, the entire overland trade of grain and cotton was in the hands of Indian groups. They knew the peasant producers and local markets better than the Europeans. Rajat Ray calls them 'bazaar firms.' The Indian firms formed an essential link between the European and Indian peasants. Claude Markovits, in the same spirit, accepts that the Europeans dominated the highways of trade but stresses 'the ability of South Asian merchants to maintain significant areas of independent international operations throughout the period of European economic and political domination.'[23]

In credit and finance, networks were critical. A merchant needed to advance money to a supplier – a transaction fraught with risks between clients who did not know each other well and when the harvest in a tropical monsoon geography was never certain. An Indian operator had a better chance of dealing with the peasant producer or local grain merchant than the average maritime trader. Land trade and sea trade, in other words, imposed different kinds of demand upon credit transactions, leading to hard, but not fixed, segmentation between the two spheres of trade.

The persistence of ethnic networks among Indians made business historians stress and sometimes overstress, the concept of the 'community.' The word may make us think business was embedded in caste and religion. Attempts to turn capitalism into an extension of the traditional society are bound to fail. Few members of the so-called business communities succeeded in business. Some, like the Marwaris, did not always pursue business. The Parsis moved away from business to skilled services. All communities were professionally too diverse and economically too unequal to enable defining these as units of analysis. It is much easier to see communities as a temporary adjustment to transaction costs drawing on the idiom of caste and religion.

The unit of an ethnic network was the family, interrelated by social and commercial ties with other families in the same network. A family firm is a firm

---

23 Rajat Ray (ed.), *Entrepreneurship and Industry in India, 1800–1947* (Delhi, 1992), 13–30; also G. Balachandran (ed.), *India in the World Economy 1850–1950* (Delhi, 2005), 10, 35; Claude Markovis, 'Structure and Agency in the World of Asian Commerce during the Era of European Colonial Domination c.1750–1950,' *Journal of the Economic and Social History of the Orient*, 50 (2007), 106–123.

that resources its capital, financial or managerial, from within a family. Most European firms recruited managers and partners from a known and trusted set but not necessarily family. Most Indian firms developed around the owner's family and recruited managers from the immediate family or families related to them. Behind the endurance (or revival) of the family firm among Indians, colonial law had a role.

V. Law

European visitors to Indian port towns in the seventeenth century observed that significant social interaction with other communities was forbidden to merchants, bankers and skilled artisans in India. Merchants lived in an insular social world and mercantile law existed as social conventions of endogamous guilds. Members of the group shared trade, married within the trade and had food with people who belonged in the same trade. Such insularity was not peculiar to Indian merchants. But in India, such rules were accompanied by a powerful moral force.

When property, succession and inheritance laws were first coded in the late-eighteenth century, the influence of this moral force on the legislators was deep, the foundation of business practices was seen to be caste or religion and there was a drive to base these laws upon indigenous religious codes. The project gave employment to scores of orientalist legal scholars and the start of schools of Hindu and Islamic traditions.

The substantial effect of that project was that property right was delivered to a 'joint family,' something in between a unitary family and a kinship group. The precise definition of the joint family was left open. The understanding was that under Indian tradition, the property was usually held joint between (typically male) descendants of a male ancestor and therefore, property should be held in common. India, however, was a plural society with not one but many religious codes. The codes existed as an ethos rather than as positive law. The government could only accord all religious laws equal status in this scenario. And to maintain strict equality, it instituted universal procedures and a universal system of courts. Combining these two principles resulted in a never-ending flow of court cases challenging the traditional succession, partition and inheritance rules (see discussion on procedural law above). These challenges were sometimes too much for the more prominent family firm, which broke into smaller family firms. But the principle of keeping recruitment of managers from the family survived.

On the other hand, the joint stock limited liability principle was a straight import from British company law into India. The main body of company law was the Companies Act, which regulated the birth, operation and death of joint-stock limited-liability companies.[24] Public shareholding created the prospect of a takeover and the family or the inner circle losing control. This was avoided using a managing agency contract when a producing company contracted its management to a firm closely held by a family or a partnership. In this way, the family and the corporate converged rather than staying oppositional.

Competition law was not a serious concern, probably because the most prominent business houses were exporters in a big world market and had little power to influence the market. The parity in law between Britain and India was believed to encourage investment and international trade. Corporate governance scandals broke out occasionally, especially after the two World Wars. But no significant departure from the Companies Act seemed needed.

During the second movement, firms and individuals emerged distinctly, sometimes as players who broke out of the community-bound patterns of enterprise. Some examples follow.

VI. Capitalistic Enterprise during the Second Transition

Most nineteenth-century European trading firms in India had India as their primary field. They were not multinationals in the modern sense. A few were survivors from the Company era, when private merchants, encouraged by the end of the Company's monopoly charter (1813), came to India to trade or operate in areas that did not interfere with the monopoly. Charles Forbes of Bombay, Thomas Parry, Binny and Finlay of south India were such survivors. Some of these companies invested in industry and plantations after 1850. While these houses survived, others engaged in indigo and, based in Calcutta, went bankrupt during a recession in the 1840s. The bankruptcy revealed two things that made the port city capitalism of that time highly unstable: Overreliance on foreign markets when information flows were limited and a banking business on the side that lent to the same trade.

After Crown rule began in 1858, steamships and the undersea telegraph brought India and Europe much closer and a new set of British capitalists came to India. Almost all had a significant stake in the cotton textile industry, as machinery vendors (James Greaves), managing agents of cotton mills (James Greaves and George Cotton), or importers of Manchester textiles (David Sassoon). Groups with a dominant interest in other articles included exporters of spices and coffee (Peirce, Leslie of Cochin), shipping agents (Peirce, Leslie; Aspinwall), exporters of coir and rice from South Indian ports (Gordon

---

24 The first Companies Act appeared in 1856; the last major amendment before independence occurred in 1936.

Woodroff), exporters of textiles (Beardsell; Brunschweiler), exporters of carpets (C.M. Hadow, Otto Weyland) and dealers in timber for the railways (Wallace). In 1851, Salomon Volkart, a commodity trader, moved from the Mediterranean to Bombay and the Greek merchant Pantia Ralli set up an operation in Calcutta. Volkart dominated Indian cotton export and Ralli wheat export.

From around 1900, several Japanese 'sogo shosha' started operations in India. The Mitsui-affiliated cotton trader Toyo Menka came to India in the 1890s. Competitive shipping rates, efficient information exchange between Bombay and Osaka, partnership with Indian businesses (Tata in Bombay and Andrew Yule in Calcutta) and the presence of Indian merchants in Kobe, Singapore and Hong Kong helped them develop their Indian interests very effectively.[25] From around 1900, several Indian cotton merchants started to form agencies with Japanese trading firms. At least one major partnership, Toyo Menka and Anandiram Podar diversified into a cotton mill in Bombay. Indo-Japanese collaboration, however, suffered from rising nationalism in both countries. Japan's iron and steel industry asked for protection from Indian pig iron in retaliation for India's textile industry's demand for protection from Japan's textile imports. The desire for military security strengthened the protectionist sentiment in Japan.[26]

Some European firms were engaged in 'agency' or 'broking.' An agency meant an undertaking to work on behalf of someone. The well-known example is the managing agency, wherein one firm manages an industrial enterprise that another firm, or the public, owns. But the agency was, in fact, much more common than this example may suggest. Many public construction sites hired workers via an agency. Railway goods were transported further into the interior (to the hill stations, for example) by European contractors called agents. The tea broker was mainly an auctioneer independent of the producers and the trader, helping the latter with price discovery. These firms had links with auction and sale houses in London's Mincing Lane. Thus, Thomas Cumberledge and Moss, later Thomas Cumberledge and Inskipp, a London broker, appear in the historical accounts of two Indian firms, J. Thomas, the premier broker of Calcutta and Warren, the tea planter group of Assam.

As India industrialized, the business of importing chemicals, metals and machines expanded. In cotton and jute textiles, the agents or branches of machine manufacturers in Britain got the goods. Since they also supplied

---

25 Naoto Kagotani, 'Up-country Purchase Activities of Indian Raw Cotton by Toyo Menka's Bombay Branch, 1896–1935,' in *Commercial Networks in Modern Asia*, eds. S. Sugiyama and Linda Grove (Richmond, Surrey, 2001); Hiroshi Shimizu, 'The Indian Merchants of Kobe and Japan's Trade Expansion into Southeast Asia before the Asian-Pacific War,' *Japan Forum*, 17 (2010), 25–48.
26 John Sharkey, 'Attitudes of the Japanese Iron and Steel Industry to Indian Pig Iron Imports, 1919–1929,' *Japan Review*, 7 (1996), 159–184.

after-sales service, replacing them with machine traders would be difficult. Platt Brothers were the largest suppliers of cotton mill machinery until the advent of ring spindles. Other machinery firms trading in India included John Hetherington and Sons, Dobson and Barlow, Asa Lees and Co. and Taylor, Lang and Co. After the advent of ring spinning, specialist machine traders played a more prominent role in the market. By 1920, a string of British engineering firms exported machine tools to India. Again, these firms were not pure traders, but their involvement in post-sale service was crucial to the success of their export business. They included Alfred Herbert, Marshall, Sons (agricultural machinery and traction engines), Stewarts and Lloyds (iron and steel tubes), Westinghouse Electric, Thornycroft (shipbuilders), George Cradock (wire rope manufacturers), Campbell Gas Engine (oil engines), General Electric (electric light equipment), Saxby and Farmer (railway equipment) and Mather and Platt (general engineering).

In the twentieth century, the range of consumer goods imported from Britain expanded to include such new articles as cosmetics, sewing machines, processed food, bicycles and cars. Manufacturing firms like Unilever, Reckitt and Colman, Singer and Imperial Tobacco Company set up sale agencies. They hired European and Indian subagents to push the products and conduct market surveys.

By far the biggest field of investment of Indian groups was in the grain and cotton trade. The prominence of the Gujarati merchants and bankers in Bombay owed a lot to the cotton export trade carried on all along the Gujarat coast, which interlinked Bombay, Broach and Ahmedabad in networks of exchange of goods, money and capitalists. The Marwaris of Bengal likewise had a firm hold on the raw jute trade. Grain trade spread out more and penetrated most villages in India.

There were three players in the local grain trade, the commission agent, the buyer's agent and the local grain merchants and landlords. The commission agent usually possessed or rented a warehouse, a costly enterprise and a major field of investment in the twentieth century.[27] The buyer's agent went around villages to contract purchases with the farmer. Local actors bought grain or cotton from the farmers and brought it to the bazaars for sale. With the growth of the grain trade, the more capital and information-intensive side of the business grew too because returns were higher and risk lower in such activities. A warehouse owner, or 'stockist' in Indian English, had access to the railways, could deal with the banks, issue bills like *hundis* and possessed carts. Europeans were almost absent from these local transactions, but they occasionally acted as buyer's agents.

---

27   Douglas Haynes and Tirthankar Roy, 'The Emergence of Marketing in the Twentieth Century: India,' in Asian Commercial History: *South Asia*, ed. Tirthankar Roy (Oxford, 2022).

Unlike the Europeans, most Indian traders are known to us by their community names rather than as firms. Thus, the Marwaris dominated the jute trade, Muslim and Eurasian merchants the leather trade and other Hindu and Jain communities the grain trade. In the exceptional cases where a local merchant firm was mentioned by name, it was a banker and issued hundi (remittance certificate, sometimes bill of exchange) bearing the firm's name. The hundi issuers concentrated in the port cities and a few large towns in the interior (Patna, Benares, Jabalpur, Ahmedabad). The formal or corporate banking system again concentrated in the cities and they accepted the more reliable hundis. All that made the cities the centres of finance. In effect, a great deal of credit funding trade moved out of the city into the countryside every harvest season to return to the town in the summer months.

Tanned hides were a semi-processed natural resource, the trading of which had some similarities with the grain trade. A similar flow of capital from outside to the interior occurred in tanned hides. Leather export was a major field for Muslim merchants of the time. Hides and skins, like sugarcane, were perishable and processed in the locality. Therefore, the local merchants and the tannery owner were often indistinct. From the last quarter of the nineteenth century, hides and skins emerged as significant exportable commodities. At the peak, 100,000 tons of hides and skins left India before World War I. After that, more hides went to the domestic market. Indian or naturalized Indian firms dominated the export trade. The Hindu and Jain traders had an aversion to hides. Therefore, Muslims, Parsis, Eurasians and the Chinese came to dominate the tanning trade. A few German trading firms (Schroeder Smidt, Schmidt Cohen and Fuchs, Wuttow Guttman) were also prominent in the business through Calcutta. In Bombay in the late nineteenth century, Bohras and Memons owned tanneries and controlled a considerable part of the export trade.

In 1947 the British Empire ended in South Asia. In India, the new state framed a development strategy formed almost point by point in reaction to how the imperial system had functioned. What was the effect?

VII. The Twentieth-Century Transition

The forty-odd years after independence in 1947 and the formal start of planned development in 1950 were marked by import-substituting industrialization with an accent on the production of capital goods. The policy encouraged domestic firms to diversify from consumer goods to capital goods and led the state into the production of oil, steel, heavy chemicals and engineering. These changes resulted in a significant expansion of the corporate groups and cooperation, sometimes collusion, between the big Indian business groups and the state. All investment and modernization plans required a government licence. Older industries like textiles and tea were discriminated against regarding licences. Mining and finance were mostly nationalized. Under capital controls, foreign investment in exports and trading dried up, whereas multinational entry was allowed on a small scale in niche consumer goods and machinery. Commodity trade was subjected to a spate of federal and provincial regulations. Starting with the Essential Commodities Act of 1955, restrictions were added on moving goods across India and private storage. There was a ban on the export of agricultural goods, a ban on futures markets, a ban on private trade and a ban in many states on the sale of farm goods except in approved sites.

These tendencies fragmented the capitalistic world. The synergy between trade, finance and manufacturing – the hallmark of the colonial system – was broken. A small subset of Indian business families diversified from textiles to metals, machines and chemicals. Most did not. Many trading and banking firms went bankrupt. Those who had their fortunes tied to textiles or plantations retreated into obscurity. British businesses suffered severely. The cosmopolitan heritage of the port cities was largely destroyed. Between 1950 and 1970, except for a few multinationals selling goods to Indians, the British firms engaged in export-oriented trading and manufacturing were squeezed out of India. A series of hostile takeovers by opportunistic Indian families sealed the global firms' fate and the future of Calcutta as a city. The retreat from the world market led to a dysfunctional dependence on the communist bloc. The tax-funded industrialization caused a waste of public resources and led to balance of payments crises.

After independence, regulation practically outlawed the entire series of indigenous banking, big or small, regional or local, in all states. The move killed the more visible top order, the family firms that commanded market reputation. What happened to the middle is a matter of speculation. At the local level, where the clients are poor but still creditworthy (with some assets and a viable trade), the credit business went 'extra-legal.'[28]

On the other hand, the size of the government increased from 3 per cent of the gross domestic product (GDP) in 1931 to 22 per cent in 1981. The enlargement of the state enabled it to intervene effectively in areas where the British Indian state would refuse to enter. For example, the long-standing problem of low agricultural productivity was partly solved by making public funds available for the subsidization of agricultural inputs. After the green revolution of the 1970s, rural industrialization added a new dimension to capitalism.

---

28 Sebastian Schwecke, *Debt, Trust and Reputation: Extra-legal Finance in Northern India* (Cambridge, 2022).

In the sphere of law, the first target for reform was the managing agency for its close association with European businesses in India. Although the agency did create a potential governance problem (it assured an income to the agent, regardless of performance), the corporate governance cases were neither so serious nor so frequent nor attributable to the managing agency system to demand deep intervention. The restrictions effectively forced some British-owned conglomerates to sell off or reduce stakes, exposing these to hostile takeovers.

By the late 1960s, when the industrialization policy was in full swing, it was apparent that adopting a protectionist industrial policy with an accent on capital goods production had made a change in corporate law inevitable. The emergence of dominant groups or 'monopolies' and bankruptcy among older industries like cotton and jute textiles required regulatory and legislative steps.

The two significant interventions to take shape in response to these new needs were the Monopolies and Restrictive Trade Practices (MRTP) Act (1965), dealing with competition, and the Sick Industrial Companies (Special Provisions) Act (SICA) (1985), dealing with insolvency. Both these laws restricted the scope of the Companies Act. A third regulatory law, the Foreign Exchange Regulations Act (FERA, 1973), made it nearly impossible for a foreign firm to buy a stake in an Indian firm.

In the 1990s, after decades of indifferent economic growth and low levels of private investment, the economy opened again to foreign capital and big business. These three laws were repealed, reformed and replaced by a competition law.

VIII. Postscript

Since the 1990s, India (and South Asia generally) entered a fourth movement. These times are too recent to infer a pattern. The years have seen a revival of private investment and the government's retreat as a market player. The transition was far more radical in India than in Pakistan or Bangladesh, where the government was not such a big player in the market except during a brief socialist interlude in the 1970s.

The impressive economic growth rates that followed can distract us from the long continuities on which this revival stands. If the colonial era can be credited for two things that made India relatively attractive to investors – an institutional–legal infrastructure and an integrated market – these factors were active in recent decades too. But lest we overstress the agency of globalization, the domestic market in both times had a significant role in shaping capitalism. The Indian home market has some unique features. It is large in scale but also regionally diverse in tastes and needs, making for a co-existence of local, regional, pan-Indian and international producers. The information technology industry, for example, supplies a range of local and global users. Another strength of the integrated market is the free movement of an enormous labour pool between regions. Nowhere in India do local labour shortages grow for a long time.

Persistence can also be seen in the stability of the family firm, even though families have become smaller than before. There is a much greater reliance across the spectrum of firms on hired managerial workers, yet management of finances or new projects is often restricted to a team of insiders.

On the other hand, if the first four decades after Indian independence went in pursuit of industrialization, the next three decades saw much of that ambition lose momentum. The fields where investment revived were primarily, not exclusively, services like information technology, trade, transport, technical education and financial services. This reorientation of capitalism has puzzled many economists, who believe regulatory laws in the labour market discouraged investments in areas that could see labour overheads build up. Others point toward the comparative advantage of Indians in labour-intensive services.

The government partially retracted from its role as a producer to concentrate more on corporate governance and competition management. The large entry of foreign capital made the legislative process turn outward and led to attempts to make mergers, acquisitions and intellectual property laws more compatible. Much of the institutional infrastructure to achieve parity between global and Indian practices remains a work in progress.

10

Capitalism, Caste and Subaltern Aspirations in India: Bengal, c.1500–1859

ANIRBAN KARAK

This chapter has four sections. In the first, I outline the conceptual and political stakes of using or rejecting 'capitalism' to thematize modern Indian histories. The aim is to specify an unresolved historiographical question and to clarify why it matters. I then suggest that the history of challenges to caste can open up a new window into this question. To show how, I explain my approach to caste and capitalism in the second and third sections, and then sketch the interrelated histories of capitalism, caste, and subaltern aspirations in late pre-colonial (c.1500–1760) and early colonial (c.1760–1859) Bengal. In the Conclusion, the fourth and final section, I outline the larger implications of my narrative for South Asia and beyond.

I. Capitalism, Colonialism, and the Politics of Historiography

The status of 'capitalism' for the writing of Indian histories has always been inseparably intertwined with the status of 'colonialism', and necessarily so. The first century of colonial rule – 1760s to 1850s – was one of massive change, and it is difficult to deny that it was a period of capitalist transition. In the 1960s and '70s, the debate was about whether longer-run political–economic changes also acted as a distinct causal factor in the rise of capitalism.

Irfan Habib, a Marxist, answered this question in the negative, and argued that pre-colonial India did not have immanent 'potentialities' for capitalism.[1] Habib emphasized the extractive, rent-hungry nature of the Mughal Empire, which effectively ruled much of the subcontinent between 1526 and 1707, when it began to crumble in the face of regional assertion. The extraction of surplus by the Mughals left little scope for reinvestment and accumulation, and there

---

[1] Irfan Habib, 'Potentialities of Capitalistic Development in the Economy of Mughal India', *JEcH*, 29 (1969), 32–78.

existed no pre-existing *telos* towards capitalism. Moreover, Habib emphasized the decisively negative effects of colonial rule, which stymied India's economic development in two ways.[2] First, through the extraction of agrarian revenues that were used to pay for India's exports, primarily in Bengal between 1765 and the 1820s. Second, in the nineteenth century, Britain kept import tariffs low in India while increasing tariffs on Indian exports to the United Kingdom. This slowed down industrialization in India and kept its market captive for British manufactures.

Habib's account, then, was a nationalist one, and it was implicitly an argument for colonialism, and against capitalism, as the meta-category for thematizing the discontinuity that marks nineteenth-century Indian history. This claim, however, immediately created another, seemingly intractable problem: how could one account for the plausibility of specifically modern norms and ideologies – such as abstract equality and liberalism – in the subcontinent? In Western and Northern Europe, where the emergence of capitalism was not coeval with extractive colonialism, the massive change in ethical and political norms that began in the eighteenth century could be practically grounded in capitalism without much anxiety. The norms of civic equality, which much of the world takes for granted today, could be thought of as an ethical aspect of capitalism.[3]

In India, however, the seemingly incomplete character of the capitalist transition, and its supposedly colonial origins, meant that such an approach could not be accepted without implicitly valorizing colonialism. This was more than just a problem; it was a dilemma in the true sense of the word. On the one hand, if capitalism was thought of as civilizationally external to India, then the norms of civic equality would have to be interpreted in the same light. One could try to ignore the problem, but the flip side was that one needed to account for the standpoint of critique, not only of colonialism and racism, but also of caste, gender, and class hierarchies. Either one would have to show that an immanent move towards such a critical standpoint occurred from within the world of pre-colonial thought and practice for reasons that Indian actors themselves recognized as important, or one would end up implicitly affirming colonialism. It is not an exaggeration to say that the first possibility has never been convincingly defended, and this dilemma is therefore yet to be resolved in the historiography of modern India.

Up to the 1960s, the problem was compounded by the fact that politically, many nationalists and Marxists – including Irfan Habib – did not think that this dilemma was something to lose much sleep over. In their judgment, if modern

---

2 Irfan Habib, 'The Eighteenth Century in Indian Economic History', in *The Eighteenth Century in India*, ed. Seema Alavi (New Delhi, 2002), 57–83.
3 For a recent, strong argument about the role of commercial capitalism in enabling the arguments about civic equality in the French Revolution, see William H. Sewell Jr., *Capitalism and the Emergence of Civic Equality in Eighteenth-Century France* (Chicago, 2021).

political and ethical norms had not grown deep roots in India, it was a result of both the rigidity of pre-capitalist norms of caste, creed, and community, as well as the deliberate underdevelopment of the region by colonial masters. The task was simple: to achieve national independence, and to work for modern economic growth and the expansion of civic equality, whilst also fighting against exploitation in a 'distorted' capitalist regime that combined the worst excesses of capitalism with pre-capitalist modes of power and privilege.

To cut a very long story very short, we can say that this line of thinking was criticized from the 1970s onward from a variety of vantage points, many of which are often clubbed together under the label of 'postcolonial' studies in Anglophone academia today. Three criticisms are most important for our purposes. First, the stadial thinking of orthodox Marxism was criticized for assuming a priori the inevitability and necessity of capitalism. Politically, this meant that Marxists failed to recognize moments of resistance to the intrusion of capitalism into pre-capitalist social forms as potentially emancipatory. Much of the work in the 1980s on the Indian peasantry as potentially a limit to bourgeois hegemony was informed by this line of thinking.[4] Second, the uncritical affirmation of the nationalist movement was also criticized. The argument here was that the hegemony of elites over subalterns in the nationalist movement was as much a result of coercion as of consent. Moreover, despite such coercion, the hegemony was perpetually incomplete.[5] Already in the 1990s, historians recognized the problems that lower-caste collaboration with the colonial state posed for historiography.[6] Recent research has further strengthened the point that the national/colonial binary is deeply inadequate to understanding the non-nationalist and even anti-nationalist politics of caste and gender in the decades leading up to 1947.[7]

Finally, the postcolonial critique differs from erstwhile Marxism in a very specific way. On the one hand, postcolonial historians remain committed to the idea that capitalism was essentially a colonial import, and here they agree with Habib.[8] To resolve the tension between seeing capitalism as a foreign import and affirming modern norms, however, postcolonials ground modern

---

4 Partha Chatterjee, 'The Colonial State and Peasant Resistance in Bengal, 1920–1947', *P&P*, 110 (1986), 169–204.
5 The classic statement is Ranajit Guha, *Dominance without Hegemony: History and Power in Colonial India* (Cambridge, MA, 1997).
6 Sumit Sarkar, *Writing Social History* (New Delhi, 1998), 358–390.
7 On caste politics, see Dwaipayan Sen, *The Decline of the Caste Question: Jogendranath Mandal and the Defeat of Dalit Politics in Bengal* (Cambridge, 2018). On gender, see Mrinalini Sinha, *Specters of Mother India: The Global Restructuring of an Empire* (Durham, NC, 2006).
8 Other scholars who were not embroiled in Indian politics also agreed that capitalism was of colonial provenance. See Immanuel Wallerstein, 'Incorporation of Indian Subcontinent into Capitalist World-Economy', *Economic and Political Weekly*, 21 (1986), PE28–PE39.

norms entirely in 'colonial pedagogy'. Thus, modern consciousness becomes essentially 'derivative', and the possibility that there was an immanent move towards modern norms is rejected outright. Partha Chatterjee, for instance, argued that only a small group of elites benefited from the arrival of capitalist modernity, and that they were the ones who subsequently led the nationalist movement by selectively appropriating 'Western' ideas and thus creating derivative discourses. For the vast majority of subalterns, this transformation was an alien and a distant one, and their resistance to colonial rule was also a rejection of modern life.[9]

We see, then, that both Marxists and postcolonials emphasized the importance of colonial agency for ushering in an era of colonial dependence and incomplete capitalist hegemony. Neither believed that there was any immanent move towards capitalist norms in late pre-colonial India. There may have been conflict and dissension, but no one ever aspired for capitalist norms or imagined that extant social tensions could be resolved by the adoption of capitalist practices. The difference between the two camps – for our purposes at least – lies in the fact that whereas the Marxists worked only with the national/colonial binary, postcolonial historians introduced the additional elite/subaltern binary.

Thus, Marxists began by mapping the national/colonial binary onto the non-capitalist/capitalist one, but they nevertheless sought modern capitalist development for the nation. Postcolonials sought to resolve this contradiction by grounding a supposedly distinct sphere of subaltern consciousness in a pre-colonial, pre-modern universe with little or no modern aspirations. This enabled a defence of the twin claims that the colonizer/colonized binary was constitutive of all differences (vis-à-vis capitalism) rather than being itself constituted and reconstituted in specific contexts, and that collaboration was of interest only to elites.

This is our historiographical legacy, but it has not been immune to challenges. The most important contributions in this regard have been made by economic and social historians of pre-colonial India, who, from roughly the early 1980s onward, began to argue that fundamental changes in social, political, and cultural life occurred between the sixteenth and the eighteenth centuries. Large-scale monetization of the economy that was helped by the influx of New World silver; commercial urbanization and the growth of commercial manufactures; an unprecedented scale of agrarian expansion; the emergence of empires that sought to both streamline revenue collection and to create a link between the agrarian hinterland and the seaboard; the arrival of European powers and the commercial opportunities that it opened up; and the cultural efflorescence associated with the spread of *bhakti* (devotion) across the subcontinent, all

---

9   Partha Chatterjee, *Nationalist Thought and the Colonial World: A Derivative Discourse* (1986); idem, *The Nation and its Fragments: Colonial and Postcolonial Histories* (Princeton, 1993).

had an effect on the scale and form of social relations and the nature of the polity. In the 1980s, Frank Perlin characterized this as a phase of 'commercial capitalism'.[10] More recently, Sanjay Subrahmanyam and Rosalind O'Hanlon, among others, have argued for a distinct phase of 'early modernity' that anticipated the modern period.[11]

The literature on early modernity has demolished the myth of pre-colonial economic stagnancy, but it has not resolved the key question about the relevance of capitalism. The category has largely been ignored, and some historians have explicitly called for an end to the 'search' for capitalism in early modern India.[12] The problem, however, is that if pre-1800 India is labelled 'early modern', then we should in principle be able to find an immanent transition to modern norms somewhere at some point. If we cannot, then one could justifiably argue that the category of 'early modern' tells us more about the present-day desire of historians to grant modernity to all parts of the world rather than the actual realities of pre-colonial India.[13] Indeed, postcolonial historians continue to insist that specifically modern political ideologies – including nationalism – can only be grounded in colonial pedagogy, even if we acknowledge the possibility of an early modern period that was 'not teleologically predetermined by the ascendancy of the colonial modern'.[14]

Historiographical turns, then, have resulted in a mixture of change and continuity. In the wake of the postcolonial intervention, however, the most important historical question can be posed thus: how would we know that the history of capitalism in India is important for understanding subaltern aspirations, and is not merely a history of the exercise of power by a colonial state acting in collusion with local elites? I show in the rest of this chapter that the history of subaltern critiques of caste can open a new window into this long-standing, seemingly irresolvable question.

10 Frank Perlin, 'Proto Industrialization and Pre-Colonial South Asia', *P&P*, 98 (1983), 30–95.
11 Rosalind O'Hanlon, 'Contested Conjunctures: Brahman Communities and 'Early Modernity' in India', *AHR*, 118 (2013), 765–787; Sanjay Subrahmanyam, 'Connected Histories: Notes towards a Reconfiguration of Early Modern Eurasia', *MAS*, 31 (1997), 735–762.
12 Prasannan Parthasarathi, 'Was there Capitalism in Early Modern India?', in *Rethinking a Millenium: Perspectives on Indian History from the Eighth to the Eighteenth Century*, ed. Rajat Datta (New Delhi, 2008), 342–360.
13 Dipesh Chakrabarty, 'The Muddle of Modernity', *AHR*, 116 (2011), 663–675.
14 Partha Chatterjee, *The Black Hole of Empire: History of a Global Practice of Power* (Princeton, 2011), 73–76.

II. 'Caste': Ideology, Practice, and Histories

Broadly speaking, two central problems remain the basis for disagreements among scholars about how to study caste. First, there is the question of sources, i.e., *what* should be the evidentiary basis for making claims about caste? This is a problem because the normative texts about what caste is and should be, i.e., texts which articulate the religious ideology of caste, were all written by upper castes, and most of them were composed before the end of the first millennium AD. Thus, even the most sophisticated analyses of these texts can only give us a partial view of what caste might have looked like in practice, and how it changed over time. On the other hand, if we want to understand how those at the bottom of the hierarchy responded to the system of caste, we can scarcely go back any further than the fifteenth century AD, and even then, the source base is extremely thin.

A related, second problem is how we approach the relationship between caste ideology and the broader social practices that enabled the reproduction of hierarchies. In other words, can we assume that there has always been a reasonable correspondence between what the ideology claimed and what caste in practice looked like? More importantly, did changes in the real world ever lead to serious problems for the ideology, or were the norms of hierarchy malleable enough to be adjusted to all kinds of social situations? These questions are at the heart of the matter as far as the history of caste is concerned, but they can scarcely be answered without simultaneously deciding upon what the sources for the study of caste can be. After all, a sole focus on texts, whatever their authorship, cannot help us answer the question of how caste worked in practice.

A discussion of the vast literature on caste that has sought to address these questions would take us too far afield. I shall focus, therefore, on clarifying my approach to the study of caste and its benefits.[15] I begin by distinguishing between the religious ideology of caste, on the one hand, and the set of practices that created, maintained, and reproduced inequalities that were then given, or attempted to be given, the *form* of caste through practices of kinship and the social organization of labour inspired by the ideology. Two practices were central in this process: the control of access to land, and the policing of access to markets.

The relationship between caste and access to land is well known. Broadly speaking, the agrarian order was structured in a way such that all caste groups inherited some kind of access to land, but that could be the right to revenue collection, a service tenure, some kind of right to tenancy or occupancy,

---

15 My framework is inspired by the work of many scholars too numerous to note here. Recent interventions with which my approach has some similarities include Sumit Guha, *Beyond Caste: Identity and Power in South Asia, Past and Present* (Leiden, 2013); and Surinder S. Jodhka, *Caste* (New Delhi, 2013).

sharecropping arrangements, the right to be an agrarian labourer, and, in the worst case, slavery. In other words, the lower a group was in the caste hierarchy, the lesser was the extent of its access to land.

This basic homology between access to land and caste was supplemented, however, by the policing of access to markets, which is an aspect that has been less highlighted in scholarly accounts. In essence, markets were treated as a form of agrarian property by upper-caste landed magnates, who were also the wielders of effective political power at the sub-regional and local levels. For lower castes, on the other hand, entry to markets required the payment of a wide variety of taxes, tolls, and fees. The control over land and markets, working in tandem, practically reproduced economic inequalities by ensuring differential access to property and power. This level of coherence in both practices can only be said to have emerged during the early medieval period (c.600–1200 AD), but that is sufficient for our narrative.[16]

To track the changing relationship over time between differential access and the religious ideology, it is also important to disentangle different aspects of the ideology itself. At the heart of the ideology lies the idea, I believe, that the maintenance of caste hierarchies is the way to ensure a homology between the divine and the secular worlds. To put it another way, the religious ideology, when considered holistically, can be interpreted as a theory of divine order *in* the secular world. To flesh out what such an order ought to look like, the ideology offers norms pertaining to two domains: kinship/marriage and the social organization of labour. In other words, for divine will to be reflected in the secular world, there had to be clear rules about who should do what kind of work, and who got to marry whom. Only then could the divine order be reproduced over time.

The most coherent theory offered by the ideology pertains to the domain of division of labour, where we find the notion of incommensurability in three interrelated spheres: people doing different kinds of labour are unequal, the different forms of labour performed by different groups are incommensurable, and the objects that are thereby produced are also incommensurable. Thus, the sword and the plough are not just objects that have 'utility'. On the contrary, they are imbued with social meaning. The Kshatriya, who is allowed, or rather *obliged* to use the sword, ranks much higher than the peasant who is not allowed to use a sword. Similarly, the maker of gold ornaments ranks higher than the maker of earthen pots, and the weaver of silk textiles ranks higher than the weaver of coarse muslins.

It is very difficult, if not impossible, to figure out which way the direction of causality runs, but all three claims about the incommensurability of persons,

---

16 See Manu Devadevan, *The 'Early Medieval' Origins of India* (Cambridge, 2020), 341–386.

labours, and objects are constitutive of this dimension of caste ideology. The ideal world is said to be one where the rules of marriage – endogamy to be precise – ensure the permanent separation of unequal groups engaged in incommensurable forms of labour. In addition, the policing of access to knowledge, which has been a constant feature of caste historically, can also be accounted for from within the theory of incommensurability. Specifically, the argument was that since knowledge, and especially the knowledge of the divine, is the purest object and pursuit, those engaged in menial occupations and dealing with impure objects – such as human waste – could not be allowed to engage in intellectual labour.

My approach allows us to make several crucial observations. First, the strength of the ideology depends fundamentally on the practical maintenance of hierarchies through differential access. Thus, if the practices of differential access were challenged, the ideology could suffer. Second, different aspects of the ideology could also be directly questioned. Indeed, for the period I am focusing on, there did emerge a critique of the idea that caste hierarchies were the best way to instantiate a divine order in the secular world. Similarly, the idea of incommensurability could be challenged when intensified commercialization and the rise of capitalism under early colonial rule weakened the correlation between caste and occupation.

Third, this means that different aspects of the ideology could get separated over time and have completely different trajectories. The most obvious possibility is a disjuncture between the norms of kinship and caste-based division of labour. Specifically, the correlation between caste and occupation could get severely weakened, but castes could continue to define themselves primarily in terms of marriage circles. Fourth, we should notice that even those who challenged caste hierarchies could have had different attitudes to different aspects of the ideology. Thus, even if the norms of incommensurability and kinship were both questioned, the overall impulse to find a homology between the secular and the divine worlds could have remained intact. I show that this is exactly what happened in Bengal, and such developments need to be taken seriously.

Fifth, my approach significantly enlarges the archive through which we can study caste, especially for the first century of colonial rule. Thus far, processes that remain reasonably well recorded in the early colonial archive – such as market conflicts, agrarian taxation and politics, and so on – have not been thought of as a window into caste dynamics. Once we think about the relationship between caste ranks and the practical conditions of possibility for their maintenance, however, it becomes possible to fruitfully use the colonial archive against its intentions.[17]

Finally, my focus on differential access allows us to study the intrinsic – and not just the contingent – effects of commercialization and capitalism on caste. After all, one would expect the rise of capitalism to have had major effects on the organization of markets and the ownership and use of land. For instance, we should expect to see an effect of capitalism on the idea of incommensurability between different labours and objects, because if the logic of incommensurability were taken to its extreme, then it would prevent the universal exchangeability of commodities. The question, then, is the following: what kind of approach to the history of capitalism would allow us to both study its relationship to caste and ground the challenges to caste in the history of capitalism in a non-functionalist manner?

III. Capitalism, Caste, and Subaltern Aspirations in Bengal, c.1500–1859

The answer to the question posed above lies in an approach to capitalism that sees it as a historically specific social form, one in which 'labour' plays an epochally unique socially mediating role. Karl Marx sought to grasp this with the category of 'abstract labour', which is often misunderstood as being merely a taxonomical abstraction that conceptually (and therefore violently, in many accounts) erases actual distinctions between different concrete labours. Yet in Marx, abstract labour names the 'essential' historical specificity of capitalism. It refers to the fact that in capitalism, labour is no longer mediated by overt social relations of dependence such as caste, serfdom, or servitude. Rather, labour itself mediates a new mode of interdependence among people.

In other words, abstract labour becomes a quasi-objective means for acquiring the products of others, and it mediates not only the relationship between humans and nature but among humans as well.[18] 'Labour' in capitalism is therefore not just a conceptual but rather a real abstraction. As Marx insisted, even the simplest category of 'labour', when 'economically conceived in [its] simplicity', is 'as *modern* a category as are the *relations* which create this *simple* abstraction'. Only in capitalism is abstract labour 'true in practice'.[19]

---

17 For a similar use of the colonial archive – including police records – to study the politics of untouchable groups in the twentieth century, see Ramnarayan S. Rawat, *Reconsidering Untouchability: Chamars and Dalit History in North India* (Bloomington, 2011).
18 This reading of Marx is deeply indebted to Moishe Postone, *Time, Labor, and Social Domination: A Reinterpretation of Marx's Critical Theory* (Cambridge, 1993).
19 Karl Marx, 'The Method of Political Economy', in *The Marx–Engels Reader*, ed. Robert C. Tucker (New York, 1978), 236–244, 239–240, 241. Emphases mine.

Additionally, abstract labour time creates 'value', and as a bearer of value, a 'commodity' is a combination of property and wealth constituted by labour. Capitalism, then, is a society based on free exchange, because it is labour that constitutes property, and the parting of individual and property – i.e., the exchange of commodities – occurs based on free volition.

Marx also argued, however, that the temporal tendency of capitalism is to destroy the property-constituting powers of labour because capitalist development is premised on the separation of labour from its product through the subordination of labour to capital. Over time, the very act of 'equal' exchange based on lateral relationships leads to vertical relationships in the 'hidden abode' of production, which is incompatible with the liberal norms of civic equality. Marx identified this as an immanent and dialectical contradiction at the heart of the relationship between liberal thought – which celebrates the sphere of exchange as 'a very Eden of the innate rights of man' where freedom, equality, property, and Bentham rule – and the realities of capitalist society.[20]

This is, of course, a theory posited at a very high level of abstraction, but it already tells us that equality and hierarchy are intrinsically related in capitalism. This implies that caste hierarchies are not incompatible with capitalism because the tendency to create new hierarchies is a constitutive internal contradiction of capitalist society. Moreover, even without narrating the history of caste, we can see how capitalist norms could enable a challenge to certain aspects of caste ideology. For instance, only the practical reality and normative force of abstract labour could negate the idea that labours, persons, and objects are incommensurable. Under capitalist conditions, commodities are universally exchangeable and equivalent, i.e., any commodity can be exchanged for any other. This is so because all commodities are material bearers of the same substance: value constituted by abstract labour. Indeed, abstract labour forms the practical basis of juridically equal abstract subjects, which liberal political theory affirms but fails to account for historically. Only abstract labour, therefore, could challenge the theory of incommensurability, and this is true not only of Bengal but of *all* pre-capitalist societies, where the non-equivalence of persons and things went hand in hand. Only with the emergence of capitalist social relations do we get a negation of such pre-capitalist norms anywhere.

My approach can thus coherently account for the plausibility of capitalist norms in India. As discussed earlier, generations of Marxist as well as non-Marxist scholars have struggled to do this; a limitation tied both to the mechanistic conception of norms and culture that informed much Marxist criticism, and to a naïve methodological nationalism that assumed capitalist development to be an iterative and modular process that is bound to repeat

---

20 Karl Marx, *Capital: A Critique of Political Economy, Volume One*, trans. Ben Fowkes (New York, 1976), 280.

itself within the spatial confines of every nation-state.[21] The obsession with 'when' India or Bengal 'became capitalist' led to a formalist approach based on the belief that one can nail down the precise moments of capitalist transition from a checklist of landmarks: primitive accumulation, wage labour, industrialization, and so on.

As Andrew Sartori has argued in a series of interventions, an approach focused on the socially mediating role of abstract labour allows for a much wider range of questions to be asked, because it attempts to discern how and when the histories of Indian practices and institutions became bound to the global histories of modern capital.[22] Instead of asking when Bengal or India became 'capitalist', the alternative Marxian approach asks when and how the reproduction of everyday life came to be fully dependent on networks of global capital. In turn, this allows us to understand why, from the nineteenth century onwards, people in Bengal found it impossible to make political arguments without reference to the role of labour in constituting social interdependence.[23]

These advantages notwithstanding, to claim that my approach has a real purchase on the historical trajectory of caste, we must be able to show two things. First, that capitalism, understood as abstract mediation, did inspire critiques of caste ideology as well as of the two practices that ensured the reproduction of caste hierarchies. And second, that when necessary and profitable, capitalism was perfectly capable of using the *legacies* of caste for its own purposes. My narrative shows that both are true.

To see this, we have to begin at the beginning. What we today call caste began to assume concrete shape sometime between 1000 and 600 BC, when the Vedic peoples who had migrated from Western Asia into North-Western India moved away from pastoral nomadism and towards settled agriculture as the primary way of life. At the time, there existed only a fourfold 'varna' classification: Brahmans (priests) at the top, followed by Kshatriyas (warriors and rulers), Vaishyas (initially cultivators and only subsequently traders), and Sudras (the ones who 'serve' the other three varnas).[24] Sometime around 600 BC, these groups also acquired the character of *hereditary* rather than

---

21 For the influence of methodological nationalism on the well-known debates regarding 'modes of production' in India, see Utsa Patnaik et al., *Studies in the Development of Capitalism in India* (Lahore, 1978).
22 See, especially, Andrew Sartori, 'Global Intellectual History and the History of Political Economy', in *Global Intellectual History*, eds. Samuel Moyn and Andrew Sartori (New York, 2013), 110–133; idem, 'The Labor Question and Political Thought in Colonial Bengal', in *Oxford Handbook of Comparative Political Theory*, eds. Leigh K. Jenco et al. (Oxford, 2020), 307–326.
23 Sartori, 'The Labor Question and Political Thought in Colonial Bengal'.
24 Although the word varna literally means 'colour', scholars agree that the fourfold classification was *not* – and could not have been – primarily based on colour. The similarity of physical features of the members of all four varnas in each region within the subcontinent

functional groups, because the inheritance of control over land could not have been streamlined otherwise.[25]

The establishment of a settled agrarian order in large parts of eastern and southern India occurred relatively late, beginning in the middle of the first millennium AD. In Bengal, the process began c.400 AD and some general points can be made about how caste evolved in the region during the early medieval (c.600–1200) period. First, the two major ruling dynasties – the Palas (c.750–1162) and the Senas (c.1070–1230) – were explicitly committed to the maintenance of a normative caste order. They made land grants on a large scale to upper castes, and the collection of revenue from these lands, cultivated by labour that was ranked as 'low caste', was the fiscal basis of the state. Between c.450 and 1230, there was continuous agrarian expansion and steady differentiation, and from the late-ninth century onward, land grants began to mention the entire caste spectrum with varying degrees of access to land: Brahmans were at the top and the Chandalas (the 'lowest of the mortals', a group classified as untouchable) were at the bottom.[26] As the scale of agriculture increased, elite groups with the right to revenue collection also developed an interest in controlling local markets that acted as nodes of distribution. This enabled control over distribution without being itinerant.[27]

Along with the establishment of political control over land and markets, attempts were made to impose a caste ideology. The Brahmans classified all non-Brahmans as Sudras, which is why there are no Kshatriyas or Vaishyas in Bengal. To distinguish between the regional elites and those below them, a further division within the Sudras was created: *sat* (pure) Sudras and *asat* (impure) Sudras. Literate groups and those with some control over land, especially the Kayasthas (scribes), the Vaidyas (the physicians) and the Magadhas (panegyrists) were classified as sat Sudras, and everyone else became asat Sudras. In short, securing the compliance and cooperation of the upper sections of rural society was important, and Brahmans had to maintain a fine

---

indicates that assimilation occurred at all levels in each region that was incorporated into the system. See Govind Sadashiv Ghurye, *Caste and Class in India* (Bombay, 1957), 116–142.
25 Devadevan, *The 'Early Medieval' Origins of India*, 356.
26 A set of classical texts known as the *Dharmashastras* (roughly 'law books') were composed by Brahmans between c.200 BC and AD 300. These texts sought to explain how a multitude of castes or 'jatis' (literally 'to be born of') could have been created from four 'varnas' through the 'mixture of varnas' (*varnasaṃkara*). The 'Chandala', for instance, was said to have been born from a Sudra father and a Brahman mother. For an extremely lucid analysis of the theory of *varnasaṃkara* and how it enabled the hierarchical ranking of a large number of groups by providing each of them with a mythical origin story, see Stanley J. Tambiah, 'From Varna to Caste through Mixed Unions', in *The Character of Kinship*, ed. Jack Goody (Cambridge, 1973), 191–229.
27 Ryosuke Furui, *Land and Society in Early South Asia: Eastern India 400–1250 AD* (London, 2020).

balance between denigrating local elites as Sudras while finding ways of distinguishing them from the larger mass of impure Sudras.[28]

Although the process moved in fits and starts, the general trend during the early medieval period was one of the gradual rooting of caste ideology. This occurred both because the establishment of a settled agrarian order most likely brought material benefits to everyone irrespective of their location in the hierarchy, and because caste norms became an inseparable part of popular religiosity. People at the bottom of the caste hierarchy who affirmed caste either implicitly in practice or explicitly – we will never know which – thought that fulfilling caste-ascribed duties inherited by birth was the way to instantiate a divine order in this world. It was also the way to get divine favour and attain *moksha* (liberation) from the endless cycle of births and deaths. Finally, given the large number of gradations that the system made possible, caste hierarchies became markers of relative status because any group could always find another below it to look down upon. This prevented the emergence of a unified opposition to Brahmanism.[29]

Between the fall of the Sena dynasty in the thirteenth century and the ascension to power of the Husain Shahis (1494–1538), nothing occurred of major significance for the history of caste. Nevertheless, two points of interpretive significance must be mentioned. First, despite the lack of an explicit commitment from the state – now controlled by Turks, Perso-Afghans, and other Muslims – to the maintenance of a normative caste order, caste continued to matter. The three upper castes – Brahmans, Kayasthas, and Vaidyas – actually managed to consolidate their position during this time. Similarly, the increased rate of agrarian expansion, coupled with the non-emergence of a Muslim peasantry, inflated the group of agrarian labourers drawn from the lowest castes. The clear implication is that caste did not need the explicit normative backing of a state to function because the practices of land and market control could continue without a commitment to the ideology of caste.[30]

Second, from the fifteenth century onwards, many hierarchical and endogamous castes with clearly defined primary occupations began to emerge

---

28 For further details on this complex process and the tensions inherent in it, see ibid., 188–249.
29 None of this is to suggest that either the practice or ideology of caste was simply accepted passively by those adversely affected by it. On the contrary, precisely because caste, state formation, and agrarian expansion were intricately interlinked, popular rebellion against high taxes and the 'state–Brahman' nexus often had a clear caste dimension. For a brief but informative discussion of such a rebellion from the eleventh century, see ibid., 169–174.
30 The lack of commitment by a state to the normative ideology of caste does not mean the lack of commitment by the state to caste. The fiscal basis of the state was agrarian revenue, and as long as access to land constituted caste hierarchies, commitment to the Brahmanical ideology was not necessary for caste to be reproduced.

among Muslims in both eastern and western Bengal.[31] Even though 'caste' had no scriptural justification in Islam, the theory of incommensurability seemed perfectly plausible to Muslims. Among weavers, for example, the Julahas, who wove only coarse muslins, formed a separate group and were universally looked down upon. The Tantis, on the other hand, who wove fine or embroidered cloth including silk textiles, were respected and usually referred to as Karigar or Jamdani Tanti.[32] Weavers of silk textiles were also given the honorific title of 'Nurbaft' or 'capturers of light'.[33] Silk, in other words, is an object that captures the play of light in ways that coarse muslins can never dream of. The two things are incommensurable, as are the people who work with them, and the labour they expend to create different kinds of textiles.

Other examples of 'low' Muslim castes devoted to specific occupations include the Beldárs, who were engaged in scavenging, cutting brushwood, and bearing torches at both Muslim and non-Muslim weddings.[34] The Lal Begis, on the other hand, were a motley collection of groups primarily devoted to scavenging and sweeping, and they could be sometimes Muslims and sometimes Hindus, or not fully assimilated into either community.[35] The fact that norms of incommensurability took hold among Muslims to this extent shows that certain aspects of caste ideology could function on their own without being tied to a larger religious worldview. This is an extremely significant point because it means that the annihilation of caste cannot be achieved solely by religious conversion.[36]

The question, then, is this: did subaltern groups ever challenge both caste ideology and the control of land and markets in ways that we can retrospectively grasp as capitalist? The answer is yes, and to see that, we have to begin with the watershed moment of the long sixteenth century (1494–1632), which witnessed major socio-economic as well as political transformations. Vast amounts of fallow and forest lands were brought under the plough with unprecedented vigour, first in western and south-western Bengal in the sixteenth century, and

---

31 A contemporary description of this trend can be found in Mukundaram Chakravarti's late-sixteenth-century text *Chandimangal*, which mentions as many as fifteen Muslim castes living in an idealized city of the time. See Mukundaram Chakravarti, *Kabikankan-Chandi*, ed. Srikumar Bandyopadhyay (Calcutta, 1952), 345–346.
32 James Wise, *Notes on the Races, Castes, and Trades of Eastern Bengal* (Delhi, 1883, 2016), 98–99, 140–141.
33 C.A. Bayly, *Origins of Nationality in South Asia: Patriotism and Ethical Government in the Making of Modern India* (New Delhi, 2001), 182–183.
34 Wise, *Notes on the Races, Castes, and Trades of Eastern Bengal*, 53.
35 Ibid., 403–406.
36 For an ethnographic account of the continued salience of caste identity, endogamy, and even untouchability among Indian Muslims, see Prashant K. Trivedi *et al.*, 'Does Untouchability Exist Among Muslims? Evidence from Uttar Pradesh', *Economic and Political Weekly*, 51 (9 April 2016), 32–36.

then in the east throughout the seventeenth and eighteenth centuries.[37] This was paralleled by the expansion of marketing, which some scholars have called the 'commercialization of agrarian relations'.[38] Indeed, the establishment of new markets was a regular affair by the late sixteenth century, and some of the markets founded at the time were still functioning in the late 1700s.[39]

Although the flourishing of commerce was initially enabled by political stability under the pragmatic rule of the Husain Shahis, commercialization continued apace even during the turbulent period of Mughal–Afghan conflict during c.1540–1620.[40] Along with an expansion of the agrarian frontier, there was commercial urbanization along riverine trade routes, which was motivated by the felt need to better integrate mercantile capital with agrarian as well as artisanal production. These towns were close to areas of rice production and were often textile-producing centres. They were usually not walled and rarely patronized by large landlords (*zamindars*). Finally, the gradual integration of Bengal into the Mughal Empire between 1575 and 1632 meant that it became part of a pan-Indian empire for the first time since the break-up of the Gupta Empire. In turn, this increased landed trade with Northern India as well as with Western and Central Asia.

The long sixteenth century also witnessed the arrival of the first Portuguese trading mission in 1518. Although the Husain Shahis were initially hostile, by the mid-1530s, faced with an attack from the Afghan Sher Shah Suri, the Bengal sultans sought to build a political alliance with the Portuguese. Between 1533 and 1536, the latter were allowed to build bases at both of the major ports – Saptagram in the west and Chittagong in the east – and to collect customs duties there. They were also given an interest in the lands adjoining the ports, and to collect rents from these areas. This can be considered the very first instance of a radically new model of urbanization in the subcontinent – that of coastal towns drawing in resources and labour from the hinterland – which eventually became the norm among European companies seeking to reduce contract risks and transaction costs.[41]

Although western Bengal was firmly under Mughal control by the 1580s, strategic alliances were still needed. A *farman* (royal order) in 1578 allowed

---

37 The classic account of the expansion of the agrarian frontier is Richard Eaton, *The Rise of Islam and the Bengal Frontier, 1204–1760* (Berkeley, 1993).
38 David Curley, *Poetry and History: Bengali Mangalkabya and Social Change in Precolonial Bengal* (New Delhi, 2008), 36.
39 Rajat Datta, 'Governing Agrarian Diversities: The State and the Making of an Early Modern Economy in Sixteenth-Century Northern India', *Medieval History Journal*, 16, 2 (2013), 473–499, 494.
40 Aniruddha Ray, *Adventurers, Landowners, and Rebels: Bengal c.1575–1715* (Delhi, 1998).
41 Tirthankar Roy, *India in the World Economy: From Antiquity to the Present* (Cambridge, 2012), 15–16.

the Portuguese to settle at the port of Hugli, which had begun to overshadow Saptagram as the main harbour. As it became a flourishing port in the late-sixteenth and early seventeenth centuries, however, direct control over Hugli became beneficial. The port was thus sacked in 1632 and control was wrested from the Portuguese, who were allowed to resettle shortly afterwards as traders. The importance of this event can be seen from the fact that all of the European companies established their first factories in Bengal on the western banks of the Hugli River: the Dutch at Chinsurah in 1635 and at Kasimbazar sometime between 1645 and 1651, the British at Hugli in 1651 and at Kasimbazar in 1658, and the French at Chandernagore in 1673.

The *bhakti* movement, at once social, religious, and cultural, emerged against this background of radical change. Derived from the Sanskrit root *bhaj*, bhakti means 'devotion' to something or someone.[42] In the sixteenth century, bhakti was invoked to suggest that universal access to the divine without the mediation of Brahmans was possible through devotion. A lot can be said about the movement, but two novel features are of the greatest importance. First, the explicit orientation towards the lowest and the most unfortunate members of society was entirely new, at least within the Hindu tradition. Indeed, if there is one message that sums up the meaning and purpose of the movement, it is that God had descended to earth in the form of Chaitanya Mahaprabhu (1486–1533) to deliver from all manner of evil all of humankind, especially those in the greatest need of such grace, namely women, sinners, and the lowest castes. Second, bhakti affirmed an individual's present birth as a wonderful opportunity to break out of stereotypical self-images rooted in a person's caste, sex, and occupation. Thus, against the Brahmanical view that one's character is determined by birth, the bhakti movement emphasized the possibility of change, transformation, and development in *this* life through divine mercy and grace. In effect, the bhakti critique asserted that caste and other ascriptive statuses could *not* be compatible with divinity or be a reflection of divine will.

One of the most lasting legacies of bhakti was its contribution to a gradual withdrawal of sacral legitimacy from external institutions to inner devotion. Although critiques of caste had long been prevalent in Bengal through Buddhism, the sixteenth-century movement and its various sectarian manifestations in the eighteenth and nineteenth centuries were different in one key respect. Poets now self-consciously reflected on the kind of practices and institutions that could enable a society free of caste. As early as the 1580s, Narottam Dāsa's (1534–1630?) remarkable poem Hāṭ Pattan ('Founding of a marketplace'), proceeded from a metaphorical identification of the 'marketplace' with congregational participation in the divine. While it is true that the object of reflection in the

---

42 Joseph. T. O'Connell, *Chaitanya Vaishnavism in Bengal: Social Impact and Historical Implications* (2019), 15.

pan-Indian bhakti tradition had always been the 'relation' between finite human beings and the infinite divine, what was new in Hāṭ Pattan was the deployment of a new set of relational metaphors – that of the 'marketplace' – to talk about what obligations to divinity and to other people could mean. By using the marketplace metaphor, Narottam's poem opened up a conceptual space for reimagining what living with others could mean in sixteenth-century Bengal.

The metaphor first used by Narottam also had a long and productive afterlife. By the time we reach the eighteenth century, we find a constant use of the marketplace metaphor as well as of metaphors of secular or *this-worldly* labouring activity by lower-caste bhakti sects such as the *Kartābhajās* (worshippers of the master), the *Sāhebdhanīs* (the wealthy Englishmen), and the *Bāuls*, and even by upper-caste *Śākta* poets such as Rāmprasād Sen (1718–1775). These poets pondered deeply and carefully about what could mediate the relationship between finite beings and their institutions in the secular world and the world of the infinite divine, if not caste-ascribed duties inherited by birth. Their short answer was: worldly labour unmarked by caste.[43]

Such reflections found *parallels* in the political and practical domain. For instance, petty merchants belonging to lower and middling castes challenged 'arbitrary' market taxes imposed by upper-caste elites and the colonial state.[44] Similarly, in the districts of Nadia and Jessore – where heterodox bhakti communities such as the *Kartābhajās* (worshippers of the master) were most active – lower caste groups fought against zamindari oppression, often with the help of Baptist missionaries.[45] The disjuncture that this created between the secular and the divine worlds, however, became a source of anxiety even among lower castes.

This is how, I insist, 'capitalism' becomes relevant for understanding even subaltern critiques of caste ideology. The idea that the sacred could emerge *immanently* from within the profane was radically new, and it went against the grain of the millennia-old idea that the material world was illusory. To be sure, references to the fleeting and illusory character of the material world continued to exist in bhakti poetry, but such claims sat in uncomfortable tension with newer impulses. Given how unprecedented the set of arguments made by subaltern poets was, it is reasonable to suggest that these claims had some relationship to the increasing importance of abstract labour as a practical reality in early colonial Bengal. The idea that worldly labour unmarked by

---

43 For a longer version of this argument backed up by textual evidence, see Anirban Karak, 'Devotional Poetry and Political Economy in Early Colonial Bengal', *Journal of the History of Ideas Blog* (11 October 2023).
44 Anirban Karak, "The Politics of Commerce in Eighteenth-Century Bengal: A Reappraisal', *Indian Economic and Social History Review*, 61 (2024), 33–66.
45 Muhammad Mohar Ali, *The Bengali Reaction to Christian Missionary Activities, 1833–1857* (Chittagong, 1965).

caste could become the means to subjective freedom became plausible precisely at the moment of capitalist transition under early colonial rule.

My reading may appear eccentric, but it becomes perfectly plausible when we place it against the background of simultaneous challenges to the policing of access to markets and land. As marketing networks expanded, market conflicts became endemic in the eighteenth century. Petitions sent by petty merchants and weavers show that those worst affected by the British East India Company's (EIC) own monopoly practices, and by the arbitrary exactions of regional elites, petitioned the colonial state in the hopes of redressal.[46] I have argued elsewhere that such conflicts over market access were deeply political, and they were embedded in longer-run histories of caste as differential access to property and power.[47] The desire for greater commercial liberties came from lower and middling castes, whereas the defence of the status quo came from upper castes and also from some upwardly mobile middling castes. The company-state had a hard time finding a balance between demands for commercial freedoms from below, the right of the state to revenue, and the privileges that local persons of status hoped to enjoy. The need for maintaining such a balance arose precisely because secular aspirations from below were making it increasingly difficult to keep the market subordinate to prevailing structures of civic authority.

In the agrarian context as well, we find similar forward-looking impulses among lower-caste peasants and agrarian slaves. For too long, scholars have ignored the fact that agrarian expansion in eastern Bengal was based on a major intensification of rural slavery.[48] Admittedly, the definition of 'slavery' was not clear cut, and neither was the relationship between slavery and caste. Nevertheless, from the testimony of upper castes recorded in the early colonial archive, we can safely conclude that caste and slavery were overlapping but not identical forms of labour control: the number of 'impure' castes set the upper limit to the total number of agrarian slaves, because 'pure' castes could be domestic slaves to castes of the same (or higher status), but they could never be agrarian slaves.[49]

Moreover, litigations by masters against those they considered runaway 'slaves' abounded between 1820 and 1850, and the testimony of the alleged slaves in these cases is remarkable.[50] It is clear, for instance, that descendants of erstwhile slaves wanted to assert a property right over their bodies and labour.

---

46 The weavers' petitions are discussed in Debendra Bijoy Mitra, *The Cotton Weavers of Bengal, 1757–1833* (Calcutta, 1978).
47 Karak, 'The Politics of Commerce in Eighteenth-Century Bengal'.
48 The only full-length study is Amal Kumar Chattopadhyay, *Slavery in the Bengal Presidency, 1772–1843* (Calcutta, 1977).
49 Indian Law Commission, *Report on Slavery in India, with Appendices* (India, 1841), II: 29, *passim*.
50 Ibid., 251–280.

They wanted to be able to choose where, how, and under whom they would work, and they preferred contractual relationships of 'loans' and 'wages' over the paternalism of a master–slave relationship. This was also a rejection of caste norms and the paternalism of caste relations, since we know that only impure castes were forced into agrarian slavery. Slaves wanted to be able to move freely whenever they wanted to, and they preferred the status of 'cultivators' or 'raiyats' over that of 'slave'.

If alleged slaves wanted to be peasants, then the resistance of peasants to greater coercion and rent extraction was not based on an atavistic vision of autarkic self-sufficiency, but rather on aspirations for participation in commercial networks on more equal terms. In a landmark study, Andrew Sartori has traced the influence of a liberalism among agrarian actors in Bengal from the 1860s onward, one that was based on the Lockean claim that it is labour that constitutes property.[51] I suggest that such claims were already present in the *Paglai Dhum* peasant rebellion (1825–1833) in the eastern frontier district of Mymensingh. Here, hill tribes such as the Garos, the Hajongs, and the Hadis, who were being incorporated into a settled agrarian order as *labouring* castes, resisted increased revenue assessment. They claimed that since it was through their labour (or of their forefathers) that forests had been reclaimed and the land made to bear fruit, the incremental profit and higher rent that resulted from the increased settlement in the region should accrue to them and not to the landlords or the state.[52] For lower-caste peasants, this was not a theoretical point, but rather a way to assert their selfhood and dignity. Indeed, by claiming that *all* labour irrespective of caste status should be seen as constituting property equally, the peasants articulated a profound critique of caste as a regime where those who laboured the most were perpetually propertyless.[53]

By the 1850s, the distinctive effects of modern capitalism on caste hierarchies began to be felt clearly and strongly. From the long sixteenth century onwards, commercialization had intensified the loosening of the caste–occupation

---

51 Andrew Sartori, *Liberalism in Empire: An Alternative History* (Berkeley, 2014).
52 For a detailed study of the Mymensingh rebellion, see Gautam Bhadra, *Iman O Nishan: Unish Shatake Banglar Krishak Chaitanyer ek Adhyay, c.1800–1850* (Calcutta, 1994), 20–164.
53 The relationship between *caste* and *abstract labour* is an exceedingly complex issue, and my historical narrative in this chapter has necessarily been a broad-brushstrokes one. I should clarify, though, that I am *not* saying that the practical reality of abstract labour reached such an extent in early modern Bengal that caste stratification ceased to matter. Indeed, in a profound sense, this has never happened anywhere on the subcontinent. Nevertheless, I do think that caste and labour bondage began to *mean* something different once production became geared towards either maintaining revenue for a colonial state or seeking profit and reinvestment in increasingly competitive and integrated markets. 'Labour', therefore, became an increasingly incoherent category by the late eighteenth century, and this *incoherence* is what poets and labouring people were responding to in distinctly forward-looking ways.

nexus.[54] As a result, kinship and the social division of labour began to have separate trajectories. Castes often engaged in multiple occupations, but most of them were still invested in defining themselves with respect to clearly delimited marriage circles. The first effect of capitalist transition under early colonial rule was to intensify this disjuncture, which was further enabled by colonial laws that began to demarcate the domains of 'labour', 'family', and 'gender'. These aspects of social life had all fallen *within* the purview of 'caste' up to the early modern period, and the rise of capitalism, along with colonial legislation, separated them for good. The temporal end-point of my narrative – 1859 – saw the passing of one such act that sealed the separation of labour into its own sphere of legislation: the Workman's Breach of Contract Act, which criminalized the breach of contract by workers.

We see, then, that even though the rise of capitalism in India depended fundamentally on British capital and colonial agency, it was Indian labour which did all the work. More specifically, it was the lowest castes and the tribes on the margins of the settled agrarian order who did the most difficult forms of labour. This would not be very significant if those communities had considered capitalism to be an entirely alien social form with no relevance to their lives. But they did not. Rather, their critique of extractive colonial capitalism was premised on an affirmation of a different vision of capitalism itself. At stake for them was the possibility of freedom from both an oppressive caste order as well as colonial rule.

Why, then, was there only limited success in overcoming caste practically? Three points can be briefly made. First, the bhakti critique of caste ideology failed because it did not have an alternative theory of the 'outer' world that could displace caste. As a result, despite an affirmation of the secular world in radically new ways, bhakti-inspired thought often tended to retreat to the 'inner' sanctum of devotion. Second, in the commercial sphere, the failure to transcend caste was largely a result of contingent political defeats, and of the continued existence of differential access to markets. Indeed, market taxes remained an important aspect of caste-based hierarchies even in the 1930s and 40s, when lower castes had to organize agitations against *hat-tola* (market tolls) extracted by upper-caste landlords and moneylenders.[55]

---

54 This is not to suggest that there ever was a perfect correspondence between caste and occupation. Nevertheless, there can be little doubt that early modern commercialization and modern capitalism have severed the link between occupation and accidents of birth in unprecedented ways. The real question is why the link has not been severed completely.
55 Sekhar Bandyopadhyay, *Caste, Protest, and Identity in Colonial India: The Namasudras of Bengal, 1872–1947* (Oxford, 2011), 231–232; Swaraj Basu, *Dynamics of a Caste Movement: The Rajbansis of North Bengal, 1910–1947* (New Delhi, 2003), 121–124.

Finally, in the agrarian sphere, the internal limitations of Lockeanism intersected in complex ways with the *legacy* of caste to prevent its being overcome.[56] By the late-eighteenth century, the practices of differential access had created a de facto separation between propertied (capital) and propertyless (labour) castes, which implies that the colonial state did not create a mass of landless, proletarian labourers from scratch.[57] Capitalism capitalized (pun intended) on this legacy, and this meant that Lockeanism was incapable of responding to the situation adequately. Specifically, the defence of capital as 'private property' from a Lockean standpoint could end up being a defence of historically constituted caste hierarchies, because the uppermost castes had historically accumulated the greatest amount of property. Moreover, Lockean liberalism could not account for the dynamic transformation of labour into capital. Especially in frontier regions with surplus land, rent-payers often became rent-receivers over time once their labour was transmuted into 'capital' and they could hire new labourers. Such processes also led to internal differentiation *within* historically oppressed groups such as the Namasudras and the Rajbansis.[58] This entanglement between extant caste statuses and capitalism's tendency to create new hierarchies meant that only an immanent critique of capitalism could properly respond to the situation, and Lockeanism stopped far short of that.[59]

IV. Conclusion

The story I have sketched above has implications for the study of caste and capitalism in South Asia, and also for the study of capitalism across the globe

---

56 By using the term *legacy*, I do not mean to suggest that caste as it exists today is merely a remnant of a pre-capitalist past. Rather, *legacy* here refers specifically to the fact that the control of land and markets over the *longue durée* had generated a de facto separation between labour and capital, implying that primitive accumulation of the classical kind was not necessary in the subcontinent for capital to constitute itself.
57 See Dharma Kumar, 'Caste and Landlessness in South India', *CSSH*, 4 (1962), 337–363; Ranajit Dasgupta, 'Factory Labor in Eastern India: Sources of Supply, 1855–1946; Some Preliminary Findings', *IESRH*, 13 (1976), 277–329; Rupa Vishwanath, *The Pariah Problem: Caste, Religion, and the Social in Modern India* (New York, 2014); and Uday Chandra, 'Kol, Coolie, Colonial Subject: A Hidden History of Caste and the Making of Modern Bengal', in *The Politics of Caste in West Bengal*, eds. Uday Chandra et al. (2016), 19–34. Cf. Ian J. Kerr, *Building the Railways of the Raj, 1850–1900* (Oxford, 1995).
58 Bandyopadhyay, *Caste, Protest, and Identity*, 3, 153–155; Basu, *Dynamics of a Caste Movement*, 21, 46, 54, 82, 103.
59 For a particularly stark example of how modern capitalism builds upon the legacy of caste and even intensifies its effects, see Shreyas Sreenath, '(Un)making the Manual Scavenger: Caste, Contract, and Ecological Uncertainty in Bengaluru, India', *American Ethnologist*, 50 (2023), 491–505.

more generally. Despite a renewed interest in histories of capitalism over the past decade and a half, there have been few attempts to explore how people in the colonized world responded to modern capitalism, and even fewer challenges to the implicit assumption in colonial studies that the categories of 'capitalism' and 'colonialism' are essentially congruent.[60] My narrative sheds serious doubt on this assumption, and my chapter is closest in substance to Chapter 6 in this volume, by Gareth Austin, who also seeks to chart the indigenous pathways to capitalism in Western Africa.

More importantly, the historical problem of how to account for the co-existence of challenges to caste and its continued salience in the present is a *general* problem in the historiography of early modern and modern capitalism. With regard to critiques of hierarchy, the way I study the relationship between capitalism and challenges to caste runs strikingly parallel with how historians of eighteenth-century Europe and the Atlantic World have identified the rise of modern commercial impulses as a solvent of settled hierarchies, and as a stimulus to greater civic equality.[61] Capitalism, however, did not lead to a gradual and inevitable overcoming of hierarchies *anywhere*. On the contrary, ascriptive hierarchies of 'race' became consolidated and strengthened in large parts of the world during the rise of capitalism between the sixteenth and the early nineteenth centuries.

The contradiction between these two developments was particularly stark in some regions such as the United States, where the century after 1776 was defined by the simultaneous existence of slavery for one group and freedom for others, and the post-1865 period has been characterized by the contradiction between racism and democracy.[62] Moreover, all 'racial' groups were incorporated into capitalism and modern nation-states through the expropriation of land and/or the exploitation of labour.[63] In Eurasia as well, the early modern period witnessed both an increasing importance of bonded labour, as well as

---

60 For important exceptions to the trend of assuming congruence between all things capitalist (such as private property in land) and 'colonialism' (or 'settler colonialism'), see Emilio Kourí, *A Pueblo Divided: Business, Property, and Community in Papantla, Mexico* (Stanford, 2004); and Paula López Caballero and Arianda Acevedo-Rodrigo (eds.), *Beyond Alterity: Destabilizing the Indigenous Other in Mexico* (Tucson, 2018).
61 For very different approaches to this question, see J.G.A. Pocock, *The Machiavellian Moment: Florentine Political Thought and the Atlantic Republican Tradition* (Princeton, 1975); and Sewell Jr., *Capitalism and the Emergence of Civic Equality in Eighteenth-Century France*.
62 Edmund S. Morgan, *American Slavery, American Freedom: The Ordeal of Colonial Virginia* (New York, 1975); Barbara Jeanne Fields, 'Slavery, Race, and Ideology in the United States of America', *New Left Review*, 181 (1990), 95–118.
63 Thomas C. Holt, *The Problem of Race in the 21st Century* (Cambridge, MA, 2000), 53. Cf. Patrick Wolfe, 'Land, Labor, and Difference: The Elementary Structures of Race', *AHR*, 106 (2001), 866–905.

an impulse towards greater integration of production and local markets with increasingly larger networks of capital.[64]

It is time, I believe, to move beyond purely cultural and religious accounts of caste, and to locate its *modern* history in South Asia within this larger contradiction between equality and hierarchy in global capitalism. By attempting this broader comparison of caste and race with regard to their instantiations *within* capitalism, we can grasp the similarities and differences between India and other parts of the world much better than approaches that seek to directly compare 'caste' and 'race' as systems of hierarchy and modes of domination.[65]

Moreover, this can be done without mechanistically applying sociological models, and without ignoring the deep specificities of the history of bhakti and caste. My narrative takes these specificities very seriously, but it also points out how the rise of capitalism affected both the practical instantiations of caste and the critique of hierarchies in fundamental ways. Even though caste was a long-standing institution, in other words, it was always a means for the control of access to resources, and it was affected in non-linear ways by the onset of modern commercial impulses.[66]

The upshot of all this for the study of South Asia is two-fold. First, my narrative about Bengal can be situated alongside a growing body of work that shows how norms of hierarchy and untouchability found a new lease of life in the eighteenth century. In the regions of modern-day Rajasthan and Maharashtra in western India, for example, the seventeenth and eighteenth centuries witnessed not only an increase in the incidence of slavery but also a renewed emphasis on 'purity' of caste and 'descent'.[67] The context in both provinces was one of regional assertions against Mughal rule and agrarian expansion. The slaves were not only war captives, but also those affected badly by famine and ongoing debt. They performed all kinds of labour including military service and agrarian labour.

---

64 Alessandro Stanziani, *Bondage: Labor and Rights in Eurasia from the Sixteenth to the Early Twentieth Centuries* (New York, 2014); Jairus Banaji, *A Brief History of Commercial Capitalism* (Chicago, 2020).
65 The literature on this question is of very old provenance. For an overview of how caste and race in India and the United States respectively have been compared in different ways for different political purposes in different eras, see Daniel Immerwahr, 'Caste or Colony? Indianizing Race in the United States', *MIH*, 4 (2007), 275–301.
66 For a recent attempt to locate caste within the history of global racial capitalism, albeit one that emphasizes only hierarchy and ignores the *impulse* to equality generated by capitalism itself, see Sheetal Chhabria, 'Where Does Caste Fit in A Global History of Racial Capitalism?' *Historical Materialism*, 31 (2023), 136–160.
67 See the essays by Ramya Sreenivasan and Sumit Guha in *Slavery and South Asian History*, eds. Indrani Chatterjee and Richard M. Eaton (Bloomington, 2006), 136–161, 162–186.

In an important new study, Divya Cherian has narrated how upward mobility among merchant castes led to a desire for greater 'distance' from those deemed untouchable, a project that was brought to fruition in alliance with the pre-colonial state of Marwar (in present-day Rajasthan) in the late-eighteenth century.[68] In a slightly different vein, Aparna Balachandran has shown that during the first half of the eighteenth century, the British East India Company in Madras tried to include both upper castes and lower-caste artisans and labourers in the process of governance. After the acquisition of a territorial empire in the 1760s, however, governance increasingly acquired a racist and high-caste character.[69]

The crux of the matter is that political and economic changes in the eighteenth century affected caste in many regions of South Asia in *non-linear* ways: it both inspired challenges to caste and intensified the exploitation and exclusion of those who were already at the bottom of the hierarchy as landless/propertyless labourers. Moreover, caste ideology and the practices of differential access both played a role in this process, and we need to understand the interplay between the two dimensions instead of one-sidedly emphasizing just one.[70]

The second implication of my account is that if we want to understand caste today, we cannot simply invoke the ideology of ritual hierarchy.[71] Rather, we have to painstakingly analyze how the intersection of capitalism with the legacies of caste as differential access to property prevented and continues to prevent the overcoming of caste. Capitalism has mattered for the history of caste in more ways than we have hitherto imagined, and the fact that the norms of ritual hierarchy have no basis in actuality today can be seen from the trajectory of caste ideology itself. Between the fourteenth and the nineteenth centuries, for example, as commercialization led to a much greater division of labour, Brahmans responded by creating entirely new rungs in the ritual hierarchy that could incorporate *new* castes with new occupational definitions into an 'expanding middle'.[72]

---

68 Divya Cherian, *Merchants of Virtue: Hindus, Muslims, and Untouchables in Eighteenth-Century South Asia* (Berkeley, 2023).
69 See Aparna Balachandran, 'Of Corporations and Caste Heads: Urban Rule in Company Madras, 1640–1720', *Journal of Colonialism and Colonial History*, 9 (2008), 1–8.
70 For a recent attempt to develop an 'affective' theory of caste that arrives at the same conclusion, see Joel Lee, 'Disgust and Untouchability: Towards an Affective Theory of Caste', *South Asian History and Culture*, 12 (2021), 310–327.
71 Cf. Hugo Gorringe, Surinder S. Jodhka, and Opinderjit Kaur Takhar, 'Caste: Experiences in South Asia and Beyond', *Contemporary South Asia*, 25 (2017), 230–237.
72 In Bengal, for example, Brahmans came up with the new category of *Navasakha* (*Nava* = nine, *sakha* = branch) or nine branches of clean Sudras to incorporate upwardly mobile groups who could no longer be denigrated as impure Sudras. For more details, see Hitesranjan Sanyal, *Social Mobility in Bengal* (Calcutta, 1981).

Crucially, however, from the mid-nineteenth century onwards, all such attempts were given up. There is no caste, for example, of software engineers, food delivery personnel, or fashion designers. From today's vantage point, it may seem absurd to even contemplate this. Yet, we should not forget that this is precisely what the ideologues of caste continued to try and do until the early nineteenth century: to account for the social organization of labour *within* a larger theory of kinship, hierarchy, and divine order. This tells us, more clearly than perhaps anything can, that the kind of social organization of labour that modern, industrial capitalism makes possible is incomparable to anything else that came before. Beginning in the 1830s, moreover, the geographical scale that determined the social organization of labour was effectively the entire globe. This is why Indian indentured labour could produce Caribbean sugar while Indians used British textiles on a large scale. The ideology of caste could not keep up with these changes.

The violence and bigotry that we see in the name of caste today are the desperate, rearguard, and reactionary actions of certain castes who recognize that the notion of ritual hierarchy no longer has any practical basis. Indeed, precisely because ritual status is no longer an immediate marker of economic status, brutal forms of violence against the ex-untouchables (Dalits) are often perpetrated by middling castes classified as Other Backward Classes (OBCs), who want to maintain both symbolic and material authority (through control over land paradigmatically) over those 'below' them. In the practical domain, caste and class remain maddeningly intertwined, but that is only because capitalism capitalized on the legacies of differential access. There can be no resolution of the caste question, therefore, without an immanent overcoming of capitalism. The abolition of proletarian labour is a necessary precondition for the annihilation of caste, and while there is no easy cure for 'prejudice', any cure must include, surely, a drastic change in the form of reality that sustains it.

11

Chinese Capitalism c.1500–1850: Institutions, Dimensions, Dynamics and Limitations

KENNETH POMERANZ

The introduction to the *Cambridge History of Capitalism* identifies four features common to all varieties of capitalism: (1) private property rights; (2) contracts enforceable by third parties; (3) markets with responsive prices; and (4) supportive governments. The fourth feature is left undefined.[1]

Some of what is left unexplored are forms of state coercion that increase the profits of certain market participants. That coercion can be of a kind almost universally condemned today: enforcing slavery or serfdom, for instance, or violently expropriating resources previously governed by customary usufruct rights, thereby accomplishing Marx's 'primitive accumulation' and creating proletarians forced to sell their labour.[2] Coercion can also take benign forms: requiring licences to sell goods which are hard to evaluate, enacting patent laws that incentivize invention, and the like. Classical Marxism's focus on primitive accumulation as a discrete moment (or moments) of coercion, ushering in a capitalist order that can subsequently rely on the economic necessity of selling one's labour, actually takes a relatively narrow view of how coercion has helped to create and sustain capitalist societies. By contrast, Fernand Braudel (1902–1985) and scholars influenced by him consider the *on-going* involvement of governments in skewing selected markets to favour certain accumulators so central that they consider 'market economy' and 'capitalism' categorically different systems. Much of the 'new history of capitalism' has followed this path, focusing especially on the early modern Atlantic world.[3]

---

[1] Larry Neal, 'Introduction', in *CHC*, I: 2.
[2] The classic account, focusing on England, is in Karl Marx, *Capital* (New York, 1967), I: 713–749; cf. Charles Tilly, 'Demographic Origins of the European Proletariat', in *Proletarianization and Family History*, ed. David Levine (New York, 1984), 1–85 for a different account of proletarianization.
[3] Fernand Braudel, *Civilization and Capitalism, 15th–18th Century*, 3 vols. (New York, 1982–1984). For three examples from a vast and varied literature influenced by Braudel see Immanuel Wallerstein, *The Modern World-System*, 3 vols. (New York, 1976–1989); Sven

Scholars in Maoist China paid at least lip service to classical Marxism. Thus their vigorous debates over to what extent pre-Opium War China had incubated 'sprouts of capitalism' largely focused on the prevalence of wage labour.[4] While large concentrations of wage labourers were found in a few mining and logging operations and some imperially sponsored factories producing high-end porcelain and cloth, even those workers were often distinguished from 'true' proletarians because their families owned some means of production, or they were victims of extra-market coercion (convict labourers, for instance), or both. (That this was also true of many European and American proletarians apparently escaped notice in China.) And everyone agreed that what were by far the biggest sectors of the late imperial Chinese economy – non-luxury cloth production, food processing, home-building and above all agriculture – used little wage labour. Even c.1930, less than 15 per cent of agricultural work was wage labour, even including numerous small land-owners supplementing their income by hiring out for a few days.[5] Thus pre-1839 China was generally deemed non-capitalist, despite having large merchants who sought profits as energetically as their peers elsewhere and enormous numbers of small-scale commodity producers who bought and sold in competitive markets undergirded by reasonably secure property rights and contract enforcement.[6]

Late imperial China was not a capitalist society, but we have learned much more than the authors of the 'sprouts' literature knew about its substantial capitalist elements and their limitations. (The 'sprouts' literature – forced within a paradigm in which all societies should naturally become capitalist – needed an external *deus ex machina* and generally chose either the seventeenth-century Manchu conquest or nineteenth-century Western aggression.) Reassessment is warranted both because of numerous new empirical findings about China and because of insights from recent studies of the history of capitalism worldwide.

Beckert, *Empire of Cotton: A Global History* (New York, 2014); Edward Baptist, *The Half Has Never Been Told: Slavery and the Making of American Capitalism* (New York, 2014).
4 See especially Xu Dixin and Wu Chengming, *Zhongguo zibenzhuyi de mengya* (Beijing, 1985).
5 For twentieth-century data, see J.L. Buck, *Land Utilization in China: A Study of 16,786 Farms in 168 Localities and 38,256 Farm Families in Twenty-two Provinces in China, 1929–1933* (Chicago, 1937), especially 293 on the relatively commercialized Yangzi Delta, where the number was under 10 per cent. For some eighteenth-century data, see Jiang Taixin and Li Wenzhi, *Zhongguo dizhu zhi jingji lun: fengjian tudi guanxi fazhan yu bianhua* (Beijing, 2005), 310; Philip Huang, *The Peasant Family and Rural Development in the Lower Yangzi Region, 1350–1988* (Stanford, 1990).
6 On contracts, see Madeleine Zelin, Jonathan Ocko and Robert Gardella (eds.), *Contracts and Property in Early Modern China* (Stanford, 2004). More generally, see Kenneth Pomeranz, *The Great Divergence: China, Europe and the Making of the Modern World Economy* (Princeton, 2000), 69–106.

Many of the empirical findings have emerged from a separate but related dialogue: the so-called 'great divergence debate' on when and why various North Atlantic economies surpassed their East Asian counterparts.[7] This debate has focused more on living standards and levels of productivity than on relations of production: indeed, the 'California school' that started this debate has repeatedly argued that a particular institutional configuration having been associated with initiating sustained per capita growth in one place did not make it necessary and/or sufficient elsewhere. The claim that capitalism did not automatically lead to *industrial* capitalism and modern growth rested on many contrary observations, including Braudel's insistence that even where institutions strongly favoured them (Venice, Genoa, the Netherlands), the most successful capitalists, over long periods of time, generally preferred re-investing their profits in commerce and finance to investing in production per se.[8] Only when favourable institutions were joined by technologies enabling significant economies of scale were they willing to tie up lots of capital via fixed investments in machinery, capital-intensive farming and so on.

In China, incentives to redirect large sums of capital from exchange to production were generally even weaker than in the early modern West. Moreover, one favourite vehicle for Western investors outside of both commerce and production – state debt – was unavailable in China, as neither the Ming nor the Qing borrowed significantly until the late 1800s.[9] Late imperial China thus featured commercial capitalism that merits comparison with European or South Asian cases, but less capitalism in agriculture or (proto-)industry. We also find less that a Westerner would recognize as high-end finance capital, though there were intricate and reasonably well-developed markets for savings and investment. Finally, the relatively slight development of high finance – relative, that is, to commercial capitalism – may be connected to the limited spread of capitalist production, at least in some sectors. The Chinese state faced less pressure to maximize revenues than did states in an endlessly warring Europe. Facing different security concerns, China preferred to extract frontier resources

---

7   Pomeranz, *Great Divergence*. The preface to the 2021 edition (ix–xx) discusses some of the ensuing debates.
8   See for instance Fernand Braudel, *Afterthoughts on Material Civilization and Capitalism* (Baltimore, 1977), 47, 60, 69–71.
9   Shanxi merchants did move government funds around the empire in the nineteenth century, often paying officials before the funds arrived, but this represented only very short-term borrowing. Wing Kin Puk, *The Rise and Fall of a Public Debt Market in 16th-century China: The Story of the Ming Salt Certificate Account* (Leiden, 2016), 85–105, has argued that the sixteenth-century salt certificate system – in which merchants sometimes received state monopoly salt years after making partial payment for it – represented a public debt, noting that a secondary market developed for the IOUs that merchants received. But this was never meant to be a regular feature of the system and was largely eliminated by reforms beginning in 1617.

in ways that officials believed would not threaten social order, sometimes sacrificing both efficiency and opportunities for private profit. This link between a less needy state and a capitalism that spread less beyond commerce is speculative, but consistent with both specific policies and general ideas in late imperial statecraft.

Officials had commented on wealthy merchants beginning long before imperial unification (221 BC); the wealthiest engaged in long-distance trade and/or provisioning armies. Unification increased state leverage over these merchants and led to state-run monopolies on salt, iron, liquor and some other lucrative trades. But imperial unity – an intermittent condition for the next 1,500 years, but a near-constant from 1273 to 1912 – also vastly expanded possibilities for private commerce.

The number of state monopolies, often leased to private merchants, waxed and waned across the centuries, but from the mid-1500s onward – the period covered by this chapter – only a handful of restricted trades remained, with salt and sometimes foreign trade being the principal examples.

I. Property, Trusts, Firms and Groups

Legally speaking, households, not individuals, owned property; for most purposes, however, household heads acted like owners. Meanwhile, wealthy families placed a great deal of property in various sorts of trusts, which had the functional equivalent of legal personhood: as in other times and places, these were often created to ensure that asset wealth was accumulated, not spent on short-term and/or individual ends.

The most important of these institutions were lineage trusts and ancestral halls. Both held assets, managed by trustees, on behalf of extended kinship groups, using earnings to support collective projects: conducting rituals; maintaining graves and temples; supporting widows, orphans and education and the like. Lineage trusts and ancestral halls (which emerged later) were not identical: among other things, ancestral halls often required significant payments from members, thereby excluding some descendants of the group's 'prime ancestor' while inviting participation from prosperous families only tenuously connected to the descent line.[10] But these differences are unimportant for current purposes; and here these entities are sometimes lumped together as 'trusts'.

Early trusts mostly owned land, receiving income from rents. But by c.1500, many mostly held money instead. They regularly lent money to profit-seeking

---

10 Joseph McDermott, *The Making of a New Rural Order in South China* (Cambridge, 2013, 2020), I: 235–368; II: 60–124.

firms or acquired equity shares in them; less often, a trust solely owned a business (including some large ones) and wrote procedures for managing it into its lineage rules.¹¹ Some lineages also stipulated that a fixed percentage of 'surplus' income – whatever exceeded the amount committed to current activities – would be retained for reinvestment, while the rest was distributed. In some large lineages, that distribution went not to families, but to lineage branches (groups descended from common ancestors more recent than the original one). Those branches might also retain a portion for reinvestment, creating additional vehicles for deferring consumption and accumulating capital.¹²

In the Qing, trusts of all sorts are frequently listed as creditors of and investors in profit-seeking firms, as well as (less often) appearing as borrowers. These trusts also advanced money both to members and to outsiders. Insiders sometimes borrowed at much lower rates, but not always and not simply because of kinship.

Moreover, some ancestral halls had begun by no later than mid-Ming to distribute some of their earnings to those who had contributed capital, according to the size of those contributions – much like corporations paying dividends. Many halls also 'hosted' affiliated organizations, such as rotating credit societies, that were explicitly devoted to money-making.¹³ Other institutions provided loans and/or equity investments to profit-seeking firms: temples, monasteries and even the government (which frequently deposited funds at interest with pawn-brokers and other firms).¹⁴

Firms took many forms. Enormous numbers of small businesses were run by individuals or members of one household and had no separate legal existence. Most other firms were partnerships. Some were *commenda*-style partnerships, in which one or more passive investors entrusted capital to a manager who undertook the enterprise – which could be a single commercial journey or something longer-lasting – with the manager compensated for his work with a pre-determined share of the proceeds; others had more than one managing partner who divided tasks and profits but were all fully liable for any losses. More complicated firms could have many passive investors, whose liability was limited to the extent of their investment, could transfer their shares to third

---

11 Madeleine Zelin, 'Chinese Business Practice in the Late Imperial Period', *E&S*, 14 (2013), 774–775.
12 Madeleine Zelin, *The Merchants of Zigong: Industrial Enterprise in Early Modern China* (New York, 2005), 85–87.
13 McDermott, *Making of a New Rural Order*, II: 107–124; Zelin, 'Chinese Business Practice in the Late Imperial Period', 774.
14 For state deposits at pawnshops, see Pan Ming-te, 'The Rural Credit Market and Peasant Economy in China, 1600–1949' (University of California, Irvine, Ph.D. dissertation, 1994), 218–220; for the state lending money at 12 per cent to Tianjin salt merchants (something that other groups did not need), see Kwan Man Bun, *The Salt Merchants of Tianjin* (Honolulu, 2001), 41–42.

parties without dissolving the firm and often included non-biological 'legal persons': lineage trusts, ancestral halls, temples and other firms. This allowed some firms to become very large, operating in multiple cities and/or operating several different businesses. A few of these firms lasted two or three centuries, until they were nationalized in the 1950s.[15] And while many firms – even large ones – recruited investors and managers entirely from within a single lineage, many others had non-kin managers and/or partners.[16] (It is also worth remembering that some lineages had hundreds or even thousands of living members; and firms based on family ties were common elsewhere, too.)

The hardest category to understand is what I have called the merchant 'group', defined by native place origin: Shanxi merchants, Huizhou merchants, Chaozhou merchants, etc. A given trade, or the trade of a particular place, was often dominated by people who claimed the same geographic origin, even if they had lived elsewhere for many years. The trade in both Anhui and Guizhou timber, for instance, was dominated by Huizhou men, and trade in specific kinds of cloth, medicine and so on by people from other particular places – frequently not where the commodity was produced. Members of these groups often preferred doing business with each other and acted together to regulate their trade, punishing members who deviated from expected behaviour.[17] At first glance, then, these groups look like scaled-up kinship groups – albeit vastly scaled up, since these 'native places' were never smaller than counties (averaging 300,000 inhabitants by the mid 1800s) and often as large as one or even two provinces, with tens of millions of residents. Like kin groups, they featured multi-stranded ties that reduced transaction costs both through affinity (based on shared dialects, foodways, worship, etc.) and by maintaining valuable networks from which miscreants could be excluded.

But solidarity was fragile, especially at large scales. Merchants within a single native-place group were often competitors, especially when they traded the same commodities. The same was true of merchants within kin groups, large or small. At least among Huizhou merchants, it appears that although some firms spanning multiple lineages were very successful, they tended to last fewer generations than single-lineage firms; firms spanning multiple branches

---

15 Kenneth Pomeranz, '"Gentry Merchants" and Partnership Revisited: Family, Firm and Financing in the History of the Yutang Enterprises of Jining, 1779–1956', *Late Imperial China*, 18 (1997), 1–38; Zelin, 'Chinese Business Practice', 769–793.
16 This was, for instance, the norm among Shanxi merchants in the frontier trade. See Zhijian Qiao, 'The Rise of Shanxi Merchants: Empire, Institutions and Social Change in Qing China, 1688–1850' (Stanford University Ph.D. dissertation, 2018), 96.
17 Zelin, 'Chinese Business Practice', 779–784, provides a useful summary of the issues surrounding regional merchant groups. See also Fan Jinmin, *Ming Qing Jiangnan shangye de fazhan* (Nanjing, 1998).

of one lineage were likewise less long-lived on average than single-branch firms and so on.[18]

Moreover, occupational groups, whether or not they shared a native place, possessed no legal personality, much less statutory authority, until the 1850s; while they often resolved trade disputes and standardized practices, these powers were informal and contingent on official tolerance. Native-place organizations were more secure, owned property and provided much of the infrastructure for merchant self-regulation, but most were not primarily mercantile organizations; their leaders were usually sojourning officials and scholars. Native-place organizations explicitly devoted to merchants (or occasionally merchants and artisans) increased over time, but remained a decided minority.[19] And sometimes merchant groups used the language of shared native place when they traded in a *commodity* from a particular place, without sharing personal origins.[20] Regional merchant groups are thus something of a black box to historians – they facilitated lots of business, but we can rarely see exactly how.

Somehow, though, native-place groups supported clusters of highly successful firms. Generally, the firms began in competitive, high-volume trades such as grain or cloth and eventually acquired enough capital, connections and experience to enter lucrative sectors where the state restricted participation, such as the salt monopolies. Firms that met these requirements could entrench themselves in high-margin trades, both through fulfilling government contracts and violating government regulations – sometimes simultaneously.

II. Two Cases: Shanxi and Huizhou Merchants in Ming and Qing

For instance, Shanxi merchants, one of the two wealthiest groups in the empire, were heavily involved in provisioning both Ming and Qing soldiers engaged in intermittent combat and long-term garrison duty along the Mongol frontier (an area too arid comfortably to feed these troops). During the Ming, trade with the Mongols themselves was often either illegal or very restricted. These same Shanxi merchants, however, frequently violated those rules, swapping tea, grain, cloth and other sedentarist products, plus silver, for Inner Asian livestock, hides

---

18 McDermott, *Making of a New Rural Order*, II: 334, 337–338, 360, 381–383.
19 He Bingdi, *Zhongguo huiguan shi lun* (Taibei, 1966), especially 101–114; Richard Belsky, *Localities at the Center: Native Place, Space and Power in Late Imperial Beijing* (Cambridge, 2005), 91–92. On general trends in 'native place' and guild structures, see William Rowe, *Hankow: Commerce and Society in a Chinese City, 1796–1889* (Stanford, 1984), 252–288 and Zhijian Qiao, 'The Rise of Shanxi Merchants: Empire, Institutions and Social Change in Qing China, 1688–1850' (Stanford University Ph.D. thesis, 2017), 222–242.
20 See, for instance, Rowe, *Hankow*, 316.

and jade. Profit margins were high since entry was limited, credit was vital and producers and consumers never met. Ming trade policy became more permissive after c.1570 and the Qing largely erased the border by conquering the Mongols in several wars between c.1680 and 1760; this greatly expanded Mongolian trade, while the new border offered possibilities for trade with Russia. Theoretically, Shanxi merchants might have faced new competitors as government restrictions eased, but by this time they were almost unchallengeable: Mongol princes owed them money, their organizations were authorized to handle many civil disputes in frontier towns (and even some criminal matters) and they controlled well-established channels for information, credit and transportation.[21]

Moreover, because supplying frontier garrisons at state-regulated prices was not in itself lucrative, the state incentivized participants by licensing them to sell government monopoly salt back in 'China proper'.[22] Thus the Shanxi merchants provisioning troops were guaranteed places in one of the few trades within China's huge domestic market that was legally protected from margin-narrowing competition. Profits were also re-invested in financial services at various levels, from pawnshops to mortgages to relatively safe low-interest loans to big merchants and other wealthy people. (Nominal rates on pawnshop loans and mortgages were sometimes quite high, but we lack sufficient knowledge about default rates to calculate profits. Foreclosing on land was particularly difficult.)[23]

In early–mid Ming, Shanxi merchants were probably the single group within the government salt monopoly. But many of them later chose not actually to trade in salt, cashing out faster by selling the certificates entitling them to do so. The buyers were mostly from Huizhou, a hilly prefecture slightly west of the wealthy Yangzi Delta.[24] These merchants, who had begun by trading in more open, competitive markets, such as those for grain and timber, dominated the Yangzi Valley salt trade by the late Ming and held that position until at least 1800. (A 1617 reform greatly reduced opportunities to speculate in salt certificates, but left Huizhou merchants even more firmly entrenched in the monopoly itself.)[25] And much as the Shanxi merchants conducted both legal and illegal trade on the northwest frontier, Huizhou merchants traded both

---

21 Terada Takanobu, *Sansei shōnin no kenkyū* (Tokyo, 1972); Qiao, 'The Rise of Shanxi Merchants', esp. 114–284.
22 Terada, *Sansei*, 80–119, 256–282.
23 Ming-te Pan, 'Rural Credit Market and the Peasant Economy (1600–1949): The State, Elite, Peasant and "Usury"' (University of California, Irvine, Ph.D. thesis, 1994); Zhang Taisu, *The Laws and Economics of Confucianism: Kinship and Property in Pre-Industrial China and England* (Cambridge, 2017); Matthew Lowenstein, 'Financial Markets in Late Imperial China, 1820–1911' (University of Chicago Ph.D. dissertation, 2021), 117–120.
24 McDermott, *Making of a New Rural Order*, II: 211–213.
25 Wing Kin Puk, *The Rise and Fall of a Public Debt Market in 16th-Century China: The Story of the Ming Salt Certificate* (Leiden, 2016), 85–101.

legal and illegal salt, clandestinely buying extra from cash-poor saltern workers and smuggling it along with their legal quotas to expand their markets.[26] Even when Ming officials delivered less salt than they had promised, this ultimately benefitted Huizhou merchants: being better capitalized than either other wholesalers or the retailers they sold and lent to, they profited by buying the entitlements of those less able to wait than they were.

Selling state monopoly salt also benefitted Huizhou merchants' other endeavours. They could often ship their salt from production sites near the mouth of the Yangzi River to destinations throughout the middle and lower Yangzi in government-protected convoys: this substantially lowered their risks on lucrative but often dangerous routes. And since salt-selling covered their expenses going upstream, they could both add high-value, low-bulk, Delta handicrafts to the upstream cargo (though this was theoretically forbidden) and return downstream with goods in which the less densely populated interior had a comparative advantage, such as grain, timber and cotton. These were the largest long-distance staple trades anywhere in the early modern world.[27]

Huizhou and Shanxi merchants thus offer the most impressive, best documented, examples of capitalist merchants gaining control of both state-run and other long-distance trades. There were other smaller but still substantial groups. Some of the largest Shanxi firms were said to have had capital in the range of 'several million' *taels* (with each *tael* worth about US$1.55 in the early nineteenth century); the Qiao merchant family was said to be worth about 10,000,000 *taels* not counting their real estate.[28] Houqua, the empire's leading tea exporter, claimed in 1834 to be worth about US$26,000,000; this has generally been considered plausible, though unprovable. Such a fortune would comfortably surpass that of John Jacob Astor, Houqua's wealthiest American contemporary; it would have exceeded 40 per cent of that year's official Qing revenues.[29]

---

26 McDermott, *Making of a New Rural Order*, II: 203–226; Ray Huang, *Taxation and Governmental Finance in Sixteenth Century Ming China* (Cambridge, 1974).
27 Pomeranz, *Great Divergence*, 242–263.
28 On the Qiao fortune, see Hu Yuxian and Wu Dianqi, 'Qixian Qiao jia bao "zai zhongtang" jianjie', *Shanxi wenshi ziliao quanbian*, Part 4, Collection 49, 1173–1174. A somewhat questionable source from the late nineteenth century (when the *tael* was worth less) lists six Shanxi families with current assets of between one and eight million *taels*: Xu Ke, *Qing bai leichao* (reprinted Beijing, 1984), 2307. My thanks to Matt Lowenstein for providing this source.
29 John Wong, *Global Trade in the Nineteenth Century: The House of Houqua and the Canton System* (Cambridge, 2016), 192. Astor died in 1848, leaving an estate estimated at $20,000,000. For silver content of the US dollar, see Alexandra Irigoin, 'The End of a Silver Era: The Consequences of the Breakdown of the Spanish Peso Standard in China and the United States, 1780–1850', *Journal of World History*, 20 (2009), 229. For Qing government

Clearly, then, Qing-era capitalists could finance large-scale ventures, including some involving considerable risk and/or a relatively long wait for returns. Until recently, however, most scholars did not think there had been much development of late imperial financial markets; and some crucial institutions of Western capitalism were absent in China. There was no public market for equities, nor publicly quoted insurance rates. Perhaps most strikingly, the state did not borrow, except in very limited, short-term ways. But this is because the needs that these activities met in the West were either not present or were met in other ways. We now have considerable evidence suggesting that financial institutions could aggregate savings on a large scale, directing them towards appropriate investments and providing long-term financing to those who could use it. The absence of certain investment vehicles is noteworthy and perhaps kept certain capitalists from accumulating wealth even faster. But there is nothing to suggest that it represented fundamental weaknesses in the financial institutions that *did* exist or that it left viable projects starved of capital.

III. Financial Markets and Capitalism during the Qing

While many Chinese firms were family-based, other firms gathered investment from well beyond any single lineage, endured for many years, trained and hired professional managers (including non-kin) and used accounting systems capable of calculating profit and changes in capital stock.[30] They seized opportunities and diversified to limit risks just as one would expect: one Canton merchant began even before the Opium War ended to have his Boston-based trading partners invest for him in American canals and railways.[31] In short we see much eminently capitalist behaviour; but we have rarely been able to look inside Chinese firms.

A flood of recently published Shanxi merchant documents – eighty-eight volumes worth so far – is changing this. Unfortunately, the documents use a special script that very few scholars know, so they are only just beginning to be reflected in scholarly writings; the major example in English so far is Matthew Lowenstein's ground-breaking 2020 dissertation and articles spun off from it.[32]

---

revenues, see Shen Xuefeng, *Wan Qing caizheng zhichu zhengce yanjiu* (Beijing, 2006), 30 and Zhou Yumin, *Wan Qing caizheng yu shehui bianqian* (Shanghai, 2000), 238–239.
30   See Matthew Lowenstein and Cao Shuji, 'Business Accounting at Fengshengtai in Late Imperial China: Is there New Evidence of Double-Entry Bookkeeping?' *BHR*, 97 (2023), 33–65; Zelin, 'Chinese Business Practice'; Kenneth Pomeranz, '"Gentry Merchants" and Partnership Revisited'.
31   Wong, *Global Trade*, 177–204.
32   Liu Jianmin (ed.), *Jinshang shiliao jicheng* (Beijing, 2018). Matthew Lowenstein, 'Financial Markets in Late Imperial China, 1820–1911' (University of Chicago Ph.D. dissertation, 2020).

This visible tip of the iceberg suggests that what remains below the waterline will revolutionize our understanding of late imperial Chinese finance.

These records include account books, contracts, internal correspondence and documents provided by counter-parties. They tell us far more than do any previously available records about how Chinese trans-regional financial networks transferred funds, discounted bills, settled balances and so on. They also show how various local institutions – lineages in some places, merchant houses in others, ad hoc 'rotating credit societies' almost everywhere – provided financial services in towns and villages: advancing long- and short-term loans against various kinds of security, accepting deposits at interest, clearing transactions between third parties and so on. These records suggest that credit was more available and at more moderate interest rates than most previous literature had suggested. There are even examples of tenants with plots far too small for subsistence (who thus probably also did wage labour) borrowing against these tenancy rights from outside lenders (rather than from their landlord or employer).[33] One reason this was possible is that more formally organized financial firms, with access to cheaper capital, regularly invested in less formal, grass-roots lenders – sometimes, for instance, holding shares in rotating credit societies – and took deposits from a wide variety of individuals, businesses, lineages and other entities.

Borrowers without adequate collateral often paid very high rates, as older literature on Chinese usury emphasized. But there was also considerable lending at rates low enough to finance grass-roots business ventures: acquiring and improving land, stocking stores, or undertaking cash crop and handicraft production. This picture contrasts sharply with the once widespread belief that most people only borrowed to deal with hunger, funerals, taxes, or other emergencies. At a higher level, credit-worthy borrowers attending merchant fairs seem to have borrowed at around 5–6 per cent per year; one sample of long-term loans had an average annual rate of 2.43 per cent and a few especially desirable customers borrowed at 0.5–1.0 per cent per year.[34] Looking at thirty-six Qing dynasty loans to agricultural tenants made against a promised portion of their future harvest incomes, Cao Shuji finds an average interest rate of 12 per cent; rates at pawnshops run by Huizhou merchants during the Qing seem to have averaged about 20 per cent, though some rates were much higher.[35]

Correspondence within and among firms also exposes the workings of trade fairs where long-distance merchants converged temporarily, much like in late medieval and early modern Europe and of remittance systems which allowed

---

33 Lowenstein, 'Financial Markets', 79–80.
34 Ibid., 46, 61, 84, 274, 349.
35 Cao Shuji, 'Diandi yu dianzu: Qingdai Minnan diqu de tudi shichang yu jinrong shichang', *Qingshi yanjiu* (2019), 68; Wang Yuming, *Ming Qing Huizhou dianshang yanjiu* (Beijing, 2012), 328.

long-distance traders to function without carrying lots of money. These fairs hosted futures markets for various commodities, including for local bronze currencies, the silver that functioned as an empire-wide currency and the notes of well-known firms; transactions among firms allowed the buying and selling of futures at any time, albeit in less competitive markets than those at the fairs. Account books also show savers routinely making anonymous, passive equity investments in commercial and, later, industrial firms.[36]

Thus it would appear that with the above-noted exceptions – public markets for equity shares, insurance and state debt – China had reasonably well-developed financial institutions, which met the needs of a highly commercialized, but not industrialized, economy. While those markets certainly did not link every village – much less every household – to a national market, solvent households in many rural areas could access a financial system with multiple urban nodes. An anecdote from Lowenstein's dissertation, describing the collapse of one Shanxi bank, provides ironic testimony to how 'modern' this system had become by the early 1900s, when most of China still had no Western-style banks. The firm's agent in one provincial city, noticing in July 1914 that notes payable in Shanghai had an unusually high silver value in another inland city, tried to profit by shorting these notes; instead, their price soared as the outbreak of World War I rippled through the global economy. The firm consequently failed, but in a quintessentially capitalist way, showing how widely even a hinterland office of a 'traditional' banking firm would reach for opportunities.[37]

State documents rarely mention high-level finance, thus limiting historians' awareness of it. Only rarely would a participant ask officials to enforce a contract: the threat that defaulting parties and guarantors could be excluded from these networks was generally enough to force private settlements. If elite commercial disputes did reach officials, they would usually ask a merchant guild or native-place association to settle them – leaving little trace in the spotty surviving archives of local and provincial officials.

Government records more often include disputes among people at the informal lower edge of the financial system: fights between neighbours who had lent and borrowed money (often without written contracts), evictions backed and/or resisted with force and people who absconded with small, borrowed sums. It was these disputes among often-desperate people that were most likely to turn violent, thereby attracting official notice.[38] Judging from the best-preserved county archive we have – from the commercial hub of Chongqing – the few non-violent cases between merchants that magistrates

36 Lowenstein, 'Financial Markets', 238–453.
37 Ibid., 454–457.
38 Thomas Buoye, *Manslaughter, Markets and Moral Economy: Violent Disputes over Property Rights in Eighteenth Century China* (Cambridge, 2000).

adjudicated usually involved very small-scale traders with no guild to handle their disputes – because they could not afford dues and/or were such small players that guilds did not bother making them join.[39] While officials who had to decide such cases generally enforced contracts, this was often tempered by reluctance to see families become completely dispossessed.

IV. Government Policy towards Commerce

Officials did debate policy towards the circulation of everyday commodities. The first Ming emperor attempted to return China to an idealized world of nearly autarkic villages; but this effort unravelled by 1430.[40] Officials thereafter recognized that many people met basic needs by both buying and selling in markets. They understood the benefits of specialization, including a regional division of labour which entailed long-distance trade in some necessities. With some qualifications, they supported competition in these markets.

Grain came first – both in real importance and official imaginations. Wu Chengming has estimated that about 30 million *shi* (about 2.4 million tons) of grain entered long-distance commerce annually in the high Qing; that figure is probably low and excludes the massive amount of grain sold in local markets, or within single provinces (many of which were bigger than almost all European countries).[41] The Qing carefully monitored harvest conditions, requiring monthly reports from every territorial official. When these conditions were normal, officials generally trusted markets to move grain to where it was needed. Keeping licences for grain traders cheap was supposed to ensure that there would always be enough participants to prevent monopolization and market manipulation.[42]

But in a huge empire, markets were rarely 'normal' everywhere. The Qing hedged against bad harvests through an elaborate system of granaries. Some, largely filled with donations, were designed to provide relief when serious hunger threatened; others, to smooth price fluctuations by officials buying when prices were low and selling slightly below market price when prices rose. While

---

39 Zelin, 'Chinese Business Practice', 779.
40 Timothy Brook, *The Confusions of Pleasure: Commerce and Culture in Ming China* (Berkeley, 1998), 17–85.
41 Wu Chengming, *Zhongguo zibenzhuyi yu guonei shichang* (Beijing, 1983), 277; Pomeranz, *Great Divergence*, 34–35.
42 On licences, see Susan Mann, *Local Merchants and the Chinese Bureaucracy, 1750–1950* (Stanford, 1987); on grain trade regulation more generally, Pierre-Etienne Will and R. Bin Wong, *Nourish the People: The State Civilian Granary System in China, 1650–1850* (Ann Arbor, 1991); Helen Dunstan, *State or Merchant: Political Economy and Political Process in 1740s China* (Cambridge, 2006).

this may have pre-empted some private, profit-driven storage, it is unlikely that it significantly inhibited capitalist accumulation; with many participants in each market, truly lucrative hoarding would have been difficult.

The bigger issue involved arbitrage across space, rather than time, as local shortages presented officials with popular demands that they forbid shipping grain to areas with even higher prices. Beijing opposed most such interventions, generally trusting markets to allocate resources fairly, especially from the 1740s onward.[43] The result was both impressively integrated long-distance grain markets and significant capacity to protect subsistence security. Many merchants presumably made normal profits through this exchange, but there were not successful 'engrossers' comparable to those in Tudor–Stuart England or sixteenth- to eighteenth-century France.[44] Some Shanxi merchants, as we have seen, were exceptions, profiting greatly by providing grain and other supplies to frontier garrisons. But they were outliers among grain traders; and their profits came, as we have also seen, not from grain itself, but from privileges the state granted to elicit grain shipments that prices alone would not justify.

Most everyday commodities purchased for private use – ordinary cloth, raw cotton, medicinal herbs and the like – came from small producers, as we will see in more detail later. The merchants who bought and re-sold these goods were often also relatively small players, incapable of exerting significant market power. Indeed Ming sources, especially Ming fiction, often portray them being extorted by government officials and clerks, local toughs and the few big merchants and merchant groups with whom they competed; it is hard to tell how typical this was, but it clearly happened enough to be considered a problem and the Qing tried various measures to make competition fairer. Firstly, they created a system of state-licenced brokers who were responsible for ensuring open access to standardized measures, information, storage space and various other features of fair markets, in return for strictly regulated sales commissions. Officials aimed to have several licensees in each market ensuring competition while allowing each broker enough business to ensure them a reasonable living; central government edicts kept licensing fees and commercial taxes low and commanded that the system prioritize regulation, not revenue. In some cases,

---

43 Dunstan, *State or Merchant*, 91–146.
44 R. Bin Wong, *China Transformed: Historical Change and the Limits of European Experience* (Ithaca, 1997), 209–229; Alan Everitt, 'The Marketing of Agricultural Produce', in *The Agrarian History of England and Wales*, ed. Joan Thirsk (Cambridge, 1967), IV: 466–592; Jean Meuvret, 'Le Commerce des grains et des farines à Paris et les marchands parisens à l'époque de Louis XIV', *Revue d'histoire modern et contemporaine*, 3 (1956), 169–203; Charles Tilly, 'Food Supply and Public Order in Modern Europe', in *The Formation of National States in Western Europe*, ed. Charles Tilly (Princeton, 1975), 380–455; Carol Shiue and Wolfgang Keller, 'Markets in China and Europe on the Eve of the Industrial Revolution', *AmEcRev*, 97 (2007), 1189–1216.

coalitions of local gentry and/or merchants themselves paid the equivalent of licensing fees and received in return the right to keep their market tax-free, if they ensured open access and fair dealing there; some community leaders saw this as an important service that confirmed their status and seem to have taken it quite seriously. While the results were highly uneven, such measures seem to have prevented outright monopolization of most local markets, helping both small producers and small merchants obtain modest but acceptable returns.[45] It was only after 1853, when the state became desperate for cash, that it allowed merchants to buy exclusive licences to trade in particular commodities in particular places, sacrificing regulatory goals to maximize revenue by selling market-distorting privileges.[46]

V. Trades with Greater State Involvement

But there were also cases where the state had very specific interests and got directly involved in production and/or transportation; and others where it feared that unfettered competition would lead to small producers being dispossessed and becoming socially 'dangerous'. The resulting interventions limited the sway of the market, while sometimes protecting profits for favoured merchants.

Most notably, the state worried about keeping food affordable in the capital – Beijing was too populous easily to be supplied by its semi-arid surroundings. It therefore collected large amounts of grain as part of taxes in more productive areas, moving and storing it in its own boats and granaries; officials and merchants then shared responsibility for local distribution.[47] We have seen, however, that frontier garrisons were fed by different mechanisms, which made participating merchants rich. The vast majority of the grain trade, meanwhile, was only lightly regulated and divided among a great many competing firms (though on some long-distance routes, most of these firms came from a few regional merchant groups); the high degree of price integration in these markets suggests that they operated fairly efficiently.[48]

---

45 On the Qing use of brokerage licences to ensure fair competition in local markets and the priority of these regulatory concerns over revenue maximization prior to the 1850s, see Susan Mann, *Local Merchants and the Chinese Bureaucracy, 1750–1950* (Stanford, 1987), 40–51, 62–69, 91–93.
46 Ibid., 94–199.
47 Li Wenzhi, *Qingdai caoyun* (Beijing, 1995); Will and Wong, *Nourish the People*, 43–74; Lillian Li, *Fighting Famine in North China: State, Market and Environmental Decline, 1690s–1990s* (Stanford, 2007), 144–165; Wu Jianyong, 'Qingdai Beijing de liangshi gongying', in *Beijing lishi yu xianshi yanjiu* (Beijing, 1989), 167–186.
48 Shiue and Keller, 'Markets in China and Europe'.

Meanwhile, grain *production* was famously dispersed among millions of small-scale producers. Officials considered an independent peasantry essential and sought to maintain it. Property law made it hard to foreclose on mortgaged farmland and allowed sellers multiple chances to re-purchase land they had sold – though this reflected custom more than statute and the consensus behind it may have weakened over time.[49] Many tenants gained increasingly strong protections against eviction during the Qing, though here law clearly followed custom – often rather grudgingly.[50] Efforts were made to protect peasants against usury, though with limited impact.[51] As noted above, the Qing made considerable efforts to ensure that peasants bought and sold in reasonably competitive markets. But while many peasant households undoubtedly benefitted from these measures, it seems unlikely that they explain the weaknesses of capitalist agriculture; as we will see, peasant production was very efficient, so it is unlikely that large farms using wage labour would have made more money for investors than collecting rent, providing loans and (in some cases) trading in debt instruments secured by land and/or future crops.

The huge old-growth timbers needed for palace construction were, by Ming-Qing times, available only in remote, rugged areas, making it unprofitable to provide them at state-set prices. The government therefore procured them itself, often using forced labour – much as it used direct appropriation of grain, a hereditary class of boatmen and a waterway partially maintained by soldiers and corvee labourers to help feed Beijing. Almost all other construction, however, used second-growth trees: mostly grown commercially by small producers, but distributed by some of the empire's richest merchants.[52]

The biggest destination for long-distance timber shipments was the Yangzi Delta, China's richest and most densely populated region, which had never been heavily forested. At first, logs mostly came from hilly areas nearby – including Huizhou, which pioneered the systematic, profit-driven planting of construction timber. These practices gradually spread to other highlands near the Yangzi and its navigable tributaries; Huizhou merchants conducted much of the trade in all these places but invested a lot less in actual production outside their native place. By c.1700, the timber frontier had reached the Qingshui River

---

49 Zhang Taisu, *Laws and Economics of Confucianism*; Buoye, *Manslaughter, Markets and Moral Economy*, 153–192, 226–229.
50 Yang Guozhen, *Ming Qing tudi qiyuen wenshu yanjiu* (Beijing, 2009); Kenneth Pomeranz, 'Land Markets in Late Imperial and Republican China', *Continuity and Change*, 23 (2008), 101–150; Zhang Peiguo, *Jindai Jiangnan xiangcun diquande lishi renleixue yanjiu* (Shanghai, 2002).
51 Pan, 'Rural Credit Market'.
52 Ian Miller, *Fir and Empire: The Transformation of Forests in Early Modern China* (Seattle, 2020), 140–159; Meng Zhang, *Timber and Forestry in Qing China: Sustaining the Market* (Seattle, 2021), 19–113.

valley in Guizhou, over 1,000 miles from the Delta and largely populated by members of the Miao and Dong minorities. It was mostly Huizhou merchants who took this region's timber from waterside markets to the Middle Yangzi, Lower Yangzi and beyond.

Thousands of Guizhou contracts survive, covering transactions for land, employment and investment in forestry and for timber itself. They provide a lens through which to view capitalist activity in this sector.

Qing officials knew that this trade was essential. However, they also worried that if 'crafty' Chinese merchants had unfettered access to the producers, these 'simple' non-Han people would wind up dispossessed and angry, endangering social stability. Consequently, they imposed regulations designed to shield producers from the market, which had no parallel in older, ethnically Han, timber regions.

Most timber-planting was small scale and labour intensive. Owners sometimes planted for themselves, but usually engaged tenants. Tenant-planters received two kinds of compensation, neither of which was a wage. During their first five years on the land, they could keep whatever they grew in between the seedlings; this often covered their basic nutrition. At about five years, the canopy closed, preventing inter-cropping; but at that point, the tenant's percentage share in the eventual sale of the trees – fixed in the original contract – would vest, becoming property that he could sell, borrow against, or hold. Most probably sold their shares soon, often beginning again as tenant-planters on other plots. This let them live off inter-planted crops for another five years; thus, part of what tenants earned by selling their share of future timber could become capital. Some acquired land this way; some probably seeded other small businesses. The vibrant re-sale market in these shares – essentially a timber futures market – allowed small players to bridge the twenty-plus year gap between planting trees and harvesting them, making their participation in sustainable timber-growing possible.[53] However, the wide availability of timber shares probably kept profit rates quite modest. Xavier Ante, using completed nineteenth-century contracts, argues that long-run annual returns averaged under 5 per cent; and even those returns were not risk-free, since trees could catch fire, be stolen, or otherwise not reach maturity. Guizhou's timber boom clearly raised average incomes and enriched a new elite that thereafter acquired land, education and local or even regional political influence, but Ante's work confirms what qualitative data also suggests – those fortunes mostly came from trading timber, not growing it.[54]

53 Zhang, *Timber and Forestry in Qing China*, 80–138.
54 Xavier Ante, 'Rewarding the Industrious: Return on Investment in Southeastern Guizhou's Forest Enterprises', paper presented at Association for Asian Studies annual conference, 14–17 March 2024; cited by permission. Rising incomes are reflected in repeated attempts by communities during this period to restrain soaring 'luxury', especially wedding

Qing policies expanded these fortunes by giving selected merchants local oligopolies. As noted, the Qing worried that big Chinese merchants would exploit supposedly naïve, often cash-poor, indigenous tree-growers; thus they forbade these merchants entering minority villages or using agents to purchase trees at the stump. 'Guest merchants' were restricted to a few riverside villages which had the right to organize timber markets, designating a limited number of agents to deal with the 'guests'; different villages would have this right each year, in a pre-set rotation.[55] These agents, or 'mountain guests', bought trees at the stump, arranged transport down the mountains (which required considerable collective effort) and sold at prices within a range agreed upon by that year's agents and far above stumpage prices. It was these men who experienced marked upward mobility, becoming significant landowners, members of local councils, leaders of militia and holders of examination degrees – or fathers of such men.[56] Their fortunes never matched those of the Huizhou guest merchants, who operated on far grander scales. But they did well enough that Qing intervention largely achieved its goals: it kept some significant portion of the gains from trade within minority communities and it buttressed social stability – albeit by nurturing a loyal *arriviste* local elite, not by preserving an imaginary world insulated from the corruptions of trade.

How different was this from non-frontier timber regions, where more laissez-faire policies prevailed? Those areas had no protected local intermediaries between producers and big merchants; consequently, the latter often combined the roles and profits of Guizhou's 'mountain guests' and 'guest merchants'. This included long-distance merchants or their relatives who were often investing in production: buying timber land and especially timber shares to guarantee themselves supplies of tradable wood. Somebody lost the land they accumulated. But the organization of production remained similar to that in Guizhou: most cultivation was on small plots, handled by tenants who, after a few years, received tradable shares in future timber. If anything, the securitization of future timber went further in Huizhou, with both tenant and landlord shares often repeatedly sub-divided as they changed hands.[57] Thus firms or other investors might own the equivalent of many acres of growing timber, but not be sole owner of any particular stand. This allowed investors – including those whose equity came from labour – to minimize their risks, but it also meant that

---

expenditures. See Xu Xiaoguang, *Kuanyue fa: Qiandongnan Dongzu xiguanfa de lishi renleixue kaocha* (Xiamen, 2012), 65–69, 74–84; Wu Daxun, *Qingchao zhili dongzu diqu zhengce yanjiu* (Beijing, 2008), 125–133; Shi Kaizhong, *Dongzu kuan zuzhi ji qi bianqian yanjiu* (Beijing, 2009), 132–134, 142–146.

55 Ante, 'Rewarding the Industrious'.
56 Ibid., 17–18. On the role of *kuan* elites and organizations in the formation of security organizations, see Shi Kaizhong, *Dongzu kuan zuzhi*, 77–81, 194–202.
57 McDermott, *Making of the New Rural Order*, I: 369–373, 398–413.

even substantial investments in 'production' did not position investors to change timber-growing practices or seek economies of scale. On the contrary: having timber holdings scattered across many plots, often in rugged terrain, made supervision extremely expensive, and owners benefited from arrangements which incentivized those actually raising trees to maximize their future value. Proletarianization would have been counter-productive; meanwhile, investors benefited when poorer tenants needed to cash out quickly. The system sustained production and served capitalist merchants well, with or without the state's paternalistic frontier policies.

The copper and zinc that the state minted also came mostly from small-scale operations; Ming and Qing licensing systems aimed to keep it that way.[58] (In theory, all mines needed licences, though this was often ignored.)[59] State policy emphasized two goals. For state-purchased minerals, it aimed to maximize output without raising offer prices (which were usually below market prices).[60] Meanwhile, all mining raised concerns about social disruption. This occasionally involved fear of disrupting indigenous communities, as with timber, but more often it revolved around two other issues: (1) concern that mining would cause environmental damage, harming and angering farmers in particular; and (2) fear that concentrations of miners – who tended to be young, single, migratory males – would constitute a rowdy, destabilizing and perhaps criminal element. (Efforts to steer mining licences to locals employing locals were apparently ineffective.)[61]

Because mining required significant up-front investment – with plenty of digging before realising any revenue – both the Ming and the early Qing made loans to producers whose output they would ultimately buy. But by the 1790s at the latest such loans had dwindled and were much less important than private financing.[62] Some private financing came from big merchants who supplied the

---

58 Copper had been used in coins since ancient times; zinc became the main metal mixed with it beginning in the 1600s. While silver circulated in large amounts, especially after the mid-1400s, and state-backed paper between roughly 1000 and 1400, China did not mint silver until roughly 1900. Richard Von Glahn, *Fountain of Fortune: Money and Monetary Policy in China, 1000–1700* (Berkeley, 1996); Hailian Chen, *Zinc for Coin and Brass: Bureaucrats, Merchants, Artisans and Mining Laborers in Qing China, ca. 1680s–1830s* (Leiden, 2019), 103.
59 Chen, *Zinc for Coin and Brass*, 175.
60 See, for instance, ibid., 636–638. For copper imports (as opposed to domestic production) and the state's insistence that the merchants licensed to conduct that trade sell large amounts to the mints at below market prices see Helen Dunstan, 'Safely Supping with the Devil: the Qing State and its Merchant Suppliers of Copper', *Late Imperial China*, 13: 2 (1992), 42–81, esp. 73–74.
61 Chen, *Zinc for Coin and Brass*, 181–183.
62 On government loans, see Li Zhongqing, *Zhongguo xinan* (Beijing, 2012), 265–269, 287–295.

mints, but more came from the retained earnings of numerous small operators. Share agreements with land-owners, not unlike those made by tree-planters, were common and the unit of ownership was often a single shaft within a mine site with many shafts.[63] Again, as with timber, richer mine owners often owned many shafts within the same general area, but rarely made the heavy bet of developing one big mine. Often, owners had begun as miners themselves and some continued working alongside their employees.[64] In some silver mines labourers had the option of forgoing cash wages, receiving food and shelter for five years and then a share of the mine thereafter; this sweat-equity system made some people rich. In some other silver and copper mines, compensation from the beginning consisted of room, board and a share of the mine's output, rather than cash wages.[65] These arrangements have striking resemblances to timber-planting contracts, despite differences in the equity that workers earned (a share of a mine versus a share of one particular harvest) and the greater risk of miners dying before they could collect.

Merchants bought the output of many small mines and smelters, mostly shipping it to distant mints. The state preferred dealing with these middlemen to buying directly from huge numbers of dispersed producers.[66] We lack sufficient data to estimate merchants' profit rates for particular times, places and metals. It is, however, suggestive that while many mines were short-lived – a product, in part, of being low tech and sometimes lacking enough capital for deep digging – merchant firms and groups in this sector were more

---

63 Xu and Wu, *Zhongguo zibenzhuyi* (Beijing, 1985), I: 513–516 on small investors and partnerships; on the involvement of big merchants (which they do not show involved intervention in production, though they did advance money for it), ibid., 516–518.
64 Ibid., I: 514–515
65 Wu Qijun, *Diannan kuangchang tulue* (1847; E-version by Airusheng shuzihua jishu yanjiu Zhongxin, Beijing, 2009), 16b; Yang Yuda, 'Silver Mines in Frontier Zones: Chinese Mining Communities along the Southwestern Borders of the Qing Empire', in *Mining, Monies and Culture in Early Modern Societies*, eds. Nanny Kim and Keiko Nagase-Reimer (Leiden, 2013), 99–100, 103–104, 106. See Also Nanny Kim and Yang Yuda, 'Mining off the Map: Fulongchang and Silver Mines in the Qing Empire's Far Southwest', *JESHO*, 64 (2021), 261, 264; Nanny Kim, 'Silver Mines and Mobile Miners in the Southwestern Borderlands of the Qing Empire', *JESHO*, 63 (2020), 130, 137, 152; Nanny Kim, 'The Tangdan Copper Mines and the 1733 Earthquake: A Mining Community Before the Boom in the Far Southwest of Qing China', *Cross-Currents*, 4 (2015), 294; Chen, *Zinc*, 155–157, 233–234.
66 Nanny Kim, 'The Tangdan Copper Mines and the 1733 Earthquake: A Mining Community before the Boom in the Far Southwest of Qing China', *Cross-Currents: East Asian History and Culture Review*, 13 (2015), 285–308, esp. 295, gives a sense of the remoteness of Qing supervision, even for copper; Yan Zhongping, *Qingdai Yunnan tongzheng kao* (Beijing, 1957), 27, notes that regulations were fairly detailed on paper, but actually implemented through multiple intermediaries.

durable.[67] Moreover, the firms supplying the mints often also sold monetary metals on private, sometimes illegal, markets, where prices were generally higher;[68] some also supplied China's numerous counterfeiters.[69] The government's mints, however, rarely made much profit – unlike many other early modern states' – suggesting that most of the profits from turning ore into money were made elsewhere along the commodity chain.[70]

Salt, a state monopoly for most of China's history, offers another revealing case. Qing salt production techniques varied across the empire, depending on natural endowments, but usually involved evaporating salty liquids found on the surface; this was rarely capital-intensive, had few economies of scale and was less lucrative than the downstream operations of big merchants. But southern Sichuan had rich brine deposits far underground, plus natural gas with which to boil brine cheaply. This made low-cost mass production possible, once the necessary wells, pumps and pipelines were in place – which required large-scale, long-term investment. Many wells were 3,000–4,000 feet deep and took 5–10 years to start yielding returns; some bamboo pipelines connecting those wells to furnaces ran over six miles, costing several times more than even the deepest wells. As people grasped these possibilities in the early–mid 1800s – when potential markets for Sichuan salt were growing rapidly – large firms that had previously concentrated mostly on distribution invested heavily in production, creating vertically integrated firms that dominated regional markets, while also expanding horizontally into other products that could be marketed along with salt. These firms remained largely lineage-owned and lineage-managed but, in other ways, they looked much like firms on the cutting edge of capital-intensive mass production in the West, with complex hierarchical structures,

---

67 In one sample of eighteenth-century copper mines, 52 out of 84 closed within 5 years and only 3 lasted over 50 years. See Lu Zhaoyi, Wu Yanqin and Li Zhinong, 'Qingdai Yunnan kuangchang de bangpai zuzhi peixi–yi Dalifu Yunlongzhou Baiyangchang wei li', *Yunnan minzu daxue xuebao*, 20 (2003), 44.

68 See, for instance Chen, *Zinc for Coin and Brass*, 636. Beginning in the 1820s, however, cheap Chilean copper began arriving in Guangzhou, driving prices there below state prices and hurting Yunnan producers very badly.

69 Chen, *Zinc for Coin and Brass*, 261–278. Both the widespread counterfeiting and the impact of Chilean copper imports will be discussed at length by Gao Xiaoyu in her forthcoming University of Chicago dissertation on the Qing copper economy. (Cited by permission.)

70 In the mid eighteenth century, margins were hefty enough that Yunnan province could also take a cut of 500,000 taels per year from 1725–1776 while output continued to rise; these revenues had essentially vanished by the 1820s. Li Zhongqing, *Zhongguo xinan bianjing de shehui jingji 1250–1850* (Beijing, 2012), 277.

professionalization and internal division of labour that their leading historian has likened to those described by Alfred Chandler.[71]

The above examples share certain patterns. With a few exceptions, production units were small, with many small-scale investors and contractual arrangements that allowed workers to acquire some equity, rather than solidifying a true proletariat. (Such arrangements also saved on wage payments and thus working capital.) The government generally liked things that way and some of their policies reinforced these tendencies. Meanwhile, capital-rich firms were much more likely to focus on shipping and commerce than production, though the Sichuan salt example shows that when it seemed opportune, they did make large fixed investments in production and innovated both technologically and organizationally. They sometimes also lent to direct producers or bought shares in their activities – as a form of vertical integration – but this was typically just one outlet for their capital and not necessarily a preferred one. Often, they were such essential partners for the government that they could simultaneously receive its protection, use it to exclude competitors and violate its laws.

VI. Producing and Marketing Ordinary Goods

The vastly larger part of the economy in which state intervention was minimal also featured a robust mercantile and financial capitalism that made few transformative investments in production. Often, this is easily explained, since small-scale, family-based production worked well. The most obvious and important example is wet-rice agriculture.

By 1600 at the latest, almost all the large rice-growing Yangzi Valley and south China estates once farmed by bondservants had been broken up, replaced by an overwhelming preponderance of very small[72] farms operated by families who either owned their land (as perhaps 50 per cent did) or had relatively secure tenancies which required high rents but gave tenants some of the same incentives and benefits as owners.[73] While some customary practices inhibited

---

71 Zelin, *Merchants of Zigong*, 12–15, 78–79, 87–114. The push for vertical integration went well beyond salt and brine to include things like raising the water buffalo who powered most pumps; horizontal expansion not only included selling other foodstuffs but tanning the hides of these buffalo (which also used salt).
72 About 1 hectare on average in the seventeenth-century Yangzi Delta and ½ and ⅔ hectare 200 years later.
73 Kenneth Pomeranz, 'Chinese Development in Long-run Perspective', *Proceedings of the American Philosophical Society*, 152 (2008), 84–87 provides a brief overview of those incentives.

land accumulation,[74] capitalist farming probably would have remained marginal in China's rice paddies regardless, given the strengths of peasant production. Per acre yields in the Yangzi Delta c.1800 were exceeded only in Japan's Kinai region. As late as 1820, agricultural output per labour day was about 90 per cent of English levels, while land productivity was over 800 per cent of England's; although the capital intensity of Delta rice-growing, with its community-operated irrigation systems, is hard to measure, it seems unlikely that it was as high as in English farming. Consequently, total factor productivity in Delta agriculture was much higher than anywhere in the West, and a capitalist reorganization would not have improved it; landowners might have increased their *share* of the crop, but not their income.[75]

North China's largely rain-dependent agriculture was much less productive, making arguments that capitalist agriculture could – and even 'should' – have replaced peasant farming seem more plausible. During the 'sprouts of capitalism' debate, Jing Su, Luo Lun and Li Wenzhi showed that managerial farms using wage labour did emerge in some particularly commercialized parts of sixteenth- to nineteenth-century North China.[76] Philip Huang later built upon this, but offered a different interpretation of why managerial farms were more efficient, but capitalist agriculture nonetheless proved abortive.[77]

Chinese and Japanese scholars claimed that managerial farms used more draft animal labour and applied more fertilizer per acre (mostly from these animals), thereby achieving higher yields. Huang argued instead that peasant and managerial farms differed little in either investment or average output; managerial farms were more profitable mostly because they hired no more labour than they needed, while peasants with average-sized farms were stuck with under-employed family labour. (All these scholars, unfortunately, had to rely heavily on data from the twentieth century, when any glut of peasant labour would have been much worse than in the high Qing.)[78] In explaining

---

74 For arguments emphasizing some of these institutions, see Philip Huang, *The Peasant Family and Rural Development in the Yangzi Delta, 1350–1988* (Stanford, 1990); Zhang Taisu, *Laws and Economics of Confucianism*.
75 Robert Allen, 'Agricultural Productivity and Rural Incomes in England and the Yangzi Delta, ca. 1620–1820', *EcHR*, 62 (2009), 525–550; Li Bozhong and Jan Luiten Van Zanden, 'Before the Great Divergence? Comparing the Yangzi Delta and the Netherlands at the Beginning of the Nineteenth Century', *JEcH*, 72 (2012), 973–976.
76 Jing Su and Luo Lun, *Qingdai Shandong jingyin dizhu jingji yanjiu*, rev. edn (Jinan, 1985), 64–159. Li Wenzhi, 'Zhongguo dizhu jingji zhi yu nongye zibenzhuyi mengya', *Zhongguo shehui kexue*, 1 (1981), 143–160.
77 Philip Huang, *The Peasant Economy and Social Change in North China* (Stanford, 1985).
78 Adachi Keiji, 'Shindai kahoku no nōgyō keieito shakai kōzō', *Shirin*, 64 (1981), 528–555; Jing and Luo, *Qingdai Shandong* (Jina, 1985), 184–195; Huang, *Peasant Economy and Social Change in North China*, 138–168.

why capitalist farming nonetheless remained atypical, Huang emphasizes that supervising hired labour became much harder when farms exceeded 200 *mu* (roughly 33 acres); and since managerial farms' main advantage was using labour more efficiently, expansion beyond 200 *mu* was less attractive than being an absentee landlord, merchant, and/or money-lender, which was also more consistent with the social advantages of living in town. And indeed, North China farms relying on wage labour were usually not much bigger than 200 *mu*.[79]

So were the limits of capitalist farming here, too, simply rational responses to limited opportunities for profitable investment in production? Even in the twentieth century, this relatively poor region had capital potentially available.[80] What North China farms most needed to raise output was to tap underground aquifers for irrigation, as happened in the 1950s–1970s; in much of the region, this would have required power-driven pumps that did not exist, and/or a scale of community organization very difficult to achieve before 1949. But this was not uniformly true; well-drilling costs varied wildly with local terrain, and some areas had lots of well-based irrigation.[81] North China's main commercial crops, cotton and wheat, were both more lucrative and more thirsty than its main subsistence crops (millet and sorghum); Ming-Qing North China had more irrigation in places that had good water transport and were relatively commercialized.[82] Some 1930s data not used in these earlier debates suggest that where access to transportation facilitated handicraft development, even small farmers benefitted by investing off-season handicraft earnings in additional yield-raising fertilizer.[83] Most of northern China, however, had limited access to water transport – especially once the Grand Canal declined in

---

79 Philip C.C. Huang, *The Peasant Economy and Social Change in North China* (1985), 171–179.
80 Carl Riskin, 'Surplus and Stagnation in Modern China', in *China's Modern Economy in Historical Perspective*, ed. Dwight Perkins (Stanford, 1975), 69–72; Lowenstein, 'Financial Markets'.
81 Chen Shuping, 'Ming Qing shiqi de jingguan, *Zhongguo shehui jingji yanjiu*, 4: 1 (1983), 36; Wang Jingxin, 'Jing li shuo' in *Huangchao jingshi wenbian* (1966 [1827]), 38: 4a–5b (1366).
82 The data directly linking commercial profit and irrigation investment are scattered and anecdotal, but given the water needs of cotton and tobacco, and the general correlation, it seems too hard to doubt. For general comments linking cotton growing in Ming-Qing North China to irrigation, noting that the irrigation had to come *before* successful large-scale cultivation (thus requiring a source of investment from outside of agriculture per se) see Wang Jialun and Zhang Fang, *Zhongguo nongtian shuili shi* (Beijing, 1989), 436. The previous page, discussing irrigation in roughly the same area for subsistence crops, notes that government loans were required to finance well-digging and defend against famine.
83 Tang Zhiqing, *Jindai Shandong nongcun shehui jingji yanjiu* (Beijing, 2004), 428–433.

the 1800s[84] – and no railroads until the 1900s (when their arrival did generally benefit nearby peasants).[85]

One agricultural sector which did undergo capitalist transformation – though mostly after 1860 – was tea. Big merchants had dominated the tea trade – especially exports – for quite some time. But there was little incentive for them to make production more efficient until China began losing overseas markets – above all to India, which went from zero to the world's biggest tea exporter within a few decades. As competition intensified, Huizhou merchants in particular began pressing both tea pickers and tea roasters – who worked in large groups and were overwhelmingly seasonal migrant wage labourers – to work harder, imposing much stricter time discipline and reducing unit labour costs. This required significant investments in means of production – buying tea-growing land, building tea-roasting 'factories' and buying or expanding warehouses, though not introducing machinery.[86] In short, Chinese merchant capitalists could mobilize large sums to change agricultural production when market pressures and/or opportunities required it, leveraging upstream processes by using their control of access to external markets. But most of China's vast agricultural sector faced no comparable pressures.

There were, then, multiple reasons why capitalist investment had limited influence on Chinese farming, which had little to do with the capitalist firms themselves. In wet-rice areas, there were no economies of scale available, while the returns to extremely careful work (encouraged by giving cultivators a share in their output) were large. In the north, there were some opportunities for output-raising investment that went unexploited, even before mechanized irrigation pumps became available; but these opportunities were limited and compatible with peasant production in those places where peasants had sufficient market access to increase cash cropping and/or pursue sidelines, raising the small sums needed to buy more fertilizer and/or tap relatively shallow aquifers. Conditions in this region also allowed for raising profits by replacing family farming with wage labour and 'releasing' under-employed labour (without raising output); but these gains were not dramatic, practical only within a fairly narrow range of farm size (roughly 16–33 acres) and required good market access – which would also give peasant families alternatives to under-employment. (Looked at differently, this suggests that where peasants were able to benefit from commercial

---

84 Kenneth Pomeranz, *The Making of a Hinterland: State, Society and Economy in Inland North China, 1853–1937* (Berkeley, 1993).
85 Ernest Liang, *China, Railways and Agricultural Development, 1875–1935* (Chicago, 1982); Lillian Li, *Fighting Famine in North China* (Stanford, 2007), 316–318, 321–331.
86 Andrew Liu, *Tea War: A History of Capitalism in China and India* (New Haven, 2020), 45–80. By contrast, the most successful tea exporter of the pre-1860 period, Houqua, lent to other merchants and invested in various other activities, but not in tea production.

expansion, this reduced any impetus towards a capitalist transformation of agriculture itself.)

What of handicrafts themselves? By far the biggest handicraft sector was textiles. This covers many fabrics and markets and enormous variations across time and place, making generalizations difficult. But there is no question that silk and especially cotton production soared during the late empire and that they were increasingly produced for sale, rather than for the producers' families.[87] There is also no doubt that the vast majority of spinning and weaving occurred in rural homes, often done by women who specialized in these activities, while the men in their households mostly farmed.[88] It is also clear that neither capitalists nor wage labourers played much role in these activities, though they were significant in calendaring, to some extent in dyeing and in producing some specialized fabrics: activities which were more urban, more full-time and featured significant economies of scale.[89] The vast majority of weaving households owned their looms and spun at least some of their own yarn (until cheap machine-made yarn became available in the mid–late nineteenth century); many, though not most, also grew cotton.[90] Merchant credit for these activities was not unknown, but also not widespread. Merchants did, however, buy and re-sell cloth profitably, often across long distances. Their control of marketing gave them influence over production without investing much in it.

The average quality of marketed textiles probably increased between 1550 and 1850; the variety certainly did.[91] Some new varieties were tailored to specific climates and/or uses, but the bigger trend was a proliferation of styles and colours. Dyeworks, which were often town-based and moderately capital-intensive, expanded rapidly.

Long-distance cloth merchants competed on quality, developing informal trademarks (sometimes embroidered on the cloth's edge) and fiercely guarding their reputations.[92] This made it vital for them to enforce standards on the

---

87 Craig Dietrich, 'Cotton Culture and Manufacture in Early Ch'ing China', in *Economic Organization in Chinese Society*, ed. W.E. Wilmott (Stanford, 1972), 109–135; Huang, *Peasant Family*; Li Bozhong, *Jiangnan de zaoqi gongyehua, 1550–1850* (Beijing, 2000), 37–85.
88 See, for instance, Li Bozhong, 'Cong "fufu bingzuo" dao "nan geng nu zhi"', *Zhongguo jingji shi yanjiu*, 11, 99–107. For some scepticism about whether these women were really mostly divorced from agricultural production see Wang You, 'Crafting the Waterscape: Environmental Governance and Rural Communities of the Lower Yangzi Delta, 100–1850' (University of California, Los Angeles, Ph.D. dissertation, 2022).
89 Tsing Yuan, 'Urban Riots and Disturbances during the Late Ming and Early Ch'ing Period', in *From Ming to Ch'ing: Conquest, Region and Continuity in Seventeenth-Century China*, eds. Jonathan Spence and John Wills (New Haven, 1979), 277–320; Li, *Jiangnan*, 61.
90 Li, *Jiangnan*, 65–77; Huang, *Peasant Family*, 53–55.
91 Li Bozhong, *Jiangnan de zaoqi gongyehua (1550–1850)* (Beijing, 2000), 53–57.
92 Gary Hamilton and Chi-kong Lai, 'Consumerism Without Capitalism: Consumption and Brand Names in Late Imperial China', in *The Social Economy of Consumption*, eds.

weavers they purchased from. Though evidence is scant, it appears that weavers became more specialized and intensively trained, while families and sometimes even whole villages that could not meet rising standards were forced out of desirable markets.[93] Thus it appears that merchants gained greater control over spinners and weavers by leveraging their control of downstream activities and generally saw no need to intervene as directly in upstream production as did 'putting out' merchants in Europe.[94] Not only did cloth quality improve without direct merchant investment; there is also evidence that labour-efficiency in spinning increased, with more households acquiring improved spinning wheels.[95]

VII. Conclusion

Most of the Chinese produced part of their subsistence directly, while also regularly participating in well-developed local and long-distance markets. Local trade was often very competitive, but big capitalist merchants dominated most long-distance trade. In some cases they entrenched themselves through privileges granted by the state, or spill-overs from such privileges, while in others they benefitted from having easier access to capital, better information and superior ability to wait for returns. These same merchants developed sophisticated mechanisms that moved money across time and space in search of maximum returns. The empire's many passive investors – including some small ones – also had access to networks that directed their savings fairly efficiently towards those seeking capital, both as loans and as equity investments. No public market for shares existed, but a variety of corporate structures allowed firms to collect investment from large numbers of people, often unknown to each other and to continue functioning when some investors withdrew from the firm, transferring their shares to others. In short, we find many characteristic features of early modern capitalism worldwide.

Henry Ruiz and Benjamin Orlove (Lanham, MD, 1989), 253–279; Li Bozhong, *Jiangnan*, 81–85.
93   Li Bozhong, *Jiangnan*, 63–64, 76, 85. Li suggests that some who could no longer compete as weavers became full-time spinners; if so, this would have been very costly for them. For differences between spinning and weaving incomes, see Pomeranz, *Great Divergence* (2021 edn.), 316–326; Pomeranz, 'Beyond the East–West Binary: Resituating Development Paths in the Eighteenth-Century World', *JAsS*, 61 (2002), 558–564.
94   The literature on putting out is vast and contentious. For particularly relevant examples see Peter Kriedte, Hans Medick and Jürgen Schlumbohm, *Industrialization before Industrialization* (Cambridge, 1981); David Levine, *Family Formation in an Age of Nascent Capitalism* (New York, 1977); for Huizhou cloth merchants abstaining from such intervention, see McDermott, *Making of a New Rural Order*, II: 341.
95   Li, *Jiangnan*, 83–84.

Ming-Qing capitalists were far more active in commerce – especially long-distance commerce – and finance than in production. It bears repeating that this was the norm everywhere before the industrial revolution, but it may have been especially true in China. We find very little agricultural wage labour, even though population growth far outstripped increases in farmland; if anything, family farming became even more entrenched and rural property less concentrated.[96] Given the exceptional productivity of China's peasant agriculture, this is perhaps unsurprising, but it is noteworthy that in sector after sector – including some like mining where there were potential economies of scale – we rarely find concentrated ownership of the means of production or mass proletarianization. Instead institutions often blurred the lines between owners and workers, giving workers opportunities to acquire small amounts of equity in lieu of higher wages.[97] In post-1860 tea production and the Sichuan salt industry, capitalists did make major investments in production, creating more intense work routines, more complex and hierarchical management systems and (in the saltworks) introducing new, capital-intensive technologies – showing that Chinese institutions could do this. But such cases are rare.

Chinese capitalism also faced other limitations, related to Ming-Qing governance. Contrary to many stereotypes, the late imperial state was not anti-merchant; it often promoted trade and division of labour across its vast territory. It was, however, anti-monopoly and offered fewer such opportunities to its merchants than did many of its contemporaries – perhaps also because, being less consistently at war (and rarely with enemies of comparable size), it felt less pressure to give merchants privileges in return for increased revenues. (Where the state did offer such opportunities, as in salt, big merchant groups took full advantage; and when it faced a chronic military–fiscal emergency after c.1850, it began granting more such privileges.) Until then, it also did not borrow, closing off an avenue of accumulation that proved quite important for early modern financiers elsewhere. And the state also did little to provide infrastructure specifically to expand private trade – though merchants did benefit from canal-building, road-building and river-dredging that was done to aid in provisioning frontier troops, feeding the capital and getting metals to government mints, while everyone benefitted from state water control investments that supported

---

96 Jiang Taixin, *Lun Qingdai tudi guanxi de xin bianhua* (Tianjin, 2011), 89–238; also see above on the on-going strengthening of tenants' usufruct rights.
97 Yet another example of this can be seen in sea-borne trade, with sailors often receiving no wages, but subsistence plus a share of the ship's cargo space with which to trade on their own account – though when it came to on-board discipline they were most definitely employees, not small-scale partners. See Ng Chin-keong, 'The South Fujianese Junk Trade at Amoy from the Seventeenth to the Early Eighteenth Centuries', in *Development and Decline of Fukien Province in the Seventeenth and Eighteenth Centuries*, ed. Eduard Vermeer (Leiden, 1990), 315.

agriculture.⁹⁸ In sum, late imperial Chinese capitalists sometimes gained from state projects, but probably less so than capitalists in some other places.

Finally, the Qing had paternalistic attitudes towards some (not all) of the non-Han peoples in their non-agricultural highlands and borderlands. This made them reluctant to sanction large-scale private investment in a wide variety of extractive activities on the frontiers, including logging, mining, harvesting Manchurian ginseng and pearls and converting steppe to farmland.⁹⁹ Such efforts did not always successfully 'protect' the locals and certainly did not prevent merchants from the Chinese heartland from profiting off trade with the frontier. They did, however, probably slow the process of mass dispossession and kept some of the profits of resource extraction per se in local hands. Thus, a capitalism that was already somewhat hemmed in at home – by strong and productive peasant property, slow technological change, a relatively small number of state-sanctioned monopolies and the absence of state debt – was also denied the 'spatial fix' of expropriating disfavoured populations in the empire's far peripheries. Those peripheries saw plenty of coercion but were not re-organized in ways that benefitted capitalists to anything like the degree that overseas conquests benefitted capitalists from Eurasia's other end.¹⁰⁰

---

98 Peter Perdue, 'The Qing State and the Gansu Grain Market, 1739–1864', in *Chinese History in Economic Perspective*, eds. Lillian Li and Thomas Rawski (Berkeley, 1992), 111–113, 123–125; Li Zhongqing, *Zhongguo xinan* (Beijing, 2012), 71–89; note 47 above on Grand Canal; Qiu Pengsheng, 'Shiba shiji Dian tong', *Zhongyang yanjiuyuan lishi yuyan yanjiusuo jikan*, 72:1 (2001), 88–91 on river-dredging to facilitate shipping copper. Of course, most other early modern states also focused most of their spending on military needs and probably did less than the Qing for agriculture; but see Steve Pincus and James Robinson, 'Challenging the Fiscal-Military Hegemony: The British Case', in *The British Fiscal–Military States, 1660–1783*, eds. Aaron Graham and Patrick Walsh (New York, 2016), 238–245 on eighteenth-century British spending aimed at stimulating economic growth, including building infrastructure designed to benefit colonial commerce.

99 Jonathan Schlesinger, *A World Trimmed with Fur: Wild Things, Pristine Places and the Natural Fringes of Qing Rule* (Stanford, 2017), 56–88; David Bello, *Across Forest, Steppe and Mountain: Environment, Identity and Empire in Qing China's Borderlands* (Cambridge, 2016), 99–105, 144–157.

100 On the 'spatial fix' as a solution to falling profits in core regions see David Harvey, 'The Spatial Fix: Hegel, Von Thunen and Marx', *Antipode*, 13 (1981), 1–12.

12

Why the Soybean Export Failed to Trigger the Reemergence of Coercive Labour Control in Eighteenth-Century Manchuria

HORUS T'AN

Immanuel Wallerstein (1930–2019) argued that Western Europe embarked on its path to capitalist development in the sixteenth century because a capitalist world-economy emerged during this period. That economic model encompassed Western Europe, Central Europe, the Baltic states and parts of the Americas and was characterized by a geographical division of labour and long-distance trade in bulk goods. China could not follow a similar path of development because it failed to establish such a world-economy. Instead, Wallerstein suggested, China's inability to create its own world-economy is because it was a world-empire, an entity that 'is responsible for administering and defending a huge land and population mass' and that this massive administration 'drains attention, energy, and profits which could be invested in capital development'.[1]

While the world-systems theory proves more effective than modernization theory in explaining the underdevelopment of certain countries, Wallerstein's interpretation of Chinese history is unpersuasive. Recent studies reveal the widespread existence of interregional trading systems and the long-distance trade of bulk goods within China during this period. These findings demonstrate that, during the eighteenth and nineteenth centuries, aided by an extensive network of rivers and coastal transportation, merchants transported millions of tons of agricultural products such as rice, wheat, cotton, and soybeans over thousands of miles. This integration of customers and producers from different parts of the Chinese empire formed vast trading networks.

---

[1] Immanuel Wallerstein, *The Modern World-System I: Capitalist Agriculture and the Origins of the European World-Economy in the Sixteenth Century* (Berkeley, 2011), 60. See also idem, *The Essential Wallerstein* (New York, 2000), 75: '… the only kind of social system is a world-system, which we define quite simply as a unit with a single division of labor and multiple cultural systems. It follows logically that there can, however, be two varieties of such world-systems, one with a common political system and one without. We shall designate these respectively as world-empires and world-economies.… World-empires are basically redistributive in economic form.'

Some of these interregional trading systems even bore structural similarities with the capitalist world-economy in the early modern period. For instance, the Manchurian soybean trade was a trading system that closely resembled the capitalist world-economy that emerged in Western Europe from the late sixteenth century, typified by the Baltic grain trade. This trading system encompassed, at least, the Yangzi Delta and Manchuria. During this period, the Yangzi Delta stood out as the most economically advanced and densely populated region within the Chinese empire. To meet the substantial food demands of its large population, peasants in this region intensified their agriculture. This intensification, in turn, generated a substantial demand for fertilizers. To satisfy this need, the Yangzi Delta imported a significant quantity of soybeans from Manchuria during the eighteenth and nineteenth centuries. This trading system exhibited a distinct geographical division of labour between the periphery and the core. In this arrangement, Manchuria served as the periphery, supplying raw materials. In exchange for Manchurian soybeans, the Yangzi Delta exported substantial quantities of manufactured commodities, primarily cotton textiles, to Manchuria. This geographical division of labour closely paralleled that observed between England and Poland in the capitalist world-economy starting from the sixteenth century. From the sixteenth century onward, Western European nations like England and the Netherlands imported vast quantities of raw materials, such as rye, from the Baltic countries like Poland to sustain their rapidly growing urban populations. Simultaneously, these Western European countries exported significant volumes of manufactured goods, including woollen and cotton textiles, to the Baltic countries.

These remarkable similarities prompt intriguing questions. Did China aim to establish its own capitalist world-economy? Why did China's economy not follow the path of capitalist development seen in Western Europe? Why did China not expand and establish overseas colonies as Western European countries did? Why did China's interregional trading system fail to catalyze technological breakthroughs like the Industrial Revolution?

This chapter addresses these questions by examining the impact of this interregional trading system on its periphery. One notable distinction between China's interregional trading system and the capitalist world-economy lies in the absence of various forms of coercive labour control in China's periphery. Coercive labour controls like slavery and serfdom were widely spread phenomena in the periphery of the capitalist world-economy in the early modern period. While coercive labour control did exist in Manchurian agricultural production during the seventeenth century, it gradually disappeared in the eighteenth century with the emergence of the soybean trade.

This contrast in labour control methods differentiates the two trading systems. This chapter compares the coercive labour control in Manchuria with labour practices in medieval and early modern Europe. This analysis elucidates why coercive labour control vanished in Manchuria by the mid eighteenth century and why, despite similar geographical labour divisions, China's interregional trading system differed significantly from the capitalist world-economy. Examining why Manchuria had coercive labour control allows us more fully to appreciate the differences between China's interregional trading system and the capitalist world-economy as well as the origin of capitalism.

I

The Manchurian soybean trade of the eighteenth and nineteenth centuries, linking the Yangzi Delta and Manchuria, resembled an interregional trading system akin to the capitalist world-economy exemplified by the Baltic grain trade between England and Poland during the seventeenth and eighteenth centuries. Both systems featured long-distance trade in bulk goods, a characteristic that Wallerstein asserts is 'only available within the framework of the modern world-economy'.[2] Additionally, they shared a geographical division of labour, a key defining feature of the capitalist world-economy.[3]

However, significant differences distinguished these two systems. One notable distinction was the absence of coercive labour control in Manchuria. Coercive labour control – like the Polish 'second serfdom' – was a prevalent practice in the periphery of the capitalist world-economy during the early modern period. Starting in the sixteenth century, Poland, along with several other regions in Eastern Europe, including Bohemia, Silesia, Hungary, and Eastern Prussia, experienced a gradual expansion of serfdom. This expansion primarily entailed the growth of landlords' demesnes at the expense of small peasants' farms and the intensification of corvée labour obligations on these demesnes. By the latter half of the seventeenth century, corvée labour requirements had escalated significantly, ranging from one or two days a week to as many as five or six days.[4] Friedrich Engels referred to this phenomenon as 'the second serfdom'.[5]

While historians disagree about the origins of the second serfdom in Eastern Europe, they agree that the second serfdom in Poland had a close relationship with the geographical labour division inherent in the capitalist world-economy. Within this global economic framework, Poland exported staple grains and imported manufactured commodities. According to Wallerstein, the Eastern European aristocrats, particularly Polish ones, embraced coercive labour

---

2 Ibid., 21.
3 Immanuel Wallerstein, *World-Systems Analysis: An Introduction* (Durham, NC, 2004), 23.
4 Péter Gunst, 'Agrarian Systems of Central and Eastern Europe', in *The Origins of Backwardness in Eastern Europe*, ed. Daniel Chirot (Berkeley, 1989), 68.
5 Frederick Engels, Marx and Engels Correspondence (1968): www.marxists.org/archive/marx/works/1882/letters/82_12_15.htm. (accessed 19/06/2024)

control because 'Eastern Europe played the role of raw-materials producers for the industrializing West'.[6]

Marian Malowist further elaborates on this notion, asserting that the export of grains from Eastern Europe to the West incentivized aristocrats in the region to expand their estates at the expense of peasants. They forced peasants into labour on their properties, aiming to eliminate competitors and capture more surplus from the grain trade.[7] Malowist argues that Poland effectively became an economic colony of the West due to the grain exports, which stifled the growth of domestic industries. The behaviour of Polish aristocrats not only worsened the living conditions of peasants but also contracted the domestic market for manufactured goods, for it eroded peasants' purchasing power and limited the customer base for local artisans in towns.[8]

The importation of manufactured goods from Western Europe further hindered the development of native industries in Poland. In their pursuit of extracting more surplus from the grain trade, Polish landlords circumvented indigenous merchants and directly engaged with foreign merchants in Gdansk to secure higher profits, which impeded the growth of an indigenous Polish bourgeoisie. Malowist underscores that the economic development of the fifteenth and sixteenth centuries led to 'a one-sided development of agriculture' at the expense of industrial production.[9]

The absence of serfdom in Manchuria poses a significant challenge to these arguments. Manchuria, like Poland in the capitalist world-economy, played a pivotal role as a peripheral region within China's interregional trading system. Both regions exported agricultural products while importing manufactured commodities. Nevertheless, despite the prosperity of the long-distance soybean trade, the historical evolution of slavery in Manchuria reveals that the soybean export did not lead to the emergence of a system akin to 'the second serfdom' witnessed in Poland during the sixteenth century. While slavery did exist in Manchuria during the fifteenth and sixteenth centuries, it more closely resembled classical slavery observed in ancient Rome and the early Middle Ages. This form of slavery markedly differed from the second serfdom that emerged in Poland during the sixteenth century. Following the end of the Ming–Jurchen wars in the mid seventeenth century, slavery in Manchuria gradually gave way to a system of tenancy. Throughout the eighteenth and nineteenth centuries, when soybean exports thrived, aristocratic estates, which were once cultivated

---

6 Wallerstein, *The Modern World-System I*, 95.
7 Marian Malowist, 'The Economic and Social Development of the Baltic Countries from the Fifteenth to the Seventeenth Centuries', *EcHR*, 12 (1959), 184.
8 Jack Kochanowicz, 'The Polish Economy and Evolution of Dependency', in *The Origins of Backwardness in Eastern Europe*, ed. Daniel Chirot (Berkeley, 1989), 106.
9 Malowist, 'Economic and Social Development of the Baltic Countries', 187.

by coercive labours, subdivided into countless small parcels that were rented out to individual small-scale peasants.

II

Why did grain exports lead to the emergence of the second serfdom in Poland but fail to do so in Manchuria? From a world-system perspective, the Polish second serfdom can be attributed to the geographical labour division within the capitalist world-economy. However, it is worth noting that world-system theorists like Wallerstein did not provide a detailed explanation of the mechanism behind the emergence of the second serfdom. This gap in understanding becomes particularly glaring considering that the soybean export in Manchuria did not lead to coercive labour control.

Tom Raster's research on the origins of the second serfdom in Poland establishes a connection between the second serfdom and grain export. Estates with better access to international markets exhibited more pronounced labour coercion. Additionally, estates located near export hubs tended to be larger. This trend emerged because grain exports incentivized estate owners to expropriate peasants' property and restrict their ability to purchase land.[10] Raster contends that the existence of serfdom on Polish estates was shaped by three factors: the subsistence wage paid to coerced labour; the wage offered to free hire labour; and the cost associated with coercion. Polish landowners employed more free labour when the wage for free workers was lower than the sum of the subsistence wage and the cost of coercion. Conversely, they resorted to more coerced labour when the wage for free labour exceeded the combined total of subsistence wage and coercion costs.[11]

In this equation, the subsistence wage remained a constant value. However, the other two factors were influenced by the grain export and the human-to-land ratio. Raster argues that Western Europe's demand for Polish grains significantly drove up local grain prices. The combination of higher grain prices and a low human-to-land ratio rendered coercion more economically advantageous.[12] So, in the absence of long-distance grain trade, tenancy was typically the preferred method for extracting surplus. In predominantly agrarian societies, economic development often entailed population growth. This local population growth increased the demand for food, similar to foreign demand. However, unlike foreign demand, local population growth suppressed labour

---

10 Tom Raster, 'Serfs and the Market: Second Serfdom and the East–West Goods Exchange, 1579–1857' (Paris School of Economics M.A. thesis, 2019), 48.
11 Ibid., 11.
12 Ibid., 60.

wages, reducing the feasibility of coercive labour control. It was only when foreign demand came into play that free labour wages saw significant increases, motivating landowners to adopt coercive labour practices in production.

The chapter adopts Raster's approach and applies it to Manchuria. Analysing the grain prices and population density in Manchuria, it compares them with the corresponding factors in Poland. This comparative analysis sheds light on the distinct historical trajectories and economic dynamics that shaped labour control practices in these two regions during the eighteenth and nineteenth centuries. By examining these variables in both contexts, we can gain a deeper understanding of the distinctive factors that influenced labour relations and the absence of coercive labour control in Manchuria.

III

Because the Qing authorities feared that foreign demand would drive up local grain prices they hesitated to lift the ban on the export of Manchurian soybeans until the mid eighteenth century. However, the Qing emperors' and their subordinates' concerns regarding the removal of the soybean export ban ultimately proved to be unfounded. Contrary to expectations, the price of soybeans in Manchuria did not experience a significant increase following the ban's removal in the mid eighteenth century. When comparing the price of soybeans in Manchuria with that of rye, the primary commodity in the Baltic grain trade, in Poland, it becomes evident that the price of soybeans in Manchuria did not experience the same level of increase as did rye.

Figure 12.1 presents the price of rye in Krakow, a significant grain-producing region in Poland, spanning the years 1371 to 1700. It reveals that the price of rye in Krakow remained relatively low before the first half of the sixteenth century.

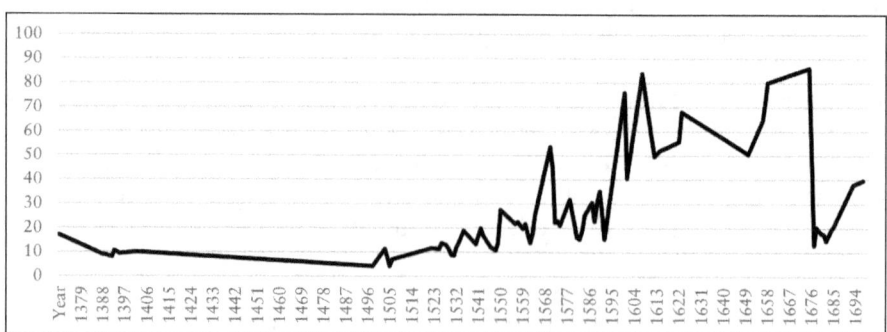

Figure 12.1. The price of rye in Krakow (gram of silver per litre), 1371–1700. *Source*: Allen-Unger Global Commodity Prices Database, http://www.gcpdb.info/data.html (accessed 19/06/2024).

However, from the mid sixteenth century onward, it saw a substantial increase. Despite experiencing sharp fluctuations after the late seventeenth century, the price of rye never reverted to the pre-sixteenth-century levels during this period.

In contrast, the historical path of soybean prices took a different course. Figure 12.2 illustrates the soybean price in the Fengtien Prefecture spanning from 1756 to 1889. It reveals that soybean prices did experience an increase from the 1750s, following the removal of the soybean export ban. However, this increase was relatively gradual and not as sharp as the rye price fluctuations. The peak of soybean prices occurred during the 1810s. Even during this decade, soybean prices were only approximately twice as high as those observed in the 1750s. In the 1820s, soybean prices sharply declined and remained in a prolonged state of depression. By the 1850s, they had reached levels even lower than those a century earlier.

After the 1860s, there was a slight uptick in soybean prices, which might be attributed to the introduction of foreign steamboats. British observers emphasized that foreign steamboats broadened the market for Manchurian soybeans. They transported soybeans directly to South China ports, eliminating the need for transshipment in Shanghai, which had been a necessary step for small native junks.[13] Even so, by the end of the nineteenth century, soybean prices had only experienced a slight increase compared to their levels in the 1750s. Soybean prices did not exhibit the same degree of extreme volatility as rye prices.

The contrast becomes more apparent when examining the price gap between grains primarily intended for export and those primarily sold in the local market. In Poland, this gap widened significantly during the sixteenth century. In the fourteenth century, the average price ratio of oats to rye to wheat in Krakow, a city located in the upper reach of the Vistula River and a primary grain production region, was 100:167:284, while in the sixteenth century, it shifted to 100:213:333.

Julian Pelc attributed this widening gap to the growing demand for rye and wheat from foreign countries. Rye and wheat were in high demand on the international market. In 1565, Poland exported 45,000 lasts of grains, with 92 per cent of them being rye.[14] Oats, by contrast, were primarily utilized as animal fodder and had limited export potential. Pelc also conducted a price comparison between grains in Krakow and Leviv, finding that the price ratio between oats, rye, and wheat in Leviv during the sixteenth century was only 100:175:240. One contributing factor to the relatively high prices of rye and wheat in Krakow was

---

13 *Reports of the Trade at the Ports in China Open by Treaty to Foreign Trade for the Year 1865* (Shanghai, 1866), 18.
14 Piotr Guzowski, 'The Influence of Exports on Grain Production on Polish Royal Demesne Farms in the Second Half of the Sixteenth Century', *Agricultural History Review*, 59 (2011), 320.

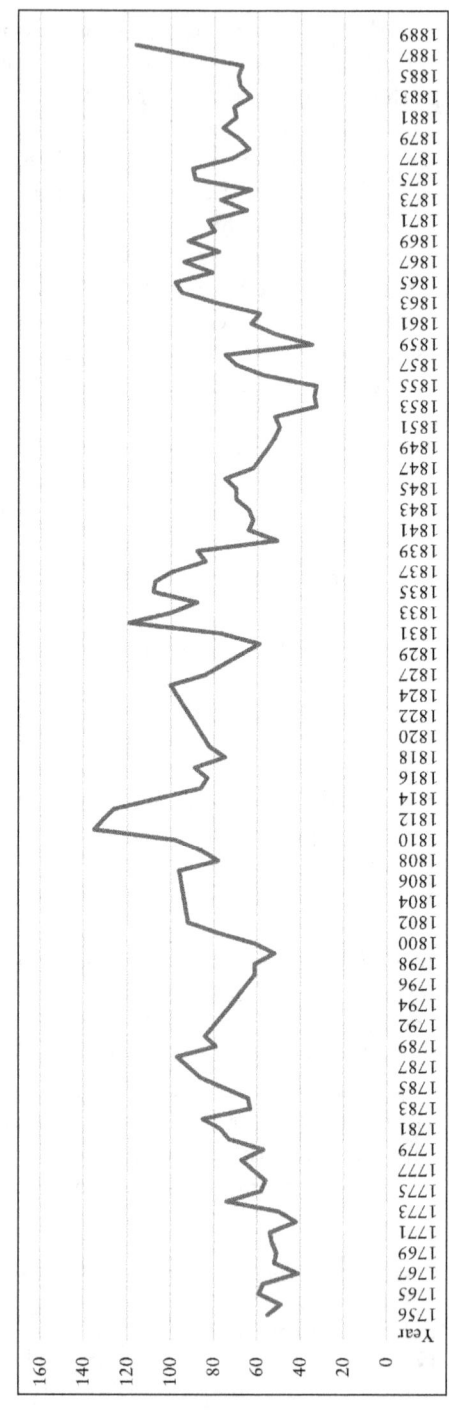

Figure 12.2. The August price of soybeans in Fengtien prefecture (tael of silver per 100 picul), 1756–1889. *Source:* Qingdai Liang Jia Zliaoku 清代糧價資料庫. [Database of the grain prices during the Qing period]. Distributed by Academia Sinica, https://mhdb.mh.sinica.edu.tw/databaseinfo.php?b=006 (accessed 19/06/2024).

the city's strategic location. Krakow's proximity to the Vistula River made it convenient for residents to transport rye and wheat downstream to Gdansk, a major port in the Baltic grain trade.[15]

Such a price gap was absent in Manchuria during the eighteenth and nineteenth centuries. Figure 12.3 illustrates the price trends of soybeans and sorghum during this period. Sorghum, a Manchurian major staple grain, was primarily consumed by local peasants. Interestingly, the price trend of soybeans closely mirrored that of sorghum. This marked similarity stands in stark contrast to the widening gap observed between oat and rye prices in Poland.

The absence of a price gap between soybeans and sorghum in Manchuria is further substantiated by Japanese diplomats. In the 1890s, they conducted a series of investigations into agricultural production in the vicinity of Newchwang. Their findings revealed that the profitability of soybean cultivation was notably low, even lower than that of sorghum. Specifically, the investigation showed that the profit per Ri (a traditional unit of measurement) from sorghum cultivation was 3.74 Yuan, while soybean cultivation in the same area yielded a profit of only 3.3 Yuan.[16]

This limited profitability helps explain why soybean cultivation occupied only a small portion of the total arable land in the region. Prior to the mid eighteenth century, both the emperor and local officials in Manchuria approached the soybean ban with caution, fearing that its removal would lead to an increase in local soybean prices; incentivize peasants to allocate more land to soybean cultivation; and potentially jeopardize local food security. However, even during the 1910s, when Manchurian soybeans gained popularity in the international market, soybean cultivation accounted for just 23 per cent of the total arable land in Liaoning Province.[17]

Foreign demand had a different impact in Poland, where it encouraged aristocrats to engage in rye production. In regions like Greater Poland and Masovia, where rye could be shipped to Gdansk via river routes, more demesnes focused on rye cultivation because rye, compared to other crops, enjoyed greater popularity in overseas markets. This expansion of rye production often came at the expense of other cereals, particularly wheat and barley.[18]

Some contemporary observers also noticed the depression of the soybean price in Manchuria. A. McPherson conducted a detailed analysis of the depression in soybean prices in Manchuria in his 1865 report in which he

---

15 Julian Pelc, *Ceny w Krakowie w latach 1369–1600* (Skład Główny, 1935), 61–62.
16 Kato Sueo, 加藤末郎, *Shinkoku shucchou fukumei sho* 清国出張復命書 (Tokyo, 1899), 12–13.
17 Komai Tokuzo, 駒井徳三, *Manshū daizuron* 満洲大豆論 (Sendai, 1912), 47.
18 Piotr Guzowski, 'The Influence of Exports on Grain Production on Polish Royal Demesne Farms in the Second Half of the Sixteenth Century', *Agricultural History Review*, 59 (2011), 324.

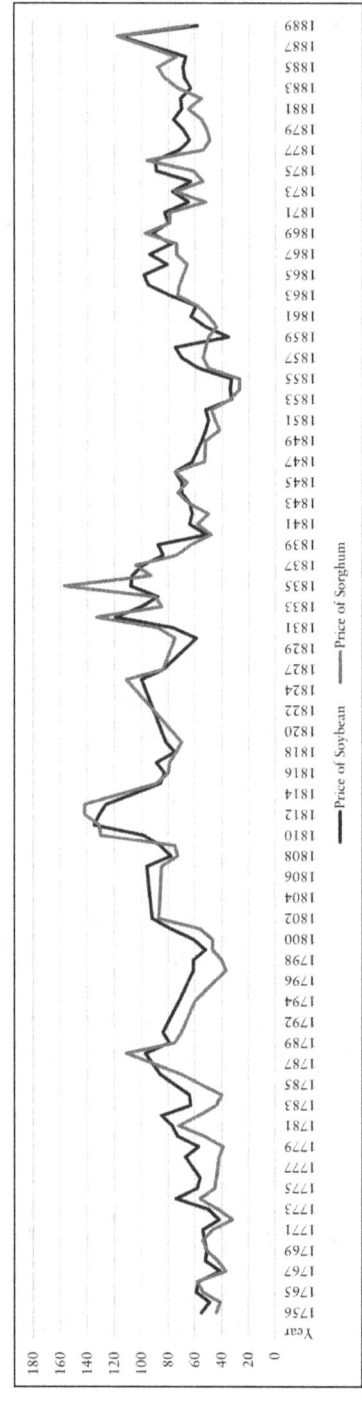

Figure 12.3. A comparison of August soybean and sorghum price in Fengtien prefecture (tael of silver per 100 picul), 1756–1889. *Source*: Qingdai Liang Jia Ziliaoku 清代糧價資料庫. [Database of the grain prices during the Qing period]. Distributed by Academia Sinica, https://mhdb.mh.sinica.edu.tw/databaseinfo.php?b=006 (accessed 19/06/2024).

made a significant observation: certain groups of merchants held a monopoly on the trade. This monopoly effectively prevented foreign merchants, as well as the merchants from China proper, from directly engaging with soybean producers. However, contrary to expectations, this monopoly did not result in elevated soybean prices. Why? McPherson discovered that the soybean trade in Manchuria began with local small soybean dealers. Unless they resided near ports like Newchwang and Mukden, soybean sellers in the region could not transport their soybean harvest directly to these ports. Instead, they had to sell their soybeans to these small dealers, who would journey into the hinterland after the harvest. These small dealers were native to Manchuria and had established relationships with local soybean sellers.

Crucially, when sellers delivered their soybean harvest to these dealers by the end of autumn, they did not receive immediate cash payment. Instead, they had to wait until the sixth month of the following year when increased rainfall and snowmelt caused the Liao River's water level to rise. During this time dealers returned by boat from Newchwang with foreign commodities such as opium and various Chinese goods.[19] This unique system of payment with credit disadvantaged foreign merchants attempting to establish direct contact with soybean sellers because it heavily relied on the trust established between soybean sellers and the small dealers, making it difficult for outsiders to compete. These small dealers effectively monopolized transportation facilities and controlled the soybean trade.

Neither were the soybean transactions in Newchwang and Mukden open business. Local yard owners tightly controlled these small dealers who had no choice but to store their soybeans in their yards, which effectively served as storage warehouses for the dealers. Some of these yards were also involved in soybean oil production. Foreign merchants looking to purchase soybeans had to rely on intermediaries, often brokers with close ties to the yards. The presence of these long-established local entities, which had operated in Manchuria for centuries, made it exceedingly challenging for foreign merchants and even native merchants from places like Sawtow or Chin-chew to establish direct contact with soybean cultivators. The competition was fierce.

Despite the monopoly that prevented outsiders from directly engaging with soybean sellers, the soybean market reached a point where further price increases were unsustainable. Once prices reached a certain level, demand decreased significantly, making it challenging to sell soybeans at even higher prices in the consuming provinces. This market constraint prevented prices from becoming exorbitant despite the monopoly.[20]

19 *Reports of the Trade at the Ports ... for the Year 1865*, 16.
20 Ibid., 17.

Merchant behaviour also highlights the disparity in demand between Manchurian soybeans and Baltic grains in Western Europe. One practice that underscored the strong demand for Baltic grains was advance payments. This practice involved merchants providing upfront cash payments to producers, creating a dependency where producers were bound to deliver products at pre-arranged prices. Advance payments were a well-known practice in medieval Europe, particularly in mining and timbering. A necessary precondition for the establishment of such an advance payment system was strong demand for raw materials in a distant market.[21] It allowed merchants to accumulate substantial quantities of commodities and effectively distribute them to distant markets.[22] In the context of the Baltic grain trade, merchants in port cities like Gdansk extended credit to grain producers. These producers, in turn, committed to supplying crops to Gdansk at their own expense and at specified prices, regardless of fluctuations caused by varying harvest conditions.[23]

Manchurian merchants, however, did not adopt the advance payment practice until the 1920s when the Manchurian soybeans became extremely popular on the international market.[24] While some prominent bankers in Mukden participated as creditors in the soybean trade, their loans did not directly benefit the soybean producers. Borrowers used these loans for speculative activities. Once the cold weather in winters had hardened the roads in Southern Manchuria, the dealers transported the soybeans they had acquired from local cultivators in wagons to cities near the Liao River, such as Tieling. From there, the cargo would travel downstream along the Liao River to reach either Mukden or Newchwang. Wealthy Mukden bankers frequently extended loans to yard owners in the city. These loans enabled the yard owners to purchase soybeans at higher prices than those in Newchwang. Subsequently, the yard owners in Mukden would store these soybeans in local yards until early spring when the soybean prices typically rose. Then, they speculated by forwarding soybeans to Newchwang.

IV

Manchuria and Poland not only differed in grain prices but also in their human-to-land ratios. At first blush, it might appear that the human-to-land ratio in

---

21 Marian Malowist, 'Merchant Credit and the Putting-Out System – Rural Production during the Middle Ages', *Review*, 4 (1981), 668.
22 Ibid.
23 Ibid., 678
24 Yasutomi Ayumu, 安富歩 and Fukao Yoko 深尾誉子, *'Manshū' no Seiritsu Shinrin no Shōjin to Kindai Kūkan no Keisei*「満洲」の成立—森林の消尽と近代空間の形成 (Nagoya, 2009), 120.

Manchuria was lower than in Poland. For instance, by the end of the sixteenth century, the population density in the Polish Lithuanian Commonwealth had reached 21.3 people per square kilometre.[25] In contrast, in the Liao River basin, the most populated area of Manchuria, population density in the early eighteenth century stood at only 2.12 people per square kilometre. By the early nineteenth century, it had increased to just 6.83 people per square kilometre.[26]

However, a closer examination of labour supply and demand reveals the opposite situation. Many historians contend that the second serfdom in Poland was influenced by labour shortages resulting from the cessation of immigration from the west of the Elbe River after the fifteenth century. Prior to the fifteenth century, Poland experienced significant German immigration from west of the Elbe River, largely linked to colonization efforts by Prussian and Polish aristocrats.[27] As more Germanic peasants moved eastward, they introduced the German tenancy system to Poland. The competition among aristocrats for these peasants prevented the increase of burdens on the tenant population. Consequently, this influx of Germanic peasants helped eliminate the old servile system in Poland. Additionally, the settlement of Germanic peasants brought changes to the legal system, with disputes now being handled by the village mayor instead of the lord's court in the manorial system.[28]

However, when the Black Death swept through the western regions of Elbe, population plummeted and immigration declined. These drops posed a serious challenge for Polish aristocrats, for the abundance of unoccupied land tempted peasants to migrate, potentially leaving the nobles without tax-paying subjects. Additionally, the land surplus drove up the wage labour costs.[29] During the fifteenth century, Polish aristocrats shifted their focus away from colonization efforts and toward income redistribution through a manorial system. They intensified socage services, increasing them from one or two days a week to as many as five or six days a week.[30]

In contrast to Poland, Manchuria did not experience labour shortages in the eighteenth and nineteenth centuries; in fact, it faced the opposite situation. During the latter half of the seventeenth and the first half of the eighteenth centuries, millions of migrants from China proper flowed into Manchuria.

---

25 Polska Akademia Nauk, *The Population of Poland* (Warszawa, 1975), 11.
26 Zhan Wen-lin 赵文林 and Xie Shu-jun谢淑君 , *Zhongguo renkou shi*中国人口史 (Beijing, 1988), 474.
27 Richard Trethewey, 'The Establishment of Serfdom in Eastern Europe and Russia', *American Economist*, 18 (1974), 38.
28 Ibid.
29 Gunst, 'Agrarian Systems of Central and Eastern Europe', 69.
30 Ibid., 68.

Between the mid seventeenth and mid nineteenth centuries, the population of Liaoning province had surged from 60,000 to over 2,000,000.[31]

By the mid eighteenth century, Manchuria began to exhibit signs of overpopulation. One indicator was the increasing release of serfs from manors. Late seventeenth-century Qing authorities had imposed strict restrictions on serfs, forbidding them from leaving their properties. Fugitive laws imposed severe penalties not only on serfs attempting to escape but also on civilians who assisted these fleeing serfs. However, starting from 1744, the authorities initiated a significant wave of serf releases. A report from the Imperial Household Department (IHD) highlighted the issue of overpopulation in many IHD-owned manors. The report recommended that the emperor authorize the release of serfs, allowing them to fend for themselves.[32] The emperor then issued an edict permitting some serfs to depart from their manors and register as civilians. He enjoined stewards not to expel elderly or disabled serfs. This report underscored how, as the population continued to grow, manors began to resemble charitable institutions. Remaining within the manor provided serfs with the security of assigned plots of land. There were instances where serfs had fled the manor but were compelled to return after a few years because they could not find sufficient land to sustain their families outside the manor.[33]

The issue of overpopulation in Manchuria was further evident in the changing policies related to the allocation of women to serfs in royal manors. In the late seventeenth century, the authorities allocated significant numbers of women to serfs in the royal manors. This allocation was a crucial measure to ensure that destitute serfs could marry and continue to expand the population. However, starting from the early eighteenth century, a different approach emerged. The practice of allocating women was generally replaced by providing material support. Authorities began offering financial assistance to help serfs marry and establish families. One contributing factor to this shift was the substantial influx of immigrants from China proper. The arrival of these immigrants also led to a decrease in the overall cost of getting married. In 1702, the average stipend for a serf was remarkably high at around 50 taels. However, by the late 1730s, this amount had decreased significantly to just 7 taels.[34]

---

31 Cao Shuji, 曹树基, *Zhong guo ren kou shi* 中国人口史 (Shanghai, 2000), 6: 481.
32 Yang Xue-chen杨学琛 and Zhou Yuan-lian 周远廉, 'Guanyu qingdai huangzhuang de jige wenti' 关于清代皇庄的几个问题, *Lishi yanjiu* 历史研究 1965 (3), 120.
33 Wu Ting-yu 乌廷玉 and Yi Bao-zhong 衣保中, *Qingdai manzhou tudi zhidu yanjiu*清代满洲土地制度研究 (Changchun, 1992), 138.
34 Liu Xiao-meng 刘晓萌, 'Baoyi nvzi hunpeizhi de wajie yu manzhou lingzhuzhi de xiaowang –yi neiwufu 'sanfan hannv' wei zhongxin de kaocha' 包衣女子配婚制的瓦解与满洲领主制的衰亡 ——以内务 府'三藩汉女'为中心的考察三藩汉女, *Qingshiyanjiu* 清史研究, 2021 (3), 10–13.

V

Theoretically, low demand for soybeans would lead to low wages for soybean producers. To compare wages between Manchuria, Poland, and England, this chapter employs Robert C. Allen's concept of the consumer price index. When comparing wages across different regions, it is common to adjust nominal wages based on grain prices. Nevertheless, in certain grain-exporting regions where grain prices were exceptionally low, deflating nominal wages with grain prices can lead to misleading conclusions. To provide a more accurate representation of wage purchasing power, Robert Allen deflated wages in England and Poland using the price of a basket of goods. This basket included not only food items like bread, beans, meat, and butter but also essential supplies such as soap, linen, candles, and fuel.[35]

A subsistence wage was set equal to 3.15 times the cost of this basket of goods, as it was assumed to support a family consisting of a man, a woman, and two children. Allen further increased the basket's cost by 5 per cent to account for rent. The welfare ratio, which measures the wage, was calculated by multiplying the daily wage by 250 and then dividing it by this subsistence wage.[36]

Using this comprehensive cost-of-living basket, Mikolaj Malinowski's study revealed that, in 1600 Poland, the welfare ratio for agricultural workers ranged from 0.61 to 0.85. In contrast, during the same period in England, this ratio stood at 1.27.[37]

Given the absence of detailed records regarding the prices of goods in the baskets used in Manchuria, this chapter adopts the annual expenses for a rickshaw puller's family as the subsistence wage. Field investigations conducted by Toa Dobunkai in Newchwang in 1900 indicated that the annual expenses for a rickshaw puller's family amounted to 120 Yuan.[38] This figure encompassed not only the cost of food but also expenses related to clothing and other essential supplies for a rickshaw puller and his family.

Furthermore, Japanese diplomats' investigations revealed that the daily income for rural labourers in the vicinity of Newchwang was a mere 15 cents.[39] Assuming that a worker would work for 250 days per year, the annual income

---

35 Robert C. Allen, 'The Great Divergence in European Wages and Prices from the Middle Ages to the First World War', *EEH*, 38 (2001), 411–447.
36 Ibid., 419.
37 Mikolaj Malinowski, 'East of Eden: Polish Living Standards in a European Perspective, ca. 1500–1800', Working Papers 0043, Utrecht University, Centre for Global Economic History, 20.
38 B03050508600_B03050508600.b10123.1-0798.00000117, 0141, B03050508300東亜同文会ノ清国内地調査一件／営口駐在班ノ部 第一巻
39 Kato Sueo, 加藤末郎, *Shinkoku shucchou fukumei sho*清国出張復命書 (Tokyo, 1899), 12.

for a rural labourer in the vicinity of Newchwang around 1900 amounted to just 37.5 Yuan. A straightforward calculation leads to the conclusion that the welfare ratio for rural labour in Manchuria in 1900 was only 0.3125. This figure was significantly lower than that observed in Poland in 1600.

VI

A comparison between Manchuria and Poland in terms of grain prices, human-to-land ratios, and rural hired labour wages helps to explain why soybean exports did not lead to a second serfdom in Manchuria. Polish aristocrats preferred coercive labour due to the prosperity of grain exports, which drove up free labour wages. In contrast, Manchuria presented an unfavourable environment for coercive labour control. Manchuria had lower grain prices, a higher human-to-land ratio, lower wages for rural labourers. These conditions rendered coercive labour control in Manchuria less profitable, at least in comparison to Poland. Consequently, despite recognizing the potential impact of soybean exports, Manchurian landowners did not prefer coercive labour practices in soybean cultivation.

The investigation into the absence of the second serfdom in Manchuria exposes a fundamental flaw of the world-system theory. Wallerstein's perspective hinges on a problematic logic. He assumes that capitalism results from the development of international labour division. This fixation on labour division has historical roots in the works of classical economists such as Adam Smith (1723–1790) and David Ricardo (1772–1823).[40] Some have recognized the close connections between Wallerstein and classical economists like Smith and David Ricardo. Robert Brenner, for instance, highlights that both Wallerstein and these classical economists share the belief that labour division, regardless of specific class structures, would enhance labour productivity. Brenner notes that both Adam Smith and Wallerstein associate capitalism with a trade-based division of labour. According to Brenner, Wallerstein follows Smith in arguing for a more or less natural emergence of increased specialization and for a resulting increase in productivity due to specialization – ultimately leading to the transformation of the productive forces.[41] For Brenner, the only difference between Wallerstein and Smith is that, for Smith, it is the separation of manufacture and agriculture and their allocation to town and country, while, for Wallerstein, 'it

---

40 Adam Smith, *The Inquiry into the Nature and Causes of the Wealth of Nations* (2007), 8–1; David Ricardo, *On the Principles of Political Economy and Taxation* (Ontario, 2001), 85–104.
41 Robert Brenner, 'The Origins of Capitalist Development: A Critique of Neo-Smithian Marxism', *New Left Review*, 104 (1977), 40.

is the division of the Atlantic World into interdependent regions, specializing in different sorts of agricultural production and/or manufacturing'.[42]

However, the fixation on labour division presents a dilemma: while labour division has been a widespread phenomenon globally for thousands of years, capitalism originated specifically in Western Europe during the early modern period. As Brenner points out, Wallerstein needs to explain 'why the rise of trade/division of labour should have set off the transition to capitalism in the case of feudal Europe' because 'the flowerings of commercial relations cum divisions of labour have been a more or less regular feature of human history for thousands of years'.[43]

Wallerstein proposed an ahistorical argument to explain this. He contended that capitalism could only emerge in Western Europe because capitalism in other parts of the world was stifled by world-empires. According to Wallerstein, a world-empire like China could not create a world-economy because it was burdened with administering and defending a vast land and population, diverting attention, energy and profits that could otherwise be invested in capital development.[44]

Wallerstein was not the first to argue thus. Max Weber (1864–1920) also posited that political institutions were a significant impediment to the emergence of capitalism in China. According to Weber, 'Chinese capital, which took part in exploiting modern opportunities, was predominantly the capital of mandarins; hence, it was capital accumulated through extortionist practices in office.'[45] The bureaucracy, which consisted of these mandarins, 'collectively opposed intervention and persecuted with deadly hatred any rational ideologist who called for 'reform' and 'prostrates rational management in administration, finance, and economic policy'.[46]

And yet, contrary to Wallerstein's assertion, China did possess a trading system which exhibited a distinct geographical division of labour between the periphery and the core. However, the absence of the second serfdom in Manchuria illustrates that this geographical labour division itself was insufficient to catalyse capitalism. The core of China's interregional trading system operated as a peasant economy. In contrast to a capitalist economy, a peasant economy struggles to sustain continuous growth. Instead, its growth typically takes the form of population expansion. In the early stages of growth, when the population is small, the overall output of the economy is low; but productivity per capita is high due to the large size of household farms on fertile

42   Ibid.
43   Ibid.
44   Wallerstein, *The Modern World-System I*, 60.
45   Max Weber, *The Religion of China, Confucianism and Taoism*, trans. and ed. Hans H. Gerth (Glencoe, IL, 1951), 242.
46   Ibid., 60, 62.

land. However, as the population grows, the overall output increases while productivity per capita declines since the average size of household farms declines. This decline weakens the ability of a peasant economy to support non-productive activities within society. Guy Bois notes that one characteristic of peasant economy growth is a decrease in the rate of levy.[47] Although the total volume of levy may increase, the percentage of the total harvest that a peasant can contribute as a levy invariably decreases.

However, the impact of a growing peasant economy extends beyond levy rates. Other sectors, such as manufacturing, are also affected. For instance, the urban population in large cities of the Yangzi Delta dwindled. The population in Suzhou, the primary textile manufacturing centre of the Yangzi Delta during the sixteenth century, also declined to only 0.5 million in the eighteenth century when most of the specialized weaving workshops there disappeared.[48] Such decline reflected 'the declining capacity of the economy to support a labour force outside of agriculture'.[49]

This process affected both non-agricultural activities and agriculture itself. The demographic pressure often resulted in a lack of investment within agricultural production. Researchers have long observed this phenomenon. For instance, in 1943, Walter W. Wilcox noted that although 'farmers saved and invested a larger proportion of their income than any other occupational group receiving similar incomes', many farm families struggled to maintain adequate working capital investments because they had to allocate their income for family living expenses.[50] This issue was particularly pronounced for small farms run by large families. Wilcox found that the absence of credit institutions was not the main cause of inadequate capital investment. Instead, many farmers were hesitant to incur debt due to the uncertainties involved.[51]

The absence of the second serfdom in Manchuria indicates that the peasant economy in the Yangzi Delta, a vital component of China's interregional trading system, faced a similar dilemma. Manchurian soybeans provided high-quality fertilizer in rice and cotton cultivation. When compared to other fertilizers like manure and silt, though, soybeans were more expensive and vulnerable to the effects of insufficient investment. The weak demand for soybeans suggested that demographic pressures prevented the Yangzi Delta's peasant economy from allocating sufficient resources to acquire fertilizers from distant sources.

---

47 Guy Bois, *The Crisis of Feudalism, Economy and Society in Eastern Normandy c.1300–1550* (Cambridge, 1984), 401.
48 Cao Shuji, 曹树基, *Zhong guo ren kou shi* 中国人口史 (Shanghai, 2000), 5: 757.
49 Robert Brenner and Christopher Isett, 'England's Divergence from China's Yangzi Delta: Property Relations, Microeconomics, and Patterns of Development', *JAsS*, 61 (2002), 628.
50 Walter W. Wilcox, 'Capital in Agriculture', *QJE*, 58 (1944), 49, 55.
51 Ibid., 62.

Additionally, the high human-to-land ratio indicated that the Yangzi Delta's peasant economy tried to mitigate demographic pressures through migration to peripheral areas.

Comparing the capitalist world-economy to China's interregional trading system reveals that the driving force behind the capitalist world-economy was the demand of urban residents within its core. During the early modern period, most bulk goods transported from the periphery to the core in the long-distance trade of the capitalist world-economy – such as coffee, sugar, tobacco, and lumber – were primarily intended to satisfy the demands of either urban residents or modern industries. Even the Baltic grains were primarily used to feed the urban population in cities within England and the Netherlands.

Agriculture in the core of the capitalist world-economy played more of a supporting role for the urban economy than driving the entire system. That is why the large-scale importation of fertilizers like bones and guano into England did not occur until the mid nineteenth century. By this time, the Industrial Revolution had already been underway for nearly a century and England's urban economy had been thriving for several centuries. The demands of the urban economy in the core, rather than the geographical labour division, drove the capitalist world-economy.

13

Property Law at the Transition to Exponential Growth: Examples from Japan

C. ALEXANDER EVANS AND J. MARK RAMSEYER

Economies grow when men and women make ever more productive use of the assets and skills they control. Growth requires shifting those resources and that labour to ever more productive uses. Before the industrial revolution, economies grew steadily, but very slowly. As they grew, people did shift resources and labour, but without much urgency.

By the twentieth century, however, most large economies were accelerating from linear to exponential rates of growth. With that change, men and women faced large incentives to shift their resources more rapidly. That shift was often a prerequisite to exponential growth – but more profitable uses also resulted from the exponential growth. We will not try to identify causation in this positive feedback loop; but exponential growth has often coincided with newly attractive opportunities for assets and labour.

Where an economy grows slowly, men and women need not worry much about their ability to shift resources to higher valued uses. After all, the slow rates of growth mean that they are not likely to want to move assets to new uses very often. So, if they worry others in their village might try to expropriate their wealth, it may make sense for them to opt for a unanimity requirement for decisions about resource transfer. This rule will make it harder to shift asset use, but with slow growth villagers will infrequently have those incentives anyway.

Where growth is slow, in other words, it may be rational to prioritize protection from opportunistic claimants over flexibility. That is why, in many jurisdictions, customary rules have often required claimants to a common resource to demonstrate unanimity in any major decision affecting the resource, a custom that Japanese courts have traditionally followed. Sometimes, however, multiple veto players delay shifts in the asset use, for protection from exploitive claims comes with diminished flexibility as a trade-off. A unanimity requirement makes every claimant a veto holder. This problem is exacerbated as increasing growth makes transfer of resources more frequently incentivized.

This chapter explores several examples from early twentieth-century Japanese property law that gave multiple parties a veto over changes in asset use. We distinguish the point from the related concept of Heller's 'anti-commons'.[1] We illustrate how these unanimity rules dampened the pace of economic change, and we discuss how courts and legislators responded.

Laws change as society changes – and as the industrial demands powering economic growth create new uses for capital. We see a general – not inevitable or uniform, but general nevertheless – shift in the interpretation of custom, as it interacts with the Civil Code, to facilitate higher-value uses of capital. These legal changes were caused by the transition to exponential economic growth – but they also then accelerated the same growth. This positive feedback loop eventually reshaped Japan's economy and its laws.[2]

I. Japan's Economic Transition

Custom in the Tokugawa Period
Despite its staid reputation, Japan's economy grew throughout the Tokugawa (1600–1868) period. Farmers carved paddies from the mountain side. Craftsmen expanded their shops into factories. Men and women migrated to the urban centres – both to national cities like Edo (Tokyo) and Osaka and to dozens of regional centres around the country.

The Tokugawa rule might have seemed stifling to the entrepreneurs of the Meiji (1868–1912) period, but the peace brought by Tokugawa conquest finally allowed ordinary people to plan out a longer economic future, after a century of civil conflict. And plan people did. They invested. They traded. They expanded coastal shipping. And they built a network of (pedestrian and horse) highways.

As they invested and traded, people formed contracts. To enforce their contracts, they turned to a variety of informal and formal sources. If they invested and traded within their social networks, they could employ the wide range of sanctions against default available to those who contract within communities with high levels of social capital.[3] But when they pushed the

---

[1] Michael Heller, 'Commons and Anticommons', in *The Oxford Handbook of Law and Economics: Volume 2: Private and Commercial Law*, ed. Francesco Parisi (Oxford, 2017), 178–199.
[2] For context on modern Japanese economic history, see Mark Metzler, 'Japan: The Arc of Industrialization', in *The New Cambridge History of Japan. Volume 3: The Modern Japanese Nation and Empire, c.1868 to the Twenty-First Century*, ed. Laura Hein (Cambridge, 2023), 293–337 and Kyoji Fukao and Tokihiko Settsu, 'Japan: Modern Economic Growth in Asia', in *CEHMW*, II: 100–128.
[3] See Robert Ellickson, *Order without Law: How Neighbors Settle Disputes* (1991); Lisa Bernstein, 'Opting Out of the Legal System: Extralegal Contractual Relations in the Diamond Industry', *Journal of Legal Studies*, 21 (1992), 115–157.

boundaries of those communities (or simply dealt with people immune to social pressure), many turned to the courts.

These courts were based in the provincial government of the quasi-independent domains, called *han*. For the most part, these domains enforced the trades, investments, and contracts in scarce resources. The Tokugawa legal system was federal rather than centralized, so generalization is dangerous – statutes, precedent, and procedure varied from domain to domain. But for the most part, domain courts enforced large-scale investments and contracts in scarce resources.

The Meiji Transition

In 1868, samurai from several outlying domains ousted the Tokugawa family. In its place, they established a government that remained nominally headed by the Imperial family, but with actual power located in a new military and business elite. In 1889, following an around-the-world mission to survey leading legal designs, the new regime promulgated a constitution based loosely on Prussian legal principles.

This new regime was central rather than federal. The regime enacted a Civil Code based explicitly on the German model in 1896 (effective 1898). The Code governed the entire country. As was typical of European civil codes, it covered contracts, property, tort, and family law.

But the new government began to rewrite its private law along western lines long before 1896. Immediately after taking power in 1868, the new regime declared that farmers (rather than the government) owned farmland.[4] Four years later, the regime made clear that farmers could buy and sell their land.[5] The new regime created a national land-titling system and instructed local administrators to document land ownership and transfers.[6] The regime followed up with a Western-style set of formal land registries.[7]

The new legal system provided the basic private property rights necessary for Japan to switch from steady but linear growth to the exponential growth rates characteristic of modern capitalist societies. The Meiji government enforced these nationally uniform and ascertainable titles to real estate by supplying

---

4 Kiyoshi Miyakawa, *Nihon ni okeru kindai teki shoyuken no keisei* [*The Structure of Early Modern Ownership in Japan*], 67 (Tokyo, 1969); Kiyoshi Miyakawa, *Meiji shonen no tochi shoyuken no hoteki seikaku ni tsuite* [Regarding the Legal Character of Early Meiji Land Ownership] Pt. 2, 21 *Rikkyo keizai gaku kenkyu* 93, 94 (1968); Dajokan fukoku 1096 of Dec. 18, 1868; Matsuo 2018, 106.

5 M5/2/15: Dajokan fukoku No. 50 of Feb. 15, 1872; Miyakawa 1969, supra note, at 67.

6 Miyakawa 1969, supra note, at 129, 168; Okura sho tatsu No. 25 of 1872; Okura sho tatsu No. 83 of 1872.

7 Miyakawa 1969, supra note, at 141, 235: Law No. 1 of 1886 (recordation act) and Law No. 13 of 1889 (land registries); Fudosan toki ho [Real Estate Recordation Act], Law. No., 24 of 1899.

mostly predictable and honest courts. These courts enforced uniform rules by which people could bind each other to most agreements about scarce resources.

II. The Rights to the Commons

Many of these agreements involved rights to the commons.[8] Japan is a heavily forested mountainous archipelago, and Tokugawa villagers used the forests. They did not farm the forests. They farmed the plains and valleys; the paddies they carved out of the mountains. In the forests, they collected firewood. They grazed their horses and cattle. They collected wild vegetables and mushrooms. Coastal villagers used the bay. Some villagers fished full-time. Some collected seaweed for food. Some found plants that they could use as fertilizer. Some farmed shellfish.

Tokugawa men and women, in other words, regularly used nearby mountains and bays as commons resources. To prevent over-use, they typically enforced on each other a variety of restrictions. Beyond those usage rights, however, they did not have much use for the mountain or the bay. And because they did not have much use for it, they did not bother specifying the residual rights. They did not care who 'owned' the mountain, because the mountain had little value beyond the uses that they made of it. No one purported to claim fee simple in the sea.

In 1967, Harold Demsetz observed that people generally find it worthwhile to define property rights only over those objects scarce enough to have significant value.[9] To define and enforce rights to property is costly. Only when those resources have sufficient value do people find it worthwhile to define their rights to the resources.

In the Tokugawa Era, neighbouring villagers found the mountain valuable enough to enforce a collective right to graze their cattle and horses or to harvest mushrooms. But they had little incentive to parcel the mountain into smaller fee-simple units. They enforced a customary collective right to use the mountain for limited purposes, and let it rest at that.

To govern their collective rights, villagers generally chose a unanimity rule. By defining commons rights by custom, the 1896 Civil Code continued this arrangement.[10] Because each member thus had a veto over any proposed

---

8   See Heller, 'Commons and Anticommons'.
9   Harold Demsetz, 'Towards a Theory of Property Rights', *AmEcRev* (1967), 347–359.
10 The 1896 Meiji Civil Code specified two forms of rights to the commons. Suppose villagers had common rights to use a property, but also held the residual right. The Code treated their usage right as a variation on fee simple, with details to follow local custom (Sec. 262). If instead they had the common rights to use a resource owned by someone else, it placed that common usage right within servitudes, but again with details to follow local custom (Sec. 294). In either case, the villagers held the usage right as a form of in rem.

change, opportunistic attempts to transform the resource were quite difficult. By contrast, under a majority rule, each member faced the risk that others might form a coalition that would expropriate his share. A veto for all helped prevent at least that worst-case possibility.

One obvious downside to a unanimity rule is rigidity in the face of new opportunities. This effect is most relevant when the group discovers a way to shift the common resource to a higher valued use. Sometimes this value-enhancing shift would enable the commons group to improve the welfare of all members. However, because unanimity is required to approve the change, a holdout strategy becomes possible. Even though the new use benefits all members, one member can try to secure a higher share of the new use by threatening to veto the move. As we see in experiment, while this sort of behaviour is uncommon it does happen.[11] Therefore, if a group is primarily concerned about moving assets to higher valued uses (rather than protecting property from tyranny of the majority exploitation), the group will do better under a majority decision rule.

When economic opportunity comes slowly, owners of a commons can rationally decide that the risk of majority exploitation is higher than the risk that opportunists might veto value-enhancing shifts. When economic change comes slowly, value-enhancing options appear slowly. Without urgency, the group has a better chance to negotiate the terms of a deal that enhances the welfare of all members – even under a unanimity rule.

At the close of the nineteenth century, Japan faced extraordinarily rapid economic growth. It needed to shift value resources to more valuable uses quickly. And in those circumstances, unanimity rules to rights in commons potentially stymied projects that could have benefited everyone.

The region along the Sea of Japan in what is now Shimane Prefecture provides a useful example. From ancient times, the beaches in this area were used for fishing and for gathering.[12] The beaches were generally 'owned' in

---

11 Perhaps the clearest experiment showing this effect is the ultimatum game. In this game, two players are tasked with splitting a reward. One player is allowed to propose a split and the other player can either accept that proposed split or refuse, in which case neither party gets anything. Player strategies vary widely when tasked with this game. While most offers are in the 50/50 range, many propose more aggressive offers. For many of the most aggressive of these offers, the other player often refuses in experiments – even though accepting the offer would benefit all players. The possibility of refusing even against one's interest – in other words, the possibility of adopting a self-harming holdout strategy – benefits the passive player by incentivizing the active player to make a more equal offer. See William Press and Freeman Dyson, 'Iterated Prisoner's Dilemma Contains Strategies that Dominate Any Evolutionary Opponent', *Proceedings of the National Academy of Sciences*, 109 (2012), 10409.
12 Kawahara Yukiko, 'Local Development in Japan: The Case of Shimane Prefecture from 1800–1930' (University of Arizona Ph.D. thesis, 1990).

common by local villagers. As the economy grew and technology improved, nearby cities expanded. With improved infrastructure, a new opportunity arose for the beaches: harvesting salt.

This proved no obstacle despite the unanimity rules required by local village leaders. With plenty of time to adapt, and with mediation available through local religious authorities, many villages transitioned successfully to a salt-harvesting focus. Soon, salt was harvested and shipped up and down the coast, from Taisha-cho to Oda.[13]

As Japan's economy developed more swiftly following the Meiji Restoration, the demand for salt was outpaced by the demand for raw metals, for use in Japan's newly growing factories. Many parts of Honshu were possible sources of metal, including Shimane, which boasted the Iwami Ginzan silver mine.[14] Towns near the mines along Shimane's coast had access to plenty of rare minerals and the whole area had promise as a source for Japan's booming industry.

However, such a radical change in use of commonly owned mountains and streams would have required unanimity from many separate villages, working together to transition from a predominantly agricultural emphasis to a new industrial economy. Unanimity rules and conservative local custom required securing consent from villagers across the coast.[15]

This proved too difficult. Objections from leaders in Hinomisaki and Taisha-cho led to dallying, and Japan's major factories had no time to waste. They quickly found other sources of copper and iron ore. By the time Matsue and Izumoshi were ready to start serious construction, the window had closed, and the opportunity had passed.[16]

Prior to the onset of exponential growth, the consensus-driven rulemaking in Shimane Prefecture was well suited to promoting stability without too much cost to growth. After the transition, the same system prevented residents from making the most of available opportunities. Today, Shimane remains one of the least economically developed of Japan's prefectures. Deeply beautiful, like much of Japan's countryside – but struggling, as it has since the Meiji Era.[17]

13 Personal conversation with Masataka Matsuura, Mayor of Matsue City, Shimane Prefecture (9 December 2015).
14 See Torigoe, 'The Fukuishi Deposit in the Omori Mine (Iwami-ginzan), Shimane Prefecture', *Japan Historical Study Group of Mining and Metallurgy*, 36 (1998), 24–30.
15 Matsuura, *supra* note 13.
16 Naoki Murakami, 'Changes in Japanese Industrial Structure and Urbanization: Evidence from Prefectural Data', *Journal of Asian Pacific Economy*, 20 (2015), 385.
17 Ibid.

III. The Perpetual Lease

The Problem
The 1896 Civil Code provided for both fee-simple ownership (Sec. 206) and for fixed-term leases (Sec. 601). The former is defined as a right *in rem*. The latter is defined as a right *in personam*. These definitions led to a predictable consequence: if a lessor sold land to a third party, the lessee had a right only for damages and only against the selling lessor. The lessee could circumvent this result only if he and the lessor agreed in advance that he would have rights against a third-party buyer. Provided they then jointly recorded the agreement, he could enforce the lease against any transferee (Sec. 605).

The 1896 Code also provided for perpetual leases – an arrangement sometimes translated as 'emphyteusis' (Sec. 270). At the close of the Tokugawa period, some farmers apparently held the right to cultivate a given field as lessee in perpetuity. Because these rights had nearly as much substance (if not more) as the 'owner' of the underlying fee simple, the drafters of the Code catalogued a perpetual lease as a right *in rem*.

The juxtaposition of term leases (*in personam*) and perpetual leases (*in rem*) created a puzzle. Suppose a tenant (and perhaps his father or grandfather) had farmed a field for decades. Did he hold a term lease that he and his lessor had regularly (if perhaps implicitly) renewed? Or did he hold a right to lease the farm in perpetuity?

Lessors and lessees renew term leases regularly. If the arrangement benefits them both, they have little reason to do anything else. But the distinction between a renewed term lease and a lease-in-perpetuity mattered, because the perpetual lease created two veto gates – and, necessarily, the risk of opportunistic hold-ups. Because both the lessor and the lessee of a perpetual lease held *in rem* rights, they could each veto any changes proposed. Even if presented with a higher valued use, they could both veto. Both had a right to hold up the other in return for a side payment.[18] Where the value of alternative uses changed only slowly, this problem was minor. But by the end of the nineteenth century, the pace of economic transformation changed the highest value uses on some assets at an extraordinary pace.

The Origins of Perpetual Lease
Most of the early twentieth-century perpetual leases seem to have dated from the Tokugawa period. According to many accounts, the parties negotiated these arrangements as compensation for the work entailed in creating a new

---

18 This situation is not totally dissimilar to perpetual lease rights on modern property; for example, a rent-control grant on a modern apartment in Manhattan. Then, as now, to make changes to the property (or to re-rent it) a landowner may need to offer a tenant an attractive side-payment, sometimes valued in the millions.

paddy.[19] Over the two and a half centuries of Tokugawa rule, farmers and entrepreneurs had massively expanded the amount of paddy land in use. To do so, they needed both money and labour. Some of them used the perpetual lease to split the returns to the collective effort.[20]

Into these construction projects, entrepreneurs invested capital. They may have earned the money in finance, in trade, or in industry. However they earned it originally, they invested in farming because they expected a market rate of return on their invested capital.

The farmers, on the other hand, invested their labour. Many were probably second or third sons. Their older brothers had inherited the small family farm. They could migrate to the city and find a job at a factory, but they preferred to farm. They located an entrepreneur who planned to build a paddy. They agreed to do the work, and for it demanded market compensation.

Rational entrepreneurs and farmers expected to earn from the new project a stream of income large enough to earn market returns on the invested capital and on the time-cost of the invested labour. Through the perpetual lease, the farmer and the entrepreneur split that income stream.

Classical economic reasoning tells us that, to make the arrangement rational for both parties, the entrepreneur would have demanded a fixed rental rate equal at least to a market return on the funds he had supplied. The farmer, in turn, would have demanded a rental charge (i) lower than the market rent on a term lease, (ii) by an amount equal at least to the market return on the value of the labour he provided.[21] Given the inevitable variation in the relative amounts of capital and labour necessary to create new paddies, a perpetual leasehold could sometimes sell for more than the residual fee simple.[22]

---

19 See, e.g., Kato v. Kitagawa, 15 Saihan minshu 790 (Sup. Ct. Apr. 24, 1936; Ito v. Ito, 3979 Horitsu shimbun 11 (Sup. Ct. Apr. 9, 1936); Nakano v. Fujii, 2568 Horitsu shimbun 5 (Osaka D. Ct. May 29, 1926).

20 Readers familiar with the English system of estates will recognize the similarity to fee simple absolute, a strong form of entitlement to property granted by the King in return for labour (originally, armed military service).

21 In its 1940 survey, the Ministry of Agriculture and Forestries calculated the average rental on a medium-grade paddy as 1.112 koku under a perpetual lease, and 0.578 koku under a term lease. It calculated an average rental on a medium-grade field as 0.568 koku under a perpetual lease, and 0.309 under a term lease. The report does not give the size of the fields in question. Norin sho, ed., Norin sho tokei hyo [The Ministry of Agriculture and Forestry Statistics] 73 (Tokyo, 1940).

22 See Ito v. Ito, 3979 Horitsu shimbun 11 (Sup. Ct. Apr. 9, 1936). This is not as incredible as it may sound at first. To return to the example of rent controlled homes, it is rare but possible for a rent-controlled desirable apartment in the city to receive a buyout offer from the landlord that exceeds the market value of the unencumbered underlying apartment.

As an example, consider a 1914 Osaka High Court opinion about Amagasaki.[23] The town is now a major coastal city between Osaka and Kobe, but much of it stands on silt washed downstream over the centuries by several local rivers. During the Tokugawa period, the local *daimyo* decided to encourage his residents to build a dike against the sea, reclaiming more land. Building the dike required an enormous amount of labour from locals. In exchange for their work, wrote the court, the *daimyo* granted the right to cultivate the reclaimed land in perpetuity (at a low stated rent) to farmers that worked on the project. This right was assignable; farmers could freely transfer the cultivation rights they had earned (Civil Code Sec. 272). Should the owner of the underlying fee simple estate in the claimed land choose to transfer his right, the perpetual lease ran with the land.[24]

The Resolution
1. The puzzles. Whether entrepreneurs and farmers chose this contractual structure varied across the country. Obviously, they could contract for funds and labour in a wide variety of economically comparable ways. Suppose farmer 'F_1' tills a field. He and his family have tilled it for decades. Every year, he pays a fixed amount of cash to wealthy villager 'W_1'.

Several formally different contracts could account for this arrangement. On the one hand, W_1 (or his predecessor) might have loaned money to F_1 (or his predecessor), who then used the money either to buy the paddy or to build it on undeveloped land. In this case, F_1 would own the land in fee simple, and would be making a regular interest payment on that loan to W_1.

On the other hand, W_1 (or his predecessor) might have funded the construction of a paddy on an undeveloped piece of land he owned. For this project, F_1 (or his predecessor) would have provided the labour necessary to build the paddy. In this case, W_1 would own the land, and F_1 would pay rent to W_1. As compensation for his work in building the paddy, W_1 might have granted F_1 the right to farm the paddy in perpetuity for a fixed sub-market rent.

Although these two arrangements are legally quite distinct, for outside observers – and for all practical purposes – the loan and the lease will appear identical.

Similarly, suppose F_2 (and his family) have similarly farmed W_2's (and his family's) field for several decades. On the one hand, F_2 might have rented the land for a term. F_2 and W_2 had both found the arrangement satisfactory, and hence renewed it regularly. On the other hand, F_2 and W_2 (or their respective

---

23 Akioka v. Kitakata, 1014 Horitsu shimbun 27 (Osaka High Ct. Dec. 15, 1914).
24 Kato v. Kitagawa, 15 Saihan minshu 790 (Sup. Ct. Apr. 24, 1936); see Yoshida v. Yoshie, 6 Saihan minroku 131 (Sup. Ct. June 22, 1900) (rights of perpetual lessee are unaffected by actions of fee simple owner).

predecessors) might have agreed that F_2 should have the right to farm the land in perpetuity.

Unfortunately for judges, Tokugawa farmers and landlords often concluded leases without drafting a written contract. Since for all practical purposes the term lease and the perpetual lease will be observationally equivalent, this posed enormous challenges for judges tasked with arbitrating landlord–tenant disputes.

2. *Judicial distinctions*. In some cases, judges deciding a lease dispute could find an explicit contract. For example, in 1906, the Supreme Court faced a dispute between two Nagano hamlets. One of the hamlets negotiated a contract to lease a piece of land from the other 'in perpetuity'. On the strength of that agreement, residents from the lessee village removed thickets, cut weeds, and slashed and burned vegetation. They worked for over twenty years to increase productivity, but now the lessor hamlet claimed to have leased the land for a term. The lower court called the agreement a tenancy in perpetuity, and the Supreme Court affirmed.[25]

Alas, most cases apparently lacked an explicit contract, and Meiji judges tended to decide that term leases were most appropriate for ambiguous cases.[26] These judges often summarily disregarded some of the claimed evidence. Just because the parties called a lease a 'tenancy', for example, did not make it perpetual.[27] Similarly, just because the lessee paid the rent in kind did not make it perpetual.[28] Indeed, judges generally presumed that leases for unspecified terms were contractual.

When a farmer could trace his lease back to a reclamation project, however, judges sometimes held that the lease was perpetual. On the one hand, the judges may have done this because the parties to a reclamation project had actually used perpetual leases. On the other hand, judges may have done this because they thought the parties had used perpetual leases in these projects. Examining early twentieth-century decisions, we observe that judges more commonly found perpetual leases in cases where the parties could trace the lease back to a reclamation project. Whether that reflected historical practice or a twentieth-century judicial decision rule, however, we cannot say.

---

25   Makisato mura v Nobuta mura, 12 Saihan minroku 1514 (Sup. Ct. Nov. 12, 1906).
26   In re Nakayama, 4291 Horitsu shimbun 17 (Sup. Ct. May 27, 1938). See also Kato v. Kitagawa, 15 Saihan minshu 790 (Sup. Ct. Apr. 24, 1936); Ishizawa v. Shiraiwa, 2011 Horitsu shimbun 22 (Sup. Ct. March 16, 1922).
27   Ninomiya v. Aizawa, 758 Horitsu shimbun 24 (Tokyo Ct. App. Oct. 7, 1911).
28   Ishizawa v. Shiroiwa, 2011 Horitsu shimbun 22 (Sup. Ct. Mar. 16, 1922).

3. Statutory modification. From the start, legislators treated perpetual leases as a complication they hoped would someday disappear.[29] So, in the Civil Code's 1898 implementation statute, reformers determined that all nominally 'perpetual' leases would expire after fifty years.[30] The Civil Code already provided property rights for fee simple, easements, and security interests, as well as contractual provisions for leases and loans. Perpetual leases seemed to serve little purpose that people could not fulfil at least as well through a mix of those other provisions.

Almost immediately, however, the men and women claiming to hold perpetual leases protested the fifty-year limit on their property rights. The shrinkage to fifty years changed the terms of their original transaction, they argued. Never mind that the present value of any stream of income more than fifty years out is effectively zero.[31] The holders protested anyway.

Legislative drafters responded with an amendment. Under the revised implementation statute, at the end of the fifty-year term a fee-simple owner of a paddy had a right to purchase any perpetual leasehold at a 'reasonable' price. Should he choose not to do so, the lessee had a right to buy the owner's fee simple interest at a 'reasonable' price.[32] This new fifty-year limit, combined with consistent judicial presumptions against perpetual leases, led perpetual leases to slowly disappear over the next half-century.

IV. The Right to Build

By the close of the nineteenth century, the Japanese were moving en masse from the countryside to the cities. Developers were replacing single-family homes with multi-family housing. They were also replacing residential units with larger scale operations. As neighbourhoods gentrified, developers replaced primitive farmhouses with more elaborate permanent structures. To do this, they purchased tracts of land – and, if a house stood on that land, they tore it down.

---

29 Western legal readers may see a parallel here to the treatment of equitable claims in the Restatements of Contract. In both cases, commentators saw the cause of action (equity in the Restatement, perpetual leases in Japan) as a historical artifact arising out of path-dependent circumstances.
30 Minpo shiko ho [Civil Code Implementation Act], Law No. 11 of 1898, Sec. 47. The original 1896 Civil Code had not included such a limitation. See Kato (1972, 157).
31 This economic point often seems to be of little relevance in these sorts of cases. In Hong Kong, for example, residents fiercely protested efforts to amend *ninety-nine-year* property leases; calling them a tyrannical taking.
32 Minpo shiko ho, supra note, at Sec. 47.

This development pattern proved to be a frequent source of conflict. When developers purchased land, sometimes the property on the land had already been rented. In such circumstances, were the new owners permitted to evict the old tenants?

Ex ante, the efficient answer was obviously to enforce whatever deal the parties had chosen. If someone wants to build a house, let him either buy the land or negotiate a clause for liquidated damages. *Ex post*, however, evicting the tenant and destroying the house could seem unfair.

Faced with this dilemma, courts and legislators tended to side with the tenant. In the process, they created yet another set of dual veto gates. In the future, should an entrepreneur create a value-increasing use for a piece of property, he potentially faced two parties that could independently veto the transaction: the fee-simple owner of the property, and the party that held a lease on the land.

To some extent, a lack of concern over veto gates appeared in the 1896 Civil Code. The Code permitted parties to negotiate for a distinctive and explicit right to build as a property right *in rem* (this right is usually translated as 'superfice'; see Sec. 265). The builder could pay for this right through regular (e.g., monthly) payments (Sec. 266).

But this new right created problems. If a builder built a house on land that she had leased for a term, she held only an *in personam* contract right; her rights did not run with the land.[33] If instead she built her house on land for which she had specifically negotiated for a right to build (even if she paid for it through regular periodic payments), she could enforce her right against anyone who bought the underlying fee simple. She could enforce this right against transferees only if she had recorded her interest, but the landowner could not block that recordation (Civil Code Sec. 177).[34]

The complexity and fact-specificity of these provisions created an obvious nightmare for judges. Given the difference between *in rem* and *in personam* interests, it obviously mattered enormously whether a homeowner held a term lease or a right to build. But this distinction was created by the Civil Code and was novel; a judge could not distinguish between the two legal rights by reading prior existing contracts.

---

33 Sato v. Asatsuma, 27 Saihan minroku 1913 (Sup. Ct. Nov. 10, 1921) (lease has no effect against 3rd party; exception for building recorded under 1909 statute).
34 Nada v. Yamagata, 3 Daihan minshu 34 (Sup. Ct. Feb. 29, 1924) (effect of recordation of chijoken); Iwafuchi v. Sugawara, 26 Saihan minroku 1935 (Sup. Ct. Dec. 8, 1920) (effect of recordation under 1909 statute); Ariizumi & Wagatsuma 1984, 341).

The Diet stepped in to solve the immediate problem by statute in 1900: all owners of existing homes sitting on land owned by someone else were declared to hold a real right to build.[35]

Although the Diet rescued *existing* lessees by the 1900 statute *ex post*, the question of future homeowners remained. Should homeowners in the future hope to build on rented land, they could explicitly specify by contract whether they held a term tenancy or a right to build. They did – and they usually specified term tenancy. Rather than contract for the *in rem* right to build, builders and landowners overwhelmingly choose the *in personam* term lease instead.

The choice to build on a term lease will strike many readers as bizarre, but in time the Diet decided to grant term lessees rights that mimicked rights *in rem* anyway. By statute in 1909, the Diet opted explicitly to protect tenants who built houses on leased land. Never mind that the lessees could have contracted for the *in rem* right to build but did not. Never mind why anyone would build a house on rented land anyway.

Initially, if one leased land for a term and built a house on it, one held only an interest *in personam*, and could not (without the lessor's advance consent)[36] enforce the new lease against a transferee of the underlying fee simple. But by statute in 1909, the Diet changed this rule: provided that a lessee recorded his building (and the owner could not block recordation), she could enforce her leasehold against any transferee of the land.[37]

Cases in the wake of the massive 1923 Tokyo earthquake and fire illustrate the problems caused by this new rule. Yoshi Negishi owned a house in the Asakusa merchant quarters of Tokyo. A fire levelled the lot, but squatters soon built two corrugated steel shacks on top of it. Effective 1 January 1924, Negishi leased the property to one Moemon Enjoji. Both parties specified a five-year term and a ban on any new buildings constructed from stone or brick. Five years later, it emerged that Enjoji had built something nonconforming (the court did not say) and now refused to leave.

The Supreme Court declared that it would decide the case according to what (it thought) the parties had *intended* – and not what they had specified. That

---

35 Chijoken ni kansuru horitsu [Act Regarding Superfices], Law No. 72 of 1900; see Nada v. Yamagata, 3 Daihan minshu 34 (Sup. Ct. Feb. 29, 1924) (presumption applied); see generally Wagatsuma & Ariizumi 1984, 338–348).

36 Consent to record – Civil Code, Sec. 605.

37 Tatemono hogo ho [Building Protection Act], Law No. 40 of 1909; Iwafuchi v. Sugawara, 26 Saihan minroku 1935 (Sup. Ct. Dec. 8, 1920) (effect of recordation under 1909 statute); Ichiura v. Matsuura, 25 Saihan minroku 1355 (Sup. Ct. July 23, 1919) (effect of recordation under 1909 statute); see Wagatsuma & Ariizumi 1984: 339–40, 363.The legislative experimentation continued. The 1921 Land Lease Act and House Lease Act added a wide variety of other 'tenant protection' provisions. By the time they were finally repealed in 1991, they had made eviction extraordinarily hard. See generally Shakuchi ho [Land Lease Act], Law No. 49 of 1921; Shakuya ho [House Lease Act], Law No. 50 of 1921.

they had signed a lease was, according to the Court, only the beginning of the inquiry. The parties agreed to a five-year term, the Court said, but they could not have meant what they said. After all, they would have realized that it would take Enjoji considerable time just to evict existing squatters on the property. Negishi, concluded the court, must have been the opportunist. In early 1924, no one knew whether Tokyo would recover. Landowners negotiated the best that they could. By 1928 Tokyo was thriving once again, and landowners like Negishi wanted better terms. Based on this analysis, the Court denied the eviction.[38]

This resolution may have seemed fair with knowledge of the parties to the dispute, but the consequences were significant. Suppose an entrepreneur located a value-increasing use for a piece of property. He now faced potential vetoes from two independent parties: the owner of the underlying property, and a tenant who had (even without the permission of his lessor) built a house upon it.

Predictably, the presence of multiple veto gates decreased the attractiveness of development. To this day, though Tokyo has some of the most active new construction markets in the world, real estate investment continues to struggle – and contemporary Tokyo is the only OECD metropolis where home values have declined or remained stagnant for an extended period.

V. Conclusions

Tempora mutantur, nos et mutamur in illis. Such is for life, and such is for law.

As observers, separated by time, we tend to view legal chance as stochastic and incremental. The rules of the game are what they are – shaped by politics, by culture, or by other forces. The economy is far more dynamic; it moves day-by-day or even hour-by-hour.

This perspective makes it tempting to look at Japan's transition to exponential growth as the story of a dynamic flexible economy adapting to growth-promoting static background rules; Hernando de Soto's rules of the game, against which market players play.[39]

This picture understates the dynamism and complexity of this turbulent era. Instead, as the Japanese economy changed, the law changed with it. Customary rules of decision making for common goods and for joint resources emphasized protection from exploitation: a prudent focus during a time of slow growth. As economic growth and Schumpeterian disruption accelerated, these rules came under pressure. Courts, tasked with balancing custom in the context of

---

38 Enjoji v. Nemoto, 1 Daishin'in hanketsu zenshu 6, 17 (Sup. Ct. Feb. 22, 1934).
39 See Hernando de Soto, *The Mystery of Capital: Why Capitalism Triumphs in the West and Fails Everywhere Else* (New York, 2000).

a new Civil Code, generally found ways to shift rights along the path of legal least resistance.

Far from static background rules, the economy's rules-of-the-road changed markedly as society's needs changed. That, perhaps, is how it should be: law is created to serve society; and if it poorly matches the economy, it probably is not serving very well. But the dynamism of the law is worth remembering. If Japan's example is typical, we should expect similar changes across societies as they transition to exponential growth.

Index

abolition 143, 147
abolitionists 61, 62, 72, 73
abstract labour 239n.53
Africa at Work (Tete-Ansá) 153
Africa 6, 18, 19, 83, 93, 112
Akim Abuakwa district 136, 149, 155
Allen, Robert 289
Amagasaki, Japan 302
American Agriculturalist 71
American colonies 4, 20, 160, 173, 176, 177
American Indians 74
American Revolution 46, 49, 85, 93
Anglo-Boer war 128
Anglo-Dutch War 115
Anglo-Mughal war 119
Anglo-Xhosa frontier war 157
anti-slavery movement 16
apartheid 124, 134, 151
Arabian Sea 203
aristocrats 277, 278, 283, 287, 290
Asante (Ashanti) kingdom 126, 127, 130, 132, 148, 152
Asia 33, 100, 165
Aurangzeb, Mughal emperor 120

Barbados 86, 87, 97
Barbarous Years, The (Bailyn) 44
Batavia, Dutch East Indiea 117
battle of al-Qasr al-Kabir 105
Bengal, India 203, 231, 232, 236, 237
bhakti movement 236
Black Death 34, 287
Bloch, Marc 14
Boer republics 128, 144
Bonsu, Asantehene Mensa 152
Borno kingdom 128
Boston, Massachusetts 38, 173
botany 169, 170, 172
Bourgeois, Nicolas-Louis 173
Brady, Mathew 76
Brahmanism 233
Brazil 87, 100, 101, 103, 104, 110, 111, 113, 136
Bristol, England 85, 90
Britain 2, 3, 8, 20, 56, 83, 112, 116, 127, 141, 162-4, 176, 178, 206, 222
British Cotton Growing Association 138

British East India company 22, 204, 238, 244
British empire 128, 143, 217
British West Africa 124, 125, 135, 139, 140, 142, 143, 149, 150, 155, 158
British West Indies 39, 44, 45, 48, 55, 60
Buddhism 236
business cycles 17, 80, 81, 82, 90, 96, 98

Calcutta, India 120
Calvinism 29
Cambridge History of Capitalism 13, 27, 28, 246
Cape Colony 128, 129, 133, 143, 156
Cape of Good Hope 165
Capital (Marx) 18
capitalist world-economy 24, 275-9, 293
cartaz system 110
caste 21, 22, 212
    hierarchies 227, 228, 230, 231, 233, 239, 241
    ideology 226, 228, 230, 231, 232, 233, 234, 237, 240, 244
Castile kingdom 103
Catholic Church 169
Ceuta, Morocco 104
Chamber of Mines 147, 151
Champlain, Samuel de 169
Charles II, King 88
child labour 42
Child, Josiah 119
China 7, 8, 23, 160, 247, 248, 255, 258, 273, 275, 291
Christianity 112
Christians 109
Civil Code 295, 296, 297, 300, 304, 305, 308
Civil War 5, 6, 16, 17, 58, 62
Clifford, Hugh 135
Coen, Jan Pieterszoon 117
coercive labour 279, 290
Coker, J.K. 147
colonial rule 124, 127, 132, 147, 155, 200, 221, 224, 228
colonial state 22, 211, 223, 225, 237, 238, 241
colonial violence 100
colonialism 112, 118, 122, 205, 206, 211, 222

colonization   18, 20, 37, 79, 120, 128, 132, 136, 140, 156, 173, 287
Columbus, Christopher   165
commodified creativity   66
Companies Act   213
Company of Merchants Trading to Africa   91
Company of Royal Adventurers   88
corvée labour   277
Cossigny, Jean-François Charpentier de   174
cotton   5, 93, 94, 167, 168
Crais, Clifton   130
creative capitalism   16, 61, 62, 64, 69, 71, 72, 73, 74, 75, 76, 77
credit creation   81, 96, 98
Cromwell, Oliver   102
Crystal Palace Exhibition   67
cultural capital   31

Dāsa, Narottam   236, 237
De Beers Consolidated Mines   133
Declarations of the State of the Colony   167
Degler, Carl   14
Democratic Party   61, 72
Dharmashastras texts   232n.26
Discourse of Western Planting (Hakluyt)   166, 167
domestic economy   176
doux-commerce   10
Dunaway, Wilma A.   39
Dutch Republic   115, 117
Dutch West India Company   101, 116

East India Company (EIC)   114, 117–21, 165, 205, 206, 238
economic creativity   61, 62, 64, 76, 77
economic development   84
economic dynamism   36
economic rationality   29
economic resource   41
economies of scale   93, 248, 264, 266, 270, 271, 273
Economy of British America, The 1607–1789   45, 46
emancipation   59, 60, 147, 156, 182, 194
Empire of Cotton (Beckert)   161
Engels, Friedrich   11
England   21, 82, 110, 198, 277, 293 *see also* Britian
enslaved labour   16, 62, 101, 127, 156
enslavers   60, 62, 70, 73, 74, 77

Essential Commodities Act   218
Estado da India   108, 109, 110, 118
Eurasia   100, 242
Europe   3, 5, 8, 20, 21, 28, 36, 99, 163, 195, 214, 256
Exhibition of the Industry of All Nations   67
exponential growth   24, 308

Fall of Rome   9
farmers   24, 70, 71, 118, 129, 130–3, 137, 138, 144, 146, 149, 152, 264, 296, 302
fee simple   297, 300, 301, 302, 304, 305, 306
Feinstein, Charles   157
feudalism   9, 180
fidalgos (nobility)   107, 108
forced labour   100, 261
Foreign Exchange Regulations Act   219
foreign trade   47
Forrest, Tom   140
Fort William   120
France   20, 119, 163, 171, 173, 175
Frankel, Herbert   142
free labour ideology   74, 76
Free-Soil Party   75
free states   73
free trade   88, 91, 141, 208
free trade imperialism   116
free whites   48, 49, 50, 56
free workers   279

Gama, Vasco da   109
gambling   41
Garrison, William Lloyd   60
Gdansk, Poland   278, 283, 286
Ghana   19, 123, 125, 127, 128, 131, 132, 135, 140, 142, 143, 148, 151, 154–6
global economy   257
global trade   117, 165
globalization   206, 209, 211
Glorious Revolution   119
gold   104, 108, 113, 133, 140
Gold Coast   104, 127, 132, 135, 142, 143, 149, 153, 155
gold rush   113, 133
Grand Design   101
Great Britain   52, 53 *see also* England
Great Depression   141
Great Divergence   7, 8, 20, 33, 160, 161
Great Indian Peninsula Railway   208
Great Transformation, The (Polanyi)   30
Greeley, Horace   68

INDEX

green revolution 218
Grim Years, The (Navin) 44
gross domestic product 218
Guizhou province 251, 262, 263

Habib, Irfan 221, 222, 223
Hakluyt, Richard 166
handloom weaving 209
Hāṭ Pattan (Dasa) 236, 237
Helper, Hinton Rowan 75
herrenvolk democracy 58
Hindus 109
Homo erectus 28
Huizhou province 253, 261, 263
human capital 30

Iberia 106
immigrants 72, 128, 129, 288
Impending Crisis, The (Helper) 75
imperialism 155
indentured servants 157
India 120, 160, 200, 201, 204, 206, 207, 208, 210, 213, 214, 217, 219, 221–5, 240
Indian Ocean 100, 104, 108, 109, 110, 112, 203
indigenous banking 206, 210, 218
indigenous capitalism 123, 142
indigenous people 19, 171
indigenous populations 100, 117, 123
Indo-Gangetic Basin 202
Industrial Revolution 2, 3, 8, 94, 159, 206, 293
industrialization 22, 52, 58, 65–8, 71, 130, 134, 142, 151, 156, 159, 201, 206, 208, 217–22
infant mortality 150
Inikori, Joseph 80
international credit crisis 94
Iron and Steel Industrial Corporation 134
Islam 234

Jamaica 88, 89, 92, 101, 102
Japan 24
Johannesburg, South Africa 133
Journal de Commerce 175

Kano, Nigeria 136, 139, 140, 148
Khoesan people 128, 129, 131
Kimberley 133 *see also* Cape Colony
Klein, Daniel B. 63
Krakow, Poland 281
Kruger, Paul 151

Kshatriya warriors 227

Labat, Jean-Baptiste 170
labour 4, 9, 30, 47, 79, 104, 131, 133, 144, 200, 226, 227, 239, 241, 294, 301, 302
labour market 125, 144, 146, 148, 150, 157, 208, 220
Labour Party 151
Lagos 127, 138, 139
landlords 23, 146, 180, 182, 185–90, 193–7, 216, 235, 239, 240, 277, 278, 303
land tenure 149, 195
Law Code of 1649 185, 189
Lever, W.H. 135
liberalism 239
Liberator 60, 72
limited-access orders 15, 54, 56
Lincoln, Abraham 75
Liverpool, England 85, 90, 94, 139
Lockeanism 241
London, England 90
Louisiana 173, 175

Malowist, Marian 278
Manchuria region 278
Mann, Horace 75
manorial courts 196
manorial system 287
manufacturers 65, 68, 176, 177, 179, 215
market economy 246
market mentalités 42
Marwaris, Indian group 211, 212, 216, 217
Marxism 223, 247
Marxists 30, 31, 32, 154, 222, 223, 224
Marx, Karl 10, 18, 99, 114, 124, 229, 230
Mataram province 117
Meiji era 295, 296, 299
merchants 9, 23, 29, 102, 105, 110, 112, 116, 119, 138, 171, 204, 206, 211, 217, 251, 253, 259, 262–4, 272, 286
  Huizhou 253, 254, 256, 261, 270
  Indian 203, 208, 213, 215
  indigenous 204, 205, 278
Middle Ages 10
middle-class parlour 67
migrant labourers 148 n.100, 149, 158
migrants 58, 157, 287 *see also* immigrants
miners 264
Ming dynasty 248, 253, 258, 259, 264
Ming-Qing imperial state 23

missionaries   169, 170, 171, 172, 237
Mississippi   70, 173, 175
modern bourgeois society   10
modern economic growth   2, 6, 8, 11
modern industrial capitalism   161
modernity   99, 224, 225
Mommsen, Theodor   28
monopolies   23, 54, 140, 153, 196, 197, 219, 249, 252, 274
Monopolies and Restrictive Trade Practices   219
monopoly   65, 88, 89, 108, 109, 119, 151, 180, 214, 238, 253, 285
Morocco   107
Morris, Morris D.   209
Mughal–Afghan conflict   235
Mughal Empire   6, 7, 22, 118, 120, 221, 235
Mughals   202, 206
Muslims   103, 106, 234

National Era   73
National Gallery   67
nationalism   151, 201, 215, 225, 230
Nationalist–Labour Pact   134
Native Americans   43, 44, 48, 51
Natives Land Act   146, 157
natural resources   20, 44, 49, 80, 162, 164, 165, 167, 170, 172, 174
Navin, John J.   44
Neal, Larry   27
Netherlands   8, 110, 115
New England   38, 44, 49, 57, 66, 70
New Historians of Capitalism   179
New History of Capitalism (NHC)   11–14, 16, 19, 31n.12, 36, 161–3
New World   100, 103, 111
New York Daily Tribune   67
Newchwang, China   283, 285, 286, 289, 290
Nieboer-Domar problem   131, 144, 157
Nigeria   127, 128, 134, 135, 141, 142, 143, 148, 154, 155, 156
North, Douglass   15
Norway   115
Nouveau voyage aux isles de l'Amerique (Labat)   170
nuclear power   41

Ohio Valley   39
Old World   100

open-access orders   15, 54, 55, 56
Opium War   255
Orange Free State   128, 133, 144, 146
Origin of Capitalism, The (Wood)   26
Osaka High Court   302
Oyo empire   126

Paglai Dhum peasant rebellion   239
palm oil   130, 132, 135, 136, 138, 141, 154
Parker, William   40
parlour culture   67, 68
Patent Office   66, 67, 73
patents   16, 65, 66, 67, 73, 75
peasants   40, 130, 138, 139, 180, 189, 192, 197, 200, 212, 261, 268, 270, 276, 278, 287
  lower-caste   238, 239
  Russian   182, 185, 187
perpetual lease   24, 300, 301, 303, 304
Physiocrats economists   175
piano trade   68, 69
pirates/privateers   101, 102, 110, 121
plague   197 *see also* Black Death
plantation system   84, 87, 97, 102, 104, 111, 121
Poland   115, 276, 277, 278, 279, 281, 283, 286, 287, 289, 290
Polanyi, Karl   30
Polish Lithuanian Commonwealth   287
political economy   175, 176
Pomeranz, Kenneth   160, 162
Portugal   103, 104, 105, 110, 112, 113, 121
Postlethwayt, Malachy   176
print matter   69
private property   182n.11
proletarianization   19, 23, 124, 125, 143, 148, 149, 154, 264, 273
property rights   24, 35, 38, 42, 50, 54, 247, 296, 297, 304
Protestantism   29
public education   16, 61, 71, 74, 75

Qing dynasty   248, 253, 258, 261, 263, 264, 274, 280

racism   242
Radburn, Nicholas   92
Rand Revolt   151
Raster, Tom   279
Republican Party   16, 61, 74, 75
Revolution of 1917   184
Rights of Man to Property (Skidmore)   72

Roe, Thomas   118
Romanov, Alexei   185
Royal African Company (RAC)   88, 89, 90, 91
royal courts   194, 196, 197
Royal Niger Company   128
Russian empire   185

Saadian dynasty   106
Saadians   107
Safi   105, 106
salt   266, 299
salt certificate system   248n.9
Sao Jorge da Mina (castle)   104
Schumpeter, Joseph   17, 63, 64, 79, 81, 82, 84
Schumpeterian growth   64
Scotland   9n.46
seigneurs   196
Sena dynasty   233
serfdom   3, 21, 38 n.26, 277, 279, 290
serfs   21, 182, 187, 188, 189, 190, 191–5, 197, 198, 288
Sérionne, Jacques Accarias de   175
settler capitalism   124, 125, 128, 143
settler-elite capitalism   19, 123, 125, 150, 156, 158
Seven Years War   163, 173
Shahis, Husain   233, 235
Sheremetyev estates   21, 187, 188, 189, 192, 195, 196, 197
Sheremetyev family   21, 182, 187, 188, 189, 190, 191–3, 194n.43, 198
Shimane Prefecture   298, 299
Sick Industrial Companies Act   219
silk   168, 178, 210, 227, 234, 271
silver   100, 101, 102, 109, 257
Skidmore, Thomas   72
slave economies   15, 133
slave labour   5, 47, 52, 117, 126, 129, 132
slave plantations   110, 121, 130
slavery   4, 11, 17–19, 36, 58–60, 62, 74, 90, 121, 131, 139, 143, 156, 161, 227, 238, 242, 278
slaves   5, 39, 44, 48, 90, 104, 111, 113, 129, 131, 132, 238, 239
slave states   72, 73, 75
slave trade   17, 53, 77, 79, 83–9, 90, 91, 93–6, 125, 136, 154, 157
slave traders   83, 85, 91, 92, 111
Slavery's Capitalism   11
Smith, Adam   8, 9, 10, 64

Smithian growth   65
Smuts political party   134
social capital   31
Society for the Encouragement of Arts, Manufactures, and Commerce   177
socio-economic organization   1
Sokoto Caliphate   19, 127, 128, 130, 152
sorghum   283
South Africa   19, 124, 128, 133, 134, 140, 142, 145
South Carolina   39, 48
South Sea bubble   90
soybeans   276, 280, 281, 283, 285, 286, 289, 292
Spain   101, 103, 105, 115, 117
St. Domingue   174
Stowe, Harriet Beecher   73
Stuart, James II, King   88, 119
subsistence wage   289
sugar   101, 102, 111, 245
sugar economy   87
sugar plantation   86
Sumner, Charles   75

Table Bay   126
tariffs   128, 141, 142, 222
Tariq ibn Ziyad   106
taxes   22, 115, 127, 128, 152, 195, 204, 206, 237, 240, 259, 260
tea   270
tenants   9, 144, 157, 180, 196, 256, 261–4, 267, 306
term leases   300, 303
Tertre, Jean-Baptiste du   171
Tete-Ansá, Winfried   153
The Philanthropist   74
Thomson, Ross   66
Tokugawa rule   295, 296, 297, 300
Tokyo, Japan   306, 307
trade cycles   79, 82, 94, 96, 98
trans-Atlantic credit crisis   93
Trans-Atlantic Slave Trade Database   84
Treaty of Tordesillas   103
trusts   249, 250

ultimatum game   298n.11
Uncle Tom's Cabin (Stowe)   73
United Africa Company   140
United Kingdom   222
United States   4, 12, 35, 94, 162, 242
Universal Dictionary of Trade and Commerce (Postlethwayt)   176

USSR (Soviet Union) 182
Usurious Loans Act   210

Vedic peoples   231
Vereenigde Oostindische Compagnie
    (VOC)   114, 115, 117, 118, 119,
    121, 165
villeins   196, 197 *see also* serfs
Virginia   167
volkscapitalisme   151
Voshchazhnikovo province   188, 192

wage labour   35, 72, 77, 125, 147, 149,
    150, 155, 157, 208, 261, 268, 269, 270
Wallerstein, Immanuel   275, 277, 290, 291
warlords   203, 205, 206

Wealth of Nations (Smith)   64
Weber, Max   1, 2, 291
West Indies   15, 56, 93, 102, 174 *see also*
    British West Indies
Western Design   102
wheat   106
Wilcox, Walter W.   292
wild rubber   131, 136
Williams, Eric   98, 163
Wilson, J.H.   95
Wood, Ellen Meiksins   26
Workman's Breach of Contract Act   240

Yangzi Delta   261, 268, 276, 292
Yangzi Valley   253

PEOPLE, MARKETS, GOODS: ECONOMIES AND SOCIETIES IN HISTORY

PREVIOUSLY PUBLISHED

1. *Landlords and Tenants in Britain, 1440–1660: Tawney's Agrarian Problem Revisited*, edited by Jane Whittle, 2013

2. *Child Workers and Industrial Health in Britain, 1780–1850*, Peter Kirby, 2013

3. *Publishing Business in Eighteenth-Century England*, James Raven, 2014

4. *The First Century of Welfare: Poverty and Poor Relief in Lancashire, 1620–1730*, Jonathan Healey, 2014

5. *Population, Welfare and Economic Change in Britain 1290–1834*, edited by Chris Briggs, P. M. Kitson and S. J. Thompson, 2014

6. *Crises in Economic and Social History: A Comparative Perspective*, edited by A. T. Brown, Andy Burn and Rob Doherty, 2015

7. *Slavery Hinterland: Transatlantic Slavery and Continental Europe, 1680–1850*, edited by Felix Brahm and Eve Rosenhaft, 2016

8. *Almshouses in Early Modern England: Charitable Housing in the Mixed Economy of Welfare, 1550–1725*, Angela Nicholls, 2017

9. *People, Places and Business Cultures: Essays in Honour of Francesca Carnevali*, edited by Paolo Di Martino, Andrew Popp and Peter Scott, 2017

10. *Cameralism in Practice: State Administration and Economy in Early Modern Europe*, edited by Marten Seppel and Keith Tribe, 2017

11. *Servants in Rural Europe, 1400–1900*, edited by Jane Whittle, 2017

12. *The Age of Machinery: Engineering the Industrial Revolution, 1770–1850*, Gillian Cookson, 2018

13. *Shoplifting in Eighteenth-Century England*, Shelley Tickell, 2018

14. *Money and Markets: Essays in Honour of Martin Daunton*, edited by Julian Hoppit, Duncan Needham and Adrian Leonard, 2019

15. *Women and the Land, 1500–1900*, edited by Amanda L. Capern, Briony McDonagh and Jennifer Aston, 2019

16. *Globalized Peripheries: Central Europe and the Atlantic World, 1680–1860*, edited by Jutta Wimmler and Klaus Weber, 2020

17. *Financing Cotton: British Industrial Growth and Decline, 1780–2000*, Steven Toms, 2020

18. *Quakers in the British Atlantic World, c.1660–1800*, Esther Sahle, 2021

19. *The Great Famine in Ireland and Britain's Financial Crisis*, Charles Read, 2022

20. *Family Firms in Postwar Britain and Germany: Competing Approaches to Business,* David Paulson, 2023

21. *Labour Laws in Preindustrial Europe: The Coercion and Regulation of Wage Labour, c.1350–1850*, edited by Jane Whittle and Thijs Lambrecht, 2023

22. *Financial Failure in Early Modern England*, Aidan Collins, 2024

www.ingramcontent.com/pod-product-compliance
Lightning Source LLC
Chambersburg PA
CBHW051559230426
43668CB00013B/1912